History of the Training College

THE Leeds Education Committee, in 1907, inaugurated a temporary College to meet an urgent need for further Training College accommodation.

For years the Training College accommodation throughout the country had been very inadequate, and many Leeds Teachers on satisfactorily completing their apprenticeship had found it impossible to obtain entrance to a Training College.

The building in Woodhouse Lane, formerly known as the Leeds Girls' High School, was secured for the educational requirements of the temporary College. For the residential accommodation of women students from districts outside Leeds the Committee decided to rent the mansion and grounds known as Weetwood Grange, and for men students the house and grounds at St. Ann's Hill.

The success which followed the establishment of the temporary Institution confirmed the Committee in their desire to place the College on a permanent basis, and it was decided to erect a permanent College to meet not only the local but the national demand for increased Training College accommodation.

The following year, owing to the large number of applications received from all parts of the country, it was found necessary to rent Buckingham House as an additional Hostel for men and to use Kirkstall Grange as an additional Hostel for women.

A special Committee had in the meantime been appointed to select a suitable site for the permanent College. The Committee after viewing several sites decided to purchase from the Right Hon. Lord Grimthorpe forty acres of the Beckett's Park Estate, including the Mansion House known as Kirkstall Grange. Subsequently additional land for the purposes of playing fields was obtained; and the total extent of the Training College Estate is now over ninety acres.

In 1910 building operations were commenced. Rapid progress has been made, and the College will be ready for occupation in September, 1912.

City of Leeds Training College
Continuity and Change
1907 - 2007

EDITED BY LORI BECKETT

© City of Leeds Training College. Continuity And Change. 1907 - 2007

First Published 2007

Published by
Leeds Metropolitan University
Headingley Campus
Leeds LS6 3QS
UK

website: http://www.leedsmet.ac.uk

British Library Cataloguing in Publication Data.
A catalogue record of this book is available from the British Library.

ISBN: 978-0-9555017-4-6

Dust jacket: Designed by Phillipa O'Byrne.
Watercolour by G. Atkinson c.1911.
(Source: Leeds Metropolitan University Archives).

Front end paper: Extract from City of Leeds Training College c.1912 Handbook.
(Source: Leeds Metropolitan University Archives).

Back end paper: Extract from Leeds Metropolitan University Vision and
Character Statement, 2007.
(Source: Leeds Met. Communications: Icon Photography)

Creative in-put by Leeds Metropolitan University Media Services

Produced by Collective (UK) Limited, Leeds.
www.collectivegroup.co.uk

Foreword

Vice-Chancellor – Professor Simon Lee

The editorial team deserves much thanks and praise from our university for their determination to tell the stories and show the images of one hundred years in Headingley of pioneering education, influential community life and significant controversy. Professor Lori Beckett has brought great determination and energy to this centenary celebration and has been inspirational in drawing on the talents of Iain Poole and so many collaborators. We have learnt much through this process of reflection and from the enthusiasm of colleagues who have such a passion for the history of education in this place.

One hundred years ago, the first students of the City of Leeds Training College arrived to study in the temporary forerunner of what is now the considerable Headingley presence of Leeds Metropolitan University. By the start of the First World War, the main features of a beautiful campus had been built in the grounds of Beckett Park, enhancing the surroundings of the original Grange, which itself is more than 250 years old. During that war, some of the tensions between pioneers led to dramatic events in the college. From the beginning, then, this is a spirited educational community with stories to tell of vision and character.

Preface part 1

Pro-Vice-Chancellor (Assessment, Learning and Teaching)

Professor Sally Brown

Assessment, learning and teaching were always central to the work of the City of Leeds Training College and today are still at the heart of everything we do at Leeds Metropolitan University, as a student centred university, committed to enabling all our students to achieve their maximum potential. My role at Leeds Met is to provide strategic leadership in this area, encouraging everyone who teaches and supports learning to focus clearly on the student learning experience. Many of the questions on which we focus now are ones that have been part of the work of our predecessor organisations for a hundred years:

- How do we ensure that students from disadvantaged backgrounds have their aspirations raised and are supported to overcome all kinds of challenges to reach their maximum potential?
- How can we make education transformative, so that students learn and grow during the years they spend with us?
- How can we make the educational experiences we offer as inclusive as possible, regardless of gender, sexuality, age, social class, race, ethnicity and religious background?
- How do we encourage students who are struggling to stay the course and make the best of their time on campus?
- How can we foster a spirit of lifelong learning, so that graduates continue to be committed to ongoing professional development?

I am supported in implementing this work by an outstanding phalanx of more than 30 Teacher Fellows, promoted on the grounds of their outstanding teaching to act as agents of changes and active advocates of innovation and scholarship and by six national Teaching Fellows who have been recognised as being among the best in Britain at motivating and inspiring students to learn. They support me in the production of out Assessment, Learning and Teaching Incubator journal, in organising events and conferences on academic pedagogy and contributing to associated regional and national events. Our Teacher Fellows were a significant contributory element in our work with enterprising students being designated by the English Funding Council a Centre of Excellence (CETL), and we are also partners in two other CETLs on Assessment of Learning in Practice Settings and Active Learning in Computing

A group of Associate Deans and other senior staff across the Faculties also work with me to shape and implement strategy and also to advise me on how we can best spend our Teaching Quality Enhancement funding to bring about institution-wide productive change. In addition, for two years I have also been leading our staff development festival here at Leeds Met, a central strand of which is concerned with disseminating outcomes of pedagogic projects and fostering innovatory approaches, including aspects of Technology Enhanced Learning that will be central to our work in the next decade.

I offer my congratulations to the editor and contributing authors of this fascinating book: Leeds Met is a university of festivals and partnerships, committed to enabling all our staff and students to use all their talents to the full, and this illuminating text enables us to reflect on our past while looking forward to an exciting future. Writers in this volume recognise the importance of understanding our history and origins, the better to help us understand our present and plan for our future.

Preface part 2

Pro-Vice-Chancellor (Research) – Professor Sheila Scraton

This book is a fitting celebration of 100 years of teacher education at Leeds Metropolitan University. The book provides a wealth of information and visual images that capture our heritage and bring alive the people, places and activities of the past. Although research does not appear as a formal aspect of teacher education over the years, critical thought and enquiry can be seen throughout the book as a part of the work of many of the staff and students, epitomised by Winifred Mercier, Vice-Principal of the City of Leeds Training College from 1913 to 1916.

Research at Leeds Met is now a central part of our vision to become a world-class regional university. Research as a running stream in the life of the University supports our constant need for intellectual engagement which, in turn, supports and underpins our learning and teaching whilst allowing selected areas of international, national and regional research excellence to flourish. Today we have 'running stream' professors who work across the boundaries of faculties and disciplines ensuring that the work we do allows for the intellectual excitement of multi- and inter-disciplinary work.

In education, research is today a formal and central part of our experiences as teacher educators. In 2007 we have research activity in four main groupings: children and childhood; pedagogy and professional learning; equity and social justice; and higher education. As chapter 5 discusses, partnerships are an increasing part of the educational experience, with research a central feature of these partnerships. Not only do we continue the tradition of close links with local schools and Education Leeds but also with organisations such as Eureka Children's Museum, Halifax who play such an important part in the educational experience of many children. Research is not separated from all our other professional activities, but focuses on current educational concerns that not only contribute to the advancement of knowledge and understanding in society, but also, applies this knowledge in the classroom through the integration of theory and practice.

Most importantly, this book is a research project in its own right. It fulfils many of the aims of our research strategy in that it crosses disciplinary boundaries, encourages staff to work in research teams, brings together researchers from different faculties and has provided the opportunity for 'new' researchers to work with more experienced colleagues. Thus, it is a research project that has not only resulted in a fascinating historical document but has also been an important aspect of our developing research environment encouraging critical reflection on our past and on the present.

C. Wright Mills[1] comments that *'No social study that does not come back to the problems of biography, of history, and of their intersections within our society, has completed its intellectual journey'*. This book is more that a descriptive history of the institutions over the past century that have become part of Leeds Metropolitan University today. By taking a rigorous approach through documentary and biographical research, this book engages in historical, social and political analysis that not only supports an understanding of the present but also helps us look forward to the future. The relationship between the past and present is always important. This book will be a significant resource for our current and future students and will be of interest to all those who have experienced aspects of this history or simply enjoy learning and understanding how the world today has been shaped by the people, places and activities of the past.

[1] Wright Mills, C. (1970) *The Sociological Imagination. Harmondsworth:* Penquin

Contents

Contributors

Dr Jill Adam was appointed as Associate Dean within the Carnegie Faculty of Sport and Education in 2004. She joined Leeds Met in 1995 following a successful career in secondary school teaching. She was formerly Principal Lecturer for secondary education and Head of the School of Education and Professional Training. She is a Governor of the University and a member of the University's Academic Board. She sits on the Board of the Yorkshire and Humber Professional Development Consortium as well as the Universities Council for the Education of Teachers Continuing Professional Development (CPD) Committee. Jill has overall responsibility for the University's partnership work with schools. Her doctoral research focused upon conceptions of expertise in teaching, and other research interests relate to teaching and educational professional development, curriculum development and student progression opportunities and experiences.

Frank Atkins MA (LeedsMet) is now retired, after a career in the Armed Forces and Business. Currently he is researching Cultural Aspects of Music 1850-1950. He is also Publicity Officer for Keighley and District Local History Society.

Professor Lori Beckett is the Winifred Mercier Professor of Teacher Education in the Carnegie Faculty of Sport and Education, the first to be appointed to the Chair, established in 2007 in honour of the City of Leeds Training College (CLTC) first Vice-Principal. Lori joined Leeds Met in February 2006, having relocated from Australia. Her teaching and research interests span education, equity and social justice, and the theorising teacher in pre- and in-service settings. Prior to her appointment, Lori was in the Faculty of Education, University of Technology, Sydney (UTS), where she was the research director of a number of contract projects, and consultant with Professor Bob Lingard et al on the Department of Education, Science and Training (DEST) funded project, *Addressing the Educational Needs of Boys,* and the Australian Research Council (ARC) funded project *Productive pedagogies, productive schools and gender reform.* Lori also worked as an academic partner in two schools in the NSW Department of Education and Training's Priority Action Schools Program, and was engaged by another school to develop and help implement its school improvement plan through intensive teacher learning and development.

Professor Alistair Black read history at both undergraduate and postgraduate levels in the University of London, taking his PhD in 1989 through the Polytechnic of North London. Having qualified as a librarian, he occupied professional posts in both academic and public libraries in the 1980s. In 1990 he became a lecturer in information and society at Leeds Polytechnic (now Leeds Met) where he is currently Professor of Library and Information History in the Innovation North Faculty of Information and Technology. He is the current editor of the international journal, *Library History.* Alistair is author of *A New History of the English Public Library 1850-1914* (1996) and *The Public Library in Britain 1914-2000* (2000), and co-author of *Understanding Community Librarianship* (1997) and *The Early Information Society:*

Information Management in Britain before the Computer (2007). He is also co-editor of the *Cambridge History of Libraries in Britain and Ireland* (2006).

Professor Anne Campbell is Professor of Professional Learning in the Carnegie Faculty of Sport and Education. She has researched mainly in the areas of practitioner research and teacher development and is interested in developing teachers' access to professional development, through action research, evaluation, fictional critical writing and narrative approaches. Her recent books include *Practitioner Research and Professional Development in Education,* (2004); *An Ethical Approach to Practitioner Research: Dealing with Issues and Dilemmas in Action Research,* (2007); and *Learning, Teaching and Assessing in Higher Education: a reflective approach,* (2007). She has also published widely in educational journals. Recent research projects are a baseline survey of Teachers' Perceptions of CPD (DfES); with Manchester and Oxford Universities the evaluation of the National Partnership Project for ITT, funded by the TTA; and the Best Practice Research Scholarship programme for the DfES, in partnership with MMU and Nord Anglia PLC.

Professor Tony Collins is a Professor in the History of Sport in the Carnegie Faculty of Sport and Education, and has published widely on rugby league and rugby union. He is involved with the Institute of Northern Studies and the Carnegie Faculty. Externally, Tony is the editor of a sports history journal. His books include *Rugby's Great Split*, *Rugby League in Twentieth Century Britain* and *Mud, Sweat and Beers: a cultural history of sport and alcohol*.

Ian Crossland started work in Leeds, for a production company, with offices in Leeds, London and Manchester, producing conferences, at a wide range of locations and with an infinite diversity of companies all over the UK. He moved to Leeds Polytechnic in 1989, just before the Polytechnic's change to University status was achieved. He worked initially within the Media Services Department, covering all. He was involved in all aspects of the department for over nine years. He then moved to Headingley, to be based in the Teacher Educational Department. He worked in the Design and Technology Centre largely supporting learning in Art and with responsibility for the dark room, potters wheel and kilns. There he first met Andy Bowles and came in to contact with the development of the on-campus school archaeological excavations which gave him a first insight into its varied history. Now in the International Faculty, and with the beginning of the Centenary Year, it has given him immense pleasure to be involved in these and future historical projects.

Jacqui Dean was Senior Lecturer in Education and Professional Development in the Carnegie Faculty of Sport and Education, Course Leader for the MEd degree and a University Teacher Fellow before her retirement. She has taught in schools and universities in South Africa, Australia and England and has extensive experience delivering teacher development courses across England. She has published widely, in both academic and history education fields. She has conducted research investigations into teacher, student and pupil learning and perspectives. She has directed three Nuffield Foundation-funded teacher development projects, the first two in post-apartheid South Africa, which influenced the national history and citizenship curricula; the third in Leeds – it investigated the citizenship potential of collaborative school and community archive construction. Jacqui is currently co-director of the Nuffield Primary History project and editor of its website for teachers and education students.

Janet Douglas was for many years a Principal Lecturer in Politics in the School of Cultural Studies in the Faculty of Arts and Society but is now retired. Her longstanding interest in the history of Leeds meant that she helped develop an MA in Social and Cultural History and with a colleague taught a module on the cultures of Northern cities in the 19th century. Janet has been active in encouraging an interest in the history of the city outside of the academy giving lectures to local societies, conducting walks and writing guide books including a contribution to recently published Pevsner Architectural Guide to Leeds. She is a council member of the Thoresby Society and the Leeds Philosophical and Literary Society, and is currently researching the work of the celebrated French photographer, Marc Riboud who, working for Picture Post, visited Leeds in 1954.

Peter D'Sena was Principal Lecturer in History and Education in the Carnegie Faculty of Sport and Education, International Teacher Fellow, and Course Leader of Primary Education, before taking up his appointment at Worcester University in October, 2007. Before moving to Leeds, Peter worked in schools for 16 years ultimately becoming Head of History in a multicultural, inner-London comprehensive. He also held schoolteacher research fellowships at both Oxford and Cambridge. Research interests include crime in eighteenth century London, school history, citizenship and cultural diversity; external consultancy includes writing Key Stage 3 history for Curriculum 2000. A trustee of the World Studies Trust, he has presented and published on the potential for the global dimension to contribute to teaching and learning at all levels. He is also a trustee of the British Postal Museum and Archive, advising on education and access.

Dr. Anne Flintoff is currently a Reader in Physical Education (PE) in the Carnegie Faculty of Sport and Education. She has been involved in school PE - as a teacher, teacher educator, and researcher for over twenty years. Her higher education teaching, research and consultancy has centred on issues of equity and social inclusion. Her doctorate research focused on gender relations in the initial teacher education of secondary PE teachers, and since then, she has been involved in researching how teachers make sense of new initiatives and policies, particularly in relation to equity issues. She publishes regularly in both academic and professional journals in the area of PE and sport, and is a member of the Advisory Board of the PE and Sport Pedagogy journal.

David Hall was born in Leicester in 1949 and moved to Leeds in 1958. He is the current chairman of Far Headingley Village Society and the author of the Society's Millennium local history book *"Far Headingley, Weetwood and West Park"*. David is a Chartered Surveyor and works for the sustainable transport charity, Sustrans.

Professor David Kirk joined Leeds Met in March 2005. He is currently Dean of the Carnegie Faculty of Sport and Education and Professor of Physical Education and Youth Sport. Professor Kirk also holds an Honorary Chair in Human Movement Studies at the University of Queensland, Australia and was an Adjunct Professor in Physical Education at the University of Limerick, Ireland from 2001-2005. He held appointments at Loughborough University, the University of Queensland, and Deakin University. He was European Editor of the Journal of Curriculum Studies from 1999-2004, and is currently Editor of Physical Education and Sport Pedagogy. He received the International Olympic Committee President's Prize in 2001 for his contribution to research in physical and sport education, the Outstanding Scholar Award in 2003 from the Research in Physical Education Special Interest Group of the American Educational Research Association, and was made a Fellow of the Physical Education Association UK in June 2005.

Professor Simon Lee became the Vice-Chancellor of Leeds Met on 1 September 2003. He studied as a Brackenbury Scholar at Balliol College, Oxford and then a Harkness Fellow at Yale Law School before becoming a lecturer in law at Trinity College, Oxford and then King's College London. Simon was appointed Professor of Jurisprudence at Queen's University Belfast in January 1989 where he also served as Dean of the Faculty of Law. Professor Lee was one of the two co-founders of Initiative '92, which established the Opsahl Commission. His work in Northern Ireland was recognised by his appointment as an Emeritus Professor of Queen's when he left in September 1995 to take up the role of Rector & Chief Executive at Liverpool Hope University College. An account of his eight years at Hope has been published by Liverpool University Press: The Foundation of Hope, edited by R J Elford. Simon is the author of several books, from Law & Morals (Oxford University Press, 1986) through to Uneasy Ethics (Pimlico, Random House, 2003). He regularly broadcasts and writes for newspapers.

Iain Poole worked at City of Leeds and Carnegie College, Leeds Polytechnic and Leeds Met between 1971 and his retirement in 2006, with a one year break at the Centre for Applied Research in Education at the University of East Anglia. During that time he has been head of history, Principal Lecturer in History and then in Education and Professional Development. He was also Deputy Head and acting Head of the School of Education and Professional Development. His main teaching and research interests have been in naturalistic evaluation, adult education, training and professional development. Laterly he worked to support staff in the creation of the regional university network partnerships.

Dr Ian Richards is a Senior Lecturer in the Carnegie Faculty of Sport and Education and Course Leader for BA (Hons) Sport, Leisure and Culture, with academic interests in sport and regeneration and a professional interest in athletics and walking. He completed his PhD on the social and economic impact of Coventry City Football Club on the city of Coventry.

Keith Rowntree trained as a Graphic Designer before progressing to study Fine Art; he continues to paint and has had several exhibitions of his work throughout the country. He has been employed in the Library at

Leeds Met for a number of years and has lately been steadily developing and maintaining an Archive which now contains material from across the University. The Archive continues to grow and is based in the Library at Headingley Campus. Keith's wide range of interests include painting, drawing, collecting books, local and family history research, creating web-pages, building computers and gardening. He hopes to develop his New Grange research with further study.

Dr Karl Spracklen is a Senior Lecturer in Socio-Cultural Aspects of Sport and Leisure in the Carnegie Faculty of Sport and Education, with research interests in sport and social identity, leisure theory and popular culture. He is currently Course Leader for BA (Hons) Leisure and Sport Studies and Teaching and Research Group Leader for the Social Sciences of Sport and Leisure.

Dr Jon Tan is a Senior Lecturer in Education in the Carnegie Faculty of Sport and Education. Graduating with a D.Phil. (Social Policy) from the University of York, his work spans issues in education and welfare, with focus on the educational progressions of children and young people, practitioner learning and the implementation of policy initiatives. Since joining Leeds Met, he has led a number of research programmes funded by the Economic & Social Research Council, the Esmee Fairbairn Foundation, and the Department for Education & Skills. His current work within teacher education examines the development of critical reflection through international teaching placement opportunities, and the support of professional learning through school-university partnership. Jon is very much involved in the supervision of PhD students, staff research development and research training. His research interests outside of the University include military history, walking the Somme battlefields, and also writing about the operations of the Royal Air Force 1939-45 drawing on oral histories. He is also an accomplished musician.

Back row standing: Prof. Anne Campbell, Iain Poole, David Hall, Prof. Alistair Black, Dr. Ian Richards, Keith Rowntree, Peter D'Sena, Frank Atkins, Dr. Anne Flintoff, Ian Crossland.
Seated: Dr. Jill Adam, Dr. Jon Tan, Dr. Karl Spracklen, Prof. Lori Beckett, Janet Douglas, Dr. Sue Warren, Prof. David Kirk
Front: Jacqui Dean, Rachel Thornton

Editor's Introduction

Lori Beckett

'We live in an age when there is great optimism about the power of education to influence the well being of individuals and nations. Parents and caregivers see education as a way for their children to improve on their own lives by building an understanding of their place in the world. It is also the principle means by which young people, by passing exams and gaining credentials, can gain an advantage in the labour market. Teachers, as they always have, hope to pass on the wisdom of generations in equipping students for the future.'

LAUDER, BROWN, DILLABOUGH and HALSEY (2006)[1]

These words open Lauder et al's edited collection, which focuses on different aspects of education, its role in the nation-state and the link with progress at the turn of this century, but the words could equally apply to the City of Leeds Training College one hundred years ago. City leaders, politicians, and personnel in the newly established local education authority, along with educationists, parents and students put great store in education because they too believed advances in knowledge and scientific understandings played a decisive role in material and social progress. Building a teacher training college in Leeds was a defining moment in history – locally, nationally and educationally. An integral part of the new national system of education that came into being after the 1902 Education Act, it was closely aligned to issues of nation building and national progress. The founders spared no cost (**Figure 1**), which allowed for the most modern technology (**Figure 2**), evident in our heritage at the Headingley campus site (**Figure 3**). The *Journal of Education*[2] reported it was intended to be the model co-educational training college for all England.

A book to mark the centenary is a fitting tribute to generations of people who have made a contribution to the institution over the years, including academic (**Figure 4**) and domestic (**Figure 5**) staff. It is addressed to Leeds Metropolitan University, its present incarnation, academic staff (**Figure 6**), estate staff (**Figure 7**), students, alumni and

Fig. 1
Council of City of Leeds Annual Report for Education Committee, 1910-1911, Appendix D. Statistics Regarding Finance. (Source: Leeds Local and Family History Library L352.02 LS17)

Right, Fig. 2
Journal report on modern technology at CLTC. (Source: Copy held by Iain Poole)

STATISTICS REGARDING FINANCE.

COMPARISON OF RECEIPTS AND EXPENDITURE.

RECEIPTS. For Year ended 31st March.							EXPENDITURE. For Year ended 31st March.					
1911.			1910.				1911.			1910.		
£	s.	d.	£	s.	d.		£	s.	d.	£	s.	d.
338,509	18	2	313,787	13	5	Elementary Education ...	327,877	4	4	325,211	6	5
103,395	1	3	93,821	17	4	Higher Education	98,725	4	4	98,211	17	7
*7,628	4	3	—				*7,628	4	3	—		
449,533	3	8	407,609	10	9	Total Revenue Account ...	434,230	12	11	423,423	4	0
—			33,709	0	0	Loans (El. Ed.)..	17,874	3	8	18,642	8	0
71,700	0	0	5,127	0	0	„ (H. Ed.)..	11,119	18	10	3,200	19	5
521,233	3	8	446,445	10	9	Total Revenue and Capital...	463,224	15	5	445,266	11	5

* Grant from Board of Education of 75 per cent. of cost of Training College Buildings in course of erection paid into Sinking Fund.

INCOME FROM LOCAL RATES.

	1911.			1910.			Rate in the £.			
							1911.		1910.	
	£	s.	d.	£	s.	d.	s.	d.	s.	d.
Elementary Education Account	153,862	10	6	153,395	3	10	1	5¼	1	5¾
Higher Education Account ...	35,678	5	4	26,677	8	6	0	4	0	3
For Education	189,540	15	10	180,072	12	4	1	9¼	1	8¼
For Medical Inspection ...	2,229	17	10	2,223	2	5	0	0¼	0	0¼
For Expenditure under the Provision of Meals Act ...	4,459	15	8	4,446	4	9	0	0½	0	0½
TOTAL	196,230	9	4	186,741	19	6	1	10	1	9

OUTSTANDING DEBT.

The outstanding debt of the Education Committee on 31st March, 1911, was £1,093,186 10s. 7d., distributed as follows :—

On Loans raised for						£	s.	d.
Public Elementary Schools	...	...	...	...	...	796,184	7	7
Industrial Schools	...	...	...	...	...	26,150	12	3
Special Schools ...	...	...	...	...	...	31,756	0	10
Offices	...	...	...	...	...	20,925	4	8
Higher Education	...	...	...	...	...	218,170	5	3

HOLOPHANE ILLUMINATION.

"The glass of fashion and the mould of form."—*Hamlet.*

Vol. III.	DECEMBER, 1912.	No. 4.

HOLOPHANE ILLUMINATION AT THE CITY OF LEEDS TRAINING COLLEGE.

The Gymnasium at the City of Leeds Training College illuminated by Tungsten Lamps and Holophane Reflectors.
(Photo. taken entirely by artificial light.)

THE HOLOPHANE System of Illumination has been widely used in educational institutions of every description. It is equally well suited to the illumination of school-rooms, laboratories, workshops, and gymnasiums.

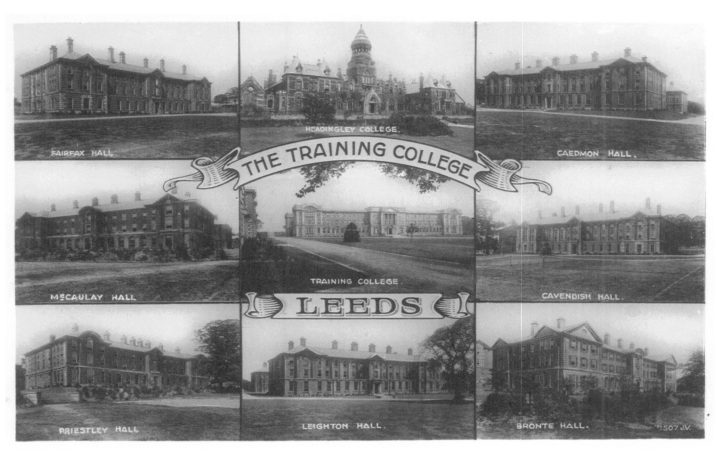

Fig. 3
Promotional postcard for
CLTC. (Source: Leeds
Metropolitan University
Archives)

local community, including Education Leeds as the descendent of the education authority responsible for bringing the College into being. It is also addressed to educationists interested in teacher education and analyses of the pioneering work done in the fledgling local authority training colleges.

This centenary book is not meant to be an academic exercise, although we showcase the work of academics with colleagues and university friends. We hope it will be of interest to a wide range of people and take its place among other anniversary books all published by the institution: to celebrate its twenty-first[3] (**Figure 8**), its fiftieth[4] (**Figure 9**), and its seventy-fifth[5] (**Figure 10**). In view of these erstwhile publications, we decided this centenary book would take as its theme 'then' and 'now' and provide a snapshot of our heritage, including the site, the genesis of the College, and its work at the turn of the 20th century, as well as a glimpse of the work done at Leeds Met at the turn of the 21st century. This centenary book has its work cut out because the history of education is complex, and like Simon (1974)[6] said, full of incident and interest, touching on all sides of life, on the outlook and interests of all classes of society.

It is crucial to acknowledge the many people who have contributed much to the publication. Carnegie Faculty Senior Lecturer Peter de Sena first mooted the idea for a centenary book project in September 2005, when I came over for interview for my position as Professor of Education. My curiosity was sparked by William Beckett (**Figure 11**) and his history, including the family estate (**Figure 12**). When packing in Australia and preparing to come back, I came across an old Deakin University[7] monograph (**Figure 13**) that focused on a prestigious independent school as an object of curriculum study.

Fig. 4
CLTC academic staff and handwritten list of names. (Source: Leeds Metropolitan University Archives)

I brought it thinking it might be useful for the centenary book. On arrival in February 2006, I talked to colleagues about making the City of Leeds Training College an object of study from different disciplinary perspectives, given the Beckett family history, local history, social and education history, including teacher training, curriculum, teaching methods, and student life.

This idea was well received. Vice-Chancellor Professor Simon Lee, Pro-Vice-Chancellor (Research) Professor Sheila Scraton, and Carnegie Dean Professor David Kirk gave me every encouragement to organise an edited collection, and so this version of a centenary book project came to fruition. Carnegie Faculty Principal Lecturer Iain Poole introduced me to records of the City of Leeds Training College (**Figure 14**) and Grier's (1937)[8] biography of the first so-called Lady Vice-Principal, Winifred Mercier (**Figure 15**), which gave me insights into the history of the institution and major players. Headingley campus library staff Helen Loughran, Keith Rowntree and Lou Charnley responded to my every question about the site, the Beckett family, and the College, and provided inestimable help with library archives, inter-library loans and photos. Carnegie Faculty colleagues Julie Harpin and Jane Barber pointed me in the direction of the Leeds Central Library and local historian David Hall's (2000)[9] millennium history (**Figure 16**), which was a wealth of information, especially in relation to the Beckett family.

The contributing authors, photographed and named in the list after the table of contents, came together throughout 2006 and slowly helped shape the book with suggestions for possible themes and chapters,

Fig. 6 Leeds Met Carnegie ITE academic staff. Back row; Liz Beasley, Dave Overton, Dave Little, Philippa Hamilton, Tom Dobson, Beverley Keen, Jonathan Doherty, Graham Turner. Third row; Kevin Williams, Chris Hines, Susan Waltham, Yinka Olusoga, Sarah Whiter, Jill Adam, Jane Barber, Avril Brock, Peter Mellor. Second row, left to right; Lori Beckett, Anne Campbell, Jean Laight, Jon Tan, Bridget Cooper, Ros Geldart. Front row, left to right; Janet Henry, Louise Nelson, Christine Allen, Pat Broadhead, Denise Gilchrist, Ruth Sutcliffe, Sue Warren, Yasmin Valli, Peter D'Sena. (Source: LeedsMet. Communications: Icon Photography)

Bottom left, Fig. 5 CLTC domestic staff. (Source: Copy of 1913 photo held by Jim Farmery; grandmother Beatrice May Craig standing on the right, aged 17)

Fig. 7 Leeds Met estate staff, top row left to right: Geoff Ibbotson, Ann Fitzgerald, Linda Foster, Frances Cooke, Sandra Noteman, Dominic Cartwright. Front row: Becky Oldfield, Carol Wright, Lauren Wright. (Source: LeedsMet. Communications: Icon Photography)

Fig. 10 Front cover of Connell's book for 75th anniversary. (Source:
Leeds Metropolitan University Archives)

each one focused on a different segment of the history guided by their
own academic interest and expertise. The Leeds Met Alumni Foundation
pledged to fund the production and publication. The Carnegie Faculty
gave me time and financial support to employ a research assistant, Ian
Kaplan (**Figure 17**), who worked tirelessly over a number of months with
me as we searched for, then travelled some miles to study, archives and
library materials. Ian also proved an invaluable source of support to the
team of contributing authors. Likewise Iain Poole (**Figure 18**) who came
back after retirement and worked for three months to help in numerous
ways with the preparation of manuscripts and images for book production.

Archivists Gilly King (Whitelands College, Roehampton

Fig. 11 William Beckett, from painting in Leeds Civic Hall. (Source: Leeds Museums and Galleries)

University), Kate Perry (Girton College, Cambridge University), Stephanie Davidson (West Yorkshire Archive Service), and Oliver Pickering (Brotherton Library, Leeds University) provided great help and guidance. Carnegie Faculty Senior Lecturer Andy Bowles alerted us to the Carnegie Faculty archives and their role in initial teacher education. Carnegie Learning Support Officers Simon Op Den Brouw and Neil Priestley scanned images, Design Officer Linda Gilhespy searched Leeds Met Communications Archives, and Copyright Officer Rachel Thornton did an extraordinary amount of work to secure copyright permission. Registrar and Secretary Steve Denton took responsibility for final decisions. Design team manager Philippa O'Byrne was responsible for the book layout.

Managing Director Tony Sidebottom along with Fred Lindop and John Parker of Collective (UK) Ltd coordinated production of the book.

We are very fortunate having such rich archival material to draw on and use, thanks to the endeavours of Keith Rowntree in the Headingley library (**Figure 19**), who preserved and organised what remained of the College records. Sadly, so much has been lost or discarded over time, but enough remains to build a small Leeds Met archive. These include maps, drawings, reports, administrative records, handwritten and typed letters, photos, Grier's book, scrapbooks of newspaper clippings, examination papers, the *Owl* student magazines, and other educational materials (**Figure 20**), which complement what we found elsewhere. The archive also holds the Leeds School Board (1899) *Yearbook* (**Figure 21**), teaching materials, students' records and recollections (memories), photos (**Figure 22**), and a study guide[10] featuring D. H. Lawrence's teaching experiences at the turn of the 20th century. We bought memorabilia at auction (**Figure 23**), and located early books and journals, Mercier's records and journal articles, the 1902 Education Act, Board of

In Affectionate Remembrance of
WILLIAM BECKETT, Esquire,
Late Banker in Leeds,
Who Represented Leeds in Parliament for many years.
He was born in the year of grace 1784, fifth Son of Sir John Beckett,
by Mary, daughter of Dr. Christopher Wilson, Bishop of Bristol.
He married Frances Adeline, third daughter of Hugo Meynell, Esquire,
and the Honorable Elizabeth Ingram, daughter and co-heiress of
Viscount Irwin, of Templenewsam.
He died on the 26th January, 1863, aged 78, without leaving issue.
His remains are consigned to the Cemetery in Kensall Green.
Eminently distinguished by his unceasing readiness to promote all plans of
benevolence and general utility ; he also took an active part
in all that concerned the welfare of Leeds.
The founder of several schools, he sought to advance and extend the
education of the people in Christian principles.
A Faithful but tolerant Member of the Church of England,
He gave to that Church on all occasions his substantial support,
largely contributing to the repairs and construction of its sacred edifices.
In business he was liberal, judicious, and public spirited.
At a period of great local pressure he merged his own interests and saved
the credit of the town.
In Parliament he was amongst the foremost in supporting and carrying
the measure for the shortening of the working hours for
women and children.
Though William Beckett has left a far nobler monument of himself
in the hearts of all those who knew him,
This humble record of so excellent a man may serve to preserve his memory
When they and their children shall have followed him to the grave,
It will thus fulfil the pious intentions of his sorrowing widow and extend
the usefulness of his example to future generations.

*Fig. 12
Dedication to William
Beckett. (Source: Moore
(1877) A History of the
parish church of Leeds)*

Portrait of The Geelong College: Continuity and Change in an Independent School

Fig. 13
Front cover of Deakin University (1979) monograph. (Source: Courtesy of Robert Ingpen and Deakin University)

Education official documents, the Connell collection known as the Leeds Local Education Authority papers, among them detailed records on the establishment of the City of Leeds Training College, for example, invoices and receipts for housekeeping needs such as a quote (**Figure 24**) from Harper's Dairies for milk supply.

Studying the archives for this centenary event gave us an opportunity to do more than peer into the past. They provided us with a variety of sources to begin a documentary-based study of the City of Leeds Training College. As the Carnegie archives study guide put it, such sources enable us

. . . to examine the witness they give and see what we think about the quality of the evidence provided in various sources . . . to consider how far this might help us reconstitute what happened . . . and to ask whether it is any use to us – are we wiser after the enquiry, and in what ways?

This approach dovetailed with McCullough's (2004)[11] approach to documentary research, particularly where he encouraged us to read between the lines. Following his lead, we studied the documentary sources, developed the storyline of the estate and identified the plot of teacher training one hundred years ago, and tried to get between the lines to analyse

meanings and deeper purpose. Of course, we could only offer our own perspectives but our investigation of teacher training 'then' in 1907 Edwardian England and 'now' in 2007 Elizabethan England sat well with McCulloch's concerns about both historical and contemporary documentary studies in education. As he said:

Education is interesting and useful partly because of its role in incorporating and transmitting cultural heritages and traditions, that is, it forms a means to develop knowledge, understanding and values from one generation to the next . . . It is also a major feature of social and economic policy in modern societies, especially in the modern period in the form of national systems of schooling, universities and, most latterly, lifelong learning (p. 4).

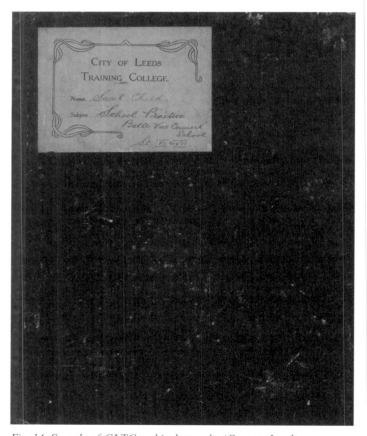

Fig. 14 Sample of CLTC archival records. (Source: Leeds Metropolitan University Archives)

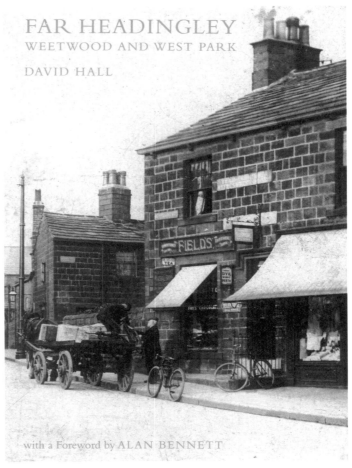

Fig. 16 Front cover of David Hall's (2000) millennium book

Left, Fig. 15 Front cover of Grier's (1937) biography

City of Leeds Training College Vice-Principal Winifred Mercier recognised this connection. Grier (1937) reported she was greatly interested in educational and social policy and encouraged her students to take part in social work in the city of Leeds, as far as their programs would allow. Writing after her departure from the College, Mercier spelt out her views in a review article[12] devoted to an analysis of educational policy, crucial at the time when the task was to conceive an organised scheme of education for schools in urban settings and training for teachers. Aware of the shift from out-of-school experience-based education to presenting knowledge in schools ready-made and remote from the child's real life of effort and action, her concern was for the reform of education:

The only way to reform education is to reform our social and industrial life. In the meantime we must work at both ends. The function of education is not only to fit young people to master the art of life as their fathers (and we would add their mothers or carers) knew it, but to make discoveries themselves. Schools must not only be repositories of tradition, but also workshops of the future.

This centenary book, reflecting current work at Leeds Met, endeavoured to work at both ends. In chapters of approximately 3,000 words with images of documentary sources used to portray the story segment, contributing authors connected education in its social, political and historical context, past and present with a vision of the future. In the early chapters it was not always possible to make explicit the connection, so we decided to top and tail the book with 'then' and 'now' to get the balance right. Throughout we engaged critical interpretations of both

Fig. 17 Research assistant Ian Kaplan. (Source: Ian Kaplan)

Fig. 18 Editor's assistant Iain Poole. (Source: Keith Rowntree)

Below, Fig. 19 Keith Rowntree in archive room, Headingley Campus library. (Source: Keith Rowntree)

historical and contemporary documentary sources, noting the significance of context. In the chapters devoted to City of Leeds Training College, we tapped into arguments and debates waged at the time, and to draw a line with work at Leeds Met, we tapped into present-day discussions and debates about different aspects of teacher education, locally and globally.

Keith Rowntree generously contributed the timeline, compiled after many years of documentary research, and while 1907 was a significant date, a close look reveals many anniversaries. 1207 was the date of Hugh de Kirkstall's written record of *The Foundation of Kirkstall Abbey*,[13] 1807 marked the visit to the Grange by William Wordsworth and sister Dorothy, and 2007 is the four hundredth anniversary of the City of Leeds charter. The timeline provided a sketch of history, a backdrop to the chapters that follow.

Keith Rowntree and Peter de Sena drew on a number of documentary sources to detail the site's history across seven centuries up to, but not including, William Beckett's occupancy. Using mediaeval manuscripts, maps, deeds, parish registers, births, deaths and marriage records, artworks, special collections, newspapers, research reports, historical and contemporary literature, they trace land ownership alongside local social and political history.

In the chapter on the Beckett family, local historian David Hall contributed much from his millennium book, which complemented detailed documentary research done by Ian Crossland, who also helped plan our meeting to interview the current Lord Grimthorpe, the Rt Honorable Mr Edward John Beckett, at his place of work in Newmarket and the family home in Yorkshire. This was a particular thrill for me, given my paternal family history, although sadly I have not made any connections!

Janet Douglas' chapter on the establishment of the City of Leeds Training College drew primarily on administrative records, the 1902 Education Act and its antecedents, plus the debates about education and teacher training evident in commentaries, public media campaigns, and local history books as well as scholarly articles on the history of education. These documentary sources allowed Janet to tell the story of the political history, including note of the personalities and conflicts that characterised the official opening on 19 October 1907.

Jill Adam and Anne Campbell contributed to the chapter on partnerships. Using information gleaned from early official documentation, photos, and scholarly work on history of education, they concentrated on

*Left, Fig. 20
CLTC blazer, example
of artefacts held by
Leeds Metropolitan
University Archives*

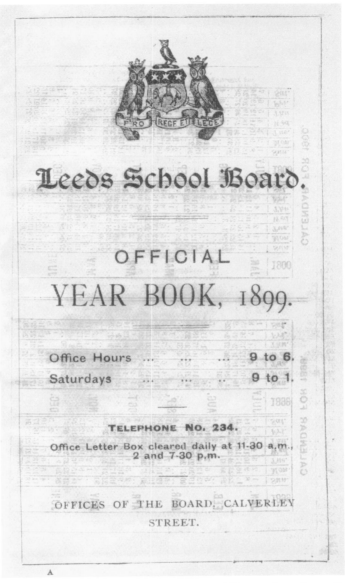

*Fig. 21 Leeds School
Board (1899) Yearbook,
example of artefacts
held by Leeds
Metropolitan University
Archives*

teacher training work in schools 'then', which was concerned with school experience for pupil teachers and student teachers in the temporary College. This lent itself to a descriptive analysis of the school-university partnerships 'now' and the documentary sources that support our work with teacher partners in continuing professional development.

Alistair Black contributed work on the built environment, which includes heritage buildings and spaces both exterior and interior on the Headingley campus, and which attracts the term *remains* in documentary research (see McCulloch, 2002, p. 3). Drawing on documentary records of the initial architectural competition for the design, maps, site plans, drawings, photos, and administrative records on costing, Alistair read the buildings and spaces, much like we read other documentary evidence, and offers a critical interpretation of their meaning and legacy.

Lori Beckett with Anne Flintoff and Sue Warren drew on official documentation and Winifred Mercier's records to concentrate on teacher training as it evolved at the City of Leeds Training College, which proved no exception when it came to debates about the preparation of young people for the teaching profession, given the shift away from the pupil-teacher system, progressive ideas about democracy and education, women's and girls' education, socialism and popular education, to name a few. Such debates fed into the scandal that rocked the College and education establishment at the outbreak of World War One, with the resignation of the first Lady Vice-Principal and eight women tutors. The lessons learned from the National Inquiry into what happened resonate

Fig. 22 Photo of former CLTC student, Rachel Ross, example of photographs held by Leeds Metropolitan University Archives.

even 'now' in efforts to reform teacher education.

Lori Beckett, David Kirk and Iain Poole wrote about the teacher training curriculum 'then', best represented in the City of Leeds Training College records of staff and subject areas, student work, the Board of Education (1912) regulations, syllabus, and accompanying examination papers. These document sources alerted us to the knowledge required by candidates for their certification as teachers or assistants, and the elementary school classroom. It must have been an onerous task of study and preparation, which gives pause to reflect on requirements 'now', especially in the light of recent Carnegie Faculty inspections by the Office for Standards in Education (Ofsted), one for the primary school programs and one for secondary school physical education.

Lori Beckett and Jon Tan drew on early scholarly work and documentary sources to concentrate on teaching methods 'then'. These were the topic of some debate, as Winifred Mercier's (1909)[14] article on experimental pedagogy show, written when she was a high school teacher engaged in a nascent form of teacher research. This lent itself to a critical discussion of pedagogies 'now', similarly characterised by debates about

teaching and learning in schools and in teacher education. Lori and Jon drew on documentary evidence from Carnegie Faculty work in initial teacher education to promote the teacher-as-researcher.

Jacqui Dean concentrated on students' experiences and used documentary records including photos and handwritten recollections of teacher training donated by past students of the City of Leeds Training College. These records are priceless and complement the scholarly work in history of education devoted to documenting teacher training. Jacqui drew on contemporary documentary sources to describe the student experience at Leeds Met 'now', especially given efforts to encourage a diversity of young people into teacher education through the *Widening Participation* project.

Sport was a regular and revered feature of student life at the City of Leeds Training College, evident in the sports facilities or *remains* still in use today. Ian Richards, Karl Spracklen and Tony Collins drew on photos, student magazines, records of fixtures, programmes, and scholarly work on the history of sport to describe the part it played in the education of young men and women 'then'. They connected the student story to historical debates about gender and class and developments in the wider world of

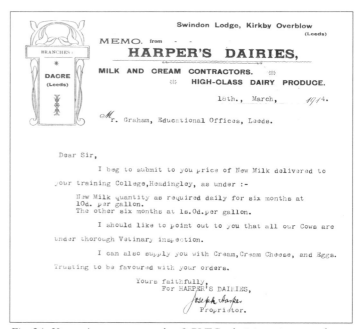

Fig. 24 Harper's quote, example of CLTC administrative records held by West Yorkshire Archive Service. (Source: WYAS, Leeds, ref. WYL863/16)

Fig. 23
Example of memorabilia
bought at auction.
(Source: Postcard held
by Iain Poole)

sport, such as the social history of football, elements of which can be seen in the student experience of Leeds Met sport 'now'.

Keith Rowntree and Frank Atkins cleverly combined their respective work on the 2nd Northern General Hospital and Masters' degree research on military hospitals, which together contributed to a chapter on the destiny of the City of Leeds Training College during the First (and Second) World Wars. They use a priceless scrapbook of photos donated by Sergeant George Sprittles, together with military documentation, including the hospital magazine produced for the wounded and medical staff, local histories and scholarly work on military hospitals.

In the final carefully crafted chapter, Vice-Chancellor Professor Simon Lee reflects on this centenary book in relation to the Leeds Met Vision and Character statement, and highlights character as the running stream through our history. He then draws on contemporary documentary sources to concentrate on Leeds Met now and to articulate his vision for the institution. This compliments the earlier chapters and provides coherence to theme of 'then' and 'now'.

In closing, I am prompted to say this centenary book has only begun the task of a documentary-based study of the City of Leeds Training College. I am grateful to the contributing authors, and I do hope they go on to use their chapters as the basis of scholarly articles for publication. I would here like to issue an invitation to anyone interested in pursuing documentary research into our heritage to please make contact. We have a wealth of archival materials waiting for systematic and methodical study of developments leading up to the establishment of the City of Leeds Training College and since, to understand and expound our contemporary educational practices. Finally, I only hope this centenary book contributes to the reflections called for by Vice-Chancellor Professor Simon Lee[15] on each generation of education pioneers who have worked in the settings we are so privileged to inherit.

ENDNOTES

[1] Lauder, H., Brown, P., Dillabough, J., and Halsey, A.H. (eds) (2006) Introduction: The Prospects for Education: Individualization, Globalization, and Social Change. In *Education, Globalisation and Social Change*. Oxford: Oxford University Press.

[2] March, 1917, issue.

[3] City of Leeds Training College *Coming of Age Celebrations Souvenir Handbook 1907-1928*.

[4] R. W. Rich (n.d) *A Short History of the City of Leeds Training College 1907-1957*.

[5] Connell, L. (n.d) *A Century of Teacher Training in Leeds 1875-1975*.

[6] Simon, B. (1974) *The Two Nations and the Educational Structure 1780-1870*. London: Lawrence and Wishart.

[7] Fitzpatrick, M., Green, H., and Lomas, L. (1979) *Portrait of The Geelong College: Continuity and Change in an Independent School*. Geelong: Deakin University Open Campus Program. School of Education CT431 Curriculum Design and Development.

[8] Grier, L. (1937) The *Life of Winifred Mercier*. London: Oxford University Press.

[9] Hall, D. (2000) *Far Headingley, Weetwood and West Park*. Leeds: Far Headingley Village Society.

[10] Fines, J., Nichol, J., and Deane, J. (n.d.) *Introduction to teaching history*. Project funded by Nuffield Foundation.

[11] McCulloch (2004) *Documentary Research in Education, History and the Social Sciences*. London: RoutledgeFalmer.

[12] Mercier, W. (1924) Review. The Children of England. A Contribution to Social History and to Education by J. J. Findlay (Methuen and Co.). *The Forum of Education*, vol.ii.

[13] Cited by Sprittles, J. (n.d) New Grange, Kirkstall. Its Owners and Occupants. Reprinted from the Publications of the *Thoresby Society. Miscellany*, Vol.13, Part 1 (original held by Thoresby Society).

[14] Mercier, W. (1909) An experiment in the teaching of history. Published in Leaflet no.17, June, by the Historical Association.

[15] See VC Reflects Thursday, 8 March 2007 (http://www.leedsmet.ac.uk/vco/reflect/vc)

CHRONOLOGY

Across the Open Field:
A Chronology of New Grange, Kirkstall Grange and Beckett Park

Keith Rowntree

This chronology is an attempt to provide an overview of the historical development of the estate site and its subsequent incarnation as the City of Leeds Training College and more recently Leeds Metropolitan University's Headingley Campus. It is based on documentary research done over a ten year period, which included work with the Leeds Metropolitan University archives, and records held by the Thorseby Society, West Yorkshire Archive Service, the Leeds Library and Information Services, and National Archives, to mention just a few repositories. The chronology also reflects collaborative work done with university colleagues, both in the Headingley campus and Civic campus libraries, as well as across faculties. Information gleaned from various conversations with past and present staff, and their contributions, must be acknowledged. The title for this chronology is taken from a line in one of T.S.Eliot's Four Quartets, East Coker, *which is a commentary on time.*

Fig. 1 Abbot Alexander, decorated tile in De Lacy Room at Abbey House Museum, Kirkstall. (Source: ©Leeds Museum and Galleries, Abbey House)

Fig. 2 Henry De Lacy, decorated tile in De Lacy Room at Abbey House Museum, Kirkstall. (Source: ©Leeds Museum and Galleries, Abbey House)

NEW GRANGE

Pre-Medieval Stone coffin and stone slab cist discovered in Beckett's Park Drive, thought to be either Roman or Saxon. Discovery opens up speculation as to extent of burials in the area and any associated settlement.[1]

1152-1182 Lands in West and East Headingley granted to Kirkstall Abbey by William de Peitivin a tenant of Henry de Lacy, Baron of Pontefract. Moor Grange and Bar Grange were established during the time of Alexander, the first abbot of Kirkstall. New Grange as the name suggests was a later grange establishment[2 3] (**Figures 1 & 2**).

1288 New Grange referred to as Planum Locum on an Extent of Kirkstall lands.[4 5]

1539 Dissolution of Kirkstall Abbey.

1539-40 Survey of dissolved religious houses in Yorkshire made by Henry VIII, mentions the demesne lands in Kirkstall which includes '... una grangia vocata New Graunge ...' also Oxmore, Friday Syke and Sawtree, field names that appear on later maps and plans.[6 7]

1541 Henry VIII leased Kirkstall monastery lands to Robert Pakeman, of the King's Household. including '... *a grange called Newgrange and a close of pasture adjacent called Oxemore ...*'.[8]

1542 Archbishop Thomas Cranmer held the Crown's interest in Kirkstall.[9]

1556 Following Cranmer's execution the lands passed back to the Crown.

1559 Some of the Kirkstall lands, including New Grange, reinstated to Cranmer family, Thomas Cranmer II, the former Archbishop's son. The Abbey site and adjoining lands already bought by the Saville family from the Crown.[10]

1559 Anthony son of Henry Wade baptised at Halifax on 26 November.

1560-80 The Foxcroft family originally from Halifax district first noted in the Kirkstall area, at Bar Grange.[11 12 13] At first probably tenants of Thomas Cranmer II or Sir Thomas Cecil, who had bought the lands from Cranmer.[14] It was during this time that Thomas Foxcroft bought New Grange.

1560-70 Thomas Foxcroft married to Joana Cliffe. Thomas Foxcroft held the 13th-century Arundel 248 manuscripts, gifted to Henry Saville.[15]

1585 Thomas Foxcroft paid 13d for a stall adjoining the old pulpit at Leeds Parish Church.[16]

1587 Will of George Foxcrofte of Barrgrange, described Thomas Foxcrofte as his nephew living at 'Newegrange'.[17]

1590 Anthony Wade married Judith daughter of Thomas Foxcroft, at Leeds Parish Church on 3 November.[18]

1590 Benjamin Wade son of Anthony Wade and Judith Foxcroft born.

1595 Wife of Thomas Foxcroft of New Graung buried at Leeds 22 April.[19]

1596/97 Thomas Foxcroft buried at Leeds 20 March, his Will left his son Isacke '. . . *all the sealing and all the glasse in the windowes which are in or about the house in Newgrainge . . .*'.[20] [21]

1596/97 Isaacke ffoxcrofte recorded living in Headingley on a Leeds Borough Subsidy.[22]

***c*.1604** Anthony Wade purchased New Grange from Isaac Foxcroft.

1610/11 Benjamin Wade (1590-1671) entered Emmanuel College, Cambridge 14 February.

1618 Benjamin Wade (1590-1671) married Edith daughter of John Shann of Leeds.[23] They had no children.[24]

***c*.1620** Anthony Wade died.

1621 Benjamin Wade (1590-1671) recorded on the Skyrack Lay Subsidy evidence that he was one of the wealthiest inhabitants of Headingley.[25]

Fig. 3
Photo of Kirkstall Abbey. (Source: Keith Rowntree, 2007)

Fig. 4
Photo of Kirkstall
Abbey. (Source: Keith
Rowntree, 2007)

1626 Benjamin Wade (1590-1671), Anthony's son, rebuilt New Grange.[26] Benjamin Wade was one of nine men who bought an interest in the manor of Leeds, making him one of the lords of the manor[27] (**Figures 3 & 4**).

1627 Benjamin Wade (1590-1671) recorded on the Skyrack Lay Subsidy, a further indication of his wealthy status.[28]

1652/53 Edith Wade formerly Shann buried at Headingley 2 January.[29]

1663 Benjamin Wade (1590-1671), Mayor of Leeds.

1664 Anthony Wade married Mary Moor daughter of John Moor of Greenhead in Lancashire.[30][31]

1665 Benjamin son of Anthony Wade and Mary Moor born, possibly in Padiham or Burnley, Lancashire.

1671 Benjamin Wade (1590-1671) died at New Grange.[32]

1671-88 Evidence of protracted Inheritance Disputes. Anthony Wade, Benjamin's nephew inherited New Grange.[33]

1672 Skyrack Hearth Tax Returns record Anthony Wade having 13 hearths, demonstrating that New Grange was a substantial house by this time.[34]

1676 Anthony Wade was Mayor of Leeds.[35]

1683 Benjamin Wade (1665-1716) on 30 March matriculated Corpus Christi College, Oxford, aged 17.[36]

1683 On 11 May Benjamin Wade (1665-1716), Anthony's son admitted to Gray's Inn, London.[37]

1683 Anthony Wade died 14 December.[38] Benjamin Wade (1665-1716) inherited New Grange.[39]

1684 Benjamin Wade (1665-1716) married Anne Calverley on 7 April.[40]

1694 A monument of white marble erected by Benjamin Wade (1665-1716) to the memory of his ancestors in Headingley Chapel. It was lost in the rebuilding of the church.[41][i]

1696 Walter Wade (1696-1726), Benjamin Wade (1665-1716) and Anne Calverley's fifth son born at New Grange 19 August.[42]

1706 Anne Wade formerly Calverley, died 7 May.[43]

1712 Benjamin Wade (1665-1716) was a Justice of the Peace for the West Riding.

1715 Benjamin Wade Esq. (1665-1716) of New Grange subscribed to Thoresby's first edition of *Ducatus Leodiensis*.[44]

1716 Benjamin Wade (1665-1716) died 17 May. His funeral at Headingley Chapel was attended by 'most of the neighbouring gentleman'.[45] Benjamin Wade (1686-1719) his eldest surviving son inherited New Grange.

1717 Walter Wade (1696-1726) married Beatrix daughter of Benjamin Killingbeck of Allerton Grange, at Weston on 2 December.[46]

1718 Benjamin Wade (1686-1719), Benjamin Wade's (1665-1716) second son was Mayor of Leeds. He died on 17 May the following year. He is the only Mayor of Leeds to die during his mayoralty.[47]

1719 Around this time Walter Wade (1696-1726), Benjamin Wade's (1665-1716) fifth son, inherited New Grange from his brother

Benjamin (1686-1719). Walter's four elder brothers had all died.[48]

1722 Walter son of Walter Wade (1696-1726) baptised at Headingley Chapel on 1 November. Walter is recorded as residing at New Grange.[49]

1725 New Grange and Estate put up for let, described as the seat of the late Benjamin Wade Esq.[50]

1726 Walter Wade senior (1696-1726) died in the early spring. His will states that Walter Wade (1722-1771) the younger of his two sons should inherit his estates along with his wife Beatrix. Benjamin Wade (1718-1759?), his eldest son, was already beneficiary of the will of Walter Wade senior's (1696-1726) brother, Benjamin Wade (1686-1719) who had died in 1719.[51]

1740/41 Walter Wade (1722-1771) son of Walter Wade (1696-1726) of New Grange matriculated 14 February University College, Oxford, aged 17.[52]

1749 Walter Wade (1722-1771) married Ann Allanson daughter of Robert Allanson of Royd.[53]

1752 Walter Wade (1722-1771) rebuilt New Grange[ii] employing architect James Paine, original design was a 'villa with wings' although now only the western wing survives much altered by the Beckett family.[54][55]

1756 Walter Wade (1722-1771) of New Grange gave a Paten and Flagon to Headingley Church.[56]

1759 Benjamin (1759-1792) son of Walter Wade (1722-1771) and Ann Allanson born 15 April.[57]

1760-71 John Smeaton drew plans for a Hand Pump for Walter Wade at New Grange.[58]

1766 Wilkinson's Plan of New Grange produced for Walter Wade Esq[59] (**Figure 5**).

1771 Walter Wade (1722-1771) died 16 December.[60] Ann Allanson his widow continued to live at New Grange, his son Benjamin Wade (1759-1792) managed the New Grange estate.[61]

1777 Benjamin Wade (1759-1792) entered Sidney Sussex College, Cambridge 6 November. He had previously attended school at Bingley under Mr Hudson and Cottesmore in Rutland under Mr Brereton.[62]

1787 Benjamin Wade (1759-1792) subscribed to Cary's New and Correct English Atlas.[63]

1792 Benjamin Wade (1759-1792) died at New Grange.[64]

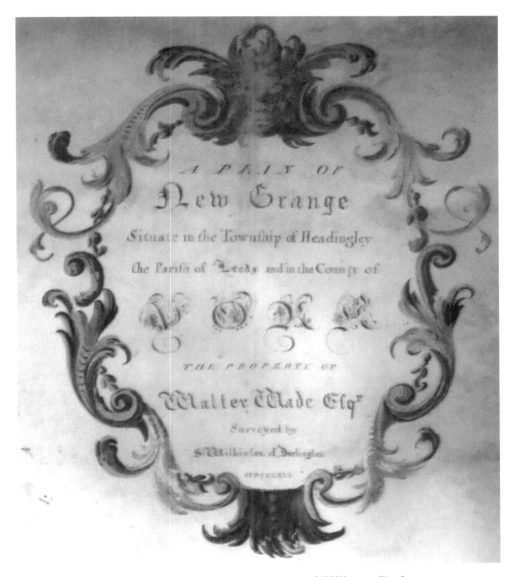

1795 John Marshall married Jane Pollard daughter of William Pollard of Halifax on 5 August.[65]

1795 Mrs Walter Wade (Ann Allanson) auctioned furniture at New Grange.[66]

1798 Thomas Benyon married Jane daughter of Joseph Dalters at Liverpool 30 March.[67]

1804 Samuel Buck, Recorder of Leeds from 1776 to 1806, rented New Grange from Wade family.

Fig. 5
Detail of cartouche from Wilkinson's 1766 plan of New Grange for Walter Wade. (Source: ©The Thoresby Society)

Fig. 6
Sketch of Kirkstall Grange, early 19th century from 'Kirkstall and its neighbourhood'.
(Source: ©Leeds Library and Information Service)

1805 New Grange advertised to be let in *Leeds Intelligencer* on 25 March[68] (**Figure 6**).

1805 John Russell RA produced pastel portraits of John and Jane Marshall.[69]

1805 John Marshall tenant occupier of New Grange.[70]

1806 Samuel Buck buried at Rotherham 1 August.

1807 William and Dorothy Wordsworth visited New Grange, Dorothy was a school friend of Marshall's wife Jane Pollard.[71][72]

1809 Mrs Walter Wade (Ann Allanson) . . . 'of Weetwood, relict of the late Walter Wade Esquire of New Grange . . .' buried at Headingley.[73]

1817 Capt. John Bastard R.N. married Frances Wade, daughter of Benjamin Wade of New Grange on 7 October.[74]

1819 John Marshall added west wing to his new house in Headingley, the now demolished Headingley House, off Kirkstall Lane.[75]

1822 Thomas Benyon leased New Grange from the Wade family. Benyon was originally from Shrewbury and had been a partner of John Marshall latterly a rival in the flax spinning business.[76]

1828 John Neave Wells married Maryann Wade daughter of Benjamin Wade of New Grange on 2 October.

1828 Thomas Benyon's wife Jane died 16 June.[77]

1828 Thompson Wade the last male child of Walter Wade was buried at Headingley on 2 February.[78]

1829 The New Grange Estate advertised in the *Leeds Mercury* on 26 September to be auctioned by George Robins in London.[79 80]

1829 A. H. Holdsworth bought the estate at auction valued at £30,000 but the sale does not appear to have been concluded.[81] It appears that this was Arthur Howe Holdsworth who was one of two MPs for Dartmouth, the other being John Bastard.

1830 New Grange and Park, in the occupation of Thomas Benyon, advertised to be let in the *Leeds Intelligencer* on 30 September.[82]

1832 William Beckett bought New Grange estate from John Bastard husband of Frances Wade.[83] It appears that Thomas Benyon was still tenant until 1833.

1833 Thomas Benyon died at New Grange 22 November.[84]

KIRKSTALL GRANGE

1834-39 Name of New Grange changed by William Beckett to Kirkstall Grange. Major alterations to the house also take place at this time, including bay windows to the south of the house, staircase and service buildings. The Lodge on Otley Road is also built[85 86 87 88] (**Figure 7**).

1838 Gardeners Cottage built.

1840 William Beckett MP married Francis Adeline Meynell on 20 November.[89]

1841 William Beckett in residence at Kirkstall grange with ten house servants.[90]

1845 John Marshall died 6 June at Hallsteads.[91]

1847 Jane Marshall formerly Pollard died 25 January.[92]

1849 Painting of Kirkstall Grange, described as the seat of W. Beckett Esq. by W. R. Robinson. This shows that the east wing of the 1752 remodelling has gone but the bays windows had not yet been built.

The south face of the building appears much as it does today and contains the Beckett Arms in the recessed arch.[93]

1851 Kirkstall Grange occupied by servants headed by Housekeeper Mary Gray.[94] William Beckett and his wife were living in Brighton.[95]

1860 Lord Palmerston was a guest of William Beckett at Kirkstall Grange.[96]

1861 Mary Gray, Housekeeper headed servants at Kirkstall Grange.[97] William Beckett and his wife Adeline at The Park, Brighton.[98]

1863 Kirkstall Grange noted in tourist guide as having fine pictures.[99]

1863 William Beckett died 26 January.[100]

1868 St Chad's Church built on Kirkstall Grange estate parallel to Otley Road. William Beckett is thought to have instigated the idea although he died before much of the plans and works were started. Edmund Beckett (who took the name Denison), his brother, continued the work and is credited as patron of the church.

1871 Kirkstall Grange occupied by servants and their families, headed by Maria Smith described as Farm Servant.[101]

1881 John Hutchison and his family occupied Kirkstall Grange, described as Gardener.[102]

Fig. 7
Artist's impression of Kirkstall Grange estate late 19th century. (Source: © Keith Rowntree, 2007)

Fig. 8
Arch in Queenswood
commemorating Queen
Victoria's visit to Leeds
in 1858. (Source: CLTC
1912 Handbook. Leeds
Met Archive)

Far right, Fig. 9
Photo of Kirkstall
Grange c. 1908. (Source:
CLTC 1912 Handbook.
Leeds Met Archive)

1886 Edmund Beckett Denison, William's nephew (already succeeded to the title of 5th Baronet Beckett in 1874) created 1st Baron (Lord) Grimthorpe.

1891 Census recorded Ernest William Beckett and family with servants living at Kirkstall Grange.[103]

1901 Edward London, Park-keeper and Caretaker lived with his family at Kirkstall Grange.[104]

1901 Edmund Beckett, 1st Baron Grimthorpe died 8 December (St Alban's Cathedral).

1905 Ernest William Beckett became 2nd Baron Grimthorpe after the death of his uncle.

1905-1907 Oscar Wilde was invited to visit the Grange.[105]

1907 Winston Churchill a guest of Ernest Beckett at Kirkstall Grange. Churchill and Beckett were friends as well as Parliamentary colleagues (**Figure 8**).

1908 Ernest Beckett wrote to Churchill asking advice on the sale of Kirkstall Grange and setting up of park. Ernest Beckett believed that the objections were politically motivated.[106] Some Leeds ratepayers objected to the sale of the land and its high cost, Walter Battle produced a pamphlet outlining his objections[107] (**Figure 9**).

CITY OF LEEDS TRAINING COLLEGE

1907 City of Leeds Training College established '. . . as a College for Men and Women who intend to become Teachers in Public Elementary Schools . . .' The main teaching block housed at Harewood Barracks on Woodhouse Lane formerly Leeds Girls High School (otherwise known as St James's Lodge demolished in the late 1960s to make way for the Central Colleges and Ring Road). Residential accommodation for students was rented, women at Weetwood Grange and men at St Ann's Hill. Walter Parsons appointed as Acting Principal.[108]

1908 Additional hostels rented at Buckingham House for men and Kirkstall Grange for women. Alderman Fred Kinder and James Graham, Director of Education began plans to construct a purpose built training college facility in Leeds. They considered several sites but the favourite was the house and grounds of Kirkstall Grange owned by the Beckett family. Ernest Beckett, Lord Grimthorpe also planned to gift some of the land as a public park. Leeds Corporation bought forty acres of land at the proposed cost of £1,200 per acre this is later reduced to £893 per acre. They leased a further 35 acres, purchased in 1912 at a cost of £550 per acre. Nineteen acres of land known as Churchwood are leased. The estate is sold with the proviso that no part of the estate was to be usd for the purpose of a racecourse and that 'no noisome of offensive trade' was to be allowed on any part of the land surrounding the College.[109] [110]

1910-12 A competition was held by Leeds Education Authority to design the new college buildings. The gentle incline of the site was

Fig. 10
Photo of the City of Leeds Training College Grand Opening at Beckett's Park, 13 June 1913. (Source: Leeds Met Archive)

Fig. 11
A ward in the 2nd Northern General Hospital, 1917. (Source: George Sprittles' Scrapbook, Leeds Met Archive)

levelled and the Education Block and seven hostels built, it is estimated that 8,000,000 bricks are used.[111]

1912 Lord Grimthorpe gifted Chuchwood to the College.

1912 Contingency plans were drawn up to prepare for the possibility of mass casualties should war be declared, the task was undertaken by Major J. F. Dobson to establish a hospital in Leeds as part of the Territorial and Reserve Forces Act of 1907.[112]

1912 The College moved into the purpose built site at Beckett Park. The Halls of Residence are: The Grange, Cavendish and Fairfax for men and Brontë, Leighton, Caedmon, Priestley and Macaulay for women.[113] Walter Parsons was appointed Principal.

1913 The official opening took place on 13 June 1913 (**Figure 10**). The proceedings were interrupted by an unnamed suffragette, who used the occasion to highlight the struggle for voting rights for women.[114] Winifred Mercier was appointed Vice-Principal.[115]

1914 On declaration of war the College was commandeered and renamed the 2nd Northern General Hospital. The first administrator was Major J. F. Dobson. Jessie Hills appointed Matron[116] (**Figure 11**).

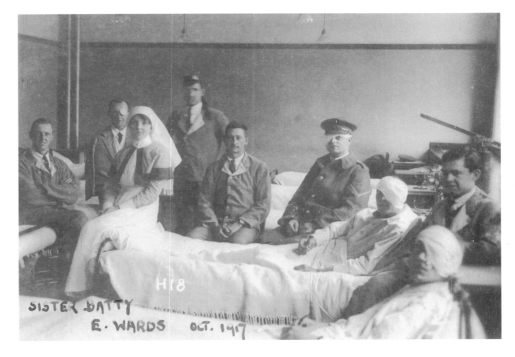

1915 Lieutenant-Colonel Harold Littlewood appointed second administrator. Mabel Whiffen was appointed Matron on Hills being posting to France.[117]

1916 Winifred Mercier resigned as Vice-Principal, eight female lecturers resign in sympathy.[118]

1918 Walter Parsons appointed head of Leeds Central High School. John R. Airey was appointed Principal of the College.

1918 WW1 ended but Army retained possession of the College buildings (**Figure 12**).

1918 Education Act.

1919 Lieutenant-Colonel H. Littlewood retired.[119]

1922 Students Representative Council was set up, a response to the increase of mature students after the war.[120]

1924 College had possession of the buildings but Military Hospital maintain presence in temporary wooden huts on the playing fields.[121]

1924 Mary E. Paine appointed Vice-Principal.[122]

1927 The Military Hospital moved from the wooden huts to new hospital at Chapel Allerton.

1928 The City of Leeds Training College celebrated 21 years.

*Fig. 12
King George V and
Queen Mary inspecting
medical staff and
soldiers based at the 2nd
Northern General
Hospital, 31 May 1918.
(Source: George
Sprittles' Scrapbook,
Leeds Met Archive)*

1929 Board of Administration for the Examination of Students in Yorkshire Training Colleges took over responsibility of examinations from the Board of Education, exams were then internal.[123]

CITY OF LEEDS TRAINING COLLEGE.
CARNEGIE COLLEGE OF PHYSICAL TRAINING

1933 Dr John R. Airey retired and Dr Rowland William Rich was appointed Principal, Helen M. Simpson was appointed Vice-Principal.[124] Carnegie College of Physical Training opened. Ernest Major appointed Warden[125] [126] (**Figure 13**).

1935 Priestley Hall occupied by Yorkshire Training College of Housecraft.

1938 Carnegie was extended including a second gymnasium[127] (**Figures 14 & 15**).

1939 Outbreak of WW2. Ernest Major joined his regiment, Carnegie College was closed.[128] The City of Leeds Training College moved to Scarborough and remained there for six years.[129] Contingency plans were brought into force to reinstate the College buildings as the 18th General Hospital.[130] As the expected number of casualties did not materialise the College became No. 11 Training Depot for the Royal Army Medical Corps and 21st Primary Training Centre.[131] Later in the war the site was used as a repatriation centre for returning POWs.[132]

1944 McNair Report (chaired by Arnold McNair) addressed issues concerning the deficiencies of the training of teachers and youth workers.

1944 Helen Simpson left to become Principal of Exhall Emergency Training College. Mary C. Parnaby appointed in her place.[133]

1945 WW2 ended in Europe and the Far East.

1946 Students from both City of Leeds Training College and Carnegie College of Physical Training returned to the Beckett's Park site. Edwin Bouffler appointed Warden of Carnegie. D. M. Scott appointed lecturer at Carnegie.[134] [135]

1947 Carnegie College of Physical Training renamed Carnegie College of Physical Education. J. H. Dodd appointed at Carnegie, he and D. M. Scott would form the backbone of Carnegie teaching staff until the early 1970s.[136]

1948 University of Leeds Institute of Education assumed

THE OWL

Left, Fig. 13
Front cover of 'The Owl'
College magazine, 1934.
(Source: Leeds Met
Archive)

1960 A three-year Certificate in Education course was introduced. Architects drew up plans for major refurbishment of entire estate.[137]

1961 Last students on the two-year course left College.[138]

1962 H. S. Pickering retired and was succeeded by Dr G. N. Westgarth, who became Deputy Principal.[139]

1963 Dr R. W. Rich retired and Dr Leo Connell appointed Principal. A common administration and governing body was established for the City of Leeds Training College and Carnegie College of Physical Education.[140] Major redevelopment of the Beckett Park Campus took place. The Refectory complex opened, 3,100 meals served each day including 4,000 eggs, 70 gallons of milk and 150 loaves of bread. The Science Block is opened and new Plant came online to provide the entire site with heating. The City of Leeds Training College Library was also extended.[141]

1963 The Robbins Report (Chaired by Lord Robbins) reviewed the state of Higher Education. A major recommendation was the expansion of universities.

1964 Following recommendations made in the Robbins Report The City Of Leeds Training College was renamed The City of Leeds College of Education. A joint governing body was set up to administer the College and Carnegie. Miss Parnaby retired and succeeded as Vice-Principal by Daphne Waite. A new hall of residence was opened the first since Carnegie in 1933 named after R. W. Rich. Queenswood, formerly the Principal's house became a hall of residence for twenty male students.[142]

1965 G. N. Westgrath moved to Shoreditch College as Principal succeeded as Vice-Principal by F. C. Willmot.[143]

1967 The Grange was refurbished. At one point the option to demolish was considered due to the dire condition of the building, which included attack by Death Watch beetle.[144]

CITY OF LEEDS AND CARNEGIE COLLEGE

1968 City of Leeds College of Education Diamond Jubilee. Merger of the City of Leeds College of Education and Carnegie College of Physical Education to form the City of Leeds and Carnegie College. Edwin Bouffler retired and John Evans appointed Director of Carnegie School. The refectory was extended and new Student Centre opened.[145]

responsibility for the curriculum and examinations in the training colleges. Post of Senior Tutor established at City of Leeds Training College, M. T. Woodhouse appointed Senior Tutor.

1953 M. T. Woodhouse died and H. S. Pickering appointed Senior Tutor.

1954 Warden of Carnegie College of Physical Education renamed Principal.

1957 City of Leeds Training College celebrated its Golden Jubilee.

Fig. 14
Group of Carnegie
students, c. 1937.
(Source: Congdon
Collection, Leeds Met
Archive)

1970-72 Building work took place at City of Leeds and Carnegie College expanding and improving the sports facilities, including a new all weather running track. The original 1912 swimming pool renovated.[146]

LEEDS POLYTECHNIC

1970 Leeds Polytechnic founded at the Central Colleges site at Calverley Street merging four colleges Leeds College of Art, Leeds College of Technology, Leeds College of Commerce and Yorkshire College of Education and Home Economics. Patrick Nuttgens appointed first Director.[147]

1972 James Report (chaired by Lord James of Rusholme) recommended reorganisation of the curriculum followed by teacher training courses.

1974 J. H. Dodd retired from City of Leeds and Carnegie College.

1976 City of Leeds and Carnegie College, and James Graham College, merged with Leeds Polytechnic. Clive Bond appointed Head of Carnegie School, John Evans became Deputy Director of Leeds Polytechnic and Arthur Nicholas became Head of School of Education

1976 Dr Leo Connell retired.

1977 D. M. Scott retired from Carnegie.

1978 Fire destroyed much of the Great Hall, part of the original Atkinson design from 1910 to 1912. After two years' work the hall was restored and renamed the James Graham Hall in honour of the Director of Education for Leeds who was instrumental in the establishment of the Training College.[148] In time the name of the Hall became attached to the whole Education Building, now known as the James Graham Building.

1983 Carnegie Golden Jubilee.

Fig. 15
Carnegie students in the
Gym, c. 1937. (Source:
Congdon Collection,
Leeds Met Archive)

1986 Patrick Nuttgens retired as Director of Leeds Polytechnic. Christopher Price appointed.

LEEDS METROPOLITAN UNIVERSITY

1993 12 February 1993, the official inauguration of Leeds Metropolitan University.

1994 Christopher Price retired Professor Leslie Wagner appointed as Principal and Chief Executive, later re-titled Vice-Chancellor of Leeds Metropolitan University.

1994-96 Extensive building work took place at Beckett Park including the creation of a new Learning Centre to incorporate and expand on the Library within James Graham Building. Phase One was completed in September 1994 when the James Graham Hall was redeveloped to house the expanded Learning Centre. The east quadrangle was in-filled with the creation of new Lecture theatre facilities. Phase Two completed in September 1996 when the 1964 ground floor reading room were demolished and rebuilt with an additional two floors, the surrounding corridors were also refurbished as group study space and staff offices. In 1996 the University had 23,000 students over half of which were part time. Improved sports and catering facilities also created.

2003 Professor Leslie Wagner retired, Professor Simon Lee appointed as Vice-Chancellor.

2005 Beckett Park renamed Headingley Campus.

ENDNOTES

[1] WYAS. (1995) West Yorkshire Archaeology Service. *Archaeology in West Yorkshire*. (3) Leeds.

[2] Lancaster, W. and Baildon, W. (1904) *The coucher book of the cistercian abbey of Kirkstall*. 8. Leeds, Publications of the Thoresby Society. pp. 57-60.

[3] Clark, E. ed. (1895) *The foundation of Kirkstall Abbey*. 4. Leeds, Publications of the Thoresby Society. pp. 178-179.

[4] National Archives (1288) *Extent of Kirkstall Lands*. E142/86.

[5] Wright, R. (2002) The granges and estates of Kirkstall Abbey in the 12th and 13th centuries. Ph.D. thesis, University of Leeds.

[6] Dugdale, W. (1846) Monasticon anglicanum: a history of the abbeys and other monasteries in England and Wales. London. p. 551.

[7] Sprittles, J. (1960) *New Grange Kirkstall its owners and occupants*. Leeds, Publications of the Thoresby Society. p. 23.

[8] Ibid. p. 23.

[9] Du Boulay, F. (1952) Archbishop Cranmer and the Canterbury temporalities. *The English Historical Review*. 67 No. 262 January, pp. 19-36.

[10] Hall, D. (2000) *Far Headingley Weetwood and West Park*. Far Headingley, Far Headingley Village Society. p. 12.

[11] Margerison, S. (1891) *Leeds Parish Church registers, first & second books, 1572-1612*. 1, Leeds, Publications of the Thoresby Society. p. 141.

[12] Treen, C. (1977) Buildings and estate development in the northern out-townships of Leeds 1781-1914. Ph.D. thesis, University of Leeds. p. 22.

[13] Brigg, W. ed. (1915-17) *Yorkshire fines for the Stuart period*. Yorkshire Archaeological Society, Record Series, 53, 58.

[14] National Archives (1558-1603) Sir Thomas Cecil v William Arthington and Edward Walker. *Bill to set aside pretended lease, woodland in Kirkstall, Adel and Leeds*. C 2/Eliz/C22/18.

[15] British Library *Arundel Mss 248*. [Internet] Available from:
<http://www.bl.uk/catalogues/illuminatedmanuscripts/record.asp?MSID=7289&CollID=20&NStart=248> [Accessed 8 February 2007].

[16] Margerison, S. (1891) op.cit., p. 82.

[17] Ibid. p. 141.

[18] Ibid. p. 268.

[19] Ibid. p. 313.

[20] Lumb, G. (1909) The family of John Harrison the Leeds benefactor. *Miscellanea*. 15, pp. 48-55. Publications of the Thoresby Society. p. 53.

[21] Sprittles, J. op.cit., p. 24.

[22] Rusby, J. (1891) Leeds borough subsidy, 39th Elizabeth 1596/97. Miscellanea. 2. Leeds, Publications of the Thoresby Society. p. 24.

[23] Clay, J. (ed.). (1909-12) *Paver's marriage licences*. Yorkshire Archaeological Society, Record Series, 40, 43, 46.

[24] Thoresby, R. amended and expanded, Whitaker, T. (1816) 2nd ed. Ducatus Leodiensis: or, the topography of the ancient and populous town and parish of Leedes and parts adjacent in the West Riding of the County of York. Leeds, Robinson, Son & Holdsworth. pp. 153-154.

[25] Stansfield, J. (1891) Subsidy roll for the wapentake of Skyrack 1621. *Miscellanea*. 2. Leeds, Publications of the Thoresby Society. p. 66.

[26] Thoresby, R. amended and expanded, Whitaker, T. (1816) op.cit. pp. 153-154.

[27] Sprittles, J. op.cit. p. 24.

[28] Stansfield, J. (1891) Subsidy roll for the wapentake of Skyrack 1627. *Miscellanea*. 2. Leeds, Publications of the Thoresby Society. p. 78.

[29] Lumb, G. (1895) *Adel parish church registers, 1606-1812 and monumental inscriptions*. 5, Leeds. Publications of the Thoresby Society. p. 40.

[30] Clay, J. (ed.). op.cit.

[31] Thoresby, R. op.cit. pp. 153-154.

[32] National Archives (1671) *Will of Benjamin Wade*. DEL 10/29. National Archives (1671) *Inventory of Benjamin Wade*. DEL 8/60.

[33] National Archives (1671-88) Court of Chancery. Inheritance dispute records concerning the late Benjamin Wade of New Grange. C5/484/5, C7/385/57, C5/172/64, C5/284/10, C5/513/13, C5/72/80, C10/500/157, C10/231/68.

[34] Stansfield, J. (1891) Return of the hearth tax for the wapentake of Skyrack (1). Miscellanea. 2. Leeds, Publications of the Thoresby Society. p. 196.

[35] Thoresby, R. op.cit. pp. 153-154.

[36] Foster, J. (1888-92) Alumni Oxonienses: the members of the University of Oxford, 1500-1714. 4. Oxford, Parker and Co. p. 1550.

[37] Foster, J. ed. (1889) *The register of admission to Gray's Inn 1521-1887*. London, Privately Published. p. 334.

[38] *Summergill collection*. Held at Leeds Local History Library.

[39] Thoresby, R. op.cit. pp. 153-154.

[40] Margerison, S. (1883) Memorandum book of Sir Walter Calverley, bart. in: *Yorkshire diaries and autobiographies in the 17th and 18th C*. Durham, Surtees Society. p. 44.

[41] Wood, R. (1957) *St Michael's, Headingley*. Shipley, The Caxton Press. pp. 78-79.

[42] Margerison, S. (1883) op.cit. p. 50.

[43] Ibid. p. 105.

[44] Thoresby, R. op.cit. pp. 153-154.

[45] Margerison, S. (1883) op.cit. p. 142.

[46] Borthwick Institute, University of York. *Marriage bond of Walter Wade and Beatrix Killingbeck*. MB W 1717.

[47] Summergill op.cit.

[48] Thoresby, R. op.cit. pp. 153-154.

[49] Lumb, G. (1916) *Registers of the chapels of the parish of Leeds, 1724-1763. 23*, Leeds, Publications of the Thoresby Society. p. 4.

[50] New Grange, To be lett. (1725) *Leeds Mercury*. 26 October to 2 November.

[51] Borthwick Institute, University of York (1726) *Admon, will and inventory of Walter Wade*. Diocese of York Prog/Exq 1726.

[52] Foster, J. (1888-92) Alumni Oxonienses: the members of the University of Oxford, 1715-1886. 4. Oxford, Parker and Co. p. 1479.

[53] Borthwick Institute, University of York. *Marriage bond of Walter Wade and Ann Allenson*. MB W 1748.

[54] *Kirkstall and its neighbourhood*. (c.1835) [Manuscript] Held at Leeds Local History Library.

[55] Leach, P. (1988) *James Paine*. London, Zwemmer. pp. 58-61.

[56] Wood, R. op.cit., p. 77.

[57] Lumb, G. (1916) op.cit., p. 297.

[58] *A catalogue of the civil and mechanical engineering designs 1741 - 1792 of John Smeaton, F.R.S.* Held at the Royal Society. Smeaton/Volume Two/Folio 120.

[59] Wilkinson, S. (1766) *A plan of New Grange situate in the township of Headingley in the parish of Leeds and the county of York, the property of Walter Wade Esq*. Held at Thoresby Society, Leeds.

[60] On the death of Walter Wade esq. (1771) *Leeds Intelligencer*. 24 December.

[61] National Archives (1771) *Will of Walter Wade*. PROB 11/976.

[62] Venn, J. ed. (1922-54) *Alumni Cantabrigiensis*. Cambridge, Cambridge University Press. p. 301.

[63] Cary, J. (1787) *New and correct English atlas*. London, John Cary.

[64] On the death of Benjamin Wade esq. (1792) *Leeds Intelligencer*. 30 April.

[65] de Selincourt, E., and Shaver, C. (1967) The letters of William and Dorothy Wordsworth: the early years 1787-1805. 2nd ed. Oxford, Clarendon Press. pp. 144-145.

66 Sale of New Grange furniture. (1795) *Leeds Mercury.* 6 October.

67 *International Genealogical Index.* [Internet] Salt Lake City, The Church of the Latter-Day Saints. Available from: <http://www.familysearch.org> [Accessed 30 October 2006].

68 Sale of New Grange. (1805) *Leeds Intelligencer.* 25 March.

69 Russell, J. (1805) *Portrait of John Marshall and Portrait of Jane Marshall.* [pastel]. Held at University of Leeds Gallery.

70 Rimmer, W. (1960) *Marshalls of Leeds flax-spinners.* Cambridge, Cambridge University Press. pp. 67-68, pp. 98-99.

71 de Selincourt, E. ed. Moorman, M. (1979) *The letters of William and Dorothy Wordsworth: the middle years 1806-1811.* pt 1, 2nd ed. Oxford, Clarendon Press. pp. 157-158.

72 Sprittles, J. op.cit., p. 30.

73 Lumb, G. (1928) Registers of the chapels of St John, Holy Trinity, Headingley, Bramley, Beeston, Chapel-Allerton and Farnley, 1763-1812. 29, Leeds, Publications of the Thoresby Society. p. 157.

74 *Pallot's marriage licence index for England 1780-1837.* The Institute of Heraldic and Genealogical Studies.

75 Rimmer, W. op.cit., p. 102.

76 Ibid. pp. 60-66.

77 Malden, R. (1923) *The church in Headingley in four centuries.* Leeds. p. 38.

78 Lumb, G. (1928) op.cit., p. 188.

79 Sale particulars of New Grange. (1829) *Leeds Mercury.* 26 September.

80 West Yorkshire Archive Service, Leeds. (1829) *Map, schedule and sales particulars for New Grange.* Dibb Lupton Solicitors. WYL160/M354

81 New Grange and Park, near Leeds. (1830) *Leeds Mercury.* 11 September.

82 New Grange and Park, near Leeds. (1830) *Leeds Intelligencer.* 30 September.

83 New Grange estate. (1832) *Leeds Mercury.* 28 January.

84 Obituary – Thomas Benyon. (1834) *Gentleman's Magazine.* 6. New Series, p. 118.

85 Hall, D. op.cit., pp. 34-36.

86 Parsons, W. (1834) *General and commercial directory of Leeds including the outtownships and principal neighbouring villages.* Leeds. Baines & Newsome.

87 Sprittles, J. op.cit. p. 31.

88 Treen, C. op.cit. p. 175.

89 (1842) Marriages. *Annual Register for 1841.* London, J. G. F. & J. Rivington.

90 Census (1841) *Headingley-cum-Burley, Leeds.* HO 107/1344/4.

91 Beresford, M. (2004) John Marshall (1765-1845). *Oxford Dictionary of National Biography.* [Internet] online ed. Oxford University Press. Available from: <http://www.oxforddnb.com/view/article/377739> [Accessed 15 January 2007]

92 de Selincourt, E. ed. Hill, A. (1988) *The letters of William and Dorothy Wordsworth: the later years 1840-1853.* pt 4, 2nd ed. Oxford, Clarendon Press. p. 847.

93 Robinson, W. (1849) *Kirkstall Grange.* [painting]. Photographic copy held at Headingley Library Archive.

94 Census (1851) *Headingley, Leeds.* HO 107/2315/342.

95 Census (1851) *Kemp Town, Brighton.* HO 107/1644/328.

96 Hall, D. op.cit., p. 59.

97 Census (1861) *Headingley, Leeds.* RG 9/3353/48.

98 Census (1861) *The Park, Brighton.* RG 9/591/152.

99 Baxter-Langley, J. (1863) *The illustrated official guide and tourists handbook to the north-eastern railway and its branches.* Newcastle-upon-Tyne, M & M W Lambert. p. 100.

100 Moore, R. (1877) *A history of the parish church of Leeds.* Leeds, Richard Jackson. pp. 33-34.

101 Census (1871) *Far Headingley, Headingley, Leeds.* RG 10/4570/24-25.

102 Census (1881) *Far Headingley, Headingley, Leeds.* RG 11/4538/117.

103 Census (1891) *Headingley, Leeds, West Riding.* RG12/3710/36-37.

104 Census (1901) *St Chads Headingley, Leeds.* RG 13/4247/25.

105 Harris, F. (2005) *Oscar Wilde, his life and confessions.* 2 vol. originally published 1916, 1918. Kessinger pp. 93-94.

106 Churchill Archives Centre. (1908) *Letter from Ernest Beckett to Winston Churchill.* CHAR 2/35/59.

107 Battle, W. (1908) *Kirkstall Grange estate, scandal, etc.* Leeds, Privately Published.

108 Rich, R. and Pickering, H. (1958) *A short history of the City of Leeds Training College 1907-1957.* Leeds. pp. 1-10.

109 Ibid. p. 5.

110 Sprittles, J. op.cit. pp. 33-35.

111 The Leeds training college. *The British Architect.* 5 July 1912. pp. 15-16.

112 Scott, W. (1922) *Leeds in the Great War 1914-1918: a book of remembrance.* Leeds.

113 City of Leeds Training College (1912) *Handbook.* Leeds,

114 Opening of teacher training college. *The Yorkshire Post.* 14 June 1913.

115 Rich, R. and Pickering, H. op.cit., p. 18.

116 Scott, W. op.cit., p. 204, p. 206.

117 Ibid. p. 205.

118 *Mercier papers.* Held at Headingley Library Archive. BPL/A.

119 Sprittles, G. (no date) *Scrapbook.* Unpublished scrapbook.

120 Connell, L. (1994) *A century of teacher training in Leeds 1875-1975.* Leeds, Leeds Metropolitan University. p. 148.

121 Ibid. p. 152.

122 Ibid. p. 149.

123 Ibid. p. 143.

124 Ibid. p. 158.

125 Furlong, B. (1983) *Carnegie 1933-1983, college and school.* Liverpool, Liverpool University. p. 13.

126 Connell, L. (1983) *A history of Carnegie College and School of Physical Education 1933-76.* Leeds, Carnegie School of Physical Education and Human Movement Studies. p. 16-18.

127 Furlong, B. op.cit., p. 18.

128 Connell, L. (1983) op.cit., p. 24.

129 Rich, R. and Pickering, H. op.cit., p. 28.

130 Platt, T. and Bramley, G. (1952) *The story of the 18th General Hospital 1939-45.* Leeds, Privately Published.

131 National Archives. (1943) No XI depot and training establishment RAMC, notes by Lieutenant-Colonel R. N. E. Watt – commandant. WO 222/258.

132 Rich, R. and Pickering, H. op.cit., p. 39.

133 Connell, L. (1994) op.cit., p. 176.

134 Furlong, B. op.cit., p. 21.

135 Rich, R. and Pickering, H. op.cit., pp. 38-44.

136 Connell, L. (1994) op.cit., pp. 251-252.

137 Porter, R. op.cit., pp. 3-4.

138 Ibid. p. 3.

139 Connell, L. (1994) op.cit., p. 312.

140 Ibid. p. 262-270.

141 Porter, R. op.cit., p. 4.

142 Ibid. p. 6.

143 Connell, L. (1994) op.cit., p. 312.

144 Porter, R. op.cit., p. 6.

145 Ibid. p. 5.

146 Furlong, B. op.cit., p. 30.

147 Pringle, D. (1980) *Leeds Polytechnic 1970-1980: a decade of achievement.* Leeds, Leeds Polytechnic. pp. 7-9.

148 Police probe college blaze. *Yorkshire Evening Post.* 28 October 1978.

i   Here is deposited the mortal remains of Benjamin Wade of New Grange, Esq; who gave the Benefit of Two Hundred Pounds to the Curate of this Chapel for ever. He departed this Life (leaving no Issue by Edith, his wife) Feb. the 15th An. Do. 1671, in the 81st Year of his Age. Truth, noble Thoughts, and Vertue met in one lye here in Shades, although his Life had none. Whose Bounty, Learning, Piety and Worth being known to all, do his due Praise set forth. Also the body of Anthony Wade of New Grange, Esq; who exchanged this Life for a better the 14th of Dec. 1683, He married Mary the only Daughter and Heir of John Moore of Green-head, in Com Pal. Lancaster, Gent. leaving Issue by her Benjamin Wade of New Grange, Esq; who (to the pious Memory of his Ancestors) erected this Tomb, An. Dom. 1694.

ii   Although many references and sources state or imply that it was Walter Wade (1698-1726) who caused the 1752 rebuilding of New Grange, establishing his death in 1726 determines that it was his son Walter Wade (1722-1771) who was responsible.

CHAPTER 1

Monks, Merchants and Industrialists:
New Grange and its occupants before 1832

Keith Rowntree and Peter D'Sena

In the 12th century, Cistercian monks became known for bringing architectural splendour and highly organised estate management to what were then the remoter parts of Europe. In Yorkshire, this led to the large monastery at Fountains and a 'daughter' at Kirkestall; and all had their own 'granges' or farms, developed from land left to them by wealthy benefactors. In 1288 the site we now know as the Headingley Campus was referred to as Planum Locum, *literally a flat open space, though by 1539, the Kirkstall Cistercians had called it* Newgrange. *The* Foundation of Kirkstall, *a 15th-century copy of a 13th-century text emphasising the hardships of monastic life in order to influence donors, indicates that an earlier religious community of hermits had occupied the site. However, the Cistercians, supported by Henry de Lacy, the 12th-century owner, cleared them from their simple wooden buildings and some chose to join the Order.[1]*

Fig. 1
Artist's impression of
New Grange c. 1752.
(Source: © Keith
Rowntree 2007)

Our understanding of what New Grange looked like during its time as a working farm is limited, though cartographical evidence suggests the original farmyard faced the current Coachhouse. Studies of other medieval granges point to common characteristics of form and function, with very basic wooden structures serving the needs of lay brothers and local labourers engaged in both arable and pastoral farming (**Figure 2**). Buildings generally surrounded an open square or oblong space and included a hall, chambers and a barn, store or animal shelter. Sometimes granges far from their abbey would have their own chapel.[2] In the case of New Grange, the presence of local quarries to the south made it possible that some of these structures may have become more substantial in the later medieval period[3] (**Figure 3**). Even so, Kirkstall Abbey syphoned the resources of the many granges and its more complex site remained the hub of activity, catering for specialised activities such as governance and the creation of manuscripts.

Monastic granges were run by *conversi* or lay brothers with practical skills, working in animal husbandry or carpentry, though Platt (1969) suggests they were more often managers or overseers.[4] Kirkstall's granges north of Leeds had an ample labour supply, especially after 1324 when the Abbey gained the manor of Headingley from John de Calverley. However, the devastating impact of endemic plague after 1349 depleted monks and labourers alike and forced the weakened monastery to lease its lands out. Consequently a strong secular presence at New Grange predates the Cistercians' departure.[5]

In the 16th century, ownership of New Grange was a mirror of political and social influence and change. The Henrician Reformation saw the dissolution of the monasteries and the swift redistribution of the Cistercians' resources. Abbott John Ripley and his thirty monks surrendered the Abbey and its estates to the King's Commissioners in November 1539 and by 1541 they were leased to Robert Pakeman, a gentleman of the King's Household.[6] By 1542 Henry VIII passed the site and possessions of Kirkstall to Thomas Cranmer, Archbishop of Canterbury – part of a series of exchanges made between them enabling a consolidation of Crown Lands in the South East.[7] Technically, Cranmer's ownership only began in 1547 on Henry's death and returned to the crown, to the catholic Queen Mary, as the counter-reformation unfolded and Cranmer was burnt at the stake (1556). The mid-Tudor religious roller-coaster, with the accession of the protestant Elizabeth I saw some of the lands granted to Cranmer's son, Thomas, in 1559. The Abbey site had already been sold to Robert Saville, eventually becoming part of the extensive estates of the Earl of Cardigan. Unlike his absentee father, deeds of 1574 and 1587 indicate that Thomas Cranmer was of resident status and hence described 'of Kirkstall'.[8] Even so, like other gentrified speculators he sold and leased out land and possessions to local families, New Grange going to the less famous, but highly ambitious Foxcroft family.

Exemplars of the post-Reformation rise of the gentry, the Foxcrofts were landowners and merchants from the Halifax area keen to demonstrate status through land tenure and political power. The family's connections with the neighbouring Barr Grange can be traced back to 1560 though by the 1580s Thomas Foxcroft of *Christall* (Kirkstall) was resident at New Grange. Late 16th-century parish registers tell of other families at New Grange and not only servants and labourers, but also those of James Brown, described as 'gent' and Robert Kent, a gentleman, whose will Foxcroft was witness to.[9] It is also possible that the Foxcrofts, having taken advantage of the massive sale of monastic treasures following the dissolutions, would have needed a library of sorts – at one time they owned a medieval gothic theological manuscript, now part of the Arundel collection held by the British Library which includes Leonardo's famous *Codex* or Notebook (**Figure 4**). Such was its value, the manuscript passed 'upwards' *via* Henry Saville, owner of Kirkstall Abbey, to the Earl of Arundel early in the 17th century.[10]

Whether the Foxcrofts gained materially from the sale of the manuscript is uncertain; more certain is their appreciation of the pecuniary as well as the societal value of a good marriage. This is illustrated by the union of Thomas's daughter, Judith, to Anthony Wade,

Fig. 2
Artist's impression of New Grange in the Middle Ages, c. 1280. (Source: © Keith Rowntree, 2007)

Fig. 3
Artist's impression of New Grange in the Later Middle Ages, c. 1450. (Source: © Keith Rowntree, 2007)

one – the addition of inscriptions at the entrances (one replaced by a copy in the 19th century – see **Figure 5**).[11] Presumably, Wade wanted a home that reflected his social aspirations and political, economic and philanthropic achievements. Returning to New Grange after his education at Emmanuel College, Cambridge, he became a co-owner of the manor of Leeds, a founding member of the town's Charter and ultimately an alderman and town Mayor (1632).[12] The Wade dynasty and its connections maintained its influence in the region into the next century: Benjamin's relative, Daniel Foxcroft rebuilt nearby Weetwood Hall; his nephew, Anthony, who inherited New Grange, became Mayor of Leeds in 1676; and his grand-nephew, the Oxford-educated Benjamin, who was later called to the Bar at Gray's Inn, married into the powerful Calverleys in 1684.[13] Marriage and the presence and power of women on the estate has greater recognition in the historical record after the Restoration, though at present our understanding, sadly, is limited in the main to that of their role as a wife or daughter. However, recent important research on Georgian England strongly supports the idea that the wealth and status of New Grange would have made it a focal point for a network of 'gentlewomen' and their educational, political and social interactivity.[14]

The 18th century saw the Wade's gentry status grow into squirearchy. Benjamin's connections as a barrister no doubt assisted his prestigious elevation to Justice of the Peace for the West Riding in 1712. Leeds historian, Thoresby, described how Wade then set about improving the New Grange estate. In his *Ducatus Leodiensis* of 1715, he enthused about the addition of 'Gardens, Terras Walks, and Other Ornaments to the house'.[15] Wilkinson's map of 1766 (**Figure 6**) also shows distinctive, oblong formal gardens that existed until the College grounds were laid out in 1910 and even today traces of Wade's terrace are visible on the Acre, running diagonally from today's Grange building towards Leighton Hall.

The greatest changes to the New Grange estate were made by Benjamin Wade's grandson, Walter (1722-1771). The untimely death of his father, Walter, in 1726 saw him inherit aged four, with his mother, Beatrix, holding the estate in trust until he reached majority. Societal and aesthetic pressures during his formative years helped shape the reconstruction. In Walpole's England mercantilists, benefiting from the

the first of a series of marriages into Yorkshire's elite and the beginning of the Wade's association with the site which was to last until 1832. Benjamin Wade, owner in the early 17th century, undertook major reconstruction work on the old monastic buildings and one very minor

first fruits of colonial trade, plantocracy and oligarchic connection, looked to make an ostentatious display of their wealth, with Palladian and other neo-classical styles especially satisfying elite taste. By 1752 the old buildings were demolished and, in the genre of Colen Campbell's highly fashionable designs of a *villa-with-wings*, James Paine, a prominent architect, erected the house we now know as *The Grange*.[16] Importantly, the present building displays layers of additions and refinements made during the 18th and 19th centuries. For example, the east wing, present in Wilkinson's map of 1766, had been demolished certainly by the mid-19th century[17] (**Figure 7**). Paine's historian, Peter Leach, compares New Grange with his other work of the 1750s at Serlby in Nottinghamshire, while his town house in Pontefract gives an indication of what it may have looked like without alterations. An illustration of the house in *Kirkstall and Its Neighbourhood* (*c*.1835) adds visual clues about changes to the external fabric. For instance, it shows the fussy treatments of some windows and the broken pediment not typical of Paine's work and there is textual evidence to show there were proposals for cosmetic modifications at the time of construction (**Figure 8**). Changes continued into the 19th century. From their arrival in the 1830s, the Beckett family were constantly renovating, adding bay windows to the surviving wing and to the exposed east wall.[18] Yet despite the many modifications, the Grange we see today is essentially the house built for Walter Wade in 1752.

The growth of newspaper publishing in the 18th century helps us to piece together the history and interests of a generation of Wades. Soon after the death of Walter's son Benjamin, in 1792, his elderly mother left the Grange and lived at Weetwood until her death in 1809. She auctioned off the furniture in 1795 when she finally left New Grange and a detailed advertisement in the *Leeds Mercury* gives us a rich textual description of the house contents[19] (**Figure 9**). This would be the last time a member of the Wade family actually lived at New Grange, even though it remained in their ownership until 1832.

The tenancy was to remain in the hands of an eminent lawyer. Samuel Buck, who had been Recorder of Leeds for almost twenty years, felt the house had an environment fit to entertain his social milieu, which included the aristocracy.[20] As industrialised Leeds worked overtime to meet the demands of the French War and ordinary men

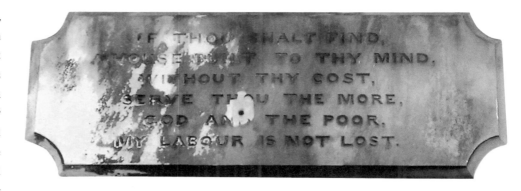

lived in fear of the pressgang, the glittering drawing rooms of New Grange played host to Leeds notables. In 1798 Buck's daughter Mary Anne married Sir Francis Lindley Wood, later Baronet Wood of Barnsley and began a dynasty of politicians which culminated with Edward Frederick Lindley Wood, 1st Earl of Halifax, Foreign Secretary, first to Chamberlain and then Churchill during World War II.[21]

Shortly before Buck's death, New Grange was again advertised for let. Its most famous tenant, John Marshall, flax merchant, factory owner and employer of almost 20,000 people, began his occupancy.[22] Described by the *Leeds Intelligencer*'s advertisement as having 'every requisite convenience for a genteel family', the physical environment of the house and gardens provided the opportunity for any fabulously wealthy industrialist to display his opulence and aspire to social greatness.[23] However, the combination of Marshall's nonconformity and riches were not guarantees of complete success. Unlike the Foxcrofts and Wades, who had been highly influential in Leeds' political and social oligarchy, he found himself marginalised by an elite dominated by Tory and Anglican sympathies. Instead, as an industrialist, with new money, and moreover as a Unitarian, his circles were friends and family, Whigs and other dissenters, particularly those attending the Mill Hill Chapel. Ultimately and paradoxically, Marshall's co-ownership of the *Leeds Mercury* gave him more influence both in the region and more recognition in posterity than all of these contemporary rivals. Though most well known for its outspoken editor, Edward Baines, and the publication of Richard Oastler's famous letter on 'Yorkshire Slavery' (1830), it was in its pages in 1826 that Marshall, possibly with an eye on Bentham's vision of a

Fig. 5
Photograph of the 19th-century replica of Wade's descriptions – North Entrance of the Grange. (Source: Keith Rowntree, 2007)

Fig. 6 A Plan of New Grange Situated in the Township of Headingley in the Parish of Leeds and the County of York, the Property of Walter Wade Esq., *by S. Wilkinson (1766).* *(Source: Thoresby Society, Leeds)*

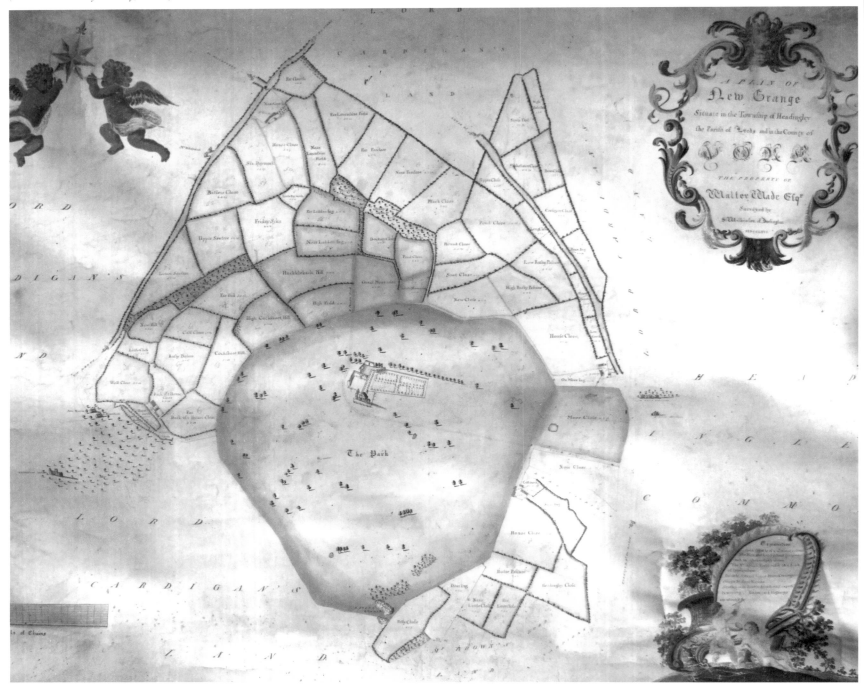

Fig. 7 New Grange Park Plan, *by G. Madeley (1829). (Source: West Yorkshire Archive Service, Leeds. WYL 160/M354)*

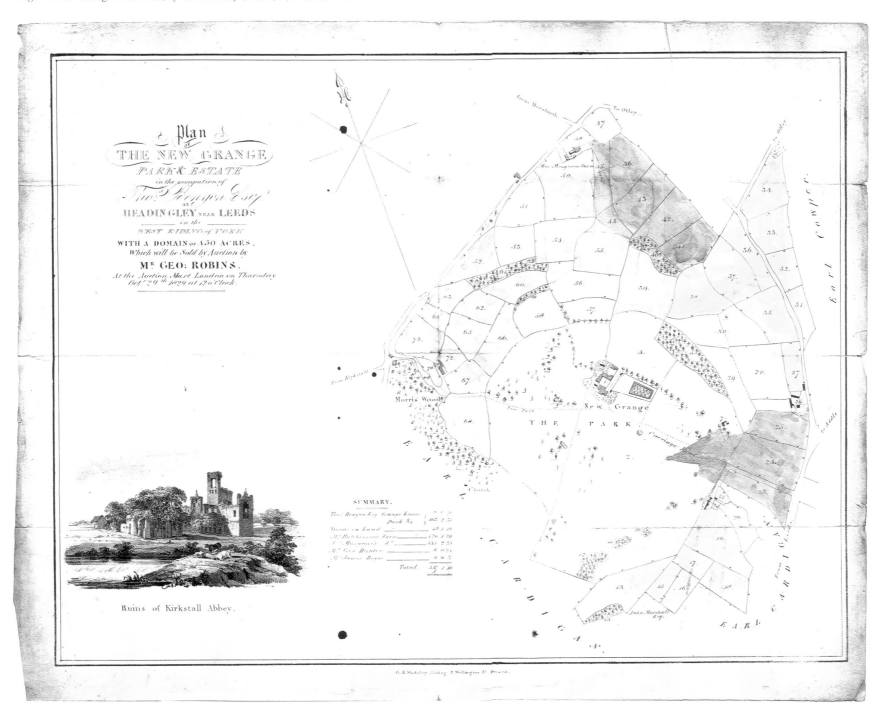

Above, Fig. 8
Pen and ink drawing
from Kirkstall and Its
Neighbourhood
(c. 1835), author
unknown. (Source:
Special Collection,
Leeds Library and
Information Service)

Fig. 9
Leeds Mercury. *The*
New Grange advertised
to let in March 1795.
(Source: Leeds Library
and Information
Service)

Sale of Furniture, &c. at New-Grange,
near Headingley.
To be SOLD by AUCTION,
By W. H. BRAZIER,
Upon the Premises, on Wednesday the Fourth Day of
November next, and the following Days,

ALL the HOUSEHOLD FURNITURE
of Mrs. WADE, at New Grange, near Headingley, consisting of Bedsteads with Damask, Chintz, and
other Hangings; Window Curtains and Chair Covers to
suit; excellent Feather Beds, Mattrasses, Blankets and
Quilts; handsome Mahogany Chairs, Tables, Chests of
Drawers, and Sophas; Floor, Stair Case, and Bedside
Carpets; Two Mahogany Cellarets; Pier and Dressing
Glasses; an Eight Days Clock; several handsome Prints;
neat painted Chairs; China and Glass; a Washing Ma-
chine; Kitchen Furniture; Brewing Vessels, and a
Variety of other Effects.
☞ The Sale to begin each Day at Ten o'Clock in the
Forenoon.
The Goods may be viewed the Monday and Tuesday
preceding the Sale.

non-denominational University College for London, first proposed the idea of higher education in Leeds.[24]

The society portraitist, John Russell, whose patrons included the royal family, presented Marshall, dressed finely, holding a leather bound book, as reminders of his undoubted wealth and his wish to be known as a man of letters. Russell's formula for Marshall's portrait draws on his earlier works, *Portrait of a Man in Blue Jacket* (c.1801), now in the Victoria and Albert Museum and *Lady Holding a Book* (1801). Depicted here, Marshall holds the book awkwardly at arms length, his expression does not appear confident; there is a trace of hesitancy about his eyes, a suggestion, perhaps, of his discomfort within Leeds society (**Figure 10**).

Marshall's portrait would have been seen by Dorothy Wordsworth on one of her visits to New Grange to see Jane, his wife, her lifelong friend (**Figure 11**). Evidence from letters between the women suggests that Dorothy would have been candid enough to dismiss any artist's flattery; indeed in 1800, after Marshall had returned

Left, Fig. 10
John Marshall.
Portrait by John Russell,
1805. (Source: Leeds
University Collection)

Right, Fig. 11
Jane Marshall.
Portrait by John Russell,
1805. (Source: Leeds
University Collection)

from one of their many stays in the Lake District, Dorothy later wrote to Jane: 'How fat your husband looks! If I had met him in the lane I would not have known him.'[25] Though they teased him about his corpulence, both William and Dorothy Wordsworth held Marshall's opinions on landscaping in high regard, referring his ideas to Lord Lonsdale a prominent landowner in the Lake District – sure recognition of his abilities in the valued and gentlemanly pursuits of literature, art, 'progressive farming', horticulture and landscaping. According to Sprittles (1960) it was Marshall's interest in landscaping that resulted in the grounds of New Grange being laid out to represent the troop movements of the Battle of Waterloo.[26]   However, evidence for this is only based on Marshall's interests rather than documented actions. Rather, in 1815, Marshall's energy had been focused on building his new summer residence, Hallsteads; and, importantly, the influence of New Grange's owners, the Wades, made such a major change by a

tenant unlikely. Moreover, Marshall left the estate soon afterwards for Headingley House, with records showing that he added a west wing there in 1819.[27]

The estate was to remain in the hands of a Unitarian industrialist, Thomas Benyon. The Benyons, already prominent lawyers and merchants in Shropshire, turned their interests to the flax industry, first with a mill in Shrewsbury and then in partnership with Marshall at Water Lane, Leeds.[28] With cheap labour, advancing technology and unremitting wartime production, profits soared, but the partnership soon strained, then soured and terminated in 1804. Even so, Thomas Benyon remained in Leeds, becoming Marshall's principal business competitor and also his successor as tenant of New Grange from 1822 where he remained until his death in 1833.

Thompson Wade's death in 1828 prompted his nieces, the heirs to the Wade fortune, to take an opportunity to realise and divide the

IN THE WEST RIDING OF YORKSHIRE.

Particulars and Conditions of Sale
OF THE

New Grange Estate,
INCLUDING ITS ALWAYS ADMIRED

MANSION AND PARK,
IN THE OCCUPATION OF

THOMAS BENYON, Esq.

Very pleasantly situate about Two Miles from Leeds, and in a County remarkable for the Wealth and Respectability of its Occupants.

THE DOMAIN

Connected with this interesting Property includes about

450 ACRES of capital LAND,

In the Occupation of a most respectable Tenantry, at Rents capable of improvement, and yielding nearly

£1,160 A YEAR.

THE EARL of CARDIGAN's WOODS

Form a pleasing Boundary to this Property;

Which will be Sold by Auction
BY

Mr. GEO. ROBINS

At the Auction Mart, opposite the Bank of England,

On THURSDAY, 29th OCTOBER, 1829, at 12 o'Clock,
IN ONE LOT.

The Property can be viewed (with permission of Mr. Benyon) on application to Mr. Teal, Land Surveyor, Albion Street, Leeds, and Particulars then had at his Offices (with Lithographic Plans and Drawings of the New Grange Estate and the Abbey of Kirkstall) Twenty-eight Days prior to the Sale; also at the Hotels, Leeds and York; Denner's Hotel, Scarborough; the Strafford Arms, Wakefield; Tontine, Sheffield; New Angel, Doncaster; of Messrs. Karslake and Crealock, Solicitors, 4, Regent Street; the Auction Mart; and at Mr. GEO. ROBINS's Offices, London.

Whiting, Printer, Beaufort House.

Fig. 12 George Robins' Particulars of Sale, 1829 – a handbill advertising New Grange. (Source: West Yorkshire Archive Service, Leeds. WYL 160/M354)

capital value of the estate. The two sales, of 1829 and 1832, might owe as much to contemporary parliamentary custom and practice as the skills of the renowned society auctioneer, George Robins.[29] While his near poetic description of the estate in the *Leeds Mercury* captured the attention of Yorkshire's elite, including John Marshall's son, Frances Wade's husband, John Bastard, MP for Dartmouth, probably touted the property in the corridors of the Commons (**Figure 12**). It is unlikely, therefore, that it was only Marshall's reluctance to lend his son enough to make a competitive bid that saw the estate sold elsewhere that October for £37,000.[30] Whether he or anybody else was surprised that the new owner was Arthur Howe Holdsworth, the other MP for Dartmouth, is not recorded. This and subsequent events are not, however, so difficult to explain. The Holdsworths and Bastards were both from Devon's elite and when the exchange of funds seemingly floundered, both MPs soon reached a settlement, speedily issuing new advertisements in 1830. At first the intention was to let the property, but by early 1832 the *Leeds Mercury* reported that the New Grange estate had been sold by its true owner, Captain John Bastard, to William Beckett.[31] The forty-year absence of an owner-occupier at New Grange was ended by a banker with an eye for social capital.[32]

ENDNOTES

[1] E. Clark (ed.), *The Foundation of Kirkstall Abbey, 4* (Leeds: Publications of the Thoresby Society, 1895); R. Wright, 'The Granges and Estates of Kirkstall Abbey in the Twelfth and Thirteenth Centuries' (University of Leeds: unpublished PhD thesis, 2002); W. Dugdale, *Monasticon Anglicanum: A History of the Abbeys and other Monasteries in England and Wales* (London: 1846). Humanities Research Institute. 'Cistercians of Yorkshire'. [[Internet] University of Sheffield. Available from: http://cistercians.shef.ac.uk/index.php{Accessed 1 February 2007.]

[2] C. Platt, *The Monastic Grange in Medieval England* (London: Macmillan, 1969); R. Donkin, 'The Cistercian Order and the Settlement of Northern England', *Geographical Review*, 59, (3), July,1969, pp. 403-416; T. Bishop, 'Monastic Granges in Yorkshire', *The English Historical Review*, 51, (202), April 1936, pp. 193-214.

[3] For detail, see S. Wilkinson, *A Plan of New Grange Situate in the Township of Headingley in the Parish of Leeds and the County of York, the Property of Walter Wade Esq.* (1766). Held by the Thoresby Society, Leeds.

[4] C. Platt, *The Monastic Grange in Medieval England* (London: Macmillan, 1969). For a summary of land use and agricultural techniques in the medieval period, see R. Bartlett, *England under the Norman and Angevin Kings, 1075-1225* (Oxford: Clarendon Press, 2000), pp. 302-12. On the corporate role of religion and the clergy, see A. Brown, *Church and Society in England, 1000-1500* (London: Palgrave Books, 2003), pp. 108-116.

[5] On John de Calverley, see SC 8/120/5964 (1324), National Archives, *Petition to King from Abbot and Convent of Kirkstall to Acquire Headingley*. On the impact of the Black Death and the mortality rates of the clergy, the classic work remains P. Ziegler's, *The Black Death* (London: Sutton, 1997); and on the plague's continuing impact, see P. Slack, *The Impact of Plague in Tudor and Stuart England* (Oxford: Clarendon Press, 2003).

[6] J. Spritles, 'New Grange Kirkstall Its Owners and Occupants', *Miscellanea*, 46 (Leeds: Publications of the Thoresby Society, 1960), pp. 22-35. On the place and importance of 'gentlemen' in the 16th-century society and earlier, see P. Coss, *The Origins of the English Gentry* (Cambridge: Cambridge University Press, 2003). For a detailed account of the Henrician Reformation and its consequences, see C. Cross, *Church and People: England, 1450-1660* (London: Blackwell, 1999), pp. 42-67.

[7] C. Treen, 'Buildings and Estate Development in the Northern Out-Townships of Leeds, 1781-1914', (University of Leeds: unpublished PhD thesis, 1977); F. Du Boulay, 'Archbishop Cranmer and the Canterbury Temporalities', *The English Historical Review*, 67, No. 262, January, 1952, pp. 19-36.

[8] For the deed naming Thomas Cranmer of Kirkstall, see the Spencer Stanhope Manuscripts, Sp/St/4/11/66/59 (1574), West Yorkshire Archive Service, Bradford. D. Hall, *Far Headingley Weetwood and West Park* (Far Headingley: Far Headingley Village Society, 2000); Treen, op.cit.

[9] S. Margerison, *Leeds Parish Church Registers, First & Second Books, 1572-1612*, 1 (Leeds: Publications of the Thoresby Society, 1891); G. Lumb, *Leeds Parish Church Registers. Ninth and Tenth Books, 1695-1722 with Armley Chapel 1695-1711 and Hunslet Chapel 1686-1724*, 13 (Leeds: Publications of the Thoresby Society, 1895). For a study of the Foxcroft's in relation to neighbouring Weetwood Hall see J. M. Collinson, Weetwood and the Foxcroft Family, *The University of Leeds Review*, 30, 1987, pp. 27-43. For an overview of land tenure and gentry status in 16th-century England, see A. G. R. Smith, *The Emergence of a Nation State*, 1529-1660 (London: Longman, 1997), pp. 182-88. For another reference to Thomas Cranmer of Christall, Yorks: see Leases, Borough of Edgcumbe, ME/1172 (1587), Edgcumbe of Cotchele and Mount Edgcumbe, Cornwall Record Office.

[10] British Library, Arundel Mss. 248. For details on the provenance of the manuscript, see the British Library Catalogue of Illuminated Manuscripts, available at:
http://prodigi.bl.uk/illcat/record.asp?MSID=7289&CollID=20&Nstart=248.

[11] R. Thoresby, amended and expanded, T. Whitaker (1816) *Ducatus Leodiensis: or, the Topography of the Ancient and Populous Town and Parish of Leedes and Parts Adjacent in the West Riding of the County of York* (Leeds: Robinson, Son & Holdsworth, 2nd edn., 1816); Spritles, op.cit. Ralph Thoresby (1658-1725), merchant, antiquarian, diarist and museum keeper is generally regarded as being the first historian of Leeds. His original work of 1715 about Leeds was brought up to date by Whitaker in the early 19th century.

[12] J. Venn (ed.) *Alumni Cantabrigiensis* (London: Cambridge University Press, 1922-54); S. Burt and K. Grady, *The Illustrated History of Leeds* (Derby: Breedon Books, 1994).

[13] Hall, op.cit.; Spritles, op.cit.; J. Foster (ed.) *The Register of Admission to Gray's Inn 1521-1887* (London: Privately Published, 1889); S. Margerison, 'Memorandum Book of Sir Walter Calverley, Bart.', *Yorkshire Diaries and Autobiographies in the Seventeenth and Eighteenth Centuries*. (Durham: Surtees Society, 1883). For a useful analysis of civic society and political office in 17th-century England, see P. Withington, 'Citizens, community and political culture in Restoration England', in A. Shephard and P. Withington (eds.), *Communities in Early Modern England* (Manchester: Manchester University Press, 2000), pp. 134-55.

[14] A. Vickery, *The Gentleman's Daughter. Women's Lives in Georgian England* (Yale: Yale University Press, 2003). For an insight into women and marriage, see A. Lawrence, *Women in England, 1500-1760* (London: Phoenix Press, 2002), pp. 41-60; and, more generally, R. Shoemaker, *Gender in English Society, 1650-1850: The Emergence of Separate Spheres?* (London: Pearson, 1998).

[15] Thoresby, op.cit.

[16] E. H. Gombrich, *The Story of Art* (London: Phaidon, 1966); P. Leach, *James Paine* (London: Zwemmer, 1988). For an excellent analysis of patterns of consumption, materialism, acquisitiveness and taste, see Maxine Berg's *Luxury and Pleasure in Eighteenth-Century Britain* (Oxford: Oxford University Press, 2007); and on social mobility and aspiration, see J. Hoppitt, *A Land of Liberty? England, 1689-1727* (Oxford: Oxford University Press, 1999), pp. 345-382. It was important for a gentleman to demonstrate an interest in culture: see J. Black, *A Subject for Taste: Culture in Eighteenth-Century England* (London: Hambledon and London, 2005). For a detailed, yet very readable analysis about the issues of social hierarchy and social change discussed throughout this chapter, see James Sharpe's *Early Modern England: A Social History, 1550-1760* (London: Arnold, 1997), pp. 133-234; and particularly on merchants and industrialists, pp. 183-89. See also S. Burt and K. Grady, *The Merchants' Golden Age, Leeds, 1700-1790* (Leeds: Grady and Burt, 1987).

[17] The sale map of 1829 appears to confirm the demolition of the east wing, but this is still open to interpretation. See *New Grange Park Plan*, by G. Madeley (1829) (Leeds: West Yorkshire Archive Service, WYL 160/M354). For more detailed comment, see Alastair Black's chapter later in this book on 'Buildings and Spaces'.

[18] *Kirkstall and Its Neighbourhood* (c.1835) (Manuscript, held at Leeds: Leeds Library and Information Service). Hall, op.cit; Spritles, op.cit.

[19] For examples of information from obituaries see, *inter alia, Leeds Intelligencer*, 23 October, 1759; 24 December, 1771; 30 April, 1792. For the sale of New Grange furniture see the *Leeds Mercury*, 6 October, 1795. G. Lumb, *Registers of the Chapels of St John, Holy Trinity, Headingley, Bramley, Beeston, Chapel-Allerton and Farnley, 1763-1812*, 29, (Leeds: Publications of the Thoresby Society, 1928). The urbanisation of 18th-century England was accompanied by the spread of news and newspapers to provincial towns. A succinct introduction to this development can be found in Bob Harris's article, 'Print Culture' in H. T. Dickinson (ed.) *A Companion to Eighteenth-Century Britain* (London: Blackwell, 2006), pp. 283-93.

[20] J. Binn and G. Brown, *A Directory for . . . Leeds, 1798* (Leeds: Binn and Brown, 1817).

[21] For Wood's obituary, *see Gentleman's Magazine* (1847), Vol. 27, New Series, p. 308; and for more detail, E. Lodge, *The Genealogy of the Existing British Peerage* (London: Hurst and Blackett, 1859).

[22] W. Rimmer, *Marshall's of Leeds Flax-Spinners* (Cambridge: Cambridge University Press, 1960); Burt and Grady, op.cit.

[23] The Sale of New Grange, *Leeds Intelligencer*, 25 March, 1805. On 'opulence and glory' during the Napoleonic period, see P. Langford, *A Polite and Commercial People: England, 1727-1783* (Oxford: Clarendon Press, 1998), pp. 615-675.

[24] *Leeds Mercury*: 14 January 1826 (Marshall's proposal for higher education); 16 October 1830 (Oastler's letter on 'Yorkshire Slavery').

[25] E. de Selincourt and C. Shaver. (eds.) *The Letters of William and Dorothy Wordsworth: The Early Years, 1787-1805* (Oxford: Clarendon Press, 1967).

[26] Rimmer, op.cit.; Spritles, op.cit.

[27] Rimmer, op.cit.

[28] On the Benyons and the course of their business relationship with John Marshall, see H. Forrest (ed.), *Shrewsbury Burgess Roll* (Shrewsbury: Shropshire Archaeological and Parish Register Society, 1924); C. Lewis and A. Thacker (2003) 'A History of the County of Cheshire. The City of Chester: General History and Topography', 5 (1) [Internet] Victoria County History, 2003. Available from: < http://www.british-history.ac.uk/source.asp?pubid=94> [Accessed 8 August 2006]; R. Somerville, *Office Holders in the Duchy and County Palatine of Lancaster from 1603* (Chichester: Phillimore, 1972); and Rimmer, op.cit. For Thomas Benyon's obituary: Gentleman's Magazine, Vol. 1, New Series, 1834, p. 118.

ENDNOTES

[29] R. Myers, 'Robins, George Henry (1777–1847)', *Oxford Dictionary of National Biography*, [Internet] (Oxford: Oxford University Press, 2004). Available from: <http://www.oxforddnb.com/view/article/23824> [Accessed 18 Feb 2007].

[30] Rimmer, op.cit.; Manuscript: 'Marshalls of Leeds', MS 200/17-19 (Leeds: University of Leeds Special Collections).

[31] In part, the story of the sale can be pieced together by tracking advertisements in the Leeds press. In the *Leeds Mercury*, see 26 September 1829 (Sale Particulars of New Grange); 31 October 1829 (Auction of New Grange); 11 September 1830 (New Grange and Park, near Leeds); 28 January 1832 (New Grange Estate).

[32] In researching seven centuries of New Grange's history, a wide range of documents, including medieval manuscripts, probate inventories, early newspapers, maps, directories and, of course, secondary publications have been consulted. It has been impossible to list them all here. In presenting a short, narrative account, there have been limited opportunities for exploring the many nuances of the historical information and interpretations. For instance, an analysis of the 18th-century Wades' business interests, which may have included the Guinea trade, is worth lengthy treatment. The authors welcome reader's comments on this and other aspects of the chapter and will be pleased to respond to enquiries from those seeking clarification about methodology and source material.

CHAPTER 2

Who were the Becketts of Beckett Park?

David Hall with Ian Crossland

In 1772 John Beckett, the 29-year-old son of a wealthy Barnsley merchant, settled in Leeds and joined the Old Bank, the first exclusively banking firm established in Leeds some twenty years earlier. Formerly in partnership with his brother Joseph, financing the transport of goods to the Continent from the flourishing inland Port of Leeds,[1] John had decided to go into banking full time. Two years later, he married Mary Wilson, whose family was also connected to the bank, and rapidly made his mark in the commercial and political life of town.

Fig. 1
Sir John Beckett
1743-1826. (Source:
National Portrait
Gallery, London)

THE BECKETTS 'THEN'

Within three years of John Beckett's (**Figure 1**) arrival at the Old Bank he was elected Alderman and then Mayor of Leeds. He played an active part in putting down the Luddite riots and was appointed Chief Magistrate of Leeds and JP for the West Riding. He was highly respected by the wealthy merchants and manufacturers of Leeds and became senior partner at the bank. His influence became so great that a contemporary said of him, 'John Beckett governs the country,

inasmuch as he governs Leeds, Leeds governs Yorkshire and Yorkshire governs Pitt'.[2] In 1813 he was created a Baronet in recognition of his services to the commercial community of Leeds.

Sir John Beckett, Bart, lived very handsomely at Gledhow Hall and raised eleven children (**Figure 2**). Two of his six sons, Christopher and William, followed their father into active management of the firm which grew in parallel with the growth of Leeds, by now the booming industrial heartland of Yorkshire's West Riding. Sir John died in 1826

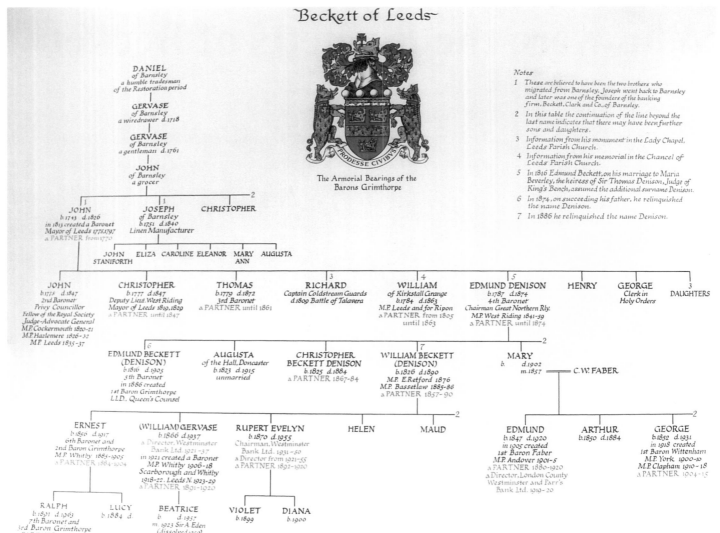

Fig. 2
Beckett family tree.
(Source: Leeds
Metropolitan University
Archives. Reproduced
with the permission of
Teddy Beckett, Lord
Grimthorpe)

leaving a fortune to his family, a hereditary title to his eldest son, John, and leaving the bank under the direction of Christopher (aged 49) and William (aged 42).

Such was the Becketts' reputation that William (**Figure 3**) was called before the Secret Committee of the House of Commons in 1832

to answer questions relating to the renewal of the Bank of England's Charter in that year. From the 1840s the Old Bank in Leeds restyled itself Beckett & Co (**Figure 4**).

At around the time William Beckett was giving evidence to the Select Committee in London he was also negotiating to buy New Grange at Headingley, an estate of 450 acres, formerly monastery farmland attached to Kirkstall Abbey and privately owned after the Dissolution by the Wade family for over 200 years. In the early 1800s it had been the tenanted home of John Marshall[3] the celebrated flax spinner who amassed a fortune, entered Parliament and moved on to greater aristocratic living in the Lake District.

William bought the estate and immediately set to work on remodelling the mansion, house, building new gate houses, and improving the estate (**Figure 5**). He also changed the name from New Grange to Kirkstall Grange. Set in the countryside, within the Manor and Township of Headingley-cum-Burley, the estate was part farmed

Left, Fig. 3
Portrait of William
Beckett. Oil on canvas
by Sir Francis Grant,
1803. (Source: Leeds
Museums and Galleries,
Temple Newsom House)

Above, Fig. 4
Beckett & Co. Bank.
(Source: Leeds Library
& Information Service
Leodis Photographic
Archive 2004122-
67991275)

Fig. 5
Entrance to the park,
Kirkstall Grange, c.1835.
(Source: Leeds Library
& Information Service
mss. Kirkstall and its
neighbourhood, nd)

Fig. 6
Beckett family coat of
arms. (Source: Ian
Crossland)

and part laid to private parkland. A new carriage drive swept through the park to the house and the whole property commanded 'a panorama which must be seen to be appreciated, there is so much of hill and dale, and such a delightful regularity in the Park, such variety and beauty in the distant prospect'.[4]

Although not Lord of the Manor of Headingley – that distinction was held by the sixth Lord Cardigan of Deene Park Northamptonshire – nonetheless Kirkstall Grange provided William with a residence befitting his status within the town's commercial life. In 1841 he married Frances Adeline Ingram, co-heir of Temple Newsam, and that same year he entered Parliament as MP for Leeds.

Hoping to impress the monarch with a visit to Kirkstall Grange in 1858, William made further improvements to his property. The Beckett coat of arms (**Figure 6**) was placed high up on the front elevation of the house (**Figure 7**), a new single-storey wing was built, deep bay windows were added to the south and east sides, and a new

entrance porch with Corinthian pillars flanking the outer doors supported a ceremonial balcony. In the grounds west of the house a long walk was formed, to a point overlooking the Aire Valley where a classical stone archway was erected commemorating the Queen's visit to Leeds for the opening of the new Town Hall. This imposing monument (**Figure 8**), framing a resplendent view of her realm from Kirkstall Grange would surely have delighted the Queen, who came to Leeds in 1858 amid great public celebration. The Queen and Prince Consort, however stayed at the home of the Mayor, Sir Peter Fairburn, in Clarendon Road, and there is no record of the royal itinerary. Sadly for William, it seems the itinerary did not include a visit to Kirkstall Grange.[5]

On other occasions, however, William did receive eminent guests to the Grange including Lord and Lady Palmerston in 1860.

The Beckett's family fortune was large and the family was generous in its patronage to many institutions and good causes, especially the Church of England. In William's case he founded several schools in Leeds 'seeking to advance and extend the education of the people on Christian principles'.[6] He made donations to Leeds Parish Church and to the rebuilding of St Michael's Church Headingley in 1838. When he died in 1863 he was honoured by the local Yorkshire community (**Figure 9**) and was commemorated in different monuments (**Figure 10**). He left land at Kirkstall Grange for the building of a new church, St Chad's Far Headingley (**Figure 11**), requesting that his body might be interred in the grounds of the new church (at Kirkstall Grange), but it took several years for building work to begin and by the time St Chad's was finally consecrated in 1868, William's remains were very much at rest at Kensal Green cemetery in London.

The responsibility for commissioning the new church fell to William's younger brother Edmund Beckett Denison. John, the eldest brother and 2nd Baronet, had died in 1847, the same year as Christopher; Richard Beckett, the fourth eldest, was killed in battle at Talavera in 1809; and Thomas Beckett, the only other brother still living in 1863, had assumed the title of 3rd Baronet and, at 84, was in retirement at Sowerby Park Gainsborough.

Edmund, the youngest brother, was 77 at the time of William's death. He had married Maria Beverley a great grand niece of Judge Thomas Denison, and took the surname Denison in acknowledgement of the eminent family connection. When Edmund, himself, briefly succeeded to the baronetcy at the grand old age of 86, he reverted to the Beckett family name. As Sir Edmund Beckett, Bart, he died 18 months later.

In his working life Edmund was a director of Beckett & Co and Chairman of the Great Northern Railway Company from 1847. In particular he established the company's railway works at Doncaster and resided at Carlton Hall, near Newark. Edmund and Maria had three sons, two of which are of particular interest in the story of Beckett's Park Leeds.

The eldest brother, Edmund Beckett Denison QC (**Figure 12**), was 47 when his uncle William died. Having been educated at Doncaster, Eton and Cambridge he was by this time a successful London barrister specialising in parliamentary and ecclesiastic law. He was also a noted amateur architect, an accomplished clock designer (**Figure 13**) and a

Fig. 7
Coat of arms on front elevation of The Grange. (Source: Photo by Keith Rowntree)

Fig. 8
The Victoria Arch built in 1858 at Headingley Campus. (Source: Photo by Susannah Marshall)

Jan. 26. At Brighton, aged 78, William Beckett, esq., of Kirkstall Grange, near Leeds, formerly M.P. for Leeds and for Ripon, and the principal partner in the eminent banking firm of Beckett and Co., of the Leeds Old Bank. "The removal of Mr. Beckett will be regarded with very great and general regret. He had filled with ability, prudence, public spirit, and we may even say with meekness, a very eminent position in the banking and mercantile world. Owing to his wealth and standing his influence was very great, and his judgment on mercantile, social, and political questions was highly respected ; but he was unostentatious in his mode of living, unambitious, calm, and always used his influence with moderation and with great respect for the rights and opinions of others. His person was noble and commanding, his manners highly popular, his talents good, his mode of speaking in public clear and effective ; so that he might have taken a more prominent position in politics if he had chosen. But his never-failing moderation led him to decline any peculiar prominence. When loudly called upon by his party in 1841, he responded to the call, and accepted a seat for the borough of Leeds in the House of Commons ; but when the Conservative party was divided on the Free Trade question, he withdrew from the representation of Leeds, and sat for some years for the borough of Ripon, from which he retired in 1857. The conduct of Mr. Beckett and his late brother Christopher, as bankers, at the alarming crisis of 1825, gave the Old Bank a strong claim on the confidence, and even on the gratitude, of the town. At that period they acted with bold liberality and yet with prudence, and so as to save many of their customers from embarrassment. Indeed, Mr. Beckett was the model of a banker, and his influence on the whole mercantile community of Leeds has been most salutary. The first Sir John Beckett, bart., went to Leeds from Barnsley, and established the Old Bank in partnership with Mr. Blayds, then Mr. Calverley. His eldest son, who succeeded him in the baronetcy, was brought up to the bar, and, entering political life, and having formed a high connection by marrying the daughter of the Earl of Lonsdale, he became Judge Advocate, which office he filled for many years to the satisfaction of his party. He sat as representative for Leeds from 1835 to 1837, but sustained two defeats for the borough —one before, the other after that period. The youngest brother of that large family, Edmund Denison, esq., sat as member for the West Riding in several Parliaments. Mr. William Beckett was also a son of the first Sir John Beckett, who married Miss Wilson, daughter of the Bishop of Bristol. Mr. Beckett was born in Leeds in 1784, and would have attained his seventy-ninth year in March. He married some years ago a sister of Mr. Meynell Ingram, of Temple Newsam, who survives him. He leaves no children."— *Yorkshire Paper.*

WILLIAM BECKETT ESQ.

*Fig. 11
St Chad's, Far
Headingley. (Source:
Keith Rowntree)*

*Fig. 12
Edmund Beckett
Denison QC from* Spy –
*Sir Leslie Ward.
(Source: Vanity Fair,
Issue 1836, 9 January
1904, courtesy of Mr
Bill Bennett and Julie's
Antique Prints)*

student of homeopathy. He was nominally the architect of St James' Church Doncaster (although the work is largely attributed to Sir George Gilbert Scott) and in 1859 he was credited with designing the most famous clock in the land – and arguably in the world – the tower clock at Westminster Palace, chiming since 1859 on Big Ben.

In the 1860s he enthusiastically threw himself into the new church project on the Kirkstall Grange estate. Edmund is acknowledged as architect and patron of St Chad's Church, however, most of the endowment came from his uncle's legacy and much of the design in the Early Decorated style, is attributed to his assistant architect William Crossland, a former pupil of Sir George Gilbert Scott. St Chad's church was consecrated on 11 January 1868 and afterwards,

*Fig. 13
The Grimthorpe clock
escapement. (Source:
Ian Crossland)*

Fig. 14 Report on death of Wm Beckett. (Source: Yorkshire Post Newspapers Ltd)

Fig. 15 Ernest William Beckett M.P., J.P. (Source: W. Herbert Scott (1902), The West Riding of Yorkshire at the Opening of the Twentieth Century, Brighton, W. T. Pike and Co.)

Edmund presided over a celebration lunch at the glebe school room on Otley Road where honours were evenly bestowed. In 1886 Sir Edmund, now the 5th Baronet Beckett, was himself created a peer and took the title Lord Grimthorpe.

By the 1860s, however, the management of the bank was firmly in the hands of Edmund's younger brother William Ernest Beckett Denison who had followed his two uncles into the business. William lived briefly at Meanwood Hall, property of his late uncle Christopher and aunts Mary and Elizabeth, and later he moved to York. His staff regarded him as a stern and benevolent dictator. He was responsible for the rapid expansion of Beckett & Co which merged with and took over other smaller Yorkshire banks. He also moved the Leeds office in 1867 from its old premises in Briggate to a new building in Park Row, designed by Sir George Gilbert Scott in a pointed Gothic style and built of red brick.[7]

William was the managing director of the bank, a Member of Parliament and the first Chairman of the Yorkshire Post. He had six children Ernest, Gervase and Rupert, and three daughters. In 1890 he was killed by a train, in an appalling accident, whilst walking beside the railway in Dorset (**Figure 14**). By this time his sons had all joined their father in the family firm. Our story, however, now focuses on the eldest.

Ernest William Beckett (**Figure 15**) was born in 1856 at Roundhay. In 1864, when Ernest was 8 years old, his father moved the family to Meanwood Hall following the death of his aunt Elizabeth. His uncle William had died the previous year and since Frances did not maintain a household at Kirkstall Grange after his death, perhaps there was a choice of homes for his nephew. In any case, he moved to Meanwood Hall and Kirkstall Grange was offered for lease. Among the tenants during this period was fellow board member at Beckett's Bank, John Metcalfe Smith who is now remembered in a memorial window within St Chad's church.

Ernest became a director of the bank and MP for Whitby. In 1883 he married an American, Lucy Tracy Lee of New York and settled at Kirkstall Grange. Lucy supported the local work of the Church of England Society for Waifs and Strays, whilst Ernest pursued his business interests at the bank and entertained celebrated guests at Kirkstall Grange, the most famous at this time perhaps being Oscar Wilde – in Leeds on a lecture tour. But within eight years of married life tragedy struck twice in quick succession for Ernest. His father died in the gruesome railway accident in December 1890 already referred to and six months later, Lucy died only days after the birth of their son, Ralph.

In memory of his wife Ernest donated £3,000 towards the building of a new Church of England home for waifs and strays in Hollin Road Far Headingley. The building is now, appropriately, part of Weetwood Primary School. The Beckett coat of arms can be seen above the entrance and three foundation stones are carved with the initials of the Beckett children, Lucille, Mabel and Ralph.

After Lucy's death, Ernest travelled widely and entertained impressively. The Prince of Wales was his guest at Kirkstall Grange in 1895 for the opening of the Leeds Triennial Music Festival that year. At some point Ernest became intimate with Alice Keppel, mistress to the future king and wife of Captain Trefusis. A love child, Violet, was born to Alice and Ernest in 1894 but a public scandal seems to have been avoided.

Fig. 16 Villa Cimbrone, Ravello. (Source: Photograph courtesy of Hotel Villa Cimbrone)

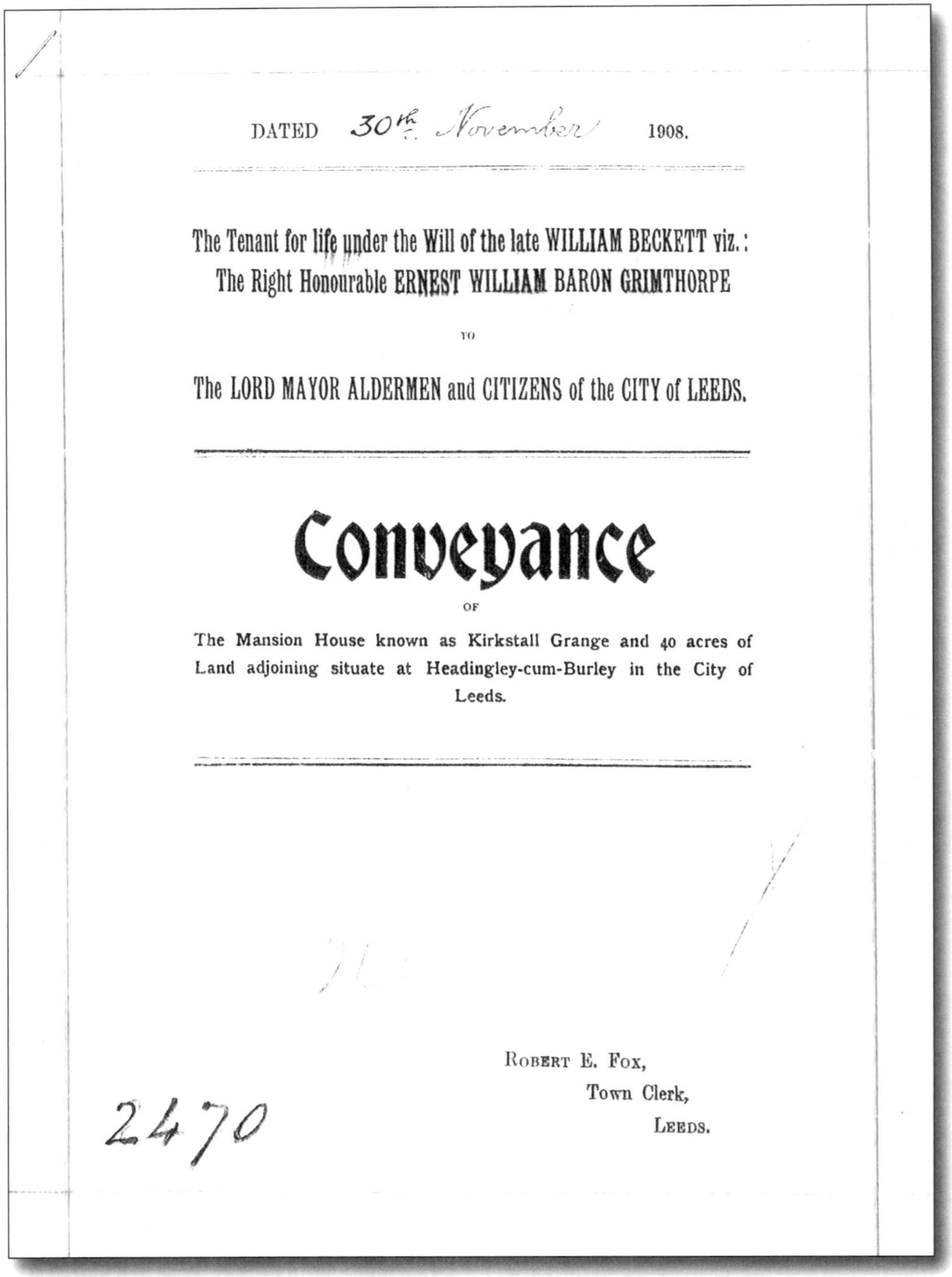

DATED *30th November* 1908.

The Tenant for life under the Will of the late WILLIAM BECKETT viz.:
The Right Honourable ERNEST WILLIAM BARON GRIMTHORPE

TO

The LORD MAYOR ALDERMEN and CITIZENS of the CITY of LEEDS.

Conveyance

OF

The Mansion House known as Kirkstall Grange and 40 acres of
Land adjoining situate at Headingley-cum-Burley in the City of
Leeds.

ROBERT E. FOX,
Town Clerk,
LEEDS.

2470

Fig. 17
Conveyance for the sale of the Beckett estate. (Source: West Yorkshire Archive Service, Ref. LC/TC deeds 2470)

In 1903 Ernest emigrated to Ravello in Italy where he acquired the 11th-century Villa Cimbrone overlooking the Bay of Salerno. (**Figure 16**) He was 46. Two years later Sir Edmund Beckett Denison died and Ernest succeeded as the 6th Baronet Beckett and 2nd Lord Grimthorpe. He died in 1917 and is buried in a pseudo-classical temple at the Villa Cimbrone.

Ernest's retirement to Italy enabled his brother, Gervase, to take possession of Kirkstall Grange with his wife Mabel and their growing family. Two children had already been born and two more, Beatrice and Prunella would be born at Kirkstall Grange. When Beatrice reached 19 years of age she married the second son of Sir William Eden, Robert Anthony. The marriage foundered after the death of their son Simon. Anthony Eden remarried. He became Foreign Secretary in 1950 and prime minister in 1955.

Beatrice's father, Gervase, was elected MP for Whitby in 1905 and in the New Year of 1908, he moved his family to Kirkdale Manor near Helmsley closer to his Scarborough and Whitby constituency. Rupert his younger brother might well have considered making his home at Kirkstall Grange but that was not to be. Instead the family, or strictly speaking, Ernest in Italy, the 2nd Lord Grimthorpe, agreed to sell the Grange and 35 acres of land to Leeds Corporation for the purpose of establishing a teacher training college (**Figure 17**). The magnificent group of college buildings, now the Leeds Metropolitan University Headingley Campus, rose on the site in 1912, designed in a Renaissance revival style by the city architect G. W. Atkinson.[8] A further 19 acres known as Church Wood was donated to the college. 92 acres was bought by the Corporation and laid out as a public park, Beckett Park, and the remainder of the estate, about 290 acres, was sold for residential development.

The sale was perhaps inevitable. Leeds had grown enormously and was by now ranked a major city, its suburbs enveloping Headingley and extending round parts of the Kirkstall Grange estate. The estate land was immensely valuable for development. Private housing further towards the countryside was by then much more attractive to wealthy businessmen. In addition, large houses like Kirkstall Grange were hugely costly to maintain and required a large number of domestic servants.

And what of Beckett & Co? In 1920 the firm amalgamated with London County Westminster and Parrs Bank, better known today as the National Westminster Bank. Rupert Beckett was appointed a director of the board and then Chairman, an office he held from 1930 to 1950.

In 1921 his brother, Gervase, formerly of Kirsktall Grange, became Sir William Gervase Beckett, Bart, having been created a baronet like his grandfather Sir John Beckett one hundred and eight years earlier, with whom, you will recall, this story began.[9]

THE BECKETTS NOW

Amongst the family's varied pursuits in industry, enterprise, politics, the military, architecture and horology, the Becketts have also had a distinguished involvement in horse breeding and racing which carries on to this day.

Ralph Ernest Beckett (the 3rd Lord Grimthorpe) served in the Territorial Army, and was involved in banking, like many in his family. Ralph was also an avid huntsman and equestrian enthusiast, serving as Master of the Middleton Hounds and owning and breeding a string of national hunt horses, the most famous of which, Fortina, won the Cheltenham Gold Cup in 1947 (**Figure 18**). Ralph also established the Grimthorpe Cup in 1922, a Yorkshire cross country race of four miles and one furlong which was known as the 'Grand National of point to pointing' and is still competed for and sponsored by the Beckett family.

Ralph was also an aviation enthusiast. He owned his own aeroplane and actively supported British aeronautics by investing his own capital and serving on the board of directors in Nevil Shute Norway's aeroplane company, Airspeed Limited (**Figure 19**). Although not a profitable business venture, Airspeed Ltd was an aviation pioneer developing the first aircraft with a retractable undercarriage (Edgerton, 1991). Nevil Shute Norway went on to become the famous novelist Nevil Shute.[10] It was this Ralph Beckett who attended the Jubilee ceremony at the City of Leeds Training College (now Leeds Met) in 1957 as a representative of the Beckett family.

Ralph's son, Christopher John Beckett, was a career soldier. Christopher served as deputy commander of the British Forces in Malta and Libya receiving an OBE in 1958 for his service to the military. He also owned, bred and raced horses and was a member of the Jockey

Fig. 18
Portrait of Fortina.
(Source: Photo Ian Kaplan, courtesy of Teddy Beckett)

Fig. 19
Nevil Shute, Hessell Tiltman, Ralph Beckett, on right of Airspeed Courier, May 1933.
(Source: Nevil Shute Norway Foundation)

Fig. 20
Westow Hall. (Source:
Photo Ian Kaplan,
courtesy of Teddy
Beckett)

Fig. 21
The Rt Hon.
Mr Edward 'Teddy'
Beckett, 5th Lord
Grimthorpe. (Source:
Photo Ian Kaplan,
courtesy of Teddy
Beckett)

Club. Christopher purchased and settled at Westow Hall in Yorkshire (**Figure 20**) with his wife Elizabeth Lumley and lived there until his death in 2003.

Christopher's son, Edward 'Teddy' Beckett is the current and 5th Lord Grimthorpe (**Figure 21**). Teddy continues in the family's equestrian tradition and has pursued a career in the horse breeding and horse racing industry.

Teddy became interested in horses at an early age and developed his knowledge and skills working on horse farms in England, Australia and the United States. He worked for eleven years as a bloodstock agent, buying and selling horses, and was a member of the British Bloodstock Agency, which, although now no longer in existence, was for many years the foremost bloodstock company. In 1999 he became the racing manager of Juddmonte Farms, a position he still holds and one which demands an encyclopaedic knowledge of horse racing pedigree. Juddmonte, owned by Prince Khalid Abdullah of Saudi Arabia, is one of the world's top horse breeding companies with stud farms in England, Ireland and the United States. Although he is based in Newmarket, Suffolk (England's centre of horse racing), Teddy's work as racing manager is global in scope.

He has three children, Harry (**Figure 22**), James and Lucy, and lives in Cambridgeshire near Newmarket.

Recently invited to the Headingley Campus, Teddy joined Leeds Met members of staff at the Civic Trust blue plaque unveiling at the Grange on 7 February 2007 (**Figure 23**). It was the first time in over a hundred years a member of the Beckett family has visited the Grange, and hopefully not the last.

The authors wish to thank Ian Kaplan and Iain Poole for their assistance.

Fig. 22
Teddy's son
Harry Beckett, aged 14.
(Source: Teddy Beckett)

Fig. 23
Visit of Teddy Beckett
(left) to The Grange for
the unveiling of the Civic
Trust blue plaque.
Pictured here on the left
with the Chairman of
the Civic Trust, Peter
Baker and Patricia Lee,
wife of the Vice-
Chancellor. (Source:
LeedsMet.
Communications: Icon
Photography)

ENDNOTES

[1] In November 1700, the Aire and Calder Navigation opened establishing Leeds as an important inland port accessible by cargo ship and barge from Hull and the North Sea trade routes. As a consequence commercial traffic on the main highways into Leeds increased substantially helping to magnetise Leeds as a business centre.

[2] Quoted in *Westminster Bank in Leeds* (nd) designed and printed by WLP Printing Group Limited.

[3] See Figure 16.

[4] A quote from the auction particulars of 1829.

[5] Some speculate that the arch was erected in Leeds as a ceremonial arch for the Queen's procession to the Town Hall and then re-erected at Kirkstall Grange after the event. This seems highly unlikely given the nature of its construction.

[6] From his memorial inscription at Leeds Parish Church.

[7] Sir George Gilbert Scott is probably best known for St Pancras Station and the Albert Memorial in London. His building in Park Row Leeds was demolished in 1963.

[8] See chapter by Black on Buildings and Spaces.

[9] For further contextual information see, D. Hall (2000) *Far Headingley, Weetwood and West Park*, Leeds, Far Headingley Village Society.

[10] Edgerton, D. (1991) *England and the aeroplane: an essay on a militants and technological nation*, London, Macmillan.

CHAPTER 3

Buildings and Spaces

Alistair Black

You don't have to be an expert in architecture to know that the buildings and spaces that form Leeds Metropolitan University's Headingley Campus, most of which began life in 1912 as the purpose-built City of Leeds Training College, are something special with a story to tell.[1] Buildings speak to us. They reflect society and communicate our aspirations, needs and values. Like books, buildings can be read and their meanings defined, debated and articulated.[2] All technology is socially determined, and the technology that is a building – including its style, internal plan and its relation to surrounding spaces and structures – is no different in this respect. Thus, having offered a description of the College's buildings and their spatial settings, this chapter proceeds to outline the influences that determined the forms they took. Finally, in light of the analysis of the College's original built form, a brief assessment is offered of its legacy today.

DESCRIPTION

Fig. 1
Site plan showing the disposition of buildings and sports areas from CLTC Handbook *(1912). (Source: Leeds Metropolitan University Archives)*

Between 1907 (when the College was founded) and 1912, when the purpose-built site at Far Headingley received its first students, training and accommodation was provided at a number of temporary premises in the Headingley area.[3] These premises are not the focus of this chapter and are well documented in other sources.[4] Rather, the concern here is with the suite of buildings and surrounding ornamental and recreational spaces designed as the College's permanent home.[5]

The location of the College in temporary premises had been approved by the Board of Education on the understanding that plans would be drawn up speedily by the council for a permanent location. No sooner had the College opened, then the Beckett Estate was identified as the preferred site for its future development. In 1909 the College acquired its first foothold on the site when Kirkstall Grange became a hostel for

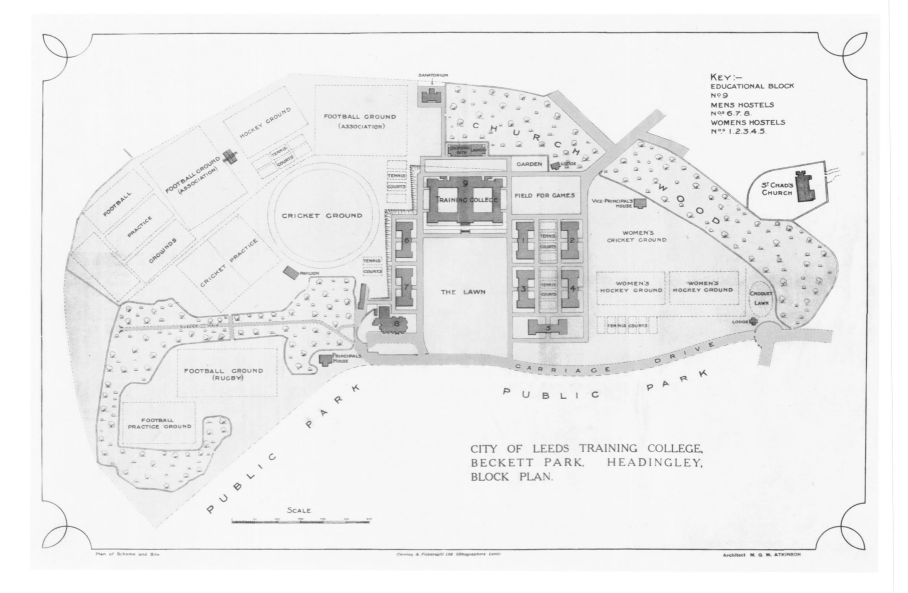

some of the College's women students. In the absence of any standard for building a training college, the representatives of the Education Committee visited a number of colleges and residential schools to obtain some 'valuable hints'; and an examination was also made of similar institutions in Europe.[6] In September 1909 the Education Committee, through the auspices of its architect F. Broadbent, issued its instructions and conditions of competition for the design, the winner to be chosen by Sir Aston Webb, who was involved at the time in re-configuring the façade of Buckingham Palace and designing the various elements in the new approach to it: Admiralty Arch, the Mall and the Victoria Memorial.

The instructions communicated a preferred arrangement of buildings on the site: a quadrangular plan with a main educational block (and smaller blocks housing a swimming bath, laundry and sanatorium) to the north, three men's hostels (two purpose-built and the existing Kirkstall Grange) to the west, and to the east five women's hostels arranged to form a mini-quad for the provision of tennis courts. The southern side of the main quadrangle was left open, and around the periphery of the site large numbers of playing fields were to be laid out. The main entrance was to be at the south-eastern tip of the site, adjoining the new public park entrance; and a tradesmen's entrance was planned at Churchwood to the north east. Churchwood was also to be the site of a house for the Vice-Principal, while a house in Queenswood, to the south west, was to provide accommodation for the Principal (both these houses eventually took the name of the woods in which they were built) (**Figure 1**).

Competitors were free to suggest a different disposition of structures and spaces, but it appears that in reality divergence from the basic plan was discouraged.[7] The style of architecture and type of materials was left entirely to competitors, although the Education Committee did insist on an avoidance of elaboration and ornamental detail. With a classical, Neo-Georgian design, the competition was won by G. W. Atkinson, who later, in the 1920s, assisted in the refurbishment

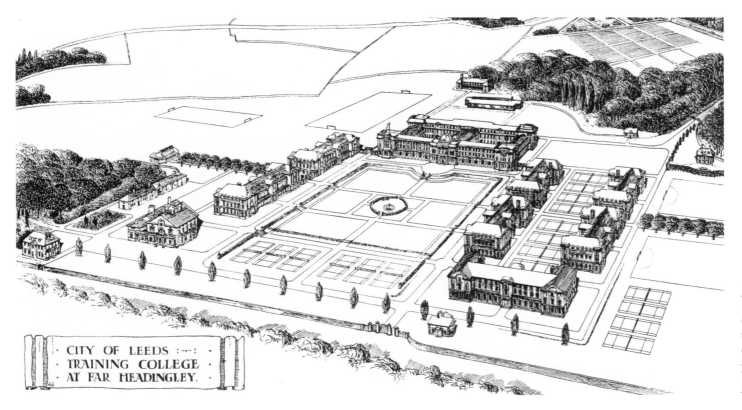

CITY OF LEEDS :—: TRAINING COLLEGE AT FAR HEADINGLEY.

Fig. 2
'Perspective View of the College', an aerial sketch which illustrates clearly the College's rural setting (from the Yorkshire Observer, *5 October 1910)*

Fig. 3
Brontë Hall's
entrance hall in 1912
from CLTC Handbook
(1912). (Source: Leeds
Metropolitan University
Archives)

Fig. 4
Brontë Hall's
entrance hall now, with
original brickwork
covered by plaster.
(Source: Alistair Black)

by virtue not only of its staff and students but also its buildings, the College 'shall take in the educational world a position second to none'.[8]

Each hostel was to house 60 students, giving a total student body of 480. In each hostel a central entrance framed by paired pilasters led over marble flooring into a large lounge area, or entrance hall (**Figures 3 & 4**). Off a corridor leading from one side of the entrance hall were a visitors' room, a tutors' sitting room and, at its end, a large students' common room. Off the corridor to the opposite side of the entrance hall was a library, as well as a dining room comprising five tables each seating twelve students (**Figures 5 & 6**). Main staircases at the end of each corridor provided access to the upper levels. To the rear of each end of the building, service wings were constructed. One of these housed a servery adjacent to the dining room, and behind the servery a kitchen, larder, dairy and a tradesman's entrance. This wing also housed a staircase for servants, leading directly up to their quarters which were cut off from the student accommodation. The opposite wing provided a students' entrance, especially useful for those returning from the playing fields because the wing also housed changing rooms, showers, baths and lavatories. From here, students could take a 'back' staircase to their rooms. Study-bedrooms were provided on the first and second floors, and were for individual occupation. A typical study-bedroom was described thus:

Behind the door is a settee, which is easily convertible into a bed. In one corner is a plain wardrobe, the inner side of the door of which shows a long mirror. Against one wall is a combination dressing chest and table, with bookshelves above; and under the window a writing table, which by 'pressing a button', so to speak, becomes a wash-stand and dressing-table, with mirror and all complete[9] (**Figures 7 & 8**).

At the centre of the corridor on each of the upper floors there was a suite of rooms for resident tutors. Electric lighting and central heating by hot-water radiators was provided throughout.

The centrepiece of the site was, and remains, the main educational block (now the James Graham Building) (**Figures 9 & 10**). Situated on high ground at the north of the site, the educational block offered a commanding view of the open land to the south, from which perspective

of the Headrow in Leeds and was primarily responsible for the design of Lewis's department store on that particular thoroughfare. Various technical aspects of the work were distributed among the creators of the six next-best designs. Atkinson was charged with designing the main educational block as well as the Brontë Hall hostel, which acted as a template for the design of the remaining hostels by the runners-up (halls differed from each other in small architectural details) (**Figure 2**).

At a cost of around £200,000, building work on the College was completed in 1912, and in the September of that year it received its first students (the official opening did not occur until June 1913). It was the opinion of two students writing in the College magazine at the time that the block appeared as an imposing structure by virtue of its elevation and its style, the latter, in red brick, with paired pilasters on the upper floors, drawing on the same Neo-Georgian-Palladian formula that informed the design of the hostels, showing 'nothing extravagant by way of ornamentation'.[10]

The main access to the building was raised and was reached by a central flight of stairs leading to a recessed portico, framed by four Corinthian pillars and a pediment above (the dome above the entrance and behind the portico depicted in various plans, as seen in **Figure 2**, was never built). Thereafter, at the rear of an adequately-sized entrance hall with vaulted ceilings, access to the upper floor was gained via a further stone staircase which split to left and right and returned upwards to the first floor. Rooms in the block were grouped around two large internal quadrangles which offered good light to all rooms, as well as a pleasant outlook. In addition to offices for the Principal, Vice-Principal and other staff, the accommodation comprised science laboratories, an educational museum, a wood-panelled library with recessed bookcases, workshops for metal and wood, and historical, geographical, art, needlework, music, lecture, class and students' common rooms. There was also a gymnasium (with changing room) for men, and another for women. The spaces were so organised as to allow for the teaching of men and women separately. At the centre of the block was the splendid College Hall, decorated with oak-panelled walls and tall, leaded, engraved arched windows. It contained a stage to its rear and, in ecclesiastic fashion, an internal balcony and organ above its entrance (**Figures 11 & 12**).

INFLUENCES

Bearing in mind the thesis that built forms are determined by social forms, that design is derived from society, how might the College's built-environment of 1912 be interpreted? What were the influences that shaped the buildings and the surrounding spaces?

The immediate derivation of the design was architectural: the ancestry provided by Kirkstall Grange and the architectural fashion of the day. The key to understanding the style adopted for the College buildings is the architectural heritage of Kirkstall Grange. The Education Committee advised that the designs for the hostels and the main educational block were to reflect the design of Kirkstall Grange, the work

*Fig. 5
Brontë Hall's dining room in 1912 from CLTC Handbook (1912). (Source: Leeds Metropolitan University Archives)*

*Fig. 6
Brontë Hall's dining room now functions as a teaching and learning space. A partition has been erected at the far end of the room to create an office. (Source: Alistair Black)*

of the country-house architect James Paine in 1752.[11] The house was a product of the wave of Palladianism that swept Georgian England and became, according to the popular architectural historian Dan Cruickshank, 'almost a religion'.[12] Andrea Palladio, a sixteenth-century Paduan, developed a form of classical design that was simple and functional. Palladian villas originated as country houses for substantial farms. One of their main characteristics was a central block flanked by two pavilion blocks, these being connected to the centre by passageways or open colonnades.[13] The pavilions acted as service and functional areas – including stables, barns, grain stores, wine cellars, farmworkers' accommodation – integral to the working life of the farm (in the Georgian era pavilions often housed administrative offices or even guest

accommodation). The effect was a 'villa-with-wings', where the impression given was of a house larger than it really was. Paine followed this Palladian prescription for a villa with symmetrical flanking wings in his Kirkstall Grange design. The eastern pavilion wing has since been removed,[14] and alterations in the middle decades of the nineteenth century, after the Beckett family had bought the house in 1832, included the addition of bay windows to the front. Otherwise, what remains (and what was there a century ago when planners constructed their vision for the College) is essentially an elegant villa plucked from the hills of sixteenth-century north-eastern Italy (**Figures 13 & 14**).

The planning of the Beckett Estate site coincided with the Edwardian Neo-Georgian revival. Around 1906 the Baroque revival, which had begun in the 1890s, gave way to a simpler, purer classicism aligned with the French Beaux-Arts School and with Georgian composition. However, the Baroque had a continuing influence in that it had highlighted the work of inspirational *English* architects like Sir Christopher Wren. Such buildings as St Paul's Cathedral, Blenheim Palace and the Radcliffe Camera, Oxford, although classical, were conceptualised as thoroughly vernacular and steeped in the cultural heritage of the English nation (it is no coincidence that the styles of the Baroque revival were also termed 'English Renaissance'). In the search for Englishness, the Neo-Georgian style proved highly attractive. A refined style, the 'Georgian' was evocative of a period in the nation's history that was one of relative calm and of increasing prosperity and colonial success (before the American and Napoleonic wars, that is).[15] The Edwardian Neo-Georgian revival was particularly strong in the area of domestic-house architecture. The styles chosen for the hostels at the College were a direct result of this aspect of the revival and were laced, moreover, with a measure of Palladianism, as seen in the 'wings' that can be detected in each, especially from the rear; although these wings were not as pronounced as those in the Kirkstall Grange design (**Figures 15 & 16**).

Beyond these direct 'artistic' influences, a number of other 'causes' of the College's design can be identified. The factors that gave rise to the design were multifarious, ranging from the economic to the political, and from the social to the cultural; and they also included, of course, the educational, which was naturally cross-cut by most other influencing factors. In view of this complexity, a useful framework for establishing the social causes of the College's built form might be considered to be what in 1910 the leading educational theorist P. E. Matheson, Fellow of New College Oxford, identified as the three core elements of education: knowledge; efficiency; and character and conduct.[16]

The 'Neo-Georgian' adopted by the planners was a refined style that mirrored the Enlightenment, when new ideas on the origins and purpose of *knowledge*, not least its role in progress, came to the fore. The Georgian period was one of increased sociability, clubbability and agricultural and industrial prosperity, driven by modern, more open and

Fig. 9
The educational block in 1912 from CLTC Handbook (1912). (Source: Leeds Metropolitan University Archives)

Fig. 10
The educational block (now the James Graham Building) today. (Source: Alistair Black)

progressive attitudes to the purpose of knowledge. Contrary to the proposition that we have only recently entered a 'knowledge society', the importance of knowledge, and learning, to industrial and imperial success was increasingly acknowledged by the pre-First World War generation. The extensive nature of the College built form reflected this new drive to invest in knowledge. The quadrangular plan paid homage to the culture of learning in the country's ancient universities where such an arrangement of space had been historically common place. The large number of student places provided in the College, requiring accommodation in terms of both residential and teaching spaces, was a reflection of the need, identified by the local authorities in Leeds and throughout the country, to train much larger numbers of teachers to meet the increasing demand of the education system.[17] To celebrate the importance and heritage of knowledge, halls were named after great figures in the history of art, literature and science who were in some way linked to Leeds or the local.[18] Each hall was endowed with its own library, while in the main educational block a pleasant and commodious general library was provided, the latter having something of the feel of an Oxbridge college library, with references also drawn from the private library of a great house.[19]

Efficiency became a touchstone for the planners of the College. The Education Committee stressed the need to provide buildings which were thoroughly efficient.[20] Buildings, it was advised, should be 'capable of easy working and effective supervision, without over-lapping waste, either in the capital outlay or in maintenance', and in reviewing the plans the Chief Inspector of Training Colleges for England came to the conclusion that there was 'no extravagance or waste', adding that the institution at Leeds would be 'the finest Training College yet projected'.[21] At the opening ceremony in 1913, Alderman Kinder said that the aim of the design had been 'simplicity with efficiency';[22] and although cloaked in a historic style, the architecture of the College was in many respects an architecture of the industrial age, anticipating the efficiency of modernism. For example, *The British Architect* described the space-saving arrangements in the hostel study-bedrooms as 'ingenious', and praised the 'mode in which space is utilised, and, indeed, economised'.[23] This emphasis on efficiency should, of course, be viewed against the backdrop of national economic decline, relative to competitors abroad.

Increasingly in the decades immediately prior to the First World War, commentators lamented the inadequacy of educational provision in Britain compared to 'Continental' nations like France and Germany. The turn-of-the-century architect M. B. Adams wrote of the need to design educational institutions well because of the need for Britain to maintain imperial power and to compete economically, noting the 'unrelenting demand for . . . educational efficiency if we are to hold our own in the cosmopolitan possibilities of the immediate future'.[24] The College's built form was a direct consequence of this sense of utilitarian urgency, which manifested itself, amongst other things, in the wide range of rooms provided in the educational block for practical, technical subjects. These were organised spatially along gender lines, a reflection of the need to recover – in the post-Boer War (defeat) era and at a time when Germany was becoming a major threat – national greatness via a division of labour into, on the one hand, competent female homemakers whose work would help reverse the degeneration of the 'race', and on the one hand, efficient manpower for the military and industrial spheres raised in a healthy fashion.[25]

Whereas notions of function and efficiency in structures are derived from scientific knowledge, views on the character of buildings are closely linked to the 'aesthetic'.[26] The importance of *character and conduct* that the College aimed to instil in its students – the stated aim being 'to mould the character of each individual student to teach them self-control and self-government'[27] – was conveyed by the many references to the dignity and imposing composition of the buildings: the Education Committee instructed that the winning submission was to be 'a dignified design expressing the character of the buildings';[28] while Edward Pease at the opening ceremony referred to their 'imposing character'.[29] The impressiveness of the buildings reflected the growing status – and indeed growing membership[30] – of the teaching profession, which the eminent education authority Sir Joshua Fitch had proclaimed to be 'the noblest of all work', characterised by a 'high purpose . . . [and] by a solemn sense of duty, and by the love of truth'.[31] The pursuit of 'character' was also reflected in the large amount of space given over to sporting activity (**Figure 1**); the College authorities, in keeping with the strong influence at the time of 'muscular christianity',[32] believing it important to produce 'fine types of men and women', not only through 'physical culture' but also through 'physical exercise'.[33]

Fig. 13
The east wing of the Grange can just be made out on this survey of the area in 1766. At some point after this, the east wing was demolished (*Source:* A Plan of New Grange Situated in the Township of Headingley in the Parish of Leeds and the County of York, the Property of Walter Wade Esq., *by S. Wilkinson* (1766). *Courtesy of The Thoresby Society, Leeds*

Fig. 14
The Grange now. (*Source: Alistair Black*)

The scheme of 1912 was very much an architecture of morality. Thus, although fine buildings, the hostels communicated a barrack-like appearance, places where order and organisation were to be engendered (it is no coincidence that in the early twentieth century, a number of military barracks were constructed in the Neo-Georgian style).[34] The 'barrack' arrangement was also designed to engender an 'esprit de corps' (one that some came to believe was not wholly compatible with overall loyalty to the institution). This said, the hostels had a certain homely charm about them, aimed at stimulating 'the home feeling rather than the institutional feeling', replete with the moral guidance that entailed.[35]

In a further attempt to build character, as well as convey knowledge, hostel walls were adorned with carefully selected

Fig. 15 Cavendish Hall in 1912 from CLTC Handbook (1912). (Source: Leeds Metropolitan University Archives)

Fig. 16 Cavendish Hall now. In recent years all the halls have undergone extensive internal and external renovation. (Source: Alistair Black)

reproductions of good paintings in order to develop in the students 'an appreciation of what was best in art'.[36] Similarly, much was made, aesthetically, of the site's natural setting. A love of nature was captured in the choice of a passage from *Macbeth* to accompany an idyllic photograph of the Grange on the front of the menu for the luncheon provided during the visit of members of the Leeds City Council in July 1912;[37] while College handbooks and other commentaries on the College celebrated the institution's easy interaction with the natural environment around it. The buildings were seen as 'worthy of the site';[38] and Edward Pease believed that the College stood in a unique situation, 'surrounded by sylvan beauty and by open spaces'.[39] Multiple references were made to the simplicity of the buildings. Such comments were derived less, perhaps, from notions of efficiency than from an awareness that simplicity was essentially rooted in nature, which was itself 'honest' and did not entertain 'superfluousness', or 'Darwinian waste'; whereas the opposite of simplicity might be judged to be 'wildness',[40] something which the clean, gently sweeping lines of the buildings patently denied, and which would possibly have prompted the writer of the souvenir handbook celebrating the College's twenty-first birthday in 1928 to recall that in 1912 the College entered what they called 'the Promised Land'.[41]

TODAY

In 1957, from a retrospective vantage point of 45 years after the College moved to its site on the former Beckett Estate, the only history of the College thus far published, other than the one you are now reading, assessed the quality of the building and spaces provided in 1912. The author wrote of the College's 'magnificent site, with its generous proportions and its completely agreeable style . . . The buildings, with no more than minor alterations, have proved adequate for all occasions . . . They show little sign of . . . parsimony . . . The hall, library, lecture rooms and laboratories are spacious and dignified'.[42] This assessment, with some minor qualification, is equally applicable today.

The history of architecture has been full of revivals. The Neo-Georgian revival of the early-twentieth century that produced the built form of the City of Leeds Training College had a long lasting effect. Between the wars it could be seen in a number of functional state buildings, such as unemployment offices, telephone exchanges, post-offices, libraries and, as said above, military barracks. The style also continued to influence domestic house design, even into recent decades. Yet it would be true to say that in the decades after 1918, as modernism came to dominate, historical architecture was not always the height of fashion (although at the Beckett Park campus it has been evident that older styles can co-exist with modern compositions, as in the case of Rich Hall, the student services block and the boiler house, all products of either the 1960s or 1970s). As modernism itself came under attack, history made a comeback. By the end of the 1970s all had changed and, as Adrian Forty reminds us, everyone thereafter wanted to show that their work had 'history'.[43]

The post-modern designs that have come to dominate architecture in recent decades are not ashamed of history. However, in its carefree approach to historical accuracy and its playful mixing of historical styles, post-modernism, it is argued, engages in shallow history and is ultimately disrespectful of the past. The retention of the historic buildings at Beckett Park and the nursing of a style that belongs to another age might on the one hand be considered to be a post-modern falsehood, a masterly deception disguising what are in effect functional office and teaching and learning spaces. It might also be seen as an investment in a 'heritage mentality' that attempts to assuage social anxieties by reminding us of supposedly safer, more cosy, more orderly and more certain times. On the other hand, it is impossible to ignore economic issues; for to replace what are solid buildings with new structures, however more attuned those new structures may be to educational needs, would be financially and, in an age when re-use is to the front of everyone's mind, possibly environmentally damaging also. Nor should an awareness of tradition and continuity be expunged: people harbour a natural curiosity about where the institutions to which they are attached came from.

Re-working old buildings to suit new demands required compromises. Over the decades the buildings at Beckett Park have undergone many internal re-arrangements. The most dramatic has occurred in recent years, with the conversion of residential accommodation (one of the attractions offered by the site in 1912) into offices and rooms for teaching, learning and meeting. In the former hostel blocks internal walls have been knocked down and partitions added. In regard to the offices of academic staff, the 'individual occupation' principle that characterised the original study-bedrooms has been abandoned, as many now share offices. This delivers much needed savings and can improve staff liaison and communication; however, it can have a negative effect on concentration and does not offer a confidential environment for staff-student relations. Many of the old 'public' and service areas – the dining, common and changing rooms and the kitchens, larders and serveries – have been transformed into bright and functional lecture rooms, with modern digital and audio-visual teaching aids.

An extensive re-working of space has also been evident in the main educational block, now the James Graham Building. The most obvious change, especially if one has the privilege of a bird's-eye view from a plane making its final approach to Leeds-Bradford Airport, is the in-filling of the internal quadrangles – by state-of-the-art lecture theatres and accommodation for modern library and computing services. Some areas, having undergone change, have reverted to an earlier function: the original library, the Acre Room, has been returned to its former function as a space for readers; while the Great Hall, having been occupied by the library in the mid-1990s, has similarly had its original purpose, and indeed decoration, restored.[44]

However, despite inevitable additions and alterations over the decades, comparing the built environment at the current Headingley Campus with the photographic record of the original buildings and spaces, what strikes one most is the *lack* of change that has taken place (this in stark contrast, of course, to the myriad academic and administrative changes that have occurred behind the built façade). True, new buildings and uses for land have appeared: the modernist structures noted above, the outdoor athletics areas, the functional blocks for indoor physical pursuits and, not least, the suite of buildings gifted by the Carnegie United Kingdom Trust in 1933, clothed in the same Neo-Georgian style as the original buildings.[45] But these additions apart, one might guess that the sense of space, proportion, dignity, aesthetic pleasure and blending with the natural surroundings that is felt today – in short the 'atmosphere of repose' which T. E. Matheson identified in 1910 as a major aim of education and as an antidote to the vulgarity, brutality and 'glitter' of what he saw as an age of 'hustle'[46] – was also experienced by those who saw the newly built site before the First World War.

ENDNOTES

[1] The Grange became a listed building in 1951. The remaining historic buildings were listed in 1996.

[2] A. King, *Buildings and society* (London: Routledge and Kegan Paul, 1980); T. A. Markus, *Buildings and power* (London: Routledge, 1993); A. Forty, *Words and buildings: a vocabulary of modern architecture* (New York: Thames and Hudson, 2000).

[3] E.g. Harewood Barracks on Woodhouse Lane for a while provided much of the teaching accommodation.

[4] City of Leeds Training College, *Coming of age celebrations souvenir handbook: 1907-1928* (1928), passim; City of Leeds College of Education, *A short history of the City of Leeds Training College 1907-1957* (1957), especially pp. 6, 14, 16, 17.

[5] The following history of the planning and the description of the permanent College site is drawn from the following sources: 'The Leeds Training College', *The British Architect* (5 July 1912), pp. 15-16; 'Leeds Training College for Teachers: a noteworthy enterprise', *Yorkshire Observer* (5 February 1910); 'Leeds Training College: official opening: Mr J. A. Pease M.P. on changing educational methods', *Yorkshire Post* (14 June 1913); City of Leeds Training College, *Handbook* (1912); City of Leeds Training College, *Handbook* (1913); City of Leeds Training College, *Coming of age celebrations souvenir handbook: 1907-1928* (1928); 'City of Leeds Training College: a review of the various stages of work' (c. September 1910), Leeds Metropolitan University Archives; City of Leeds Education Department, *City of Leeds Training College: instructions to architects and conditions of competition* (1909); 'City of Leeds Training College: cost of the scheme (c. 1907), Leeds Metropolitan University Archives; City of Leeds College of Education, *A short history of the City of Leeds Training College 1907-1957* (1957), pp. 1-16.

[6] 'City of Leeds Training College: a review of the various stages of work' (c. September 1910), Leeds Metropolitan University Archives, p. 1.

[7] As implied in 'City of Leeds Training College: a review of the various stages of work' (c. September 1910), Leeds Metropolitan University Archives, p. 3.

[8] Quoted in City of Leeds College of Education, *A short history of the City of Leeds Training College 1907-1957* (1957), p. 14.

[9] 'The Leeds Training College', *The British Architect* (5 July 1912), p. 16.

[10] Ibid. p. 16. Many would disagree that the building has a 'lifeless frontage', an observation to be found in S. Wrathmell (with J. Minnis), *Leeds: Pevsner architectural guide* (London and New Haven: Yale University Press, 2005), p. 264.

[11] P. Leach, *James Paine* (London: Zwemmer, 1988).

[12] D. Cruickshank, *A guide to the Georgian buildings of Britain and Ireland* (London: Weidenfeld and Nicolson, 1985), p. 7.

[13] L. H. Heydenreich and W. Lotz, *Architecture in Italy 1400-1600* (Penguin: Harmondsworth, 1974), pp. 313-14.

[14] As evidenced by Wrathmell, op. cit., p. 264.

[15] A. Service, *Edwardian architecture: a handbook to buildings design in Britain 1890-1914* (London: Thames and Hudson, 1977), especially chapters 10, 11 and 12 on, respectively, 'High Edwardian Baroque', 'The Beaux-Arts Influence on Edwardian Classicism' and 'The Neo-Georgian House'.

[16] P. E. Matheson, 'Ideals in Education' (1910), reproduced in his *Education Today and Tomorrow* (London: Humphrey Milton and Oxford University press, 1917), p. 33.

[17] City of Leeds Higher Education Sub-Committee, The present position of the question of training colleges and training teachers (22 November 1906).

[18] See Endnote 22 in the following chapter on the *Genesis of the City of Leeds Training College* by Janet Douglas.

[19] G. Barber, *Arks of learning: a short history of Oxford library buildings* (Oxford: Oxford Bibliographical Society, 1995); P. S. Morrish, 'Domestic libraries: Victorian and Edwardian ideas and practice', *Library History*, Vol. 10 (1994), pp. 27-44.

[20] City of Leeds Education Department, *City of Leeds Training College: instructions to architects and conditions of competition* (1909), paragraph 7.

[21] 'City of Leeds Training College: a review of the various stages of work' (c. September 1910), Leeds Metropolitan University Archives, pp. 1, 2.

[22] 'Leeds Training College for Teachers: a noteworthy enterprise', *Yorkshire Observer* (5 February 1910).

[23] 'The Leeds Training College', *The British Architect* (5 July 1912), p. 16.

[24] M. B. Adams, 'Public libraries, their buildings and equipment: a plea for state aid', *Library Association Record*, Vol. 7 (1905), p. 162.

[25] A. Davin, 'Imperialism and motherhood', *History Workshop*, No. 5 (Spring 1978).

[26] A. Forty, *Words and buildings: a vocabulary of modern architecture* (New York: Thames and Hudson, 2000), p. 121.

[27] Words of Alderman Kinder, Chairman of the Board of Governors, 'Leeds Training College: official opening: Mr J. A. Pease M.P. on changing educational methods', *Yorkshire Post* (14 June 1913).

[28] City of Leeds Education Department, *City of Leeds Training College: instructions to architects and conditions of competition* (1909).

[29] 'Leeds Training College: official opening: Mr J. A. Pease M.P. on changing educational methods', *Yorkshire Post* (14 June 1913).

[30] The number of male certified teachers had risen from 6,395 in 1870 to 21,223 in 1895, the number of female teachers rising from 6,072 to 31,718 in the same period: D. R. Jones, *The origins of civic universities: Manchester, Leeds and Liverpool* (London: Routledge, 1988), p. 78.

[31] J. G. Fitch, *Lectures on teaching* (Cambridge: Cambridge University Press, 1881), pp. 434, 435. Fitch gave evidence to Cross Commission, the report of which, in 1888, paved the way for the establishment of day training schools for teachers.

[32] D. Newsome, *Godliness and good learning: four studies on a Victorian ideal* (London: John Murray, 1961), pp. 26-27. 'Muscular Christianity' stressed manliness and high spirits over piety, and games-playing on an organised basis became an important aspect of the school curriculum, as well as the curriculum of those training to teach.

[33] Words of Alderman Kinder, Chairman of the Board of Governors, 'Leeds Training College: official opening: Mr J. A. Pease M.P. on changing educational methods', *Yorkshire Post* (14 June 1913).

[34] For example, the Royal Air Service base at Mount Batten, Plymouth: James Douet, *British barracks 1600-1914* (London: Stationery Office, 1998), p. 196. It might be argued that the efficiency and clean lines inherent in the Neo-Georgian suited the air service, as the latter was seen as the modern wing of the armed forces.

[35] 'The Leeds Training College', *The British Architect* (5 July 1912), p. 16. Of course, some opposed to the erection of the College argued the residential system a 'wholesome and desirable moral and domestic atmosphere': Words of Walter Battle, author of the pamphlet *Kirkstall Grange Estate. Scandal, Etc.* (1908), which opposed the scheme; quoted in City of Leeds College of Education, *A short history of the City of Leeds Training College 1907-1957* (1957), p. 7.

[36] 'Leeds Training College: official opening: Mr J. A. Pease M.P. on changing educational methods', *Yorkshire Post* (14 June 1913).

[37] 'City of Leeds Training College: Visit of the Members of the Leeds City Council: Luncheon, Monday 1st July 1912', Leeds Metropolitan University Archives.

[38] Alderman Kinder at the opening ceremony: 'Leeds Training College: official opening: Mr J. A. Pease M.P. on changing educational methods', *Yorkshire Post* (14 June 1913).

[39] 'Leeds Training College: official opening: op. cit.

[40] A. Forty, *Words and buildings: a vocabulary of modern architecture* (New York: Thames and Hudson, 2000), p. 251.

[41] City of Leeds Training College, *Coming of age celebrations souvenir handbook: 1907-1928* (1928), p. 13.

[42] City of Leeds College of Education, *A short history of the City of Leeds Training College 1907-1957* (1957), p. 9.

[43] A. Forty, *Words and buildings: a vocabulary of modern architecture* (New York: Thames and Hudson, 2000), p. 203.

[44] The Great Hall was re-named the Ghandi Hall on 9 June 2007.

[45] Records relating to the origins and early history of the Carnegie Physical Training College can be found in the Scottish National Archives, files GD281/65/34-37; and in the minutes of the Carnegie United Kingdom Trust, 7 March 1930, 19 March 1930, 12 July 1930, 11 March 1932, 16 June 1932, 7 October 1932, 6 March 1936, 5 June 1936 and 2 October 1936.

[46] P. E. Matheson, 'Ideals in Education' (1910), reproduced in his *Education Today and Tomorrow* (London: Humphrey Milton and Oxford University press, 1917), p. 37.

CHAPTER 4

The Genesis of the City of Leeds Training College at Beckett Park

Janet Douglas

The concern of this chapter is to chart the developments and decision making that led to the establishment of a teacher training college in Leeds in October 1907 and the opening of the purpose built premises at Beckett Park, Headingley in 1912. Leeds was not the first local council to establish a training college but it was one of the earliest. More significantly, this college was the largest in the country and with its lavish accommodation, was to become the model which other local authorities followed. It is not fashionable these days for historians to explain events in terms of the activities of individuals. Instead the emphases of the current history-writing are on economic, social and cultural forces. Even political history has become marginalized. The analysis that follows, however, stresses the importance of both political processes and the role of certain personalities.

Fig. 1 Fred Kinder, Liberal Party Leader 1904-10, Chairman of the Education Committee 1904-07. (Source: National Federation of Assistant Teachers Conference Souvenir 1907, in Leeds Metropolitan University Archives)

Fig. 2 James Graham, Secretary for Higher Education 1906, Secretary for Education 1908-18 and Director of Education in Leeds until 1931. (Source: City of Leeds Training College Coming of Age Celebrations Souvenir Handbook 1907-1928, Leeds Metropolitan University Archives)

Fig. 3 Charles Wilson, Leader of the Conservative Party 1906-28. (Source: Scott, W. c. 1903. The West Riding of Yorkshire at the turn of the century, courtesy of Leeds Library & Information Service)

BACKGROUND

What historians like to call 'structural factors' may explain why a training college was opened in Leeds, but to explain why the college was built on such a scale, we need to turn to the motives and ambitions of particular people and how they realised these in specific political contexts. Three names stand out: Fred Kinder, a woollen manufacturer and barrister and leader of the Liberal Party in Leeds (**Figure 1**); James Graham, an educational administrator (**Figure 2**); and Charles Wilson, an accountant who became the leading local politician in Leeds after the Conservative Party took control of the Council in 1907 (**Figure 3**).

The building of teacher training colleges began in the 1840s and is obviously bound up with the growth of popular education in the 19th century. The first colleges were small with rarely more than a hundred places, and were controlled by one of two religious educational societies, one representing the Church of England and the other, the Non-Conformist denominations (most training colleges were Anglican institutions). The majority of teachers however did not attend college, they were recruited through a pupil-teacher system which involved a five-year apprenticeship beginning at the age of 13. For five years, pupil teachers continued their own education in an elementary school on a part-time basis receiving special tuition from the headmaster, and because they also taught in the school (*'learning by doing'*), they received a small salary. It was this small salary which enabled working class children to stay in education and enter the teaching profession. At the end of their apprenticeship, pupil teachers could take the competitive Queen's Scholarship examination and if successful be awarded a grant to study at a training college for three years.

A milestone in the history of education in England was the passing of the 1870 Education Act which introduced universal elementary education between the ages of 5 and 11 (later raised to 12). The delivery of education was no longer the monopoly of the religious societies, instead elected School Boards were established throughout the country to build and manage what was intended to be a vast expansion of educational provision. The increased demand for teachers that the 1870 Act entailed was not matched however by any commensurate expansion of training college provision. By 1902 there were still only 46 colleges offering 4,200 places – the vast majority still controlled by the Church of England. Thus elementary education system remained reliant on the pupil teacher and the 'uncertificated' teacher (ie those who had not attended a training college). In the case of the Leeds School Board in its early years, only 18 per cent of its teachers were college trained.

Although there was pressure from some School Boards to be allowed to open their own training colleges, the Board of Education (the equivalent of the Department of Education), were anxious to avoid antagonising the Anglican Church by allowing the establishment of a rival system of training colleges. Instead incremental changes were made to the pupil-teacher training system. In 1880, for example, it became possible for pupil-teachers from a number of schools to be taught together in evening or at Saturday morning classes, and from here it was a short step to School Boards opening their own pupil-teacher centres with specialised staff and their own curriculum. Challenges to these developments encouraged by a Conservative Government that deplored 'the ambition' of school boards,[1] led to *the Cockerton Judgement* of 1899 which declared that School Boards were exceeding their powers by providing pupil-teacher centres, and indeed any institutions of secondary education (at the time referred to as 'higher education'). Other pressures not least from the Anglican Church which feared that competition from Board schools was leading to the closure of their own schools, prepared the way for the radical reorganisation of education embodied in the 1902 Education Act. The Act abolished the School Boards and vested the provision of education in local councils including the opportunity for the new Local Education Authorities (LEAs) to establish secondary schools and teacher training colleges (**Figure 4**).

THE

PUBLIC GENERAL ACTS

PASSED IN THE SECOND YEAR

OF THE REIGN OF HIS MAJESTY

KING EDWARD THE SEVENTH;

BEING THE

THIRD SESSION OF THE TWENTY-SEVENTH PARLIAMENT

OF THE

UNITED KINGDOM OF GREAT BRITAIN AND IRELAND:

WITH AN INDEX, AND TABLES SHOWING THE EFFECT OF THE YEAR'S LEGISLATION ON THE PUBLIC GENERAL ACTS; ALSO THE TITLES OF THE LOCAL AND PRIVATE ACTS ARRANGED CONSECUTIVELY AND IN CLASSES.

Published by Authority.

Royal Coat of Arms removed in accordance with copyright regulations

LONDON:
PRINTED FOR HIS MAJESTY'S STATIONERY OFFICE,
BY THE KING'S PRINTER.

And to be purchased, either directly or through any Bookseller, from
EYRE AND SPOTTISWOODE, EAST HARDING STREET, FLEET STREET, E.C., and
32, ABINGDON STREET, WESTMINSTER, S.W., or
OLIVER AND BOYD, EDINBURGH; or
E. PONSONBY, 116, GRAFTON STREET, DUBLIN.

Price Three Shillings.

Fig. 4 Cover of Public General Acts, 1902 – includes 1902 Education Act. (Source: Courtesy of Leeds Library & Information Services)

The first mention of opening a training college in Leeds appears in minutes of the Higher Education Committee of the City Council for June 1906 but discussion was deferred to the next meeting when it was deferred for a second time.[2] That a training college was on the agenda *at all*, was due to two crucial developments. At the end of 1904, unexpectedly political control of the council had passed to the Liberal Party whose leader, Fred Kinder was passionate about education and chaired both the Education Committee and its Higher Education Sub-Committee (first set up in April 1906). It was also the Liberal Party that was responsible for 'poaching' James Graham from the neighbouring West Riding local authority where Graham was employed as an inspector for schools. In May 1906 he was invited to take charge of the city's post-elementary educational provision as Secretary for Higher Education. As well as local support, Graham came to Leeds on the recommendation of Robert Morant, architect of the 1902 Education Act and now Permanent Secretary at the Board of Education (**Figure 5**). Working in tandem, Kinder, the politician, and Graham, the administrator, pushed through a rapid expansion of secondary education in the city and became the major force behind the decision to open a training college.

The reasons why the city needed a college were rehearsed at various meetings and in various reports written by Graham. The aim of the LEA was eventually to employ only college-trained teachers but in 1906 these made up only a quarter of the staff in its schools. The problem was that there simply were not enough training college places in the country. As the 1906-7 Annual Report of the Education Committee noted that *'the provision of training college accommodation has been under the consideration of the committee at various times, and this year the extreme urgency of the matter was illustrated by the fact that no less than 60 Leeds students who desired to enter a training college but could not do so owing to the inadequacy of the accommodation available. Having trained teachers to a certain point* (ie through the pupil-teacher system), *there was an obligation on the Council to provide if possible, the means for the completion of their training'.*[3]

At the third meeting of the Higher Education Sub-committee, Kinder pointed out that the Board of Education had recently increased its grant for the capital costs of building training colleges from 25 per cent to 75 per cent, and no doubt bearing this financial inducement in mind, in September, Kinder and Graham were authorised to begin discussions with the Board of Education. But Kinder, the elected politician needed to be ever vigilant about the prospect of rate increases. At the November meeting of the Higher Education Sub-committee, this problem was tackled head-on: how does the establishment of a training college benefit Leeds ratepayers? In a report prepared by Graham, it was pointed out that due to the increasing demand for training college places, it was difficult for Leeds pupil teachers to find training college places, yet the city needed 220 new teachers every year due to the expansion of provision and the retirement of existing teachers. Ideally according to Kinder and Graham, the city needed a training college with 400 places but if for the present, only half that number were to be trained, the annual costs would be between £2,000 and £2,500 a year including buildings and maintenance and there was the possibility of a grant from the Board of Education. Perhaps appealing to the Yorkshireman's antipathy to waste, Graham pointed out that a third of all male pupil teachers and half of all women who were already costing Leeds ratepayers £16,000 a year, would not be able to enter a training college at the end of their apprenticeship.[4]

By April 1907 speaking at the annual meeting of National Federation of Assistant Teachers held in Leeds, Graham was sufficiently confident to announce that *'the provision of a Training College in Leeds cannot be long delayed as further provision in this direction is a matter*

of urgent necessity',[5] but it was not until 18 July that the Higher Education Sub-committee actually passed a resolution that:

'a building in Woodhouse Lane which until recently accommodated the Leeds Girls High School be rented for the purpose of a temporary Training College and the period for which the premises be taken be two years in the first instance, this period to be renewable if found necessary'.[6]

The building mentioned was St James's Lodge built in the 18th century and although it was demolished in the 1970s, its site now forms a part of the Civic Campus of Leeds Metropolitan University (**Figure 6**).

The temporary Training College was to open in September or early October 1907, leaving only two months to prepare the building, organise a syllabus, employ staff, make arrangements for residential accommodation and obtain the approval of the Board of Education. Through the good offices of Robert Morant, approval was quickly obtained but only on the understanding that the arrangements were to be temporary. Why the haste? Probably both Kinder and Graham were aware that at the next municipal elections in November, the Liberal Party was likely to lose control of the City Council and feared that the new council might not be sympathetic to their plans. Due to the temporary nature of the college, staff were not given permanent appointments, most were recruited from existing secondary schools including the new Principal, Walter Parsons who had taught in Leeds since 1882 and served as headmaster of two elementary schools before becoming head of a Leeds Pupil-Teacher Centre in 1895 (**Figure 7**). Despite the short notice, the Authority was inundated with requests for places in the new college, receiving over a thousand applications from all over the country, for 141 places.

At the end of 1907 the Liberal Party did lose its majority on the Council. For the next twenty years, Leeds local politics would be dominated by the Conservative Party and its leader, Charles Wilson, who is the third figure in our story. Wilson believed in *'stringent economy in every direction'.*[7] Chairing the Council's Finance Committee, he kept a tight control over the municipal purse strings, and because education was the largest single item of expenditure in the Council's budget (*'a money-burner'* in Wilson's words), he was a member of the Education

Committee and chaired its Finance Sub-committee. At any moment he could have pulled the plug on the future development of the training college. That he did not do so is due to another aspect of Wilson's political *credo*: his personal identification with Leeds and ambition see *his* city surpass every other city in Yorkshire.[8] We might speculate that he saw in the training college project the opportunity to insert Leeds-trained teachers into elementary schools all over the county, not to speak of other parts of England (**Figure 8**).

In the years before the First World War, the political environment was changing: the growth of the Labour Party meant the old two-party system of Liberals versus Conservatives was coming under threat. Although there were only a handful of Labour councillors on the City Council

Fig. 10
Front cover of Walter
Battle's pamphlet.
(Source: Leeds
Metropolitan University
Archives)

KIRKSTALL GRANGE ESTATE

SCANDAL,

ETC.

1908.

Copies of this Pamphlet may be obtained gratis on application
to Mr. ASPINALL, 15, Queen Victoria Street, Leeds.

Fig. 11
Edmund Beckett,
Lord Grimthorpe.
(Source: Ernest William
Beckett M.P., *by Spy (Sir*
Leslie Ward), Vanity
Fair, *Issue 1836, 9*
January 1904. Courtesy
of Mr Bill Bannett and
Julie's Antique Prints.

and often presided over meetings in Clarke's absence (**Figure 9**). Against all previous practice, Kinder remained chairman of the Higher Education Sub-committee and later became the chairman of the new Training College Sub-committee.

It is hardly surprising then that there was considerable continuity in policy and that Wilson (and his placeman, Clarke) and Kinder aided and abetted by Graham, were prepared to use the local rates to provide Leeds with a large and handsome training college. These four men formed an inner circle, a clique no doubt resented by others. Outside of office hours, they socialised together, dining in each other's homes and at good restaurants; with the exception of Graham, they were all masons. When in London on official business they stayed in the Russell Hotel and at weekends joined shooting parties on Wilson's North Duffield estate. Graham anxious to build alliances with other municipal Secretaries of Education against imperious central power, often sent them braces of pheasants!

In the last year of the Liberal administration, there had been plans to purchase the whole of the 264-acre Kirkstall Grange estate, the home of the Becketts that was on the market for £240,000. The intention was to open a public park, provide a site for a permanent training college and offset the cost of the expenditure by selling the remaining land for housing development, a self-funding model that had already been employed for financing the purchase of Roundhay Park in the 1870s. Although the scheme had been defeated because it was believed that the estate was over-valued, plans had been sufficiently advanced for a successful application to the Board of Education for a grant towards the purchase of 25 acres for the site of the new college.

Writing to the Education Committee in February 1908, the Board of Education reminded the committee that approval of the temporary training college had only been granted on the condition that a permanent college would be built and inquired what progress was being made in regard to this matter.[10] Prompted by the letter, the Higher Education Sub-committee set up of special sub-committee of Kinder, Clarke, C. F. Tetley and G. Portway, to investigate a new site for the training college. The sub-committee all of whom with the exception of Kinder, lived in Headingley (Kinder lived in neighbouring Kirkstall), inspected ten possible sites and perhaps not surprisingly given previous

in 1905, in a letter to the *Yorkshire Post*, Wilson asserted that the aim of the Labour Party was, *'to smash both the old parties, first the Liberals and then the Tories and the end might be that men would join together upon the same platform for mutual protection'.* [9] Wilson's answer to this threat was to nurture a concordat between the two parties ('collusion' in the eyes of the Labour Party). For example, in 1907 they reached an agreement over budgetary estimates so that the municipal finances would no longer provide ammunition at elections. In the spirit of bi-partisanship, Wilson was prepared to countenance Liberal over-representation on the aldermanic bench and in terms of committee membership. This careful fostering of Liberal support meant that Fred Kinder continued to play an important role in the making of education policy. Although Kinder lost his chairmanship of the Education Committee to the Conservative, W. H. Clarke, he became its vice-chair

plans, selected part of the Kirkstall Grange estate. Graham on behalf of the Education Committee wrote back to London that a college for over 400 students was being proposed and that a site of 50 to 60 acres had been seen and approved by some of the Board's own officials.[11] Reminding them that the Board had already given approval for the purchase of 25 acres, he now applied for an increased grant which the Board approved at the beginning of April. Surely here we can see the hand of the inner circle, the City Council had not yet approved the purchase, yet a site had been selected, had been shown to officers of the Board of Education, grants had been applied for and approved?

It was not until May 1908 that the scheme came before a full meeting of the Council. In recommending the plan, Graham wrote:

The maintenance of the training college would bring into Leeds an annual expenditure of from £25,000 to £30,000, almost all of which would go into the pockets of Leeds tradesmen; in addition there would be the expenditure of the students in residence on personal needs such as clothing, boots and other things. Their estimate of the local patriotism of Leeds ratepayers has caused the Education committee . .

. to take prompt action with a view to fixing Leeds once and for all as the most important centre in Yorkshire for the training of teachers.

What Graham failed to mention in his memorandum,[12] was that the cost of the Beckett's Park site at £42,000, was the most expensive of the sites inspected by the sub-committee. Nevertheless, the Council approved the purchase. So much for Wilson, the stickler for economy! But matters were not yet completely settled: in Leeds, there was vigorous opposition to the scheme and because the local authority needed to borrow money to finance its share of the purchase price, approval was needed from the Local Government Board in London. In a 13-page pamphlet addressed to the ratepayers of Leeds entitled *'Kirkstall Grange Estate. Scandal, etc.'*, Walter Battle argued that with an increasing city debt of £12 million and rising rates, the purchase of Beckett Park was *'a preposterous project'* (**Figure 10**). The site was too expensive compared with other sites, and it was inconvenient due to its distance from the tramway. He went on to argue:

Fig. 12 Lord Leighton (1890) by Mayall. (Source: Hulton Archive/Getty Images Ref 3322338)

Fig. 13 Thomas Babbington Macaulay by John Partridge c'1849-53. (Source NPG 1564)

Fig. 14 Memorial to Caedmon, St. Mary's Churchyard, Whitby. (Source Richard Thomson & licensed for reuse under this Creative Commons Licence:
http://creativecommons.org/licences/by-sa/2.0/)

Fig. 15 *The Bronte Sisters By Patrick Branwell Bronte c. 1834. (Source: NPG1725)*

Fig. 17 *Lord Frederick Charles Cavendish by John D. Miller, 1883. (Source: NPG D7677)*

Fig. 16 *Sir Thomas Fairfax. (Source: Leeds Library and Information Services)*

Let it be asked what is the need of the additional education that is to be provided? Is it to enable those who receive it to fight the battle of life? I say 'No'. Pupil teachers are at a discount. Multitudes of young people who have qualified themselves are now unable to get employment as teachers . . . Does Mr Kinder propose to offer a superior training to that offered by Principal Bodington and his colleagues at Leeds University (where a small teacher training course had existed since 1891)*? I venture to say that any training received at this admirable institution is immeasurably superior to that which would be afforded by any branch of the Corporation.*[13]

Battle was a publican, representing the views of the small tradesmen who felt the burden of the rates far more keenly than wealthy manufacturers and professional men. Others reiterated Battle's criticisms, demanding an enquiry by the Board of Education that was duly held in the Town Hall in October 1908. Given the close relations between Kinder and Graham and the Board it's hardly surprising that the Corporation won their case, but there was still the matter of Local Government Board approval. On 24 October, Lord Grimthorpe, the owner of Kirkstall Grange was sufficiently anxious to write to his friend, Winston Churchill, recently appointed a cabinet minister and President of the Board of Trade (**Figure 11**). What is clear from his letter is that he and others in Leeds feared that the opponents of the purchase might make successful representations to the Local Government Board. What this letter divulged was that if the purchase was successful, Grimthorpe planned to give a further 40 acres to the city to form a public park. *'I leave it to you my dear Winston to do what you think best'*.

It is clear from a letter written a fortnight later is that Churchill did intervene:

Fig. 18 Joseph Priestley by Ellen Sharples, c.1796. (Source: NPG 175)

*Fig. 19
Priestley Hall name
plate. (Source: Keith
Rowntree)*

Inspector of Training Colleges had been consulted at an early stage and had declared that the College *'would without doubt be the finest Training College yet projected'*,[16] it was not over-optimistic for Graham to report to the Education Committee in January 1910 that he expected Board of Education approval.

However, Graham was wrong. A fierce champion of local autonomy and resentful even in public, of central interference, Graham had been involved in a number of skirmishes with the Board and even Morant's patience was wearing thin. The Board on viewing the detailed plans felt that they were more ambitious than was necessary (*'they took our breath away'*) and therefore announced that it was not possible for the Board to award the full 75 per cent grant.[17] Kinder and Graham rushed to London for a meeting with Walter Runciman, the President of the Board of Education and Morant. Constrained by Treasury controls, the two explained that the Board could only make a grant on the basis of £280 per student whereas the Council's plans were calculated on a

A thousand thanks. I am glad it is all right and the proposed purchase has received the sanction of the Local Govt. Board . . . A friend in need is a friend in deed and I am infinitely grateful to you.[14]

With all the necessary approvals now obtained, a Training College Sub-committee was established in November 1908 with Kinder as its chairman. Determined to build an impressive college, it sought advice from the Board of Education but were informed that the Board did not know of any suitable model.[15] Much of the early planning work was carried out by James Graham himself and he even financed some professional consultations out of his own pocket. Provisional plans showed an educational block for teaching purposes and a library, and eight residential hostels, one of which would be the original Beckett house, Kirkstall Grange. These plans formed the planning brief for an architectural competition announced in September 1909. As the Chief

*Fig. 20
The opening of the
College. (Source:
Photograph from the
collection in Leeds
Metropolitan University
Archives)*

VII. BATTALION PRINCE OF WALES' OWN
WEST YORKSHIRE REGIMENT
(LEEDS RIFLES)

Programme

2 to 3 p.m.

1	Grand March	... ... "Tannhauser"	Wagner
2	Selection ...	... "Our Miss Gibbs" ...	Caryll, Monckton
3	Suite	... "Spanish Dances"	Moszkowsky
4	Fantasia	"San Toy"	Sidney Jones
5	Idyll ...	..."The Whispering of the Flowers"...	... Von Blon
6	Selection	... "The Gondoliers"	... Sullivan

4.30 to 7 p.m.

7	Overture	"Mirella"	Gounod
8	Selection	"The Dollar Princess"	Fall
9	Suite	"From Foreign Parts" ...	Moszkowsky
10	Selection ..	"Carmen"	Bizet
11	Valse	... "The Quaker Girl" ...	... Monckton
	Veil Dance	... "Mystic Beauty"	Fincke
12	Interlude Minuet	... ...	Boccherini
13	Reminiscences of Tosti	... ... Arranged by Pougher
14	Gabotte	"Fifinette"	Fletcher
15	Excerpts from ...	"Cavalleria Rusticana"	.. Mascagni
16	Selection	"The Count of Luxembourg"	Lehar

Regimental March   The Prince of Wales

God save the King

Fig. 21 The West Yorkshire Regiment band's programme of music for the official opening of the College. (Source: Photograph from the collection in Leeds Metropolitan University Archives)

costing of £300 per student. Unable to pressurise the Board further, the Training College Sub-committee had two options: either to trim the scheme, or else fight it on an incremental basis to save various details They did both: the sanatorium behind the main building and the tennis courts in front were sacrificed, but with much patient negotiating over many meetings, Graham and Kinder managed to retain most of other features of the original plans.

Building was due to begin in July 1910 but negotiations and according to Graham, the Board's cumbersome procedures were delaying matters. In July, he wrote:

These delays are most annoying. We have been working day and night to meet your original requirement that the College should be built and open in September 1911. If we get on with the job at once, this can be done . . . I have arranged to forgo my holiday and all my men engaged on this particular job are doing without holidays this year in order that the work may be sent forward at the greatest possible speed . . .[18]

Another early disagreement with the Board concerned the College principalship. For what would be the largest and grandest college in the country that the Board wished to be a model for the rest of the country, it felt that only a highly qualified Oxbridge man (sic!) should fill the post of principal. The Local Authority wished to appoint Walter Parsons, the principal of the temporary college but he had no degree! After much arm-twisting, the Board accepted Parson's appointment but insisted that it must remain temporary, and that given that two-thirds of the students would be women, there must also be a Lady Vice-Principal. Conflicts such as these were fuelled by rival values and interests and would continue long after the opening of the college: the Board with its elitist view of education,[19] wanted to consolidate its control over education, dilute the power of what they regarded as ill-qualified local councillors and in particular, they sought to prevent the over-control of education by local officers. The Local Authority's interests were precisely the opposite, and as for Graham himself, his own immense power over education in Leeds rested on local control and he was fierce in the protection of that power.[20] During a later conflict with the Board, William Clarke shrewdly observed that '*an Education Secretary's lot is not a happy one but James Graham was a man who could be happy with unhappiness*'.[21]

With building finally underway, Graham was indefatigable in his supervision of the project, no detail however small escaped his attention. For example he selected all the furniture and furnishings himself – the former was of special interest as he himself was a noted collector of Chippendale and Hepplewhite furniture. Even the names of the hostels were selected by the Secretary for Education: Leighton (**Figure 12**), Macaulay (**Figure 13**), Caedmon (**Figure 14**), Brontë (**Figure 15**), Fairfax (**Figure 16**) and Cavendish (**Figure 17**) – he had wanted to call one of the colleges after William Forster, the architect of the 1870 Education Act but as a Liberal MP for Leeds' great rival, Bradford, the sub-committee vetoed this choice and it was replaced by Priestley (**Figure 18**) as a representative of science and someone born just outside of Leeds[22] (**Figure 19**). The college was not ready for opening in September 1911 as had been planned, and for a year classes were taught in a newly built elementary school on Kirkstall Road but a year later the first cohort of 480 students, 300 women and 160 men began their studies at the City of Leeds Training College at what now was renamed Beckett's Park.

The College was formally opened on 13 July 1912 by J. A. Pease, the President of the Board of Education (**Figure 20**). After a splendid lunch in the Town Hall, two special trams conveyed the party to the gates of the College. Bands played in the quadrangle (**Figure 21**) hymns were sung and the Bishop of Ripon read a prayer (**Figure 22**). In his address, Pease referred to the College as '*a great possession for the city of Leeds*' and how '*it will be in the future a national asset*'. The summer of 1913 was a high point of suffragette militancy and though 'precautions' had been taken, Pease's speech was disrupted and a lady was escorted away, later in the afternoon another suffragette was thrown into the swimming pool and had to be rescued by a group of trained life savers! Next day, the college grounds were visited by thousands of Leeds citizens.[23] Reflecting on the progress that had been made, the Education Committee's Annual Report for 1912-13 boasted that '*everything now augurs well for the college rapidly becoming one of the leading training colleges in the country*'.[24]

OFFICIAL OPENING in
the COLLEGE HALL

Ald. F. KINDER, J.P., CHAIRMAN OF THE GOVERNORS OF THE COLLEGE
will take the chair at 3 o'clock

Programme

1 Hymn ...   ...   " Now thank we all our God "

2 Prayer   .   THE LORD BISHOP OF RIPON

3 Chorus ...   ...   " O Gladsome Light "
                        THE COLLEGE STUDENTS

4 Introduction of the Rt. Hon. JOSEPH A. PEASE, M.P., *President of the Board of Education*
                        THE CHAIRMAN OF THE GOVERNORS

5 Address to the Students and Declaration of Opening of College
   Rt. Hon. J. A. PEASE, M.P.

6 Vote of Thanks to the *President of the Board of Education*
                To be Proposed by Alderman W. H. CLARKE
                        Chairman of the Leeds Education Committee
                To be Seconded by Councillor F. BOWMAN
                        Governor of the Training College
                To be Supported by Sir JOHN C. HORSFALL, Bart.
                        Chairman of the West Riding County Council

7 · RESPONSE of the *President of the Board of Education*

8 Vote of Thanks to the CHAIRMAN
                To be Proposed by Councillor G. RATCLIFFE, J.P.
                To be Seconded by Alderman C. H. WILSON, J.P.
                To be Supported by Alderman J. BADLAY

9 RESPONSE of the CHAIRMAN
                        ———
                God save the King

Fig. 22 The programme for the official opening of the College. (Source: Leeds Metropolitan University Archives)

ENDNOTES

[1] B. Simon (1965), *Education and the Labour Movement 1870-1920*, Lawrence and Wishart, p. 208.

[2] ₁ West Yorkshire Archives Service (WYAS): LC/ED/29/1 Minutes of the Higher Education Sub-committee 19 June 1906.

[3] Local Studies Department of Leeds Central Library: L352.24/L517 Annual Report of the Education Committee of Leeds Corporation 1906-07.

[4] WYAS: LC/ED/29/1 Minutes of the Higher Education Sub-committee 20 September and 22 November 1906.

[5] National Federation of Assistant Teachers (1907), *Conference Souvenir* p. 110.

[6] WYAS: LC/ED/29/1 Minutes of the Higher Education Sub-committee 18 July 1907.

[7] M. Meadowcroft (1978), *Transition in Leeds City Government 1903-1926*, unpublished M.Phil thesis, University of Bradford, p. 158.

[8] W. R. Meyer (1993), James Graham versus the Board of Education, *History of Education Bulletin 51*, p. 22.

[9] W. R. Meyer (1998), Charles Henry Wilson: the man who was Leeds, *Thoresby Society Miscellany* Vol. 8 (2nd series).

[10] H. S. Pickering, A Short History of the City of Leeds Training College 1907-1957 (typescript) p. 3 (Leeds Metropolitan University Archives).

[11] Ibid p. 3.

[12] L. Connell (no date), *A Century of Teacher Training in Leeds 1875-1975*, Leeds Metropolitan University, p. 91.

[13] Beckett's Park Archive: Walter Battle, Kirkstall Grange Estate. Scandal etc.

[14] Churchill Archive: CHAR 2/35/59-60. Letters from Ernest Beckett to Winston Churchill.

[15] Connell op.cit., p. 92.

[16] Ibid p. 92.

[17] Meyer, James Graham versus the Board of Education, op.cit., p. 26.

[18] Pickering op.cit., p. 8.

[19] Simon op.cit., p. 237.

[20] L. Connell (1973), The Administration of Secondary Schools: Leeds versus the Board of Education 1905-11, *The Journal of Educational Administration and History* Vol. 5 Part 2.

[21] Meyer, James Graham versus the Board of Education op.cit., p. 3.

[22] Of the names selected by Graham probably only Brontë is well known today. Cavendish refers to Lord Frederick Cavendish a West Riding MP and promoter of the Yorkshire College which later became the University of Leeds. Cavendish was murdered at Phoenix Park, Dublin in 1882; Fairfax commemorates Sir Thomas Fairfax, commander in chief of the Parliamentary Army during the Civil War; Caedmon was a 7th-century poet based at Whitby; Leighton refers to Lord Leighton, painter and President of the Royal Academy who was born in Scarborough; Thomas Babbington Macaulay was a famous historian and was MP for Leeds between 1832 and 1833.

[23] Accounts of the opening of the College in *Yorkshire Post* 13, 14, 16, 19 June; *Leeds Mercury* 14 June; *Yorkshire Observer* 14 June; *Leeds Weekly Citizen* 13 and 20 June; *The Times* 13 June; the *Morning Post* 13 June.

[24] Connell, *A Century of Teacher Training in Leeds* op.cit., p. 94.

CHAPTER 5

School Partnerships

Jill Adam and Anne Campbell

Teacher education and training has always facilitated partnership working with schools, not least the specific 'training' by those working in schools, the provision of teaching 'practice' opportunities for student teachers in schools and further professional guidance by staff from across different school disciplines and contexts. Whilst, perhaps unsurprisingly, many of the expectations and operational dimensions of school partnerships have altered and shifted considerably over the past 100 years, specifically, the broader concept of school experience rather than teaching practice, this chapter also outlines some of the continuities and consistencies in such work, closing with a consideration of new opportunities that partnership work with schools may now invite.

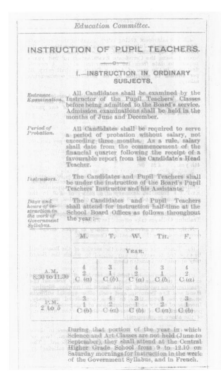
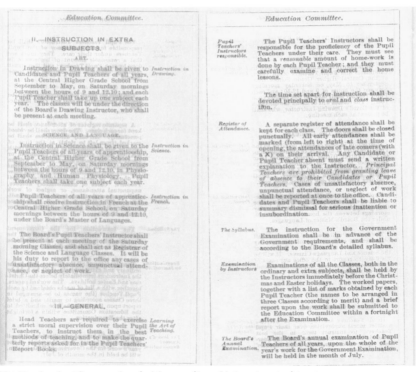

Fig. 2 Extract from Leeds School Board (1899) Yearbook. (Source: Leeds Metropolitan University Archives)

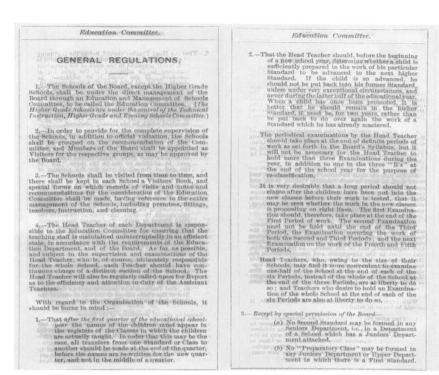

Fig. 3 Extract from Leeds School Board (1899) Yearbook. *(Source: Leeds Metropolitan University Archives)*

SCHOOL PARTNERSHIPS 'THEN'

The pupil teacher system of teacher training was the dominant model for supplying the profession with a 'trained' workforce prior to the 1902 Education Act (**Figure 1**). Although the term 'partnership' with schools was not used at that time, from the early years of its establishment in 1846, there was an arrangement between school boards and local schools. According to the National Archives, by the turn of the 20th century elementary school children were selected as pupil-teachers and received three years' concurrent training and education. At 18, they were prepared for the Queen's/King's Scholarship examination, later termed the Preliminary Examination for the Certificate. Originally both training and education were provided at their elementary schools under the supervision of the headmaster, but following the 1870 Elementary Education Act, they received instruction at separate establishments called Pupil-Teacher Centres run by local school boards, and embarked on teaching practice in their elementary schools.[1]

The work of educational historian Brian Simon[2] and former City of Leeds Training College (CLTC) Principal Leo Connell[3] alerted us to ways the pupil-teachers were taught in the schools during school hours under the supervision of the head teacher concerned. In addition, head teachers provided a minimum of seven and a half hours 'instruction' for the pupil-teachers outside of school hours. This 'instruction' was given to all of pupil-teachers in the school regardless of their stage or year of study, and the head teacher concerned received additional payment. An outline of the instruction provided to pupil-teachers is clearly demonstrated in the Leeds School Board[4] *Yearbook* (**Figure 2**).

Structured around the demands of a school day, the time available for this instruction, or one might

thus make their pupils imitative rather than reflective, monkey teachers rather than intelligent instructors of their class.

Such dissatisfactions with the quality and focus of instruction continued to be raised; whilst at the same time, the number of pupil-teachers in schools grew significantly. Eventually the demands for improvements in the training led to the establishment of 'centres' for instruction. Connell[7] further elaborated that here, groups of pupil-teachers would attend the same school or 'centre' for more tailored instruction – provided by a number of teachers, who were not necessarily from the pupil-teacher's own school. These 'teacher trainers' were individuals who had been identified as capable practitioners during their own training.

Fig. 4
Photo of former Pupil-Teacher Centre. (Source: Keith Rowntree)

argue 'training', appears very limited from a C21st standpoint, as it usually took the form of all pupil-teachers meeting with the head teacher before the start of the formal school day. That said, the work undertaken by the head teachers was subject to strict guidance and expectations of practice, which did provide some measure of comparable practice across the sector. These requirements and guidance were issued by the associated School Board, as we can see in an example from the Leeds School Board[5] (**Figure 3**).

Connell[6] suggested that the number of head teachers capable of giving adequate instruction to pupil teachers was extremely limited and that the quality of the instruction, or 'training' received was often brought in to question:

In many schools they leave them all to themselves . . . or they stand by and watch the often awkward attempts of the young teacher, and embarrass rather than assist him (sic) by untimely criticism. In other cases they give a lesson before the apprentices without either explaining the principles on which it is given or the rules which it proceeds, and

Education Committee.

TEACHERS CRITICISM LESSONS

1.—Shall be given in all Schools weekly, as follows :—
Senior and Junior Departments, on alternate Wednesdays and Thursdays .. .. .. 3.45 to 4.30.
Infants' Departments, on alternate Wednesdays and Thursdays .. .. 3.30 to 4.15.
(The above times may only be departed from if permission in writing is previously obtained from the office.)

2.—The whole of the classes, except the one detained, shall be dismissed in time for the Criticism Lesson to begin punctually. The lessons should occupy not more than twenty-five minutes in delivery. At the close the scholars shall be dismissed, and the various teachers present called upon by the head teacher for their criticisms, after which the head teacher should offer such hints as the lesson suggests.

3.—All Teachers shall attend these lessons and enter their criticisms in books provided for the purpose. These books must be preserved and shewn to H.M. Inspector on the occasion of his visits.

4.—All Pupil Teachers and Ex-Pupil Teachers shall take turns in giving the Criticism Lessons, and Certificated Teachers are strongly recommended to do so.

5.—A *Time Table*, showing subjects, names of teachers, and dates of delivery of lessons shall be prominently exhibited in each school.

6.—No teacher shall be required under the above rules to give a Criticism Lesson oftener than once a month. If there be not sufficient teachers in any Department to allow of Criticism Lessons weekly, either Model Lessons or Hints on Practical School Management suggested by the School routine should be given by the Head Teachers, in order that there may be no interruption in the weekly course of these lessons.

Fig. 5 Extract from Leeds School Board (1899) Yearbook. (Source: Leeds Metropolitan University Archives)

Whilst undoubtedly more efficient in terms of resources, centre-based training was not met with universal support. The centre system meant that the head teachers, previously responsible for instruction, no longer received an income for such work; and there was also concern that the personal, professional relationship established between 'master and student' was lost. In reflecting back on the system, former CLTC Principal Dr R. W. Rich[8] reported that the system instituted at Leeds whereby pupil-teachers were farmed out in groups to selected masters, but allowed no time off from school, was condemned by the inspectors. Nevertheless, the centre system of instruction did become established in Leeds, and the number of pupil-teachers attending grew considerably; growth which eventually led to classes being moved in 1901 to a purpose built Pupil-Teacher Centre in the city (**Figure 4**).

An important dimension to the school-based elements of training and the support offered to the pupil-teachers by teachers, were the weekly 'criticism lessons'. These lessons were either observed or taught by the pupil-teacher, in line with the strict rules and guidance issued by the Leeds School Board (**Figure 5**). The pupil-teachers were expected to maintain thorough records of their weekly teaching experiences, together with details of the school, their timetable and planning. These records were to be kept and presented in two exercise books; one for work associated with actual teaching, including the criticisms received; the other for recording all work done other than actual teaching.[9] The only extant examples we found was in the work of student teacher Samuel Childs, attending the temporary CLTC in 1908-1909 and doing school practice at Belle Vue Council School (**Figures 6a & 6b**), which suggests that criticism lessons and written records were an on-going part of the education and training of teachers.[10]

We also know there was an inspection system, with school work inspected by Her Majesty's Inspectorate (HMI), the first of which were appointed in 1891.[11] We found records of such activity in a Leeds School Board Log Book,[12] which details a report on the school's work and how it was enforced by the Inspectorate, along with additional information on the grants received, the pupil-teachers' examination results, and staffing (**Figures 7a, 7b & 7c**). Simon[13] further broadens our insights by highlighting the rigid and severe discipline that occurred as a necessary corollary, evidence for which was found in a Corporal Punishment

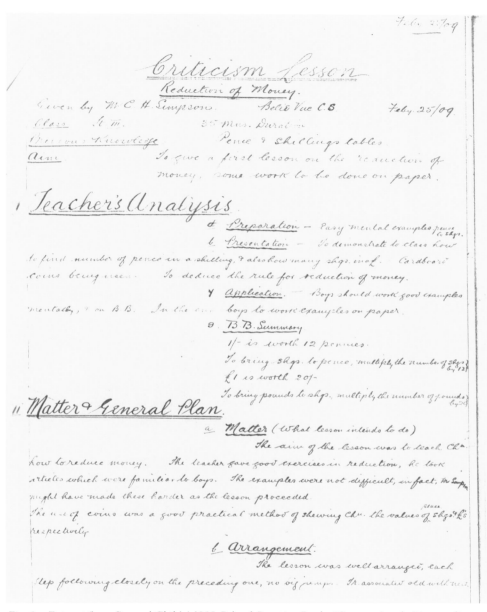

Fig. 6a Extract from Samuel Childs' 1909 School Practice Book. (Source: Leeds Metropolitan University Archives)

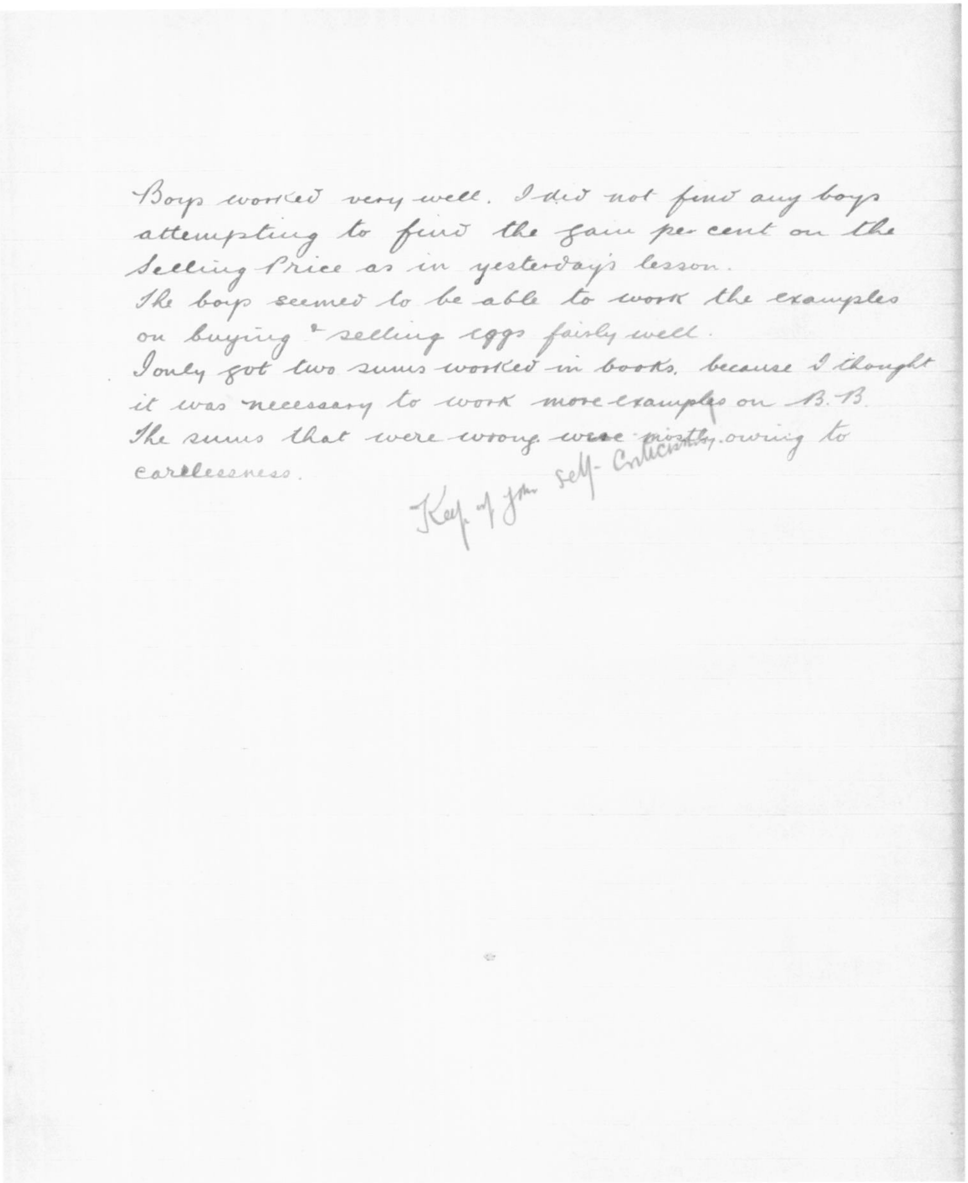

Boys worked very well. I did not find any boys attempting to find the gain per cent on the selling Price as in yesterday's lesson.
The boys seemed to be able to work the examples on buying & selling eggs fairly well.
I only got two sums worked in books, because I thought it was necessary to work more examples on B.B.
The sums that were wrong were mostly owing to carelessness.

Keep up your self-Criticism.

Fig. 6b Extract from Samuel Childs' 1909 School Practice Book. (Source: Leeds Metropolitan University Archives)

Book[14] (**Figure 8**). We can only imagine that every misdemeanour, including those behaviours now recognized as being symptomatic of 'learning difficulties and disabilities'[15], was punished.

In addition to work with pupil-teachers, other 'partnership' arrangements between the Leeds School Board, local schools, the Pupil-Teacher Centre, and then the CLTC specifically related to the use of facilities. For example, the science laboratories at the Thoresby High School[16] (**Figure 9**) and the facilities at the School of Art (**Figure 10**) were both used, particularly during the time of temporary accommodation for CLTC, prior to it settling on the Beckett Park site.

Successive Annual Reports on the Leeds Education Committee[17] furnished to the Council of the City of Leeds in the decade following the Education Act 1902, provide helpful insights into the demise of the pupil-teacher system and the introduction of the new Training College system. However, it is important to set this in context. Educational historian Eric Eaglesham,[18] in writing about the infamous Cockerton judgement in the lead-up to the 1902 Education Act, shed some light on the new teacher training system, which came about because of disputes over higher elementary education. At issue was the education of the School Boards' pupil teachers, ex-pupil teachers and assistant teachers, given the Education Department insisted on their further education, past elementary standards, which then consisted primarily of the three Rs. Under Morant, their further education became really secondary education, and hybrid elementary-secondary education finished.[19] The 1902 Education Act was not without controversy, as the political cartoons of the day showed (**Figure 11**).

In the 1906-1907 Annual Report (**Figure 12**) Chairman Fred Kinder noted that important modifications to the existing scheme had been made by the Committee, made possible by the release of new Pupil-Teacher Regulations issued by the Board of Education in the spring. The most important was to allow the 'Bursar Scheme' to run concurrently with the Pupil-Teacher Scheme, which allowed pupils receiving their educational training under the new provisions to be styled 'bursars'. They were to receive free secondary school education for one year and a maintenance allowance. This was the Committee's preferred option, no doubt tied to the fact that a large proportion of funds for the training of intending teachers were drawn from the Imperial

Exchequer rather than local rates.[20] The requirement was for pupils to pass the Preliminary Examination for the Teachers' Certificate or equivalent qualifying them for entrance to a Training College. The 'notes' section of the Board of Education[21] *Regulations and Syllabus* is instructive in this regard[22] (**Figure 13**).

The intention, according to Kinder, was to let the Pupil-Teacher Scheme lapse, since most of the pupils who proposed to enter the teaching profession attended secondary schools, in marked contrast to the situation where pupils did not attend a secondary school or a Pupil-Teacher Centre prior to becoming pupil teachers. Kinder further justified the new 'Bursar Scheme' on the grounds of the maintenance allowance and one can see that there were deliberate moves to scale down payments to pupil-teachers, no doubt as an incentive to become bursars. Again, Eaglesham[23] sheds some light on this situation:

The pupil-teacher was undoubtedly 'elementary' in the social sense: he (sic) sprang from the working classes, his education was part of his contract within an elementary school, and under an elementary school board.

Chairman Fred Kinder also noted the establishment of the temporary College and the decision of the Education Committee not to attach members of teaching staff full time, but rather to utilise the secondary school staffs of the city on a part-time basis.[24] Here we see the use of well regarded teachers, drawn from secondary rather than elementary schools, taking a prominent role in elementary teacher training in what could be called a campus-based professional model spliced later with professional practice in schools.

SCHOOL PARTNERSHIPS 'NOW'

Our documentary research suggests that partnership arrangements with schools have existed within and across different systems of teacher education and training (**Figure 14**). The 'training' of apprentice teachers within schools, facilitated by established practitioners is a common thread, and so too is the use of facilities. A defining moment in the more recent history of partnership was the legislation of 1992,[25] whereby the government made it a requirement that all initial teacher education (ITE)

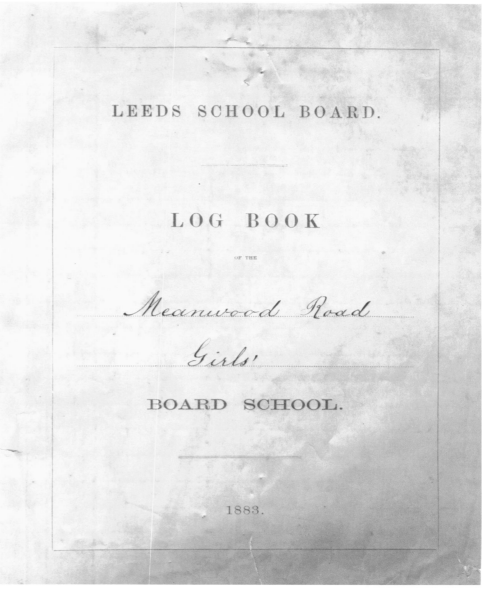

Fig. 7a Extract from Leeds School Board Logbook for Meanwood Road School for Girls. (Source: Little London Community Primary School)

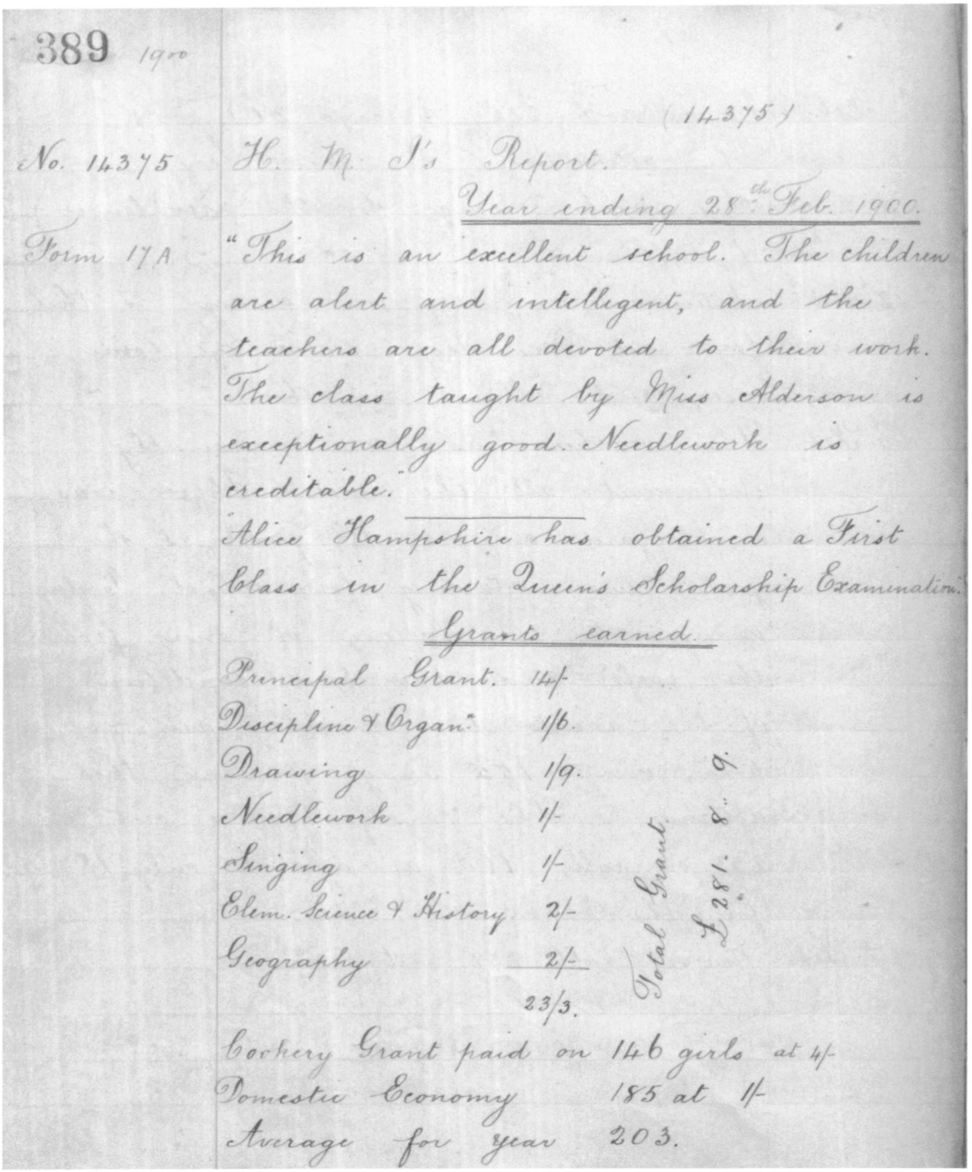
389 1900

(14375)

No. 14375 H. M. I's Report.

Year ending 28th Feb. 1900.

Form 17A "This is an excellent school. The children are alert and intelligent, and the teachers are all devoted to their work. The class taught by Miss Alderson is exceptionally good. Needlework is creditable."

Alice Hampshire has obtained a First Class in the Queen's Scholarship Examination.

Grants earned.

Principal Grant.	14/-
Discipline & Organⁿ	1/6.
Drawing	1/9.
Needlework	1/-
Singing	1/-
Elem. Science & History	2/-
Geography	2/-
	23/3.

Total Grant £281. 8. 9.

Cookery Grant paid on 146 girls at 4/-

Domestic Economy 185 at 1/-

Average for year 203.

Fig. 7b Extract from Leeds School Board Logbook for Meanwood Road School for Girls. (Source: Little London Community Primary School)

in England had to be achieved through formal partnership arrangements between individual Higher Education Institutions (HEIs) and individual schools. Partnership became one of the core principles of teacher education in England. Recently a team of researchers[26] from Manchester, Oxford and Liverpool investigating partnership argued that it is the concept and practice of partnership that is ***the*** distinguishing feature of ITE in England today.

Despite a lot of international interest and debate about the concept of partnership in ITE in Scotland,[27] about Professional Development Schools in the USA,[28] partnership development in Australia[29] and in New Zealand,[30] it is only in England and Wales that partnership has become institutionalised at a national level as the core principle of provision. For all teacher education institutions in England, partnership is a major dimension of their work and one that is at the heart of their courses and regularly subjected to inspection. Following this landmark legislation came the establishment of the Quasi Autonomous National Government Organisation (Quango), the Teacher Training Agency (TTA) in 1994, now renamed the Training Development Agency (TDA).

As noted above, researchers[31] evaluating the recent practice of partnerships in ITE in England in the National Partnership Project (NPP) 2002-05[32] suggested that, although the programme did probably contribute to increasing the numbers of partnership places in schools during its lifetime, the NPP did not alter the underlying model of partnership. Indeed, they suggested that in many cases the practice of partnership in England had changed little since the mid 1990s. However, many partnerships continued to thrive despite the regulatory framework, as we show below. Reflecting upon school partnership work in our centenary year, one striking development since partnerships 'then' to partnerships 'now' is the many varied forms Leeds Met's work with schools now takes.

Leeds Met's partnership work with schools continues to include school experience for trainee teachers,[33] although we prefer the term student teachers to signify the complexities of teacher education and training, which is not simply tied to a 'training' agenda. Leeds Met offers both undergraduate and postgraduate teacher education and training programmes, across the Early Years, Primary and Secondary school age groups. Requirements for placements, for example the number of days needed in school(s) across the duration of a course, are dictated by the TDA. This agency also outlines the professional expectations student teachers must achieve at successive stages of their career, including the initial stage of teacher education, leading to Qualified Teacher Status (QTS)[34] (**Figure 15**) – a function not too dissimilar to that undertaken by the Leeds School Board at the turn of the last century. This suggests that control of entry requirements to the teaching profession has not been relinquished by local and national governments, unlike those of other professions such as medicine. More recently, there has been much controversy and debate about teaching standards and about the role of teacher education and training and the teaching profession in the construction of these standards. Now as then, each of the teacher education and training programmes and the school based work are also subject to the external scrutiny of Her Majesty's Inspectors (HMI), currently in the form of the Office for Standards in Education (Ofsted).

In 2007, student teachers in schools are supported by a number of staff in school 'a mentor', who has responsibility for their school-based learning whilst on placement; subject co-ordinators; class teachers with whom they are placed; and a range of support and interagency staff.[35] Aims and objectives for each school experience are individually determined and agreed between student, mentor and university tutor. These are linked to the professional standards set by the TDA. Advantages of partnerships are the professional learning opportunities offered to all partners as identified by Johnston et al:[36]

Emerging partnership efforts between schools and teacher preparation programs have encouraged more frequent and intense involvement of undergraduate education students with schools, classrooms and teachers. In these partnership models, university and school-level educators have an opportunity to influence the professional culture of schools and positively impact the quality of teaching and learning. Importantly these collaborative models create an even greater need to consciously attend to the socialisation that naturally occurs in settings that link new and experienced educators.

Each school has a key 'link tutor' from the University, an

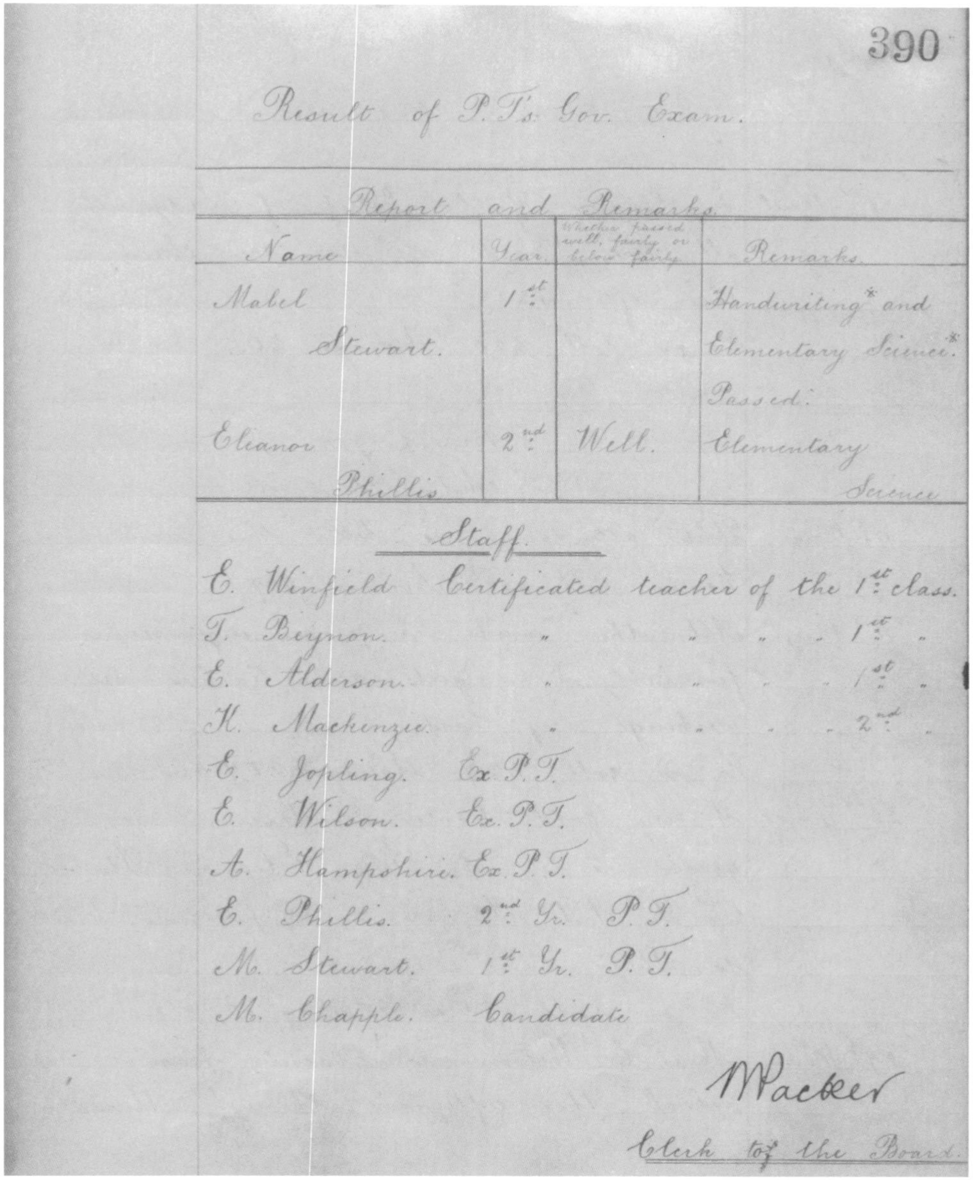
390

Result of P.T.'s Gov. Exam.

Report and Remarks

Name	Year	Whether passed well, fairly or below fairly	Remarks
Mabel Stewart.	1st		Handwriting* and Elementary Science.* Passed.
Eleanor Phillis	2nd	Well.	Elementary Science

Staff.

E. Winfield Certificated teacher of the 1st class.
T. Beynon " " " " 1st "
E. Alderson " " " " 1st "
K. Mackenzie " " " " 2nd "
E. Jopling. Ex P.T.
E. Wilson. Ex. P.T.
A. Hampshire. Ex. P.T.
E. Phillis. 2nd Yr. P.T.
M. Stewart. 1st Yr. P.T.
M. Chapple. Candidate

W Packer
Clerk to the Board.

Fig. 7c Extract from Leeds School Board Logbook for Meanwood Road School for Girls. (Source: Little London Community Primary School)

Date.	Name of Child.	Age of Child.	Nature of Offence.	Nature and Amount of Punishment.	Signature of Teacher who administers the Punishment

Fig. 8
Extract from Corporal Punishment Book for Meanwood Road School for Girls. (Source: Little London Community Primary School)

Above right, Fig. 9 Photo Thoresby High School. (Source: Keith Rowntree)

academic who liaises and works with both school colleagues and the student teacher in relation to the achievement of the expectations of the placement to describe the 'triad'. This applies to primary education (**Figure 16**) and secondary Physical Education (**Figure 17**). Payments for school-based education and training continue to be made, although these are now made directly to the placement schools rather than to individual head teachers!

Regardless of the teacher education and training route being pursued, all student teachers now undertake placements in at least two contrasting schools, covering work across at least two Key Stages or age phases. Primary school student teachers also gain experience of teaching in the secondary sector. In contrast to the pupil-teacher system and the use of the Pupil-Teacher Centres, school placement partnerships in 2007 are available in over 400 schools. Each of these school partners agree to common requirements of education and training whilst offering

distinctive strengths and specialisms. For example, a school may hold a specific specialist school status, or schools are located in contrasting catchment areas with intakes that reflect different school populations marked by family, social and cultural diversity. The placements of the student teachers are determined, in part, to ensure a breadth of experience that allows all of the TDA standards to be met, as well as giving contrasting educational challenges to the student teachers across their course. All of the staff involved in teacher education and training are provided with 'preparation and development' at the university to ensure a high quality of support and assessment practices. Further, schools are clustered geographically to allow for reciprocal support, collaborative learning and moderation.

Current examples of partnership initiatives, apart from ITE, include:
• externally funded research-based projects focusing upon assistive and creative technologies;

Fig. 10
Photo of art facilities at
the School of Art.
(Source: Leeds Library
& Information Service
Leodis Photographic
Archive 20031031-
49380130)

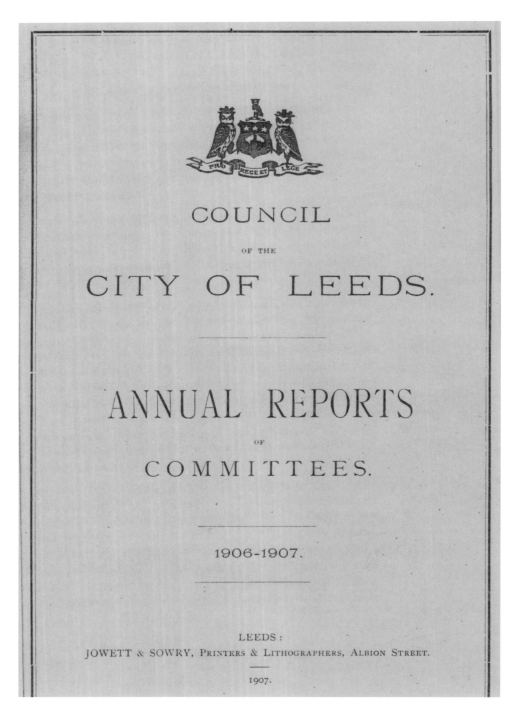

Fig. 12 Front cover of 1906-1907 Annual Report Finance. (Source: Leeds Local and Family History Library L352.02 LS17)

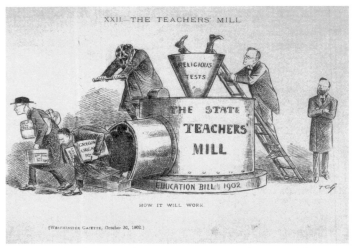

Fig. 11 Political cartoon from the Westminister Cartoons. (Source: Institute of Education library, University of London)

- the development of subject specific curriculum extension activities, especially in History;
- school and University staff professional learning and development programmes including accredited Postgraduate programmes, Master Classes and subject/discipline specific provision, eg disability awareness training and National College for School Leadership (NCSL) Programmes (**Figure 18**);
- non-teacher training student placements including sports coaching and dissertation project work;
- reciprocal access to specialist facilities – especially in relation to examination level studies in sport, music and technology, student volunteering, Enterprise and Business Enterprise activities including the planning and organisation of University corporate events;
- student and staff volunteering;
- school governance work and residential and non-residential summer school study opportunities;
- progression articulations for post 16 students through the Regional University Network and Leeds Met's Progression Module (**Figure 19**).

The Leeds Met Progression Module initiative[37] is an access vehicle into higher education. Leeds Met works with partner schools and colleges to inform and prepare students for university, particularly students who would not ordinarily follow this career path. This connects

NOTES.

(1.) **No** student admitted to a Training College in 1907 or afterwards will be allowed to be prepared for an Examination forming a recognised stage towards a University Degree as a part of his Course, unless he has either

(*a*) passed the Preliminary Examination for the Certificate and obtained in that Examination distinction in English, History, and Geography, and also in four optional subjects, including two languages, one of which must be either Greek, Latin, French, or German; or

(*b*) passed some other Examination which may have been accepted by the Board for the purpose.

(2.) The standard required to pass the Preliminary Examination for the Certificate as a whole will be roughly equal to the standard which has been required to pass the King's Scholarship Examination in recent years. To obtain distinction in any subject a standard will be required which may be regarded as equivalent to that of a pass (not "distinction") in the Leaving Certificate Examination of the London University. In English and in History, however, the standard will be rather higher; and it is hoped that the development of the Pupil Teacher Centres may make it possible before long similarly to raise the standard in other subjects.

Fig. 13 Extract from Board of Education (1907) Regulations and Syllabus. *(Source: The National Archives ED24/441)*

Fig. 14
Photo of Leeds Met Carnegie student, Rebecca Low, on school placement at Carr Manor Primary School. (Source: Jane Barber)

with a school partnership initiative, successfully launched with the formalisation of work with Skipton Girls' High School in January, 2006 (**Figure 20**). *Termed Outreach* (**Figure 21**), it is governed by a shared vision of partnership work with schools and of Leeds Met as a learning community concerned to influence students for life, linking and engaging our local community and those across the globe.

As noted above, one striking development of Leeds Met's work with schools now is the diverse range of opportunities being pursued in partnership covering research and development. What seems to be emerging is a re-conceptualisation of partnerships with schools. Research partnerships with schools,[38] professional learning partnerships and networks,[39] and the recent networked learning communities initiative[40] all illustrate how relationships between higher education and schools are being developed in innovative ways to strengthen the learning of teachers and education workers and their academic partners.

The reasons for this expansion and diversification may seem obvious. For example, the interest of both parties in learning, intellectual development and socialisation; the pursuit of 'seamless' progression for school pupils to further and higher education; the training and preparation of future workforces and continuing professional development

opportunities for those already working in the various sectors and professions. But there is also Leeds Met's commitment to community engagement, to 'working beyond boundaries' and to 'making a difference'. We can only agree with Richmond:[41]

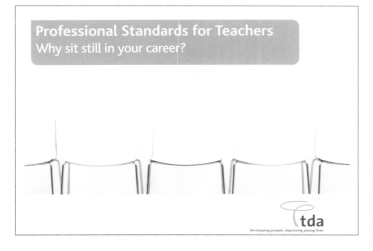

Professional Standards for Teachers
Why sit still in your career?

tda
developing people, improving young lives

Fig. 15
Front cover of new TDA standards. (Source: Copyright Training and Development Agency for Schools 2007)

Fig. 16
Extract from Carnegie
Faculty Primary
Partnership Handbook.
(Source: Carnegie
Faculty courses office)

INTRODUCTION

Dear Colleagues

This handbook provides a single resource for school and university based tutors to use in relation to the school based elements of Initial Teacher Education at Leeds Metropolitan University.

The handbook is an overview document which needs to be read in conjunction with other documents, such as specific placement booklets, Link Tutor files, which contain more specific information on the individual expectations for each placement. All our documentation can be found online at www.leedsmet.ac.uk/carnegie/placements.htm

The handbook has been provided at the request of partnership schools who prefer to have key documents all located in one place. Leeds Met partnership bases itself on the quality engagement of large numbers of very different schools. This enables our trainees to experience a diverse range of placements and a variety of methods in managing the training process. We are lucky to be at the forefront of regional activity with TDA Partnership Promotion Schools as well as Training Schools in the area.

We are continually remodelling our systems to maximise placement opportunities whilst retaining our commitment to quality experiences for all our trainees irrespective of mode or duration of training.

Our current provision has been revalidated and remodelled in response to partnership needs and national directives. Trainees follow two distinctive routes into primary teacher training.

A   Early Childhood Education 3-7
     (specialising in Foundation Stage and Key Stage 1)

B   Primary Education 5-11
     Specialising in a subject English or Maths or French or Design Technology or History or Physical Education Key Stage 1 and 2

These routes will enable trainees to focus on particular age phase settings and develop their career profiles accordingly. The Children's Workforce Strategy should provide a diverse range of job opportunities for which our trainees will be well qualified.

We are pleased to work in an increasing collaborative regional and national context with other providers, LEAs and partners to provide first class work-based learning experiences.

Thank you for your continuing support for our partnership.

Denise Gilchrist
Associate Dean Initial Teacher Education
Tel. 0113 283 6122
E-mail d.gilchrist@leedsmet.ac.uk

H:\CFSR\Placement&LiasonOffice\Handbooks\2006-07 FINAL\Primary\Primary Partnership Handbook 2006-2007.doc

- 1 -

LEEDS METROPOLITAN UNIVERSITY ITE PARTNERSHIP

Leeds Metropolitan University is a higher education provider of Initial Teacher Education and training both at the undergraduate and postgraduate level. The Partnership is based on an agreement between selected schools and Leeds Metropolitan University to provide a suitable quality learning environment for the education and training of trainee teachers.

The core activity centres on the placement and assessment of trainees in schools and/or other settings in the progression towards recommendation and award of Qualified Teacher Status (QTS).

Partnership activity is underpinned by some of the following assumptions:

- That ultimately, the quality education of school children remains the focus of the partnership's activities.
- That initial teacher education and training is just one phase of an individual teacher's developing career and that the partnership's activity is set in the wider context of recognising individual student needs both on entry to ITE, and early and continuing professional development following the achievement of QTS.
- That all partners feel the benefits of partnership. This includes: trainees, whose experience is enhanced by a rigorous joint school-University approach; schools and LEAs, whose children experience creative and diverse teaching and whose staff are professionally developed as School Based Tutors; and, the university, whose courses and staff are enhanced by close involvement with schools.

All programmes of Initial Teacher Education in England must meet the requirements laid down in Qualifying to Teach (02/02) and all trainees must meet the Standards for the award of QTS laid down in Qualifying to Teach. However, this does not mean that all ITE providers are the same. The programmes provided by Leeds Metropolitan University's Secondary Partnership are distinctive in a number of ways.

Distinctive Feature	How this is Achieved
Trainees are supported and encouraged to develop the personal qualities which will make them enthusiastic, energetic, caring, valuing and valued members of the teaching profession.	• University tutors share a commonality of values. • Personal support, formal and informal, is given a high priority, both in university and in school.
Trainees are encouraged to develop as reflective academics and intellectuals.	• Courses include academic qualifications which are subject to rigorous quality assurance procedures. • Courses provide opportunities for trainees to move into Masters degree level work.
The role of the subject specialist teacher is central to all courses.	• A high proportion of the training is delivered through the specialist subject. • Subject specialist School Based Tutors support trainees in school • A strength of the partnership is in the links between subject tutors and School Based Tutors.
Good teaching practice is modelled and mirrored throughout the courses	• School Based Tutors are successful practitioners who are able to make explicit the basis for their own and others' practice. • A criterion for the appointment of University tutors is successful practice as school teachers.
Variety is valued	• Recruitment and admissions strategies actively seek to make teacher education available to any who have the potential to become good teachers. • Partner schools reflect the diversity of British education.

OUR MISSION

To be a world class regional centre for professional development in education, leadership and change management.

AIMS

- To provide professional and leadership development opportunities for teachers, school and public sector staff across the Yorkshire and Humber region.
- To be a high quality provider of professional development nationally.
- To become a centre of excellence in leadership development and change management dedicated to promoting high quality provision across the region.

WHO ARE WE

We are a partnership of Leeds Metropolitan University (Leeds Met) and CCDU Training and Consultancy Ltd who together have extensive experience in leadership development and are committed to excellence.

We work together to provide development opportunities to meet the needs of public sector staff throughout our region.

Working closely with the Yorkshire and Humber Professional Development Consortium of local authorities, universities, diocesan authorities and headteachers from the region, we are able to ensure that our programmes respond to local, regional and national needs as well as legislative changes, and to plan our provision accordingly.

WHERE ARE WE

We are based on the prestigious Headingley Campus of Leeds Metropolitan University. We are located at Churchwood and North Lodge and our programmes are delivered throughout the region in locally based centres close to our participants as well as on Campus.

WHAT WE DO

We provide leadership development programmes for leaders at all levels in schools and other educational settings including the following programmes on behalf of the National College for School Leadership:

- National Professional Qualification in Integrated Centre Leadership
- National Professional Qualification for Headship
- Headteacher Induction Programme
- Leading from the Middle
- Developing the Capacity for Sustained Improvement
- Working Together for Success
- Leading Small Primary Schools

WE ALSO PROVIDE CONSULTANCY SUPPORT FOR STAFF IN EDUCATIONAL SETTINGS ON REQUEST.

Additional provision includes:

- Higher Level Teaching Assistant assessment throughout Yorkshire and Humber and the North East by CCDU.
- Masters programmes in Leadership and Management by Leeds Met.

Fig. 18 Extract from Carnegie Leaders in Learning brochure. (Source: Carnegie Marketing Manager Michael Ainsworth)

Fig. 19
Leeds Met Progression
Module. (Source:
Carnegie Marketing
Manager Michael
Ainsworth)

Opening the doors to Higher Education

INTRODUCTION

The decision about what and where to study is becoming increasingly difficult to make. With newer, more exciting courses being introduced year on year, coupled with the rising costs of studying at university, young people are under pressure to make sure that the choice they make is the right one.

The Progression Module is a formal programme of study which helps young people through the decision making process and provides the opportunity for them to make an informed choice as a result of their research.

Through following this programme, which is delivered in schools and colleges, students will explore their own strengths and weaknesses, develop career action plans, research courses, discover the real costs of higher education, deliver a presentation, take part in a mock interview and develop a personal statement.

Fig. 20
Skipton Girls' High
School Collaboration.
(Source: Leeds
Metropolitan University
website, Images,
11/01/06)

A partnership fit for the Dales

Skipton Girls' High School became the first school to join Leeds Met's expanding Regional University Network at a launch which saw Chancellor Brendan Foster, Vice-Chancellor Professor Simon Lee, school head Jan Renou and Chair of Governors John Goodfellow formalise a new partnership.

As a result of joining one of the country's most innovative universities, students at the school will benefit from access to a range of foundation courses and progression opportunities, which, in future, will help prepare them for entry into higher education.

Leeds Met has also been working closely with the school, offering advice and support for their new fitness centre which Brendan Foster officially opened on the day of the signing.

Students from the enterprising partner school were inspired when they were invited to meet Dame Kelly Holmes at our summer graduation festival.

Head teacher Jan Renou was thrilled with the new agreement and said: "I'm really excited about the partnership. We wanted to do something in the community and I was interested in Professor Lee's outreach programme. We hope to realise some of the Vice-Chancellor's vision and hope he can help our girls look at undergraduate study."

School pupil Abigail Lockwood, 12, agrees: "The extra-curricular activities brought about through the opening of the new fitness centre and the introduction of the foundation courses will help us to achieve what we want at our own level."

Having arrived in Skipton following the Headingley Carnegie Stadium press conference, Chancellor Brendan Foster commented on what an eventful day it had been for Leeds Met: "It is great to see the university reaching out to the wider community."

The fact is that people bring several kinds of knowledge, some helpful and some detrimental, to a successful partnership. In addition, professionals from different cultures see the usefulness of the discipline's knowledge base in different ways. The challenge is to understand the cultures of the various players and to foster a sense of belonging, regardless of the cultures involved.

Partnership working with schools has undoubtedly changed and expanded over the past 100 years. It is a dynamic and evolving dimension to the work of a university and Leeds Met is proud both of its heritage in this area and of the opportunities to work with prospective students, current students, university and school staff and our increasing network of alumni. In line with our aspiration to be a 'world class regional university with world wide horizons, using all our talents to the full', the next 100 years promise to be exciting times for Leeds Met and all our school partnerships.

The authors wish to thank Jane Barber, Lori Beckett and Iain Poole for their help and contributions to this chapter.

WELCOME

outreach
outreach
outreach

INTRODUCTION

This document provides a starting point for conversation and collaboration. Leeds Met recognises the individuality of each school and the strengths and opportunities each brings to partnership.
We are a student centred university, where everything we do focuses upon optimising the student experience, including the transition to higher education.

Leeds Met is striving to be a world-class regional university, with world-wide horizons, using all our talents to the full. We are aligning every aspect of our work with this bold vision and we look forward to working with you in reaching our aim.

FOR STUDENTS & PARENTS
- Specialist talks to final year students and parents e.g. financially surviving at university
- Invite university students & staff to attend schools specialist events
- Subject talks at schools, where possible linked to the curriculum
- Opportunities for Leeds Met to contact parents and community for HE initiatives
- Free taster session for the new game Rock-it-Ball
- Revision classes
- Student life workshop
- Gifted and Talented
- Curriculum extension projects e.g. History/Enterprise & Healthy Schools initiative. FIA (Lisa Gannon & Andy Smith Exercise in Schools for Yr 6 Primary - informing about exercise/healthy eating) and Gifted and Talented (Dave Morley)
- Development of the Curriculum

FOR STAFF
- Collaborative research
- Joint development in pedagogies etc
- Curricular activities which involve staff, possibly summer school activity, specific areas of focus agreed with the school
- Opportunities for school admin staff to join admin staff development programmes
- Specialist sports coaching or similar session at Carnegie or other Faculty i.e. training sessions
- Fee discount for teaching staff on range of CPD opportunities. Offer CPD opportunities for admin staff/ECDL (INN)

FOR SCHOOL GOVERNACE/MANAGEMENT
- Opportunity to take a student placement
- Delivery platforms e.g. Pod casts
- University marketing/branding for key activities and events e.g. sports certificates
- PR and marketing advice for Schools
- Forum for Schools to met other schools to exchange ideas/best practice/staff etc
- Access to partners/partners event e.g. Leeds Rugby (Leeds Rhinos & Tykes), Yorkshire Cricket Club, Black Dyke Band, Harrogate International Festival, Northern Ballet, West Yorkshire Playhouse

ASPIRATION RAISING
Getahead Team's Aspiration Raising activities, on and off campus activities:
- Work with Primary Schools
- Work with 11 to 16yr olds
- Post 16 - Progression Module
- Work with Parents/Carers

- Student Ambassador Scheme
- Summer Schools Residentials/non Residentials Work with specific target groups: BME groups, Looked after Children

THE CARNEGIE EXPERIENCE
- Introduction to Leeds Met ● Lunch
- Tour of Carnegie Stand ● Free t-shirt
- Campus tour ● Option for sporting activity
- Being a Carnegie student

LEEDS MET EXPECTATIONS:
What would we expect in return
- Display presence within the school e.g. plaque, images etc. This would be regularly updated by Leeds Met
- Attendances at parents evenings - especially yr 11 & 6th form, open evenings and progressions evenings
- Use of facilities as appropriate for provision e.g. CPD
- Badging for Leeds Met in some way i.e. logo prominent on letter headings, in entrance hall (all signed up in an agreement)
- Recognition in Schools prospectus with brief description of partnership activities
- Use of facilities as appropriate for HE Hub & CPD programmes
- School available to lead staff development sessions for Leeds Met staff on latest in schools curriculum/ ALT/pedagogy etc
- University marketing/branding for key activities and events e.g. sports certificates

Fig. 21 Extract from Leeds Met Outreach flier. (source: Carnegie Marketing Manager Michael Ainsworth)

ENDNOTES

1 See www.nationalarchives.gov.uk/catalogue/Leaflets/ri2170.htm

2 Simon, B. (1974) *Education and the Labour Movement 1870-1920*. London: Lawrence and Wishart, pp. 180-181.

3 Connell, L (nd) *A Century of Teacher Training in Leeds 1875 – 1975*. Leeds: Leeds Metropolitan University.

4 Leeds School Board (1899) *Yearbook* (original copy held by Leeds Met Archives, Headingley Campus library).

5 ibid.

6 Connell, L (nd) op.cit.

7 ibid.

8 Rich, R. W. (1933) *The Training of Teachers in England and Wales During the Nineteenth Century*. London: Cambridge University Press, p. 239.

9 We found a similar instruction in the City of Bradford Education Committee (1915) *Scheme for the Training and Supervision of Student Teachers* (original held in WYAS ref: LEA file 763).

10 Samuel Childs' 1908 workbook on Demonstration Lessons and 1909 School Practice book (copy and original held by Leeds University Archives).

11 Godsen, P.H.J.H. and Sharp, P.R. (1978) *The Development of an Educational Service, The West Riding 1889-1974* (Oxford), who noted Leeds Secretary of Education James Graham's first appointment as an assistant inspector in 1893.

12 Leeds School Board Log Book of the Meanwood Road Girls' Board School, 1883-1906, on loan from Little London Community Primary School, formerly Meanwood Road Girls' Board School, and one of our flagship school partners engaging with Lori Beckett and Jon Tan in a joint school-university project, 'Patterns of Learning', on teacher learning and development devoted to teacher research.

13 Op.cit.

14 Corporal Punishment Book of the Meanwood Road Girls' Board School also on loan from Little London Community Primary School.

15 For example, see Carnegie Faculty Module Handbook for PVKP: Promoting and Supporting Learning and Integration – Inclusive Education. Module CRN: 64034. Level 2 Semester 2, 2006-7. See also research papers, like Whitty, G. (2005). Policy and Practice for Inclusion: The role of initial teacher preparation an continuing professional development in England. Paper presented at the international conference on teacher development, special education needs and early years education, Lanzhou, Gansu Province, People's Republic of China, October.

16 Connell, op cit, p.17 noted the CLTC use of Thoresby High School following the outbreak of WW1, because of expedience. It met each afternoon, the pupils of the Thoresby School using the building each morning. This 'Box and Cox' arrangement was not satisfactory – the pupils had the school from 9 to 1, and the College had it from 1:30 to 5, so that there was not much chance of a change in the air. This arrangement continued until Easter 1916 when the 450 students were moved and accommodated in The Grange, which thus became the College.

17 For detailed discussion of Education Committee activities, see Janet Douglas' chapter, The Genesis of the City of Leeds Training College at Beckett's Park.

18 Eaglesham, E. (1956) *From School Board to Local Authority* (Oxford).

19 The judgment disallowed the expenditure of the London School Board, which lost its appeal on expenditure for some higher grade and evening classes because it was not on elementary education. This led to the destruction of the higher grade schools in their original form and precipitated the abolition of school boards and the creation of a new system designed by Robert Morant. In 1899, he was private secretary to Sir John Gorst, Vice president of the Committee of Council on Education, and helped pilot the Board of Education Bill through the House of Commons. Morant was then invited by Balfour to prepare the draft of the 1902 Education Bill. See p.2 in Eaglesham (1956) ibid.

20 This was part of TUC policy, in line with the demands of the Labour movement, says Simon, op cit p. 256.

21 Board of Education (1907) *Regulations and Syllabuses for the Preliminary Examination for the Elementary School Teachers' Certificate* (original copy held by The National Archives ref. ED24/441).

22 We learned more about the bursarship from archival materials donated by CLTC student, Rachel Ross, reported in Jacqui Dean's chapter on Student Participation.

23 Eaglesham op. cit. p. 153.

24 For detailed discussion of staffing, see Janet Douglas's chapter, op.cit.

25 See 1994 Education Act. London: HMSO; and Department for Education and Science (1992) *Initial Teacher Training (Secondary Phase)* (Circular 9/92). London: DES.

26 Furlong, J., Campbell,A., Howson, J., Lewis.S. and McNamara, O. (2006) Partnership in English Initial Teacher Education: Changing times, Changing Definitions. Evidence from the TTA National Partnership Project, *Scottish Educational Review*, vol. 37, pp 32-45.

27 See Brisard, E., Menter, I. and Smith, I. (2005) *Models of Partnership in Programmes of Initial Teacher Training: a systematic review*. Edinburgh: General Teaching Council of Scotland.

28 Darling-Hammond, L. (1994a) (ed.) *Professional Development Schools: schools for developing a profession*. New York: Teachers College Press; and Darling-Hammond, L. (1994b) 'Developing Professional Development Schools: early lessons, challenge and promise' in Darling-Hammond, L. (ed.) *Professional Development Schools: schools for developing a profession*, pp. 1-27. New York: Teachers College Press.

29 See Department of Education, Science and Training (DEST) (2003) *Australia's Teachers, Australia's Future*, Main Report. A report by the Committee for the Review of Teaching and Teacher Education. Canberra: Commonwealth of Australia; and Grundy, S., Jasman, A., Newbound, P., Phillips, A., Robison, J., Strickland, L., & Tomazos, D. (1999) 'Exploring an Emerging Landscape: a metaphor for university teacher educators working with, in and for schools', *Australian Educational Researcher*, 26 (3), pp. 37-56.

30 McGee, J. (2001) 'Enhancing School-University Partnerships', *Waikato Journal of Education*, 7, pp. 129-145.

31 Furlong et al (2006) op.cit.

32 The National Partnership Project (NPP) was established to strengthen and promote partnerships between schools and higher education.

33 The Universities Council for the Education of Teachers (UCET) recently agreed to use Initial Teacher Education and Training (ITET) in the hope of emphasising the *education* element of teacher preparation in universities and colleges. Throughout the text education and training are used to re-inforce this.

34 Recently released by the Training and Development Agency for implementation in September, 2007.

35 For detailed discussion of the school-based tutor see Lori Beckett and Jon Tan's chapter on Teaching Methods, Pedagogies and Professional Learning.

36 Johnston, B, et al (2002) Teacher Socialisation: Opportunities for University- School Partnerships to Improve Professional Cultures. *High School Journal*, 00181498, April/May 2002, Vol 85, Issue 4.

37 See www.leedsmet.ac.uk/metoffice/access/index

38 such as described by McLaughlin, C., Black-Hawkins, K., Brindley, S., McIntyre, D. and Taber, K. S. (2006) *Researching Schools:Stories from a Schools-University Partnership for Educational Research*, London: Routledge

39 Day, C. (1999) *Developing Teachers: The Challenges of Lifelong Learning*, London: Falmer.

40 McGregor, J. , Holmes, D. and Temperley, J. (2005) Collaborative enquiry in Networked Learning Communities, paper BERA Conference Glamorgan, 2005.

41 Richmond, G. (1996) University/School Partnerships: Bridging the Culture Gap. *Theory Into Practice*, vol. 35, no. 3, pp. 214-218.

CHAPTER 6

The Education and Training of Teachers[1]

Lori Beckett with Anne Flintoff and Sue Warren

The City of Leeds Training College handbook[2] opening statement declared:

'The City of Leeds Training College is a College for Men and Women who intend to become Teachers in Public Elementary Schools, and is conducted under the Regulations of the Board of Education for the Training of Teachers for Elementary Schools . . .'

Given such a formidable introduction, one wonders what the students and their parents made of it. The fact there were over one thousand applications for 142 places in 1907[3] suggests some enthusiasm because enrolments continued to grow steadily during the years of the temporary College, then with the occupation of the permanent College in 1912, and beyond.[4]

Report on opening of
CLTC at Beckett's Park,
Yorkshire Post 14 June,
1913. (Source:
Yorkshire Post)*

TEACHER TRAINING 'THEN'

Such enthusiasm was proclaimed by the *Yorkshire Post* article on the Official Opening[5] (**Figure 1**), which documented a veritable 'who's who' of civic leaders and educationists including MP and Board of Education President Mr J. A. Pease (**Figure 2**), who did the opening address. From this one article, we learned that the City of Leeds Training College was the realisation of a vision, a political coup, a model for the UK and the Colonies, central to national education and nation-building, part of a new system, and not immune from sensations of dissonance.[6]

The article showcased the educational politics, notably the administration of teacher training. Pease's mention of the principle of the central authority attaching conditions to the subsidies and grants, and the exercise of control over expenditure of the money to local authorities or to governors of training colleges, was telling because it harked back to the infamous audit appeal case, or Cockerton Case.[7] Educational historian Eric Eaglesham[8] reckoned the resultant 1902 Education Act revealed the forces to be reconciled: exercising some control over the expenditure of public money, and subjecting education to rules and regulations without risk of damage to educational progress. Pease's comments were also prophetic, given what was to come at the City of Leeds Training College, a reflection of the extraordinary powers given to the administration by the Act.

Such rules and regulations are stark in the tiny Leeds School Board *Yearbook*,[9] given information on the old system of teacher training, regulations and instructions to staff. The Instruction of Pupil Teachers and Instructions to Teachers[10] (**Figure 3**) show the organisation and management of teaching, which came to be called professional expectations, no doubt a carry-over from the 'payments by results' system that dominated elementary schools up to its abolition in 1897.[11] Educational historian Brian Simon[12] noted the immediate aim was to radically reduce government expenditure on education, and a further aim was to concentrate the efforts of teachers on the 3 Rs (reading, writing and arithmetic). While it was partially successful, it was at the cost of enforcing entirely mechanical drill methods of teaching on the schools.[13]

We presume the students' and parents' enthusiasm for the City

of Leeds Training College bore witness to the new system of a two-year residential course of study leading to better teaching (**Figures 4**). Cambridge alumnus Lynda Grier[14] called it a revolution in teacher training, and evidence is in the Board of Education regulations[15] (**Figure 5**). These regulations were embedded in the prospectuses and successive handbooks[16] as 'Conditions of Admission' (**Figure 6**), and were reflected in letters sent to students[17] (**Figure 7**). The same sources[18] provided details of life on campus (**Figure 8**), where four

hours a day, five days a week, were devoted to instruction in classroom-based subjects like English, history, geography, mathematics, art, needlework, method, science and hygiene.[19] The afternoons were given to school practice, possibly criticism lessons,[20] excursions, exercise and recreation.

Regulations also applied to staffing. Grier's biography of Winifred Mercier[21] recorded the Board of Education's stipulation that when the new buildings were completed a woman should be appointed

Fig. 2
Photo of Official Opening. (Source: Leeds Metropolitan University Archives)

Fig. 3
Leeds School Board
Official Yearbook, *1899,
Instructions to Teachers.*
(Source: Leeds
Metropolitan University
Archives)

Education Committee.

INSTRUCTIONS TO TEACHERS.

1.—The Regulations approved by the Board must be strictly observed by the Teachers.

2.—The Principal Teacher is held directly responsible for—

(a) The moral training and oversight of the pupil teachers ;

(b) The organization and discipline of the School ;

(c) The cultivation of habits of cleanliness and punctuality in the scholars ;

(d) The general arrangement and tidiness of the School-rooms ;

(e) And the supervision of the faithful discharge of the duties prescribed for the schoolkeeper.

The organization must also, at all times, provide for his direct intervention in giving the lessons. "He ought, as a rule, to have one or more of the classes (to be varied from time to time) in a group or in the gallery, under his own immediate charge. He must, indeed, at times leave himself at liberty to observe the manner in which his assistants or apprentices teach, and to watch the collective working of his School; but his duties will be very ill performed if (what is called) general superintendence forms the sum or principal part of them."*

3.—The Registers and requisite books of account, as directed by the Clerk to the Board, must be promptly and accurately kept, and the proceeds of sales handed over quarterly, together with the various books for examination as directed. Head Teachers are responsible for the safe custody of the school-fees and proceeds of sales, and for their due payment at the Offices of the Board. Teachers are strongly urged to avoid the unnecessary exposure of money during School hours, or the leaving of the same overnight in the Schools; which if done must be at the Teachers' own risk.

A cash bag is provided by the Board, to facilitate the safe delivery of school money at the Board Offices, for which the Head Teacher is responsible. The bag must be locked before being sent by the Caretaker, and will be opened by a duplicate key kept in the Board Offices.

* Committee of Council on Education.

50

Education Committee.

While the Principal Teacher must be held responsible for the regularity and accuracy of this work, the Assistant Teachers may fairly be charged with the marking and keeping of the registers of their several classes. The latter should, moreover, be required to give assistance out of School hours in the preparation of the monthly and other returns, the examination and preparation of papers or lessons, and in the fixing of the needlework of girls ; none of which duties should be allowed to take the time of either Principal or Assistant Teachers during the very limited hours at command for actual instruction.

4.—Every case of scholar's absence should be promptly reported to the parent on the form provided for the purpose ; all children absent for a week should be visited by the Assistant Teachers, and cases of repeated absence, without satisfactory reasons, should be visited by the Head Teacher. Pupil Teachers are relieved from the work of visiting irregular children at their homes, and the necessary assistance required in this duty by the Head Teacher is to be rendered by the Assistant Teachers.

5.—Home lessons must be strictly limited to work which may occupy in preparation not more than thirty minutes for children up to Standard III.; not more than one hour for children of Standard IV. and upwards. Cases of delicate or ailing children must be most carefully discriminated, and all pressure, both at School and in home lessons, must be strictly avoided.

6.—Valuable apparatus and stationery are committed to the care of the Teacher. He is responsible for the proper and careful use of apparatus and furniture, and for the economical use of all books and stationery. Extravagance or wasteful and careless use of books and stationery would be a serious reflection upon the discipline of the School. No stock—such as books, maps, &c.—may be written off as consumed without previous permission.

7.—It is particularly undesirable that large classes should be crowded in class-rooms, or the babies left in the sole charge of a Candidate or Junior P.T.

8.—The Head Teacher of each department must keep a record of the amount of the accommodation for which the School has been approved by the Education Department, and will be held responsible for compliance with the regulations of the Department in keeping the average attendance for the school year within the accommodation.

51

Education Committee.

9.—No child may be refused admission to school, and no name may be removed from the Registers, except by written permission of the Clerk to the Board ; and all such cases of removal from the Registers must be entered fortnightly in the duplicate Registers.

10.—The interval of 15 minutes for Recreation in the morning and 10 minutes in the afternoon school, provided for in the Official Time Table, is imperative, and must on no account be omitted.

11.—Children should not be sent out of school on messages after the closing of the registers.

CORPORAL PUNISHMENT.

1.—Assistant Teachers and Pupil Teachers are absolutely prohibited from inflicting corporal punishment in any manner whatever ; and Head Teachers are required immediately to report to the Board any violation of this regulation.

2.—The Board are of opinion that the frequent use of corporal punishment is a mark of incompetence on the part of the Head Teacher. Head Teachers must exercise the utmost caution in inflicting corporal punishment, and must never strike a child on any part of the head, either with the hand, or with any instrument whatsoever.

3.—All cases of corporal punishment, however slight, inflicted with the hand, the cane, or in any manner whatever, must be recorded *at the time* in the book provided for the purpose.

4.—Any Teacher, whether Head Teacher or subordinate Teacher, offending against the foregoing regulations, may be suspended by the Clerk to the Board, until the case shall have been dealt with by the Education Committee.

MEMO.—The Corporal Punishment and Teachers' Time Books shall be sent to the Offices for inspection on the closing of the Schools for the Midsummer and Christmas vacations.

52

---

as Vice-Principal, a position of considerable responsibility. Mercier's acceptance of the post was conditional on its scope for initiative and independence to carry out her ideas, which derived from work experience in so many institutions (**Figure 9**).[22] Her many accomplishments[23] included a reorganisation of the library, curriculum development, and schemes for a third-year course. She set out to strengthen the intellectual life of the College, further develop the curriculum, invite guest lecturers, and encourage students to undertake social work in the community as well as school appointments further afield.

Grier's book, scrapbooks of newspaper articles[24], and snippets in consecutive issues of the *Journal of Education*[25] indicated a scandal erupted at the City of Leeds Training College in the early years of World War 1, prompted by Mercier's resignation on 17 May 1916, within three years of her appointment. City of Leeds Secretary of Education James Graham followed with a 'pep' talk to the whole staff, and eight women tutors resigned in protest (**Figure 10**). This provoked a call for a national inquiry (**Figure 11**), conducted by the Board of Education in the Council Hall, Leeds, over seven days, 15-18 and 22-24 August 1916, inclusive (**Figure 12**). The proceedings were private, and according to the *Journal of Education*, the *Yorkshire Post*, and City of Leeds Training College staff member H. S. Pickering, the report was never released.[26] It makes for fascinating reading because it documents the scandal as if it was a legal case[27] (**Figure 13**). Mercier described it as 'like a great State Trial for treason, full of passion and drama: a most wonderful experience'.[28]

The problems for Mercier came down to differences of opinion and approaches to education and teacher training, particularly management and organisation, with all its complexities and political machinations. Professor John Dover Wilson[29] described the major players – Mercier, Graham, and Principal Walter Parsons – as

19

Key to Diagram (on following page).

This diagram is intended to represent the various ways in which a person may proceed through the different stages of the teaching profession.

The rectangles represent the status of the teacher at the various stages of his or her career; the dotted lines represent the several means of progress of the teacher through these stages; the letters enclosed in circles represent the examinations which the teacher has to pass in this process.

It will be observed that the lines leading from the rectangles representing the early stages of the teaching career meet in an ellipse, from which other lines proceed leading to the rectangles representing the later stages. It is intended by this to represent the fact that teachers who have passed through these earlier stages by any one of the alternative routes indicated by the dotted lines, may then proceed to the later stages either by entering a Training College, whether as an ordinary or a Degree Student, or by becoming Uncertificated Teachers. The Examinations to be passed in each of these three cases are shown on the diagram by their appropriate letters. It should be observed that Bursars and Pupil-Teachers may have passed one of these Examinations during their period of recognition as such, and that Student-Teachers will have done so, as a rule, previous to the beginning of their recognition.

The minimum age at which intending teachers passing through a Secondary School Course and going direct to a Training College can pass each stage is shown on the left-hand side of the Diagram; for those passing through the Pupil-Teacher course it is shown on the right-hand side.

The various Examinations are indicated in the diagram by the following letters :—

(A) = One of the Examinations mentioned in Appendix I. A.

(B) =   „   „   „   I. B.

(D) =   „   „   „   I. D.

(E) = An approved Final Examination, conducted wholly or partly by a University.

(F) = The Board's Final Examination for Students in Training Colleges.

(G) = The Board's Certificate Examination for Teachers in Elementary Schools.

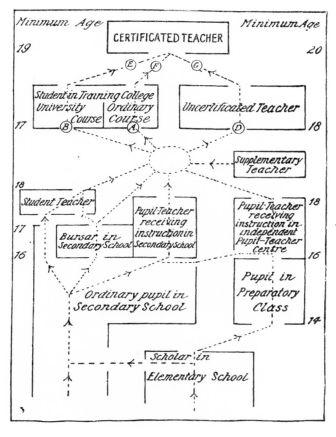

Fig. 4
Extracts from Board of
Education (1912) How
to Become a Teacher,
London, HMSO.
(Courtesy of Special
Collections, Leeds
University Library, Shelf
mark 93/032)

protagonists unaware at the beginning of the coming clash and of each other's point of view. Clearly not one for political disillusionment, Mercier recorded her reasons in her letter of resignation, which had to do with the constraints on her office.[30] Although the Board of Education completely exonerated Mercier and the eight women tutors, and ascribed the 'Responsibility for failure' to Parsons and Graham, there was divided opinion. We learned of Parsons' popularity from Graham's letter,[31] the Board of Governors' testimonial,[32] and Pickering,[33] who noted honorary doctorates conferred on both men.

We know Mercier had her detractors who described her pejoratively as a feminist,[34] as well as supporters, no doubt thrilled with her exoneration. The *Journal of Education,* representing the education profession, showed overwhelming support for Mercier and her colleagues.[35] Dover Wilson said she was 'a great social artist, and

will take her place in history with Robert Morant, Albert Mansbridge and Margaret Macmillan. What they did for secondary, adult and infant education, she did for the English training college'. This was some reputation to live up to, and we learned that before Morant became assistant director of special enquiries in the Education Department and crafted the 1902 Education Act, he sat as a model for W. B. Richmond's Redeemer in St Paul's, London[37] (**Figure 14**). The suggestion was that this top level bureaucrat was god-like.

Mercier's work is a pivotal part of the story and plot line of teacher training at City of Leeds Training College, for many reasons. It throws into stark relief the impact of tight control and regulation. These were the forces named by Eaglesham,[38] who said they must be reconciled if damage to educational progress was to be averted. Sadly, we can only ponder the damage done. Dover Wilson[39] claimed the

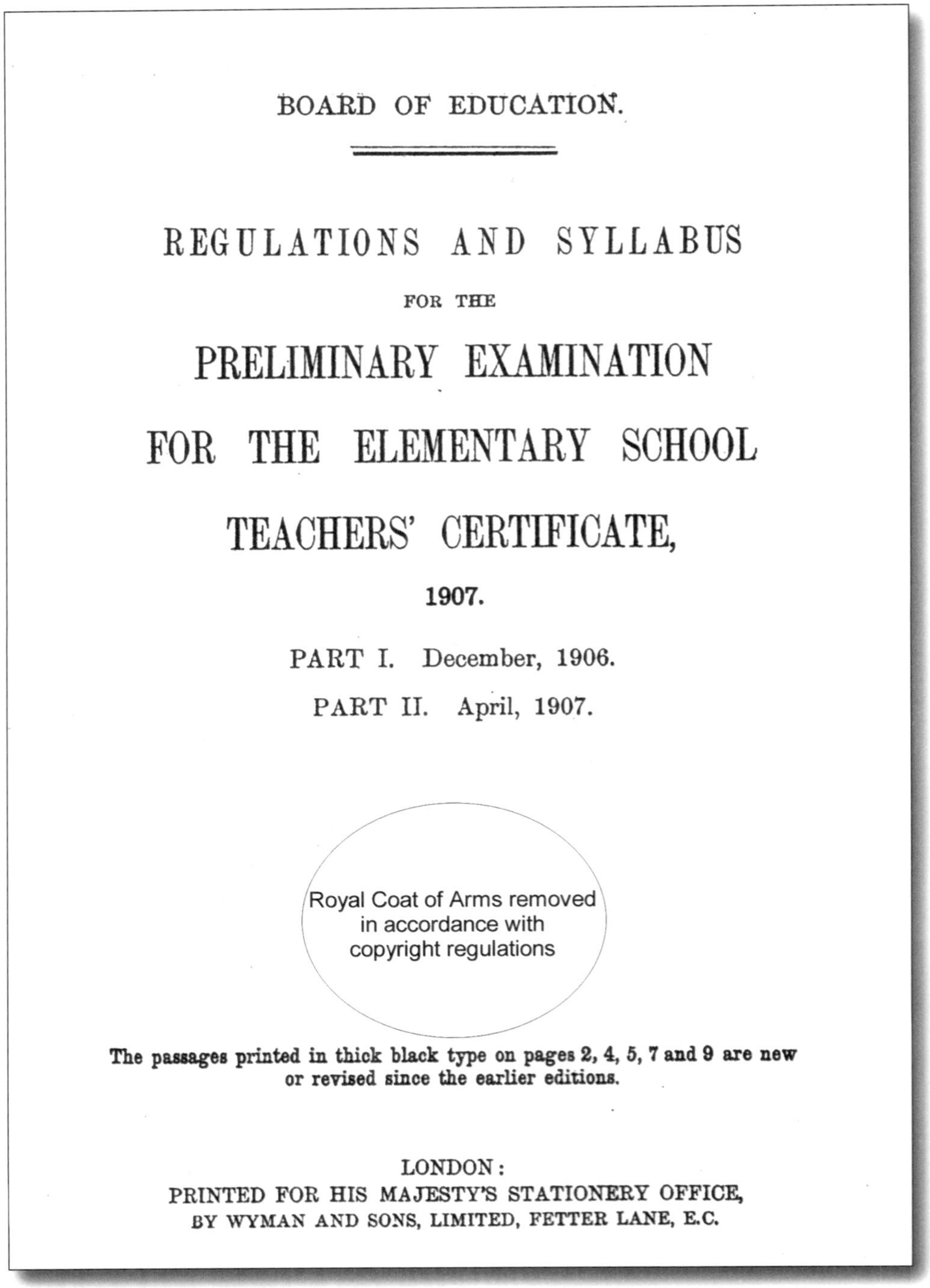

BOARD OF EDUCATION.

REGULATIONS AND SYLLABUS

FOR THE

PRELIMINARY EXAMINATION

FOR THE ELEMENTARY SCHOOL

TEACHERS' CERTIFICATE,

1907.

PART I.   December, 1906.

PART II.   April, 1907.

Royal Coat of Arms removed
in accordance with
copyright regulations

**The passages printed in thick black type on pages 2, 4, 5, 7 and 9 are new
or revised since the earlier editions.**

LONDON:
PRINTED FOR HIS MAJESTY'S STATIONERY OFFICE,
BY WYMAN AND SONS, LIMITED, FETTER LANE, E.C.

*Fig. 5 Front cover of Board of Education Regulations and Syllabus for the Preliminary Examination
for the Elementary School Teachers' Certificate. (Source: The National Archives ref.ED24/441)*

issue at the heart of the scandal was 'the issue of the modern world': on the one hand, a smooth and imposed efficiency offering quiescence, creature comforts, and security in exchange for servility, and on the other, spiritual freedom with all the risks and uncertainties that freedom for spiritual adventure implies. This suggests Mercier was a progressive thinker, a woman of ideas, not surprising given the evidence of her reading and writing, where she critically interpreted and re-oriented the ideas of prominent male thinkers towards girls' education and teacher training for women.[40] She was a reform-minded intellectual, moving on to lead Whitelands College and the Training College Association, and helping establish psychology and philosophy as foundation disciplines of teacher training.[41] She was awarded the OBE in 1933 for services to education.[42]

The scandal at City of Leeds Training College strikes us as a central problem, not only for historians of the education and training of teachers then and now, but for feminist and pro-feminist researchers,[43] especially those of us concerned with contemporary educational politics and policy debates where economic efficiency, not social inequalities, are the central concern.[44] Then as now, we must address ourselves to educational theory, research, policy and practice, and engage in critical analyses of the education and training debates, including the ideas that drive different teacher education policies and program constructions in different educational and socio-political contexts (**Figure 15**). These ideas have changed and developed over the course of a hundred years, but the task of negotiating professional expectations remains.

TEACHER EDUCATION 'NOW'

The Carnegie Faculty of Sport and Education takes carriage of teacher education, both initial teacher education (ITE) and continuing professional development (CPD).[45] A cursory glance at the marketing materials, including the handbook on undergraduate courses 2006-7 (**Figure 16**) and web-based advice from Leeds Met[46] (**Figure 17**), and the Training and Development Agency (TDA),[47] indicate what is required to secure a place in the undergraduate bachelor degree programs and Post Graduate Certificate of Education (PGCE) programs leading to Qualified Teacher Status (QTS). Advice provided to candidates for interview includes reference to the latest directions:[48]

CITY OF LEEDS TRAINING COLLEGE

CONDITIONS OF ADMISSION

CANDIDATES for admission to the College as Two Year Students must, as a rule, be over 18 years of age on the 1st of August in the year of admission to the College, and must have passed within two years and six months of their admission one of the qualifying Examinations set out in Appendix A (I. or II.) of the Regulations of the Board of Education for the training of Teachers.

The following are the principal qualifying Examinations :—

(a) The Preliminary Examination for the Certificate which is conducted by the Board of Education.

(b) The Matriculation Examination of the University of London and of the Joint Matriculation Board of the Universities of Manchester, Liverpool, Leeds, and Sheffield.

(c) The Cambridge Senior Local Examination and the Oxford Senior Local Examination.

BECKETT'S PARK   FAR   HEADINGLEY

Fig. 6 Extract from CLTC 1912 Handbook, Conditions of Admission. (Original copy held by Leeds Metropolitan University Archives)

CITY OF LEEDS TRAINING COLLEGE

HOME LIFE IN THE COLLEGE

THERE are eight Halls of Residence in close proximity to the Educational building, each under the supervision of a matron and two resident tutors.

The Halls of Residence are arranged in order to stimulate as far as possible the home feeling rather than the institutional feeling. Each student is provided with a Study Bedroom, so furnished that during the day it has the appearance of a sitting room. In addition to these private rooms each House possesses its Library, Dining Room, and Common Room. Students, therefore, have the advantage both of privacy in work and of opportunities of corporate life.

BECKETT'S PARK   FAR   HEADINGLEY

Fig. 8 Extract from CLTC 1912 Handbook, Home Life in the College. (Source: Leeds Metropolitan University Archives)

Telephone Nos. 234, 1240, 2352.

City of Leeds.

EDUCATION DEPARTMENT,

CALVERLEY STREET,

LEEDS.

15th May 1918.

Dear Sir (or Madam),

I have to inform you that you are appointed Trained Certificated Assistant Teacher under the Leeds Education Committee at a salary at the rate of £100 per annum.

It is understood that you will take up duty in any School to which you may be located, and the engagement may be terminated at any time by one month's notice on either side to expire on the last day of any calendar month.

Please complete and return the enclosed form of acceptance of appointment.

You will be informed in due course as to the School to which you are appointed.   Kindly inform me if you desire to be furnished with a list of apartments in the neighbourhood of the School to which you are appointed.

I am,
Yours faithfully,

Miss R. Ross.

James Graham

Secretary for Education.

P.S.   Clause (1) of Article 15 of the Elementary School Code is applicable to this appointment, namely :-

"The Teacher shall not be required to perform any duties except such as are connected with the work of a Public Elementary School, or to abstain, outside the school hours, from any occupations which do not interfere with the due performance of his duties as Teacher of a Public Elementary School".

Fig. 7 Letter of Appointment, 1918, Rachel Ross documents. (Original copies held by Leeds Metropolitan University Archives)

MR. GRAHAM'S "TALK" WITH THE STAFF.

RELATIONS OF TUTORS AND HOUSE-KEEPERS.

THE CONDUCT OF THE STUDENTS

The following are notes of Mr. Graham's "Talk with the Residential Staff as to Economy and Conduct in the working of the various Halls," to which references were made at the meeting of the Education Committee yesterday. We have inserted some cross-headings :—

The reason I have asked to see you is that owing to the war we are losing gardeners, firemen, and ronukers, and experiencing considerable difficulty in maintaining the domestic staff of the halls. The prices of foodstuffs have risen seriously, and the cost of everything we require in connection with the maintenance of the halls and of the work of the College generally has risen rapidly. With the help and cordial co-operation of the residential staff of the Training College, we feel convinced it is possible to go a very long way by preventing waste (without being stingy in the direction of all that is necessary), by preventing unnecessary work (without curtailing the reasonable liberty of the students), and by preventing avoidable damage to property, furniture, and equipment. Before adopting the policy of cutting down or reducing expenditure on the College on hard and fast lines, we want to see how much can be done by preventing waste, preventing unnecessary work, and preventing unnecessary damage. This will lead me to deal with many points, and to cover much ground. As this is the first time that I have met the whole of the staff who are particularly interested in the residential side of the work of the College, I think it advisable to touch upon a variety of questions which need your consideration if the object in view is to be accomplished.

Although the prices of foodstuffs have risen rapidly and the best English-fed butchers' meat is now very dear, and difficult to obtain, the Governors have decided that there shall be no tampering with the quality of the food, particularly butchers' meat, supplied to the hostels, and that, as the Governors do not eat margarine themselves, they will continue to supply the best fresh butter to the students. This has been the attitude of mind of the Governors throughout. With care and economy, the standard of quality can be maintained. The greatest economy should be exercised as regards food, and comparative food values should be carefully studied. It is the duty of resident tutors, as well as the housekeepers, especially at the present time, to see that there is no waste or extravagance at table. At breakfast, for instance, no student should be allowed to eat both butter and bacon. At all meals moderate helpings of food should be served in the first instance, as it is always possible to have a second helping, whereas if the first helping is more than can be eaten, what remains is waste. Considering the high price and scarcity of milk, it should be made clear that any one who does not intend to drink the whole of the allowance served in the morning should not take a sip and leave the rest. The provision of this morning milk costs something like £400 a year. If untasted the milk can be used for household purposes, otherwise it is wasted. In the main the milk is apparently appreciated, and as the portion for each person is small (about a quarter of a pint), there is no excuse for any being left.

SOME HOUSEHOLD MATTERS.

The Governors are always pleased to see students or staff entertaining visitors. It would, however, be a distinct gain if notice were always given to the housekeeper, in order that she may have reasonable time in which to provide the meals. If it is desired that visitors should stay overnight or for the week-end, the permission of the Principal and Vice-Principal should be obtained previously, and records should be made in the book provided for the purpose. This is not for the purpose of my personal scrutiny, but for the purpose of systematising official records.

A QUESTION OF RESPONSIBILITY.

The Chairman read a letter from a number of teachers and others in the employ of the Committee, stating that the resignation of Miss Mercier (the vice-principal) would be a serious loss to the educational work of the city and asking if pressure could be brought on Miss Mercier to withdraw her resignation. "Of course, that is quite impossible," the speaker added. He had promised to read a letter, signed by Mrs. Kitson Clark as secretary, from the Yorkshire Ladies' Council of Education. This letter viewed with grave anxiety the statements made in the Press concerning the staff of the College, stating that a woman of the eminence of Miss Mercier was not likely to resign without grave reason, and continued: "The Training College is an institution of national importance, and being a college for the training of teachers any lowering of its aims must be widely felt in the education of women and children throughout the country. Under the circumstances we are calling an emergency meeting of our Executive to consider whether there is any action which we can usefully take in this connection." He had given an assurance in reply that there was no intention on the Committee's part of allowing the aims of the College to be lowered in any way whatever. The Chairman went on to say that he could understand the grievances of the tutors if they were responsible to Mr. Graham; but they were responsible to the vice-principal and the principal. Looking at the question impartially, he thought it was an ideal method to have the business person responsible to the business head and the educational staff responsible to the educational head, and he did not see how any friction could arise. When he asked the tutors to "pin" themselves to any portion of Mr. Graham's address they did not do so.

THE DISCUSSION OF OUTSIDE SUBJECTS.

As far as he could see, the Chairman remarked, the work of the College was to fit teachers for their future educational career; it was not the discussing of outside subjects in educational lectures and the putting of one side only by a teacher. If a matter were to be discussed it could be done in debating societies, which were formed for that purpose, where the "pro" and the "anti" might be put. "If they want to thrash out a subject like woman's suffrage or the abolition of breach of promise, let them do it in debating societies," the speaker added.

Mrs. Connon: Has that been done?

The Chairman: It is just as much a short time since we had to stop a Socialist society in one of these halls.

Mr. Escritt: Shame!

The Chairman: It is just as much a shame as if we stopped a Conservative society. I should stop it as well. The Chairman continued that he had heard it stated by ladies outside that Mr. Graham said they were not to join any outside societies. Mr. Graham had not said anything of the sort. "As a matter of ordinary administration, we have no alternative but to accept these resignations," the Chairman said. "If we do not, all control of our College and policy will have gone. There is no reason why the members of the Higher Education Committee should not go to their hearts' content into the question of the constitution of the College, and the way it is worked. All the information is before you. You must accept these resignations, because there is no good reason for them, and we cannot be left in the lurch by people who are not loyal."

Mrs. Hudson agreed that the Committee should accept the resignations, but she thought that in order to justify themselves in the eyes of the public, it would be wise for the Committee to start an inquiry into the matter.

Alderman J. R. Ford agreed with Alderman Kinder's observations, but felt that there was something behind the trouble which ought to be investigated. He could not support the amendment, because he thought they would be in a false position if they did not accept the resignations. The tutors should have made a formal protest before taking action.

Alderman Kinder, in replying to the discussion, said he had never been a party to any "hole and corner" meeting. He agreed with Mr. Graham that the Committee were responsible to the public, but they were not responsible to eight teachers. The latter were responsible to the Committee, and if they chose to relieve themselves of responsibility without any cause there was only one course open to the Committee. He did not agree that trouble would arise out of this question; he believed they were getting rid of it. He had no objection to the whole scheme of administration at the Training College being placed before the Higher Education Committee, even at the next meeting, if it were possible to be ready then. He only made one condition—that none of the disaffected ones should be asked any questions—because he was not going to put in a defence before he had a statement of claim. Two of the signatories to the document of resignations had lived in the same hall for twelve months, and had not spoken to one another.

The amendment was rejected by nine votes to four, the minutes being then confirmed.

Fig. 10 *James Graham's talk to the staff,* Yorkshire Post, *29 June 1916. (Source: Leeds Metropolitan University Archives)*

1909

MERCIER, WINIFRED LOUISE: *b.* 20 May 1878, at Ilford; *dau.* of Lewis Mercier, of Huguenot ancestry, and Agnes Stedman. *Educ.* Wynaud House Sch., Bower Park; Maria Grey Tr. Coll. 1897–99; Camb. Teachers' Cert. 1899; Somerville Coll., Oxford, 1904–07; Margaret Evans Hist. Prize 1905; Hons. Mod. Hist., Cl. I, 1907; M.A. (Oxon.) 1921. A.M., St George's Sch., Edinburgh, 1899–1904; Hist. M., Manchester H. Sch. 1904–09; Res. Lecturer and Director of Studies in Hist. and Econ., Girton, 1909–13; Vice-Principal, Leeds Municipal Tr. Coll. 1913–17; Lecturer in Educ. and Tutor to Secondary Tr. Students, Univ. of Manchester, 1917–18; Principal of Whitelands Tr. Coll. 1918–34. F.R.Hist.Soc.; Member of Council, Hist. Soc. 1928–31; Member of the Archbishops' first Cttee. of Enquiry into the Teaching Office of the Church 1917; Pres. of the Tr. Coll. Assoc. 1919, 1927; Member of Exec. of Central Council for Sch. Broadcasting and Chairman of its Sci. Cttee. 1929. O.B.E. 1933. See *Who was who 1929–40*; *Somerville Coll. Register*; Lynda Grier, *The life of Winifred Mercier* (O.U.P. 1937).

Died 2 Sept. 1934. (n.c.)

Fig. 9 *Winifred Mercier Biography from 1909 Girton Review. (Source: Girton College library, Cambridge)*

All courses leading to Qualified Teacher Status must fulfil the standards for the award . . . The standards are grouped under three headings: Professional Attributes (Relationships with children and young people; Frameworks; Communicating and working with others; Personal professional development); Professional knowledge and understanding (Teaching and learning; Assessment and monitoring; Subjects and curriculum; Literacy, numeracy and ICT; Achievement and diversity; Health and well-being); and Professional skills (Planning; Teaching; Assessing, monitoring and giving feedback; Reviewing teaching and learning; Learning environment; Team working and collaboration).

This sort of edict typifies the current system of government regulation and bureaucratic control of teacher education, put in place after decades of reform to the structure and content of teacher education, subject to different legislation. The most recent is the Education Act 2005.[49] Contemporary theorists Furlong et al[50] ascribed such reforms to the phenomenon of teacher education becoming a key issue of government educational policy with a dramatic increase in central control, given the establishment of the Council for the Accreditation of Teacher Education (CATE) and subsequent modifications, the revision of conventional training courses including government specification of course content, along with the development of largely school-based 'articled teacher' and 'licensed teacher' routes to QTS. The system has been marked by ideological struggle,[51] and more recently, by further radical reform with the abolition of CATE and the establishment of the Teacher Training Agency (TTA), now called the Training and Development Agency (TDA), which took over the functions of CATE and the funding of ITE in England, plus the development of the new inspection framework for ITE from the Office for Standards in Education (Ofsted), ending the articled teacher scheme and the establishment of school-centred teacher training (SCITT) schemes. Furlong et al posited these policy initiatives were framed with the explicit aspiration of changing the nature of teacher professionalism, and with it, to influence the nature of professional knowledge, skills and values.[52]

Currently Carnegie Faculty is contracted by the TDA to supply 263 qualified teachers, given the 2007 intake, with funding tied to targets, a prescribed national curriculum[53] and standards for ITE,[54] including school partnerships, and accountability through Ofsted inspections.[55] Once candidates satisfy the TDA's Trainee Entry requirements and make an application for either full- or part-time study through the Universities and Colleges Admissions Service (UCAS) and the Graduate Teacher Training Registry (GTTR), they are subject to a competitive selection process, including interview and an English proficiency exercise. If successful, a formal offer of acceptance is made (**Figure 18**), but the offer of place is conditional upon satisfying a medical questionnaire and criminal records check. Students are provided with a Leeds Met student handbook (**Figure 19**) and Carnegie Faculty course handbook (**Figure 20**), and while attendance is not compulsory, the expectation is that students provide evidence that they meet the Standards set out by the TDA.[56] Students are also advised that in order to become a qualified teacher, they must pass the TDA Skills Test, and preparation is provided throughout the course.

Carnegie Faculty enjoys an excellent reputation, locally, nationally and internationally, and in 2007 attracted 3,382 applications

Fig. 11
Example of public call for Inquiry. (Source: Courtesy of Special Collections, Leeds University Library, mark MS1343)

Fig. 12
Telegram to Secretary of Leeds Education Board informing of Committee of Enquiry. (Source: Courtesy of Special Collections, Leeds University Library, mark MS1343)

No. 4.

BOARD OF EDUCATION.

CITY OF LEEDS TRAINING COLLEGE.

REPORT TO THE BOARD OF EDUCATION on the system under which the City of Leeds Training College is controlled and managed, with special reference to the recent resignations of members of the staff.

SUMMARY.

1. In accordance with our instructions we went to Leeds and opened an inquiry on Tuesday, August 15th, into the system under which the City of Leeds Training College is controlled and managed, with special reference to the recent resignations of members of the staff. The inquiry was held in the Council Hall and extended over seven days, viz., August 15–18 and 22–24 (inclusive). By direction of the Board the proceedings were private, and were attended only by Governors of the College, members of the Local Education Authority, the Secretary for Education, the Principal, the late Vice-Principal and the Tutors, including the Tutors who had resigned, and the House-keepers of the Halls of Residence. In the course of the inquiry we heard evidence from the Chairman of the Education Committee, the Chairman and other members of the Governing Body, the Secretary for Education, the Principal of the College, Miss Mercier (the late Vice-Principal), the members of the staff who had resigned, other Tutors (men and women) still in the service of the College, some of the Housekeepers of the Halls of Residence, and an ex-student. We desire to take this opportunity of acknowledging the readiness shown by the Chairman, Vice-Chairman, members and officials of the Local Education Authority to assist us in every way.

The Chairman of the Education Committee, at the opening of the proceedings, stated that in view of the public interest which had arisen his Committee welcomed the inquiry, and that they would give us every possible facility to pursue it. This assurance was amply fulfilled. Nothing was lacking to the efficiency of the arrangements made by the City for the convenient transaction of business, or to the readiness of its representatives to comply fully with any desire which we expressed for information upon any point.

Origin of the Inquiry.

2. The City of Leeds Training College for Elementary Teachers was founded in 1907. It was begun in temporary premises and on a comparatively small scale ; but from the first the Authority made it clear that in this exercise of their powers under the Education Act, 1902, they were determined to spare neither trouble nor expense in order to establish a College worthy of the best traditions of a great municipality, and fitted to play an important part in the system of national education. In point of size the College was designed to be, with one exception, the largest Training College for Elementary Teachers in England : its full complement of students was to be 180 men and 300 women. Its permanent buildings, which were planned and equipped

A (33)1545 Pk 50 125 10/16 E & S   A

Fig. 13 Front cover Board of Education Report. (Source: Leeds Metropolitan University Archives)

for the 263 places (**Figure 21**). It has the highest application rate in the university, 13:1 overall in teacher education, and has sustained its market position as a national provider, but also locally and regionally.[57] Successive Ofsted inspections have returned positive reports, noting the professionalism and commitment of student teachers, the excellence of ICT, library and other resources and competences using them; the high quality of student teachers' planning, management and organisational skills; the strengths of partnership relationships and communication with a wide range of schools and agencies, and forward thinking about the *Every Child Matters* developments, peer involvement with mentors, teacher fellows and school-based research. Such records provide contemporary evidence of the regulatory work in teacher education, which dovetails with the reform and regulation of teaching standards in schools, the National Curriculum, testing and accountability, league tables, and teacher appraisals.[58]

Carnegie Faculty is also building international links, with collaborative work being negotiated with France, Australia and Jordan,[59] which speaks to the intention to develop not only a distinctive brand of research-informed teaching for both academics and graduates but also a research program in the light of international comparative work on models of teacher education, including quality teaching, inclusion and equity implications, multi-agency work, and globalisation. The organisational structure of Teacher and Research (T&R) groups is intended to facilitate this work. Inspired by Boyer,[60] the directed focus is on defining and rewarding work expectations in academic groups who share the same or similar subject matter knowledge expertise, to be updated and refreshed regularly through scholarly activity undertaken by an 'intellectual community' of scholars.[61] Other Carnegie Faculty initiatives include the establishment of the teacher fellows program (**Figure 22**), the ITE freshers' residential experience (**Figure 23**), and international school placements, all intended to ensure innovative work.

In a similar vein, Carnegie Faculty academics[62] concerned with debates on the nature and complexities of ITE reform, teacher professionalism, and the student teacher experience have established the Research in Initial Teacher Education (RITE) group. This is intended to support theorisations of policies like *Teaching for the C21st*, *Every Child Matters* and *Sure Start*, the new National Curriculum, pedagogies and assessment, school partnerships, and our existing approaches to program construction in view of local, national and international research. The RITE group is also keen to support Faculty through the shift into the proposed new era of Ofsted inspections and internal academic review cycles (formerly called revalidation), which both generate huge amounts of documentation and data ripe for critical analyses feeding into staff research projects, publications, and policy-making[63] (**Figure 24**).

This sort of work reflects our efforts at what contemporary commentator Michael Young[64] called the 'reflexive modernization' of teacher education, particularly extending the process of *public learning* about teacher education, both initial teacher education and lifelong learning. The RITE group has made meaningful links with the Carnegie Research Institute, Carnegie Leaders in Learning, and

Fig. 14 Morant, model for W. B. Richmond's The Redeemer in St Paul's Cathedral. (Source: Jarrold Publishing)

Below left, Fig. 15 Conference flier for centenary event, International Women's Day, 2007. (Source: Carnegie Faculty Marketing Manager Michael Ainsworth)

Below right, Fig. 16 Extract from Leeds Met handbook on undergraduate courses 2006-7. (Source: Carnegie Faculty archives)

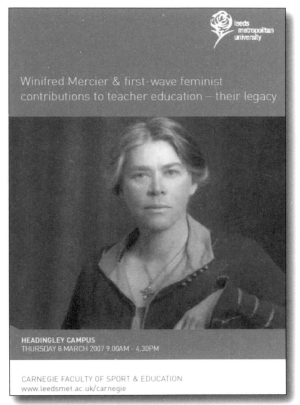

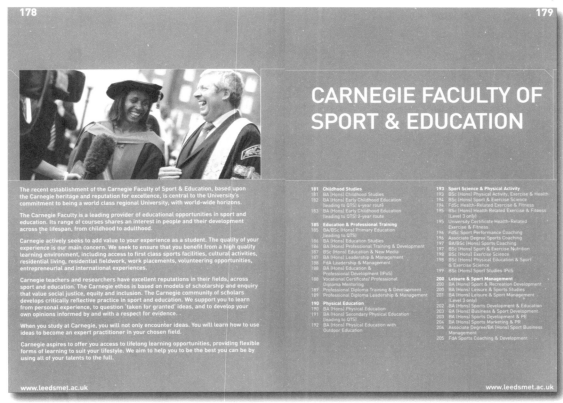

pan-university research groups, and built strategic research partnerships with local schools, Education Leeds, and other universities. At issue are joint interests in the concept of teacher learning and development and its form and content in the pre-service and in-service settings, but also the conceptualisations of school work and the bringing together of teachers' professional knowledge and academic research knowledge through teacher research in communities of learning.[65]

Taking a cue from such research and the scholarship of teaching and learning, Carnegie Faculty work can be summarised as preparing teachers to be professionals of the future.[66] The Leeds Met submission to the Qualifications and Curriculum Authority (QCA) *Futures* project[67] spelled this out, noting a national conversation must be seen in relation to a future British society and a global society, both witness to the meta-transformation of the economy, politics and statehood. Quoted three times in the QCA report, our concern was to draw attention to many options for the future, guided by a social theory and a theory of social change, in what is sometimes called the second modernity[68] (**Figure 25**).

The Carnegie Faculty 'reflexive modernization' of teacher

Fig. 17
Sample of Leeds Met Web info. re BA Primary Education

Right, Fig. 18
Current Leeds Met letter on formal offer of acceptance. (Source: Carnegie Faculty admissions office)

COURSE DETAILS

BA(Hons) Primary Education - Full-time

UCAS CODE: X120 BAQ/UPR

BANNER CODE: QPREB/F - FT

ENTRY REQUIREMENTS:
Click Here for General Entry Requirements
220 points
160 points
International Baccalaureate Diploma: 28 points.
You need to show evidence of attainment in ICT. Evidence is sought of work experience with children in the 5-11 age range.
GCSE (or equivalent) passes are required in English Language, Mathematics and a science.
Checks on applicants' medical fitness and a lack of criminal records are made after they have been offered a place.
Please be aware that you will be required to attend an interview as part of the selection process.
NOTE:
Please be aware that this course is currently undergoing a module review.

Course Content
This degree in Primary Education is available as a full time and a part time course, leading to Qualified Teacher status. The four year full time course provides students with a broad range of experiences in preparation for primary teaching including a practical component in school during each year of study. This includes experience in at least two key stages. The part time route enables students to access the same course content but on a more flexible basis.

All students access core modules in English, Maths and Science to develop subject knowledge in preparation for primary teaching.

Level 1
Modules include: Professional Values, Knowledge and Practice, English, Mathematics, Science, Curriculum Studies and subject elective modules.

Level 2
Modules include: Professional Values, Knowledge and Practice, English, Mathematics, Science, Curriculum Studies and subject elective modules.

Level 3
Modules include: Professional Values, Knowledge and Practice, Managing the Learning Process in the Core Subjects, Educational Developments and Initiatives, Dissertation and subject elective modules.

Assessment
A variety of teaching methods and approaches are used, including lectures, seminars, workshops, small group tutorials and individual tutorials. Each module is assessed usually by written assignment, presentation or practical activity, for which support is available for all students.

Career Opportunities
The vast majority of students completing this course become primary school teachers. To become a qualified teacher, students must also pass the Training and Development Agency Skills Tests, for which preparation is given throughout the course. Alternative career opportunities include positions in schools and other educational settings, eg within the area of learning support.

VACANCIES
NOTE: This Section is only available inside Leeds Met
Vacancies available: No
Def apps accepted: Yes
PT mode details: N/A
Modules: N/A

KEY FACTS
Faculty: Carnegie Faculty of Sport & Education
School: Education and Professional Training
Programme: QPREB
Place of study: Headingley Campus
Length of study: 4 years
Start dates: September
Term dates: See student calendar
Graduate employability: 73.1% of graduates in employment or further study within six months.
Intake: 144
How to apply: Apply through UCAS.

COURSE LINKS
Related Courses
BA(Hons) Physical Education
PGCE Primary
Course Keywords
Education
Education (Primary)
Education (Teacher Training)
ITT
QTS
Teacher Training
Teaching

COURSE CONTACTS
Frazer Shelton(Course Administrator)
F.Shelton@leedsmet.ac.uk 0113 283 2600 ext 27490

Paula Kearton(Course Administrator)
P.Kearton@leedsmet.ac.uk 0113 283 2600 ext 23519

Paul Hurst(Admissions Tutor)
P.J.Hurst@leedsmet.ac.uk 0113 283 2600 ext 23544

Peter D'Sena(Course Leader)
P.DSena@leedsmet.ac.uk 0113 283 2600 ext 23553

Course Enquiries
Leeds Metropolitan University
Civic Quarter
Leeds
LS1 3HE

Tel: 0113 283 3113
Fax: 0113 283 3148

Carnegie Faculty of Sport & Education

Carnegie Hall   Tel: 0113 283 2600
Headingley Campus   Fax: 0113 283 7410
Beckett Park   Web: www.leedsmet.ac.uk
Leeds LS6 3QS

1 March 2007

Dear

Re: BA (Hons) Primary Education Leading to the Award of Qualified Teacher Status (age range 5 – 11)

Thank you for attending an interview; I trust you found it a worthwhile and enjoyable experience.

I am pleased to inform you that we are making you an offer of a place on your chosen course. The full details of the offer will be sent to you via UCAS in the near future but in the meantime the following summary might assist you with your career planning:

220 UCAS Tariff Points to include 160 points from 2 six or 1 twelve unit award
Health and Police Check

We hope you will continue to manage your studies successfully and achieve your predicted grades in the forthcoming examinations – may I wish you good luck.

Additionally, looking ahead to you joining a course of Initial Teacher Training, we offer a personal action plan with an identified target for you to work on and record your progress before you start the course. We intend to use this in the initial stages of your training at Leeds Met and hope you will find it useful as professional development wherever you choose to commence your studies.

Yours sincerely

Paul Hurst
Assistant Director of Undergraduate Studies

Enc: Post Interview Personal Target and Development Plan

PS If you do choose to take up this offer at Leeds Metropolitan University and there is a little 'blip' in your results in August – **do** contact Frazer Shelton or Paula Kearton, Programme Administrators, on 0113 2837490 or 0113 2832600 ext 3519 before contacting other institutions or Clearing. We **may** still be interested in you.

ACADEMIC CALENDAR   000

Academic calendar

Many students in the professions, especially in health, education and law, work through the calendar year, as do many postgraduate students. This academic year, the University is introducing short summer schools. Planned for both early and late summer, these are intended to create flexibility for as many students as possible to take one module in an intensive four week period, in early or late summer, in addition to the two traditional twelve week semesters which each have associated periods for assessment. In Harrogate, a three term system reflects the travel arrangements of public transport.

Dates of significance for many students are the following:

HIGHER EDUCATION STUDENTS

University semesters - 2006/07
Semester 1:
Monday 25 September 2006 -
Friday 19 January 2007
Semester 2:
Monday 22 January 2007 -
Friday 1 June 2007

Standard full-time and sandwich attendance dates:
18 September 2006 - 15 December 2006
8 January 2007 - 30 March 2007
23 April 2007 - 1 June 2007

FURTHER EDUCATION STUDENTS:
LEEDS MET HARROGATE

Autumn term:
11 September 2006 - 15 December 2006
Spring term:
2 January 2007 - 30 March 2007
Summer term:
16 April 2007 - 6 July 2007

Full-time students have the following reading weeks:
23-27 October 2006
12-16 February 2007
28 May - 1 June 2007

Graduation ceremonies
Winter Graduation will take place on Thursday 23 and Friday 24 November 2006. Summer Graduation – the provisional date for this is week commencing 16 July 2007.

THE COURSE HANDBOOK FOR

BA/BSc (Hons) Primary Education (Leading to Qualified Teacher Status)

Level 1/Year 1

2006-2007

Carnegie Faculty of Sport and Education

Admissions Data 2006/07 UCAS/GTTR - QTS Data

UCAS Code	PROGRAM Code	Course Title	Target	Total Number of Applications to Date
XC16	QBSPE	BA (Hons) Secondary Physical Education (leading to QTS)	30	391
X9C6	QPGSP	PGCE Secondary Physical Education (leading to QTS)	20	302
X110	QECPB	BA (Hons) Early Childhood Education (leading to QTS)	60	382
X111	ECPBQ	BA (Hons) Early Childhood Education (leading to QTS) 2 Year Route	15	86
X121	ECEPG	PGCE Early Childhood Education (leading to QTS)	22	192
X120	QPREB/QPBSC	BA/BSc (Hons) Primary Education (leading to QTS)	104	1550
X100	PGPEQ	PGCE Primary Education (leading to QTS)	12	479
		TOTALS	**263**	**3382**

Above left, Fig. 19 Extract from current Leeds Met Student Handbook. (Source: Carnegie Faculty office)

Above right, Fig. 20 Carnegie Faculty Course Handbook. (Source: Carnegie Faculty courses office)

Fig. 21 Spreadsheet on current applications for places. (Source: Carnegie Faculty courses office)

Fig. 22 Advert for Teacher Fellowship Opportunity. (Source: Carnegie Faculty Human Resources office)

education sits well with the Leeds Met statement[69] on the vision of a Great North Uni, combining mass participation and world-class performances with the intention to be, among other things:

A healthy, ethical, environmentally-friendly and sustainable community which values well-being, diversity, taking risks as pace-setters, the efficient and imaginative use of our resources, good governance and professionalism.

CONCLUSION

The stories and plot lines of the education and training of teachers 'then' at the City of Leeds Training College one hundred years ago and 'now' in the Carnegie Faculty expose similarities, differences and lines of continuity. Despite the years and the passage of time, a constant seems to be a genuine concern for the professional experiences provided for young people wanting to be teachers.[70] There have been many changes to policies and programs but the task of constructing a new generation of teachers with adequate knowledge, skills and values is the ever-present challenge. The supply and demand for teachers during the 20th and 21st centuries has been a constant influence on teacher education provision, as has been that old chestnut – a training or an education for teachers resulting in a complete 'workforce reform'.[71]

In closing, it is difficult to go past the conclusions of educational historian Eric Eaglesham,[72] echoed by Winifred Mercier and others more recently, about political power and administrative control, and the urgency to make education as independent of politics as considerations of public finances will allow. Behind the politicians, bureaucrats and administrators are children and young people whose paramount need is expert, unbiased teaching. We concur and acknowledge teacher educators with a keen sense of professionalism who must deliver on the complex tasks of teacher preparation for work in different and diverse school communities in England and beyond, but also for democracy and a peaceful but equitable and just global society. This is something that requires our diligence, now and in the future.

Thanks to Professor Anne Campbell, Dr Julia Lawrence, and Iain Poole for valuable inputs and critical feedback on this chapter.

Fig. 23 Photo ITE Freshers' residential in the Lake District. (Source: LeedsMet. Communications: Icon Photography. October 2006)

Making sense of 'disadvantage' through professional dialogue

This symposium brings together teacher and academic partners working in an urban school in Leeds, England, who report on a whole-school teacher learning and development project that is geared towards helping staff think critically about what to do to tailor a school improvement program in a challenging school. We engage both descriptive and critical analyses of urban schools and particular issues of concern, the 'Patterns for learning' project as a pilot study, and the implications for teacher education. The intention is to share our experiences of what it takes to move past generic school improvement responses to work with staff, through professional conversations about their lived experiences, their commitments, and developing self-determined teacher research projects that are clustered around issues of concern. It connects, theoretically and practically, with work done in disadvantaged schools in Australia.

Mixed messages in urban schools
Jill Wood

This paper reports one headteacher's perspective on the urban challenges in inner-city schools in England's north, from the particularities of staff practices in different schools, community and social contexts, to national policy directions and funding streams to support staff learning and development. It highlights the policy requirements and what these mean for staff – management, teachers and teaching assistants – set against the background of practitioners' critical urban educational concerns. The paper draws on English and Australian literature to shed light on practitioner research being developed in one Leeds school to support staff make sense of the their work given different policy messages about what they need to be doing.

'Patterns for learning' project
Jon Tan

This paper reports on the experiences of academic partners working with staff on a pilot study in an inner-city Leeds school to articulate their critical urban educational concerns and the theories that inform their practices. It begins with what it means to build a school-university partnership that empowers school staff to engage in professional conversations about the urban school setting and urban education, leading to staff developing a shared language for discussing and acting on issues of concern, theoretical analyses, and teacher research projects that draw on English and Australian literature. It follows with a progress report on the developmental activities engaged to support staff learning, teacher research, the school's improvement plan, and learning outcomes, especially for students.

Tough teaching in teacher education
Lori Beckett

This paper reports on the teacher education implications of staff professional learning and development sessions done in English and Australian urban schools, where academic and teacher partners worked together to jointly investigate the complexities of teachers' work and initiate school-based research. The focus is on evidence trails in the form of school data, documents and policies, classroom observations, and interviews with school staff as well as pre-service teacher education programs. The analyses highlight the need for teacher educators to take into account the experience of teaching in schools marked by structural disadvantage, poverty, oppression and exclusion in the pre-service and in-service teacher education settings. Ideally, there needs to be seamless continuity in professional learning so that student teachers and newly qualified teachers are prepared for the challenging experiences of teaching in tough schools.

Play needs to be reinstated as a form of creative expression across the primary age range; its erosion has diminished learning opportunities. Creativity is the springboard for innovation.

Leeds Metropolitan University

This is not simply about redefining new knowledge contents, but rather about the complexities of new forms of knowledge, including emerging knowledge, and the knowledge and learning needed to negotiate the challenges of the global age.

Leeds Metropolitan University

There should be less focus on teaching institutions and structures (schools, colleges, etc) and more focus on building truly cross-regional, cross-national equitable learning opportunities and outcomes available to pupils regardless of their social and family background, geographical location and other social markers.

Leeds Metropolitan University

ENDNOTES

[1] This title is taken from an article by Mercier (1923) The education and training of teachers, *Education Forum*, vol.1, pp. 78-81, which speaks to on-going debates about teacher training versus teacher education. See note on education and training in chapter on School Partnerships by Jill Adam and Anne Campbell, who report that the Universities Council for the Education of Teachers (UCET) recently agreed to use Initial Teacher Education and Training (ITET).

[2] City of Leeds Training College (*c*.1912) Handbook (original copy held by Lori Beckett). See City of Leeds Training College (n.d) temporary prospectus (original copy held by West Yorkshire Archive Service [WYAS] ref.WYL863/7S).

[3] City of Leeds Training College (n.d) *Coming of Age Celebrations Souvenir Handbook 1907-1928* (original copy held by Leeds Metropolitan University Archives).

[4] Different sources noted the details of student enrolment numbers. See City of Leeds Training College ibid and Pickering, H. S. (n.d) Part 1 1907-1933, in *A Short History of The City of Leeds Training College 1907-1957* (original copy held by Leeds Metropolitan University Archives).

[5] Article titled Leeds Training College. Official Opening. *The Yorkshire Post, Saturday,* 14 June 1913.

[6] This is a phrase used by Edwards, Gilroy and Hartley (2002) in *Rethinking Teacher Education* (RoutledgeFalmer) to describe a sense of negotiating a series of ambivalences – and indeed outright contradictions – in professional life, which produced an uncomfortable feeling of inconsistency between what was professed through teaching and writing and the lived experience in a department of teacher education. This seems most apt, given the conflicts and contestations at the time.

[7] This was described by Janet Douglas in the chapter, The Genesis of the City of Leeds Training College.

[8] Eaglesham, E. (1956) *From School Board to Local Authority* (Oxford).

[9] Leeds School Board (1899) *Yearbook* (original copy held by Leeds Metropolitan University Archives).

[10] See image of Instructions to Pupil Teachers, in Jill Adam and Anne Campbell's chapter on partnerships.

[11] Simon, B. (1965) *Education and the labour movement, 1870-1920, London, Lawrence and Wishart* p. 118.

[12] Ibid.

[13] See chapter 8 on Teaching methods, Pedagogies and Professional Learning by Lori Beckett and Jon Tan, who documents the traditional whole-class didactic teaching style, as described by Edwards et al (2002) op.cit.

[14] Grier, L. (1937) *The Life of Winifred Mercier* (Oxford University Press).

[15] Board of Education (1907) *Regulations and Syllabus for the Preliminary Examination for the Elementary School Teachers' Certificate* (original copy held by The National Archives ref: ED 24/441). These regulations are noted, and an image shown, in Beckett et al's following chapter on curriculum.

[16] City of Leeds Training College op.cit.

[17] Ibid.

[18] Pickering, author of Part 1 of the *Short History,* noted lectures of one hour duration from 9am to 1pm, with no break on the timetable.

[19] Given evidence from staff lists of responsibilities printed in the prospectus and handbooks. Lori Beckett et al report on the details of the Training College curriculum in the next chapter.

[20] This facet of teacher training is described in the preceding chapter on school partnerships by Jill Adam and Anne Campbell.

[21] Op.cit.

[22] These included Mercier's teacher training at Maria Gray Training College, teaching experience at St.George's School, Edinburgh and The Manchester Girls' High School, interrupted by her studies at Somerville College, Oxford. At the time of her appointment to City of Leeds Training College, Mercier held the post of Director of Studies in History and Economics and Lecturer in History at Girton College, Cambridge.

[23] According to Grier, these included a reorganisation of the library, curriculum development for women students wanting to be infants teachers, separate from teachers of the upper school, and schemes for a third-year course for both men and women. Her major concerns were to strengthen the intellectual life of the College, further develop the curriculum to accommodate more variety, invite guest lecturers to talk on topics such as economic conditions of the war, and encourage students to undertake social work in the community as well as school appointments further afield.

[24] One set is held in the Leeds Metropolitan University Archives, and another in the Connell papers held by Special Collections, Brotherton Library, Leeds University (ref: MS 1343; Shelf Mark 93/032).

[25] See *Journal of Education* (1916) August, pp. 451-452 on The Leeds Training College; September, p. 504 on Leeds Training College; *Journal of Education* (1917) January, p. 11 on The Leeds Training College; March p. 137 on The Leeds Training College; April, p. 199 on The Leeds Training College; August, p. 465 Jottings on James Graham's appointment; September, pp. 508-509 on The Association of Headmistresses' protest and p. 516 Jottings on James Graham's appointment; November, p. 645 on Leeds – the latest not the last; also Journal of Education (1918) February, p. 75 on The Leeds Training College; October, p. 604 on Parsons' re-appointment.

[26] *Journal of Education* ibid; *Yorkshire Post* articles in scrapbooks, ibid; Pickering ibid.

[27] Copy held in the Leeds Metropolitan University Archives.

[28] Grier (1937) op.cit., p.140.

[29] See Introduction to Grier (1937), op.cit.

[30] Original copy in Connell papers op.cit.; typed copy done for the Board of Education Inquiry held in the Leeds Metropolitan University Archives.

[31] Original copy in Connell papers op.cit.

[32] Original copy in Connell papers op.cit.

[33] Pickering op.cit.

[34] The Board of Education report on the National Enquiry p. 23 indicated that partisans of the Principal referred to the women as feminists. Graham's letter to Kinder dated 13 September 1916 (original held in Connell papers, op.cit.) claimed Mercier's evidence to the Inquiry was pure fabrication. In writing the history, Pickering (op.cit.) reported the controversies on Mercier, but suggested p. 18 co-education was the issue and that Principals, staff and students rejected what Mercier stood for. Similarly, Meyer (1985) indicated a partisan view in his report (see *Introduction to the Papers of the Leeds Education Authority [1903-60],* copy held by Leeds Metropolitan University Archives). He claimed the College was an institution for women during WW1, where difficulties arose in connection with the discipline of the girls in training and the behaviour of some of the lady tutors. Further, Meyer suggested his disagreement with the findings of the National Inquiry. 'Whether or not a candid and rational investigation of the evidence bears out these judgements can regrettably not be stated in a neutral Introduction.'

[35] *Journal of Education* op.cit.

[36] In Grier, op.cit.

[37] See Palmer, J. A. (ed) (2001) *Fifty Major Thinkers on Education.* London and New York: Routledge, pp. 143-45.

[38] Eaglesham op.cit.

[39] In Grier, op.cit.

[40] See Mercier (1923) op.cit.; also Mercier, W. (1909) An Experiment in the Teaching of History. *The Historical Association,* Leaflet no.17, June; (1919) President's Address to Training College Association. *Journal of Experimental Pedagogy and Training College Record,* Vol.5, no.1, March; (1924) The Children of England. Critical Notices. *The Forum of Education,* Vol.11; (1928a) The Training College Curriculum. The Forum of Education, vol.V1, no.1, February; (1928b) Prologue in Davis, V. (ed) *The Matter and Method of Modern Teaching* (Cartright and Rattray).

[41] Mercier was on the Editorial Board of *The Forum of Education*. See article on The Future of 'The Forum of Education', Vol.111, No.3, November 1930, which advised on the development of the journal, given the British Psychological Association approached the Training College Association with a proposal for a new journal, called *The British Journal of Educational Psychology.*

[42] Medals and citation held in Whitelands Archives, Roehampton University.

[43] See Purvis, J. (1985) Reflections Upon Doing Historical Documentary Research From a Feminist Perspective. Chapter 7 in Burgess, R. G. (ed) *Strategies of Educational Research: Qualitative Methods* (The Falmer Press).

[44] See the Series editors' preface, by Weiler, K., Weiner, G., and Yates, L., to Lingard, B. and Douglas, P. (1999) *Men Engaging Feminisms.* Buckingham and Philadelphia: Open University Press; also Coffey, A. and Delamont, S. (2000) *Feminism and the Classroom Teacher. Research, Praxis and Pedagogy.* London and New York: Routledge Falmer.

[45] The City of Leeds Training College (which became the City of Leeds College of Education, following the re-designation recommendations of the Robbins Report in 1963) merged with Carnegie College in 1968 to become the City of Leeds and Carnegie College. This in turn, following the James Report, merged with Leeds Polytechnic Department of Education and James Graham College to form the Department of Education in the new Leeds Polytechnic in 1976. The department became a School of Education in 1985. In 1987 the Polytechnic was restructured into faculties and teacher education became part of a Faculty of Educational and Leisure Studies. A further re-organisation established a Faculty of Education and Cultural Studies in 1990 which subsequently supported a school of Teacher Education Studies and a School of Professional Education and Development (which provided part-time in-service courses; education leadership and management, training and professional development courses; and research and HE training – largely for in-house learners). Following the establishment of a new Carnegie Faculty of Sport and Education, now divided into Teaching and Research Groups, initial teacher education has been led by Denise Gilchrist and the area of practitioners' lifelong learning by Dr Jill Adam. Margaret Christian is the Director of Carnegie Leaders in Learning.

[46] See www.leedsmet.ac.uk for detailed course information.

[47] See www.tda.gov.uk for guidance on admissions.

[48] Part of the university information package supplied to candidates, which provides advice on the selection process, including interviews, expectations and evidence in support of the applications.

[49] See Part 3: Training the School Workforce at www.opsi.gov.uk/acts/en2005/05en18-b.htm for the most recent developments at the time of going to press.

[50] Furlong, J., Barton, L., Miles, S., Whiting, C., and Whitty, G. (2000) *Teacher Education in Transition. Re-forming Professionalism?* Buckingham and Philadelphia: OUP.

[51] See Richards, C. (1999) *Primary Education- At a Hinge of History?* London: Falmer Press, for an historical review of primary education.

[52] They demonstrate through their research that throughout the 1980s and 1990s the New Right and other critics were increasingly successful in establishing the issue of teacher professionalism as a legitimate topic for government policy, a concern taken on by the Blair New Labour government, linked to maintaining supply of well-qualified applicants and creating greater accountability within a national framework for teaching. Other commentators agree that successive conservative governments adopted neo-liberal economic policies associated with Thatcherism, which treated public education, including teacher education, as an instrument of economic policy. See Young, M. F. D. (1998) *The Curriculum of the Future*. London and Philadelphia: Falmer Press, esp. chapter 11, Towards a New Curriculum for Teacher Education.

[53] The Qualifications and Curriculum Authority (QCA) launched the new secondary curriculum at Lord's Cricket Ground on 12 July, 2007. See www.qca.org.uk

[54] TDA released the new standards booklet *Professional Standards for Teachers. Why sit still in your career?* for implementation from September 2007. See www.tda.gov.uk/standards.

[55] See www.ofsted.gov.uk/

[56] See TDA *Qualifying to Teach* Handbook of Guidance at www.canteach.gov.uk

[57] Source of information - Denise Gilchrist, interview at Leeds Met, February 2007.

[58] The QCA has no immediate plans for a new primary curriculum, but the new secondary curriculum has implications for Carnegie Faculty's brief for initial teacher education and practitioners' lifelong learning.

[59] Carnegie academics Christine Allan and Dr Jon Tan are working in partnership with the Instituts Universitaires de Formation des Maitres (IUFM) Montpellier, geared to research on professional learning, which includes placements in French schools for Carnegie ITE French specialist students, and host teacher and university staff exchanges. Professors Lori Beckett and Anne Campbell with Dr Jon Tan are working on links with academic and teacher research partners in Australia, and Professor Lori Beckett and Dr Jon Tan are working with Little London Community Primary School Headteacher Jill Wood on links with academic and teacher research partners in Jordan.

[60] See Boyer, E. L. (1990) *Scholarship Reconsidered. Priorities of the Professoriate*. New York: John Wiley and Sons, particularly the analysis of faculty work under the headings of discovery, integration, application and teaching. Also see our namesake, The Carnegie Foundation for the Advancement of Teaching, at www.carnegiefoundation.org

[61] As noted by Carnegie Faculty Dean Professor David Kirk in a briefing paper, one of a series on Faculty restructuring, to academic staff in 2005. These developments are increasingly being made available to and taken up by partners in schools and agencies supporting children's learning and development. See Jill Adam and Anne Campbell's report in the Partnerships chapter.

[62] These include Jonathan Doherty, Christine Hines, Carol Potter, Jane Barber, Sarah Squires, Anne Flintoff, Julia Lawrence, Denise Gilchrist, Anne Campbell and Lori Beckett as the core group.

[63] These efforts sit well with the University Council for the Education of Teachers (UCET), given Professor Pat Mahony and Dr Jean Murray's presentation, *Developing Research Capacity in Teacher Education*, to the Management Forum meeting on March 1, 2007.

[64] See Young (1998) op.cit.

[65] For example, Carnegie academics Professor Lori Beckett and Dr Jon Tan together with Little London Community Primary School Headteacher Jill Wood submitted an abstract for a symposium at the Australian Association for Research in Education (AARE), Fremantle, 2007, which was accepted. The papers reported on the school-university partnership project work.

[66] See Newby, M. (2006) *Teaching 2012 The regional seminars, Autumn 2005 – Spring 2006*. Report for the TDA; also Newby, M. (ed) (2005) Looking to the future, journal of education for teaching. *International Research and Pedagogy*, vol.31, no.4, November.

[67] Carnegie Faculty Professors Lori Beckett and Pat Broadhead authored the Leeds Met submission to the QCA Futures project, as organisations were invited to comment on a curriculum for the future. See QCA (2006) *Futures. Meeting the Challenge* at www.qca.org.uk/futures/

[68] See Beck, U. (2005) *Power in the Global Age*. Cambridge: Polity Press.

[69] See Leeds Metropolitan University *Vision and Character* statement (printed inside back cover).

[70] Also, in line with LeedsMet's policy of widening participation, a significant feature of teacher education in 2007 has been success in attracting mature candidates who are committed to a career in teaching and who access QTS through alternative routes including 2+2, part-time and school-based training in conjunction with Education Leeds.

[71] Tony Blair in his electioneering in 1997 indicated the prominence of education under New Labour in his 'Education, Education, Education' speech and the government has certainly lived up to its promises given the amount of legislation governing schools and teacher education in the decade since.

[72] Op.cit.

CHAPTER 7

Curriculum for Teacher Education and Training

Lori Beckett, David Kirk and Iain Poole

*The acquisition of knowledge was a striking feature of the quest to become a teacher in the early years of the 20th century. A cursory glance at the Board of Education Regulations and Syllabus[1] indicate a prominent place for the Preliminary Examination for the Elementary School Teachers' Certificate, 1907 (**Figure 1**). This shows definite rules about entry into the profession, and the body of knowledge required of young people wishing to be certificated teachers. It also suggests the Board of Education had firm theories about what knowledge was deemed important for prospective teachers, and they made this knowledge available on request.[2]*

CURRICULA 'THEN'

The regulations reveal that candidates had to be Pupil-Teachers, or over eighteen years of age, and present for examination on set topics, three compulsory subjects, and one optional. These knowledge requirements were spelled out in the 'Detailed Syllabus of the Subjects of Examination' (**Figure 2**). Here we can see what they were expected to have learned during this time in training, no doubt considered a form of craft knowledge for prospective teachers. Specific subject matter knowledge was outlined in the Part II of the Detailed Syllabus, which is divided into compulsory (**Figure 3**) and optional subjects.

Copies of the examination papers in English Language and Literature I and II, English Composition, Mathematics I and II, Elementary Science, French, German, Latin, Welsh, Hebrew, Spanish, Geography, History were attached to the Regulations and Syllabus. These show both the kinds of knowledge valued and the hierarchy of knowledge in the Pupil-Teacher training curriculum (**Figure 4**). We also find what we would nowadays call higher order cognitive skills being tested – evidenced in commands such as compare and contrast and justify – with an emphasis on

Fig. 1
Extract from Board of Education Regulations and Syllabus *for Preliminary Examination 1907. (Source: The National Archives ref. ED24/441)*

REGULATIONS AND SYLLABUS FOR THE PRELIMINARY EXAMINATION FOR THE ELEMENTARY SCHOOL TEACHERS' CERTIFICATE, 1907.

REGULATIONS.

(1). The Preliminary Examination for the Elementary School Teachers' Certificate (which replaces the former King's Scholarship Examination) for the year 1907, will be divided into two parts. All candidates must be either Pupil-Teachers, or persons not being Pupil-Teachers who will be over 18 years of age on August 1st, 1907. No Pupil-Teacher will be admitted to the examination before the beginning of the last year of his engagement. Persons employed in Elementary Schools in Scotland will not, as a rule, be admitted to the Preliminary Examination for the Certificate held in England.

(2). Part I. will consist of Reading, Repetition, Penmanship, Composition, Arithmetic, Drawing, Music, and (for women) Needlework.

In Part II. all candidates will be examined in (a) three Compulsory Subjects, viz.: English Language and Literature, History, and Geography, and also in (b) one Optional Subject, which may be either Elementary Mathematics, Elementary Science, or one of the following languages: Greek, Latin, German, French, Italian, Spanish, Portuguese, Welsh, or Hebrew.

Candidates may offer more than one of the Optional Subjects; but two only of these may be languages; and if two languages are taken, one must be either Greek, Latin, German, or French.

(3). Candidates who are recognised by the Board as Pupil-Teachers at the date of Part I. of the examination, or who, not being Pupil-Teachers, have been employed in Public Elementary Schools in some recognised capacity other than that of a monitor for not less than a year during the two years immediately preceding that date, will be credited with an allowance of marks towards the result of Part II. of the examination, unless an unfavourable report upon their teaching capacity has been received from the Inspector.

(4). Part I. will be taken on either Thursday, Friday, or Saturday, December 13th, 14th, and 15th, 1906, at Pupil-Teacher Centres and such other places as may be necessary. It will be open to all candidates, whether Pupil-Teachers or not, who are qualified under the conditions of Regulation (1) above, and who intend to complete their examination by taking Part II. in April, 1907.

(5). Part II. of the examination will be open only to candidates who have satisfied the examiners in Part I. Part I. will be a qualifying test merely, and no marks for the subjects included in it will be credited towards Part II. It is not, however, intended that the test in these important subjects should be of a perfunctory character.

(6). Part II. will be held on April 9th, 1907, and the following three days, at such places as may be necessary. Information as to these places will be given to candidates. If the Board has arranged to hold the examination at any Training College, candidates may, with the consent of the authorities of the Training College, be examined at that College. Such candidates must make their own arrangements with the authorities of Training Colleges.

(7). The names of candidates for the Preliminary Examination for the Certificate should be notified to the Board of Education, Whitehall, London, S.W., before October 1st, 1906. The notification must be made on Form 12 (Exam.), a stock of which will be supplied to Local Education Authorities and Managers of Pupil-Teacher Centres. The form can also be obtained on application to the Board.

9632. 8,000.—Wt. 26342. 1/07. Wy. & S. 5721r. A

4 *Preliminary Examination for the Certificate.*

As it frequently takes some time for candidates to procure the information asked for on Form 12 (Exam.), these Forms should be procured in good time.

Late applications, when some good reason is shown for the delay, may be received during October on payment of a fee of 5s.; but no application will under any circumstances be received after October 31st.

(8). Candidates who pass Part I. of the examination need not make a special application for permission to attend Part II. A Form admitting them to Part II. will be sent to them in due course.

(9). Candidates who have not been Pupil-Teachers and who have not previously supplied a satisfactory medical certificate to the Board, must produce such a certificate on an approved Form as a condition of admission to Part II. of the Examination. When necessary, such Forms will be sent to the candidates for completion together with the Forms admitting them to Part II. of the Examination. No candidates need obtain a medical certificate unless one of these Forms is sent for completion.

(10). Candidates who obtain a suitable aggregate of marks in Part II. will be held to have passed the Examination, but for the purpose of this aggregate no marks will be counted for more than one optional subject, and if a candidate attempts more than one optional subject, the marks for that only in which he does best will be counted toward his aggregate. All candidates who pass the Examination will be regarded as qualified by Examination for recognition as Uncertificated Teachers and may be proposed by the authorities of a Training College for admission as recognised students for a two years' course of training. It will further be possible for any candidate who passes the Examination as a whole to obtain distinction in any or each of the three compulsory subjects and of four optional subjects in Part II., and such distinction will be shown by appropriate signs in the list of results. This list will give the names of all candidates who pass the Examination in alphabetical order without classification.

(11). The results of examinations for University Extension Certificates will not, in and after 1907, be accepted as substitutes for any portion of the Preliminary Examination for the Certificate.

(12). Candidates will be informed by letter from the Board of Education of the result of their examination.

(13). Arrangements will be made for a special examination in the Summer of 1907 of Blind Candidates proposing to enter a recognised Training College for the Blind.

(14.) Copies of these Regulations and Syllabus may be obtained on application to the Secretary, Board of Education, Whitehall, London, S.W., or from the Local Education Authorities, to whom a supply will be sent for this purpose.

DETAILED SYLLABUS OF THE SUBJECTS OF EXAMINATION.

Defective spelling or handwriting will be taken into account in estimating the value of a Candidate's work.
The use of rulers will not be allowed except for Mathematical questions where actual measurements are necessary.

PART I.

I.—Reading:—

To read with clear enunciation, ease, and intelligence, from a work of a standard prose author and a work of a standard poet.

Candidates are required to draw in outline with pencil or chalk, on a half imperial sheet of paper, the objects placed before them as they appear from the point of view in which candidates may be seated. No ruling, measuring, or use of instruments is allowed ; but the pencil may be held between the eye and the objects for the purpose of estimating their apparent relative size. For the examination the groups will be composed of an imperial drawing board and, placed upon it, two or more geometrical models or vases, or a simple common object or a group of objects.

Candidates should have gone through a graduated series of exercises in drawing from geometrical models, common things of simple form, &c., with the object (i.) of studying their structure and character, as well as the effect of perspective in modifying the appearance of such things, and (ii.) of representing them accurately and intelligently.

II.—Repetition:—

To repeat 100 lines of Shakespeare or some other standard English author with clearness and force, and knowledge of the meaning. In place of 50 lines of English, candidates from Welsh districts may substitute 50 lines from a standard Welsh author. The exercises in Reading and Repetition will be performed at the Examination Centre and not during the visits of Inspectors to Public Elementary Schools.

III.—Penmanship:—

To set copies in large and small hand.

IV.—Composition.

V.—Arithmetic:—

The Theory and Practice of Arithmetic
The following will be excluded :—

Troy and Apothecaries Measures.
The rules for finding Square and Cube roots.
N.B.—Candidates may be asked to determine the square (or cube) roots of numbers that can readily be expressed as the product of the squares (or cubes) of small factors.
Practice.

Ratio.
Proportion except by the unitary or fractional method.
Stocks and Shares.
True Discount.
Scales of Notation.
Foreign Exchanges.
Recurring Decimals and Complicated Fractions.
The metric system will only be applied to measuring length, area, and volume.
Questions may be set on the mensuration of rectangular surfaces and solids.
The use of algebraic symbols will be permitted.
As a rule, (a) the questions will not involve long operations or complicated numbers, (b) the answers to money sums will not be required beyond the nearest penny.
The papers will be sufficiently long to allow the candidates some latitude in the questions selected, but no limit will be placed on the number of questions which may be attempted.

VI.—Drawing :—

Candidates will be required to undergo a test at the discretion of the Examiner, in either (1) or (2) below.

(1). Freehand Drawing in outline.

Candidates are required to make a drawing in outline with pencil or chalk, on a half imperial sheet of paper, from diagrams of ornament, or natural foliage and flowers. The drawing must not be of the same size as the example supplied. No ruling, measuring, tracing, or use of instruments is allowed.

Candidates should have gone through a graduated series of Exercises in drawing from diagrams, and, where possible, actual specimens of ornament of good form, and of foliage and flowers from nature, with the object of cultivating a power of drawing freely and accurately, and with an appreciation of the structure, proportions, and beauty of the originals.

(2) Model and Object Drawing in outline.

Fig. 2
Extract from Board of Education Detailed Syllabuses *of Subjects of Examination 1907. (Source: The National Archives ref. ED24/441)*

testing students' propositional knowledge. This is a curriculum dictated by the question 'What should they know?'.[3]

Of particular interest were the final two pages attached to the Board of Education *Regulations and Syllabus*. The first documented the expectations for the Penultimate Stage, that is, the results to facilitate young people's entrance into a Training College program of study (**Figure 5**).[4] We are prompted to ask why this knowledge was considered appropriate for the 1907 Pupil-Teacher? Former College Principal Leo Connell[5] pointed out that the Training Colleges had a dual role, to provide professional training but also to continue the student's general education. We found an example of a Leeds elementary school subject timetable in a 1907 student's workbook[6] (**Figure 6**), which shows a close match with the knowledge required of prospective teachers. This is not surprising because they were being tested on knowledge gained in schools, either as Pupil-Teachers or as school graduates (**Figure 7**).

We can identify some assumptions about the subject-based curriculum, established at the end of the 19th century. Knowledge offered at school was separate to knowledge acquired in everyday life; it was

Fig. 3 *Board of Education Detailed Syllabuses: Compulsory Examination Subjects 1907. (Source: The National Archives ref. ED24/441)*

PART II.

A. COMPULSORY SUBJECTS.

I.—English Language and Literature:—
(1.)—English Grammar.
(2.)—The elements of English Composition and Literature.
Questions will be set to test such knowledge as may be derived from books like Abbot and Seeley's "English Lessons for English People."
All candidates should have undertaken as wide a course as possible of general reading, which should include, amongst other books, one or two of Shakespeare's plays, some historical novels, and an anthology of verse. It is recognised that such reading cannot be wholly tested by examination, but a large number of alternative questions will be set, some of which all candidates may reasonably expect to be able to answer.
Candidates will also be expected to write an Essay.
Opportunity will be given to shew a knowledge of Welsh.

II.—History:—
(1.)—The outlines of British History, including the main landmarks of European History as they directly affect British History.
Candidates will be called upon to answer
(a.) the whole of a small number of elementary questions relating to the period of 1017-1870;
(b.) a selection from a large number of questions requiring a more advanced knowledge of some substantial part of that period. This part of the paper will be arranged in five sections, dealing with: (i.) 1017-1399; (ii.) 1399-1603; (iii.) 1603-1714; (iv.) 1714-1815; (v.) 1815-1870. Candidates will be allowed to select questions from one, more than one, or all of these sections.
Some of the questions under (a.) or (b.) will relate especially to Welsh History.
(2.)—The elements of the duties and rights of citizenship.

III.—Geography.—(1) The elements of general and physical geography. (2) The drawing of simple sketch maps. (3) Political and economic geography, with special reference to Europe, including the British Isles. Some of the questions in (2) and (3) will relate to Wales.

considered cognitively superior, and could take pupils beyond what they gained through experience; and school subjects were located within communities of specialists. Contemporary curriculum theorist Michael Young[7] reckoned these were the fundamental principles, which gave the subject-based curriculum credibility, and not just because of its association with elite institutions. Young goes on to emphasise the importance of acknowledging the crucial social conditions for knowledge acquisition and production that are independent of the specific social contexts in which they are located.

These social conditions of knowledge are evident in the case to support the decision to establish a temporary Training College in Leeds. The Higher Education Committee Chairman Fred Kinder[8] noted that the Board of Education indicated clearly that the Training College Course should be the normal course for all intending teachers.

The efficiency of the instruction given to the children in the Public Elementary Schools of the country is, to a very large extent, dependent upon the nature and quality of the training given to the students. It is essential therefore that all Teachers should have the best possible training and should possess the highest qualifications. For it is to them that the country must look to turn out material fitted to take advantage of the educational and industrial opportunities that now exist.

The earliest prospectuses for students and parents[9] show that the curriculum for the two-year course, leading to the Board of Education Teacher's Certificate, included as compulsory subjects English language and literacy, history and geography, elementary mathematics, elementary science, hygiene, theory of music, principles of teaching, practice of teaching, reading and repetition, drawing, needlework (for women), singing, physical training and manual instruction (for men). Connell[10] noted that the Board regulations also permitted twenty optional subjects at a higher level, of which the City of Leeds Training College offered only one, a class in French for about fifteen students. The staffing (**Figure 8**) for the new training college reflected the balance of the knowledge curriculum (**Figure 9**).

The distribution of physical resources at the City of Leeds Training College (**Figure 10**) hints at the dominance of a curriculum that favoured knowledge transmission, although resources were devoted to what we would call a vocational curriculum and a personal development curriculum. Inclusion of staff and facilities to teach hygiene and physical training reflects the contemporary national concerns[11] about the need to improve the health of Edwardian children (pioneered by Margaret Macmillan in Bradford).[12]

By 1913 the Board had issued substantial revisions to the Teacher's Certificate[13] in recognition of the fact that increasing numbers of students were undertaking the course with a higher level of general education, with many receiving a secondary education until the age of 17.[14] This revision of the curriculum led to an increase in time devoted to professional subjects such as principles and practice of teaching and other College assessed subjects. The core elementary school subjects of English, mathematics, history, geography and elementary science remained compulsory, however, and the Board examinations continued to test propositional knowledge.

There were alternative views of the Training College curriculum. Before her appointment, Vice-Principal Winifred Mercier had experimented at the Manchester Girls' High School with a modified history curriculum, which developed the individual learner. The focus was on the acquisition of appropriate history knowledge, self-motivation, and self-development or 'learning how to', which relied heavily on the availability

A.

PRELIMINARY EXAMINATION FOR THE CERTIFICATE, 1907.

PART II.

ELEMENTARY SCIENCE.

Thursday, April 11th, 10.15.—12.45.

You should answer SIX *questions*—ONE *from General Section* (i), ONE *from General Section* (ii), *and* FOUR *from Special Section A.*

GENERAL SECTION (i).

1. Some lead shot are given you. Describe how you would find in a practical manner the average volume of a single shot.

2. How would you determine the melting-point of a small quantity of paraffin wax, and the boiling-point of 2 or 3 c.c. of methylated spirits?

GENERAL SECTION (ii).

3. Describe the appearance of any two salts with which you are well acquainted, and state how they may be prepared.

4. When chalk is strongly heated it is converted into lime. What experiments would you make to show that the change had taken place and how could you prove that it was a complete one?

SPECIAL SECTION A.

5. Describe carefully all that might be observed on the addition of cold nitric acid to copper turnings. Draw the apparatus you would use to collect any gas evolved. Explain how you would attempt to show that the gas contains both oxygen and nitrogen.

6. Compare and contrast the properties of common petroleum, tallow, linseed oil, and olive oil. From which of these are soaps commonly made? How would you proceed to make one of them on a small scale?

7. What experiments would you make to show that paraffin oil contains both carbon and hydrogen?

8. How would you proceed to see whether carbonic acid gas is soluble in olive oil or petroleum; also whether it is absorbed by a small lump of lime?

1 47033—9. 8500.—3/07   [OVER

PENULTIMATE STAGE.

A.(1)
Board of Education's Preliminary Examination for Certificate.

*Part I. Professional Subjects.

Satisfactory Report from H.M.I. on Reading and Repetition.

Satisfactory aggregate in Penmanship, Composition, Arithmetic, Drawing, Music, Needlework

Reach certain standard in Arithmetic. and also in Composition.

Part II. Satisfactory aggregate (English Language and (Literature, History, (Geography, and a fourth (subject either Mathemat- (ics, or Science, or a (Language.

A.(2) If going into Degree Course)English Language & Literature, he must pass separately in)History, Geography, Mathematics,)Science, Two Languages.

B.(1)
University Matriculations, etc.
*No professional subjects.

(London; Victoria; Manchester, Liverpool and York Joint Matrics. (Matriculation; Birmingham; Wales (Durham (but must pass in History or Geography); Royal (University of Ireland; Trinity College, Dublin.

Higher Certificate of Oxford & Cambridge Schools Examination Board, but must pass in English or History.

Oxford & Cambridge University Extension Certificate.

Oxford Higher Local.

Cambridge Higher Local.

Oxford Senior Local, but satisfy in Arithmetic, and in either History or English Language & Literature and in either Geography or Political Economy.

Cambridge Senior Local but include English.

Durham Local but include both History or English Literature. and Euclid or Algebra.

Preceptors First Class but pass in History or Geography. and in Euclid or Algebra.

Central Welsh Board Senior, but pass in Elementary Mathematics, and History or English Literature.

Scotch Leaving Certificate, but Higher in 3 subjects - English, Mathematics, One Language.

B.(2) If going into a Degree Course he must in these examinations pass separately in each of the seven subjects named above at the end of the Preliminary Examination of B.ofE. but no professional subjects.

20th-century elementary schools.

Three years after she left City of Leeds Training College, Mercier was publicly involved in curriculum debates. In an Address to the Training College Association,[16] she posited that the Training College must provide higher education that is neither school work nor university:

The nature of this course, the number of subjects to be included, their relation to each other and their right treatment, we are now, it seems to me, engaged in discovering. It is thus extremely important that under the new regulations there should be a very large liberty for the Colleges, so that there must be as much experiment and discovery as possible.

of a wide variety of books and a good library.[15] Once in post, there were opportunities to experiment further, given the new central library in the Education Building and a Library in each hostel (**Figure 11**), emphasis on collegiality (**Figure 12**), societies and sport (**Figure 13**). However, such curricular developments were greatly constrained by the demands of Board regulations and the absence of a wide variety of reading materials in early

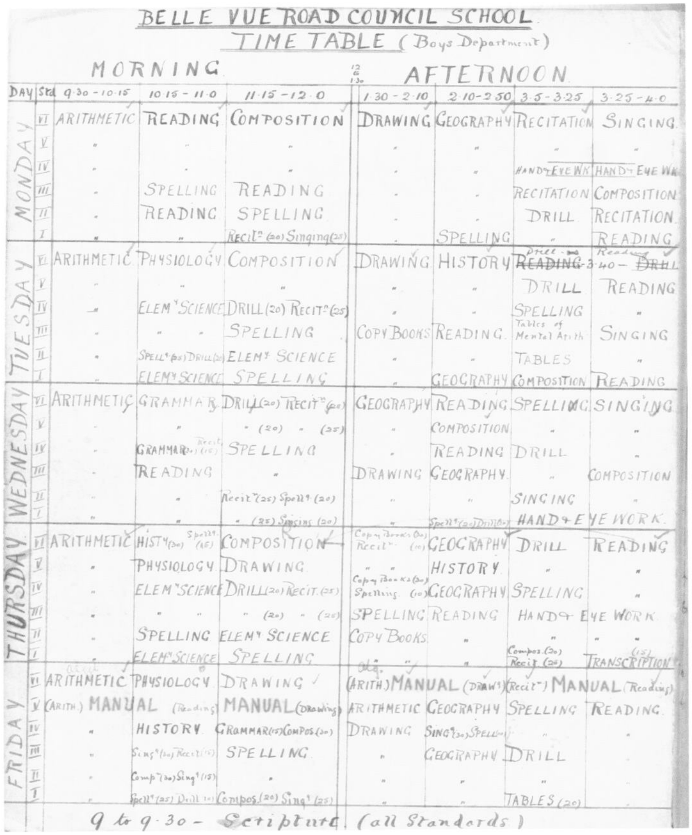

BELLE VUE ROAD COUNCIL SCHOOL
TIME TABLE (Boys Department)

MORNING — 12 to 1.30 — AFTERNOON

DAY	Std	9.30 - 10.15	10.15 - 11.0	11.15 - 12.0	1.30 - 2.10	2.10 - 2.50	3.5 - 3.25	3.25 - 4.0
MONDAY	VI	ARITHMETIC	READING	COMPOSITION	DRAWING	GEOGRAPHY	RECITATION	SINGING
	V	"	"	"	"	"	"	"
	IV	"	"	"	"	"	HAND & EYE WK	HAND & EYE WK
	III	"	SPELLING	READING	"	"	RECITATION	COMPOSITION
	II	"	READING	SPELLING	"	"	DRILL	RECITATION
	I	"	"	Recit^n (20) Singing (25)	"	SPELLING	"	READING
TUESDAY	VI	ARITHMETIC	PHYSIOLOGY	COMPOSITION	DRAWING	HISTORY	~~READING~~ Drill - 3.40	~~DRILL~~ Reading
	V	"	"	"	"	"	DRILL	READING
	IV	"	ELEM^Y SCIENCE	DRILL (20) RECIT^N (25)	"	"	SPELLING	"
	III	"	" "	SPELLING	COPY BOOKS	READING	Tables of Mental Arith	SINGING
	II	"	SPELL^G (25) DRILL (20)	ELEM^Y SCIENCE	"	"	TABLES	"
	I	"	ELEM^Y SCIENCE	SPELLING	"	GEOGRAPHY	COMPOSITION	READING
WEDNESDAY	VI	ARITHMETIC	GRAMMAR	DRILL (20) RECIT^N (25)	GEOGRAPHY	READING	SPELLING	SINGING
	V	"	"	" (20) " (25)	"	COMPOSITION	"	"
	IV	"	GRAMMAR (30) Recit (15)	SPELLING	"	READING	DRILL	"
	III	"	READING	"	DRAWING	GEOGRAPHY	"	COMPOSITION
	II	"	"	Recit^n (25) Spell^g (20)	"	"	SINGING	"
	I	"	"	" (25) Singing (20)	"	Spell^g (20) Drill (20)	HAND & EYE WORK	
THURSDAY	VI	ARITHMETIC	HIST^Y (30) Spell^g (15)	COMPOSITION	Copy Books (30) Recit^n (10)	GEOGRAPHY	DRILL	READING
	V	"	PHYSIOLOGY	DRAWING	" "	HISTORY	"	"
	IV	"	ELEM^Y SCIENCE	DRILL (20) RECIT. (25)	Copy Books (30) Spelling (10)	GEOGRAPHY	SPELLING	"
	III	"	" "	" (20) " (25)	SPELLING	READING	HAND & EYE WORK	
	II	"	SPELLING	ELEM^Y SCIENCE	COPY BOOKS	"	"	"
	I	"	ELEM^Y SCIENCE	SPELLING	"	"	Compos. (20) Recit. (25)	TRANSCRIPTION (15)
FRIDAY	VI	ARITHMETIC	PHYSIOLOGY	DRAWING	(ARITH.) MANUAL (DRAW^G)		(Recit^n) MANUAL (Reading)	
	V	(ARITH.) MANUAL (Reading)		MANUAL (Drawing)	ARITHMETIC	GEOGRAPHY	SPELLING	READING
	IV	"	HISTORY	GRAMMAR (15) COMPOS. (30)	DRAWING	SING^G (30) SPELL^G	"	"
	III	"	Sing^g (30) Recit^n (15)	SPELLING	"	GEOGRAPHY	DRILL	
	II	"	Comp^n (30) Sing^g (15)	"	"	"	"	
	I	"	Spell^g (25) Drill (20)	Compos. (20) Sing^g (25)	"	"	TABLES (20)	

9 to 9.30 – Scripture (all Standards)

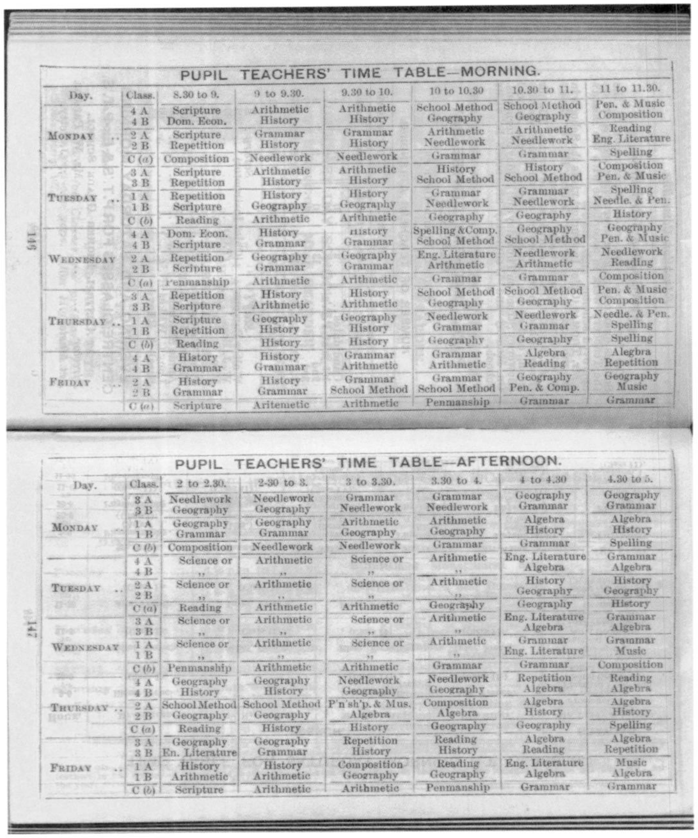

PUPIL TEACHERS' TIME TABLE—MORNING.

Day.	Class.	8.30 to 9.	9 to 9.30.	9.30 to 10.	10 to 10.30	10.30 to 11.	11 to 11.30.
MONDAY ..	4 A 4 B	Scripture Dom. Econ.	Arithmetic History	Arithmetic History	School Method Geography	School Method Geography	Pen. & Music Composition
	2 A 2 B	Scripture Repetition	Grammar History	Grammar History	Arithmetic Needlework	Arithmetic Needlework	Reading Eng. Literature
	C (a)	Composition	Needlework	Needlework	Grammar	Grammar	Spelling
TUESDAY ..	3 A 3 B	Scripture Repetition	Arithmetic History	Arithmetic History	History School Method	History School Method	Composition Pen. & Music
	1 A 1 B	Repetition Scripture	History Geography	History Geography	Grammar Needlework	Grammar Needlework	Spelling Needle. & Pen.
	C (b)	Reading	Arithmetic	Arithmetic	Geography	Geography	History
WEDNESDAY	4 A 4 B	Dom. Econ. Scripture	History Grammar	History Grammar	Spelling & Comp. School Method	Geography School Method	Geography Pen. & Music
	2 A 2 B	Repetition Scripture	Geography Grammar	Geography Grammar	Eng. Literature Arithmetic	Needlework Arithmetic	Needlework Reading
	C (a)	Penmanship	Arithmetic	Arithmetic	Grammar	Grammar	Composition
THURSDAY ..	3 A 3 B	Repetition Scripture	History Arithmetic	History Arithmetic	School Method Geography	School Method Geography	Pen. & Music Composition
	1 A 1 B	Scripture Repetition	Geography History	Geography History	Needlework Grammar	Needlework Grammar	Needle. & Pen. Spelling
	C (b)	Reading	History	History	Geography	Geography	Spelling
FRIDAY ..	4 A 4 B	History Grammar	History Grammar	Grammar Arithmetic	Grammar Arithmetic	Algebra Reading	Alegbra Repetition
	2 A 2 B	History Grammar	History Grammar	Grammar School Method	Grammar School Method	Geography Pen. & Comp.	Geography Music
	C (a)	Scripture	Aritemetic	Arithmetic	Penmanship	Grammar	Grammar

146

PUPIL TEACHERS' TIME TABLE—AFTERNOON.

Day.	Class.	2 to 2.30.	2-30 to 3.	3 to 3.30.	3.30 to 4.	4 to 4.30	4.30 to 5.
MONDAY ..	3 A 3 B	Needlework Geography	Needlework Geography	Grammar Needlework	Grammar Needlework	Geography Grammar	Geography Grammar
	1 A 1 B	Geography Grammar	Geography Grammar	Arithmetic Geography	Arithmetic Geography	Algebra History	Algebra History
	C (b)	Composition	Needlework	Needlework	Grammar	Grammar	Spelling
TUESDAY ..	4 A 4 B	Science or "	Arithmetic "	Science or "	Arithmetic "	Eng. Literature Algebra	Grammar Algebra
	2 A 2 B	Science or "	Arithmetic "	Science or "	Arithmetic "	History Geography	History Geography
	C (a)	Reading	Arithmetic	Arithmetic	Geography	Geography	History
WEDNESDAY	3 A 3 B	Science or "	Arithmetic "	Science or "	Arithmetic "	Eng. Literature Algebra	Grammar Algebra
	1 A 1 B	Science or "	Arithmetic "	Science or "	Arithmetic "	Grammar Eng. Literature	Grammar Music
	C (b)	Penmanship	Arithmetic	Arithmetic	Grammar	Grammar	Composition
THURSDAY ..	4 A 4 B	Geography History	Geography History	Needlework Geography	Needlework Geography	Repetition Algebra	Reading Algebra
	2 A 2 B	School Method Geography	School Method Geography	P'n'sh'p. & Mus. Algebra	Composition Algebra	Algebra History	Algebra History
	C (a)	Reading	History	History	Geography	Geography	Spelling
FRIDAY ..	3 A 3 B	Geography En. Literature	Geography Grammar	Repetition History	Reading History	Algebra Reading	Algebra Repetition
	1 A 1 B	History Arithmetic	History Arithmetic	Composition Geography	Reading Geography	Eng. Literature Algebra	Music Algebra
	C (b)	Scripture	Arithmetic	Arithmetic	Penmanship	Grammar	Grammar

147

Fig. 6
Example of elementary school timetable from Samuel Childs' Demonstration Lessons workbook *September 1908. (Source: Leeds Metropolitan University Archives)*

Far right, Fig. 7
Leeds School Board Official Yearbook, *1899, Pupil Teacher Timetable. (Source: Leeds Metropolitan University Archives)*

In Mercier's advocacy, we can see a notion of the teacher training curriculum in terms of 'what should they know?' contrasted with a notion of liberal education curriculum associated with some universities and underpinned by the question 'What should they become?'. As she put it:

(Our students) have as much need for a liberal education such as will 'free the human spirit', and lead to a worthy maturity as any other students in the country. Old ideas die hard, but unless a young teacher has a worthy vision of his (sic) work, and has gained, through the study of even one subject only, some idea of the value of knowledge, and the joy of imparting it, it is but waste labour to prepare him assiduously to reach (sic) all the subjects ordinarily taught in Elementary School. The machine may have been provided with material, but the power that should make it productive has never been generated.[17]

Mercier expressed confidence in the view that a shift was underway in teacher training with proposals for extension courses, but a further comment suggested that old ideas did indeed die hard. Revealing, perhaps, the influence of John Dewey's ideas about education as experience on her own thinking, she said of the regime of examination of propositional knowledge:

The professional certificate could then be awarded on an examination mainly of the student's own records of experience rather than on answers to questions which test his (sic) reading and lectures, but do not test his power of applying his knowledge in the classroom, or the ideas by which he himself is inspired.[18]

Reading between the lines of the documentary sources – the

*Fig. 8
Photo of teaching staff,
deposited in archives by
certificate student
Rachel Ross. (Source:
Leeds Metropolitan
University Archives)*

*Fig. 9'
List of CLTC teaching
staff from CLTC
Handbook (1912).
(Source: Leeds
Metropolitan University
Archives)*

regulations, syllabuses, examinations, and other archival materials – the curriculum question that seems to dominate is 'What should they know?'. Examinations tested Pupil-Teachers' and Trainee Teachers' propositional knowledge. There is evidence to show, however, that City of Leeds Training College provided additional, optional and higher level knowledge that offered opportunities to develop the teacher as a person, and so focus on the teacher they may become.[19]

THE CURRICULA 'NOW'

The Initial Teacher Education (ITE) curricula in the Carnegie Faculty of Sport and Education in 2007, while governed by the Training and Development Agency (TDA)[20] and the Leeds Met Academic Regulations, reflect a self-conscious awareness of the distinctive role of knowledge in the preparation of young people for the teaching profession. There is a concerted effort to involve academics in curriculum debates, and opportunities happen at many levels. One is the National Curriculum for ITE[21] and Carnegie Faculty efforts to provide a meaningful and worthwhile curriculum for student teachers, given the wider socio-cultural contexts for school placements and school appointments, locally, nationally and internationally.

A second area of debate is the development of programs of study

CITY OF LEEDS TRAINING COLLEGE

STAFF.

PRINCIPAL - - Mr. W. PARSONS.

ENGLISH STAFF.
Mr. G. C. DENT, B.A.
Mr. G. E. WILKINSON.
Mr. H. LACEY, M.A.
Miss E. P. GOODFELLOW, M.A.

HISTORY AND GEOGRAPHY.
Mr. G. C. DENT, B.A.
Mr. C. H. JARVIS, M.A., LL.B.
Mr. J. R. FIRTH, B.A.
Miss E. BIRDSELL.

MATHEMATICS STAFF.
Mr. W. TAYLOR, B.A.
Mr. J. E. PARKINSON, M.A.
Mr. E. HARRISON.
Mr. F. E. RELTON, B.Sc.
Miss J. L. MACKAY, M.A.

ART.
Mr. R. H. PARKER, A.R.C.A.
Miss D. B. MARTIN, A.R.C.A.

NEEDLEWORK.
Miss A. E. MITCHELL.

HANDWORK.
Mr. J. BERRY.
Mr. E. HAMNETT.
Mr. W. OSBORN.
Mr. G. UNWIN.

METHOD STAFF.
Mr. T. P. HOLGATE, B.Sc., L.C.P.
Mr. J. E. PARKINSON, M.A.
Mr. R. KERR, B.Sc.
Miss E. MELVILLE, M.A.
Miss M. A. SLADDIN, B.A.
Miss E. FOSTER, B.A.
Miss M. E. EGGAR, Higher Froebel
Certificate.

SCIENCE STAFF.
Mr. H. T. TODD, B.Sc.
Miss CRAWSHAW, B.Sc.

HYGIENE.
Mr. A. WEAR, M.D., B.S.
Mr. R. V. CLARK, M.A., B.Sc., M.B.,
Ch.B., D.Ph.

MUSIC.
Mr. W. GODSON.
Mr. J. F. JACKSON.
Miss A. E. MITCHELL.

ELOCUTION.
Mr. J. B. CROSSLEY.

PHYSICAL EXERCISES.
Mr. H. G. BROWN.
Miss HANSINE ANDERSON.
Miss K. HOLST.

FRENCH.
Mr. J. F. JACKSON.

MEDICAL OFFICER - - Mr. A. WEAR, M.D., B.S.

BECKETT'S PARK FAR HEADINGLEY

10

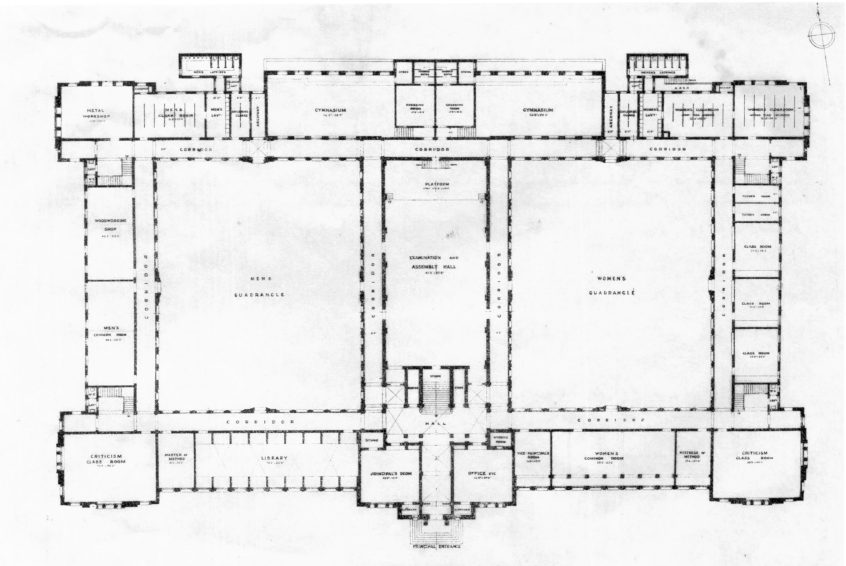

GROUND FLOOR PLAN.

CITY OF LEEDS TRAINING COLLEGE.
PLANS OF EDUCATIONAL BLOCK.

Fig. 10
Diagram of original intended use of the three floors of the CLTC teaching block from CLTC Handbook *(1912). (Source: Leeds Metropolitan University Archives)*

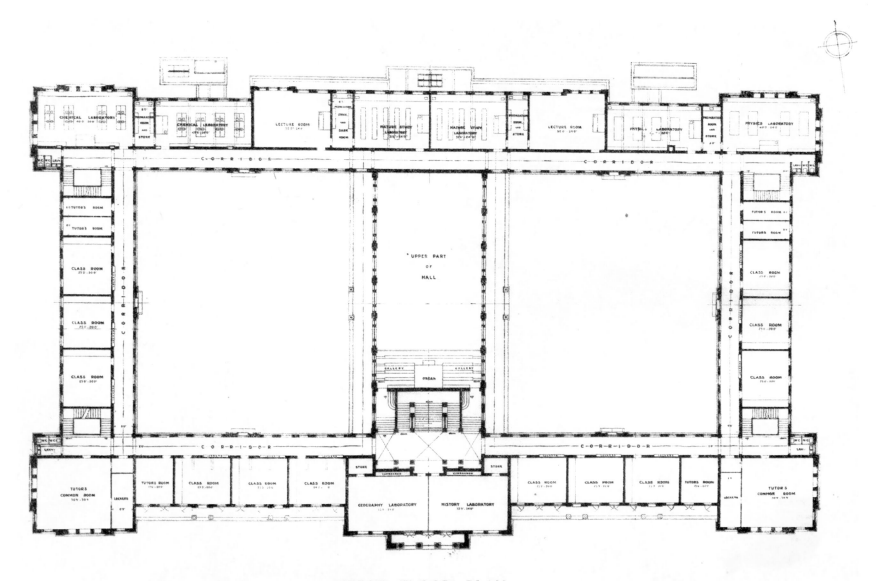

FIRST FLOOR PLAN.

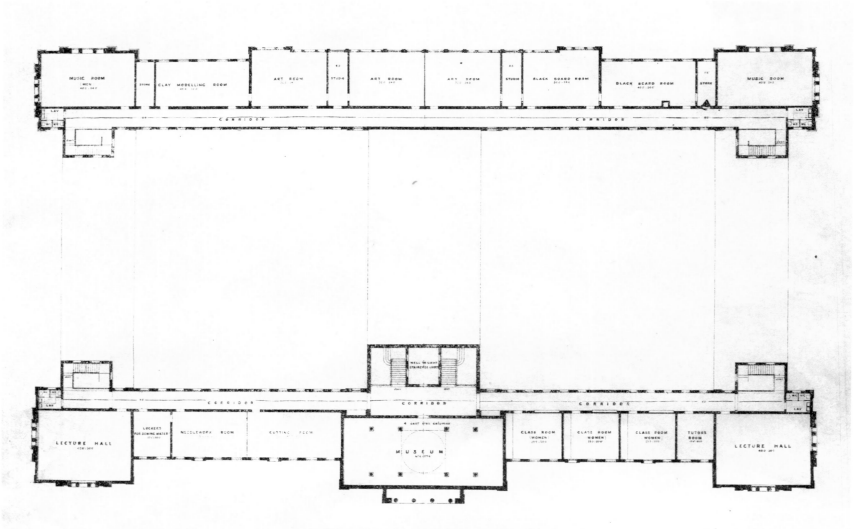

SECOND FLOOR PLAN.

leading towards Qualified Teacher Status (QTS), in England and beyond. This can be a three- or four-year undergraduate degree or a one-year post-graduate certificate,[22] currently Early Childhood Education (3 – 7), Primary Education (5 – 11), Secondary Physical Education (11 – 16 with post 16 curriculum enhancement) (**Figure 14**). Such debates are critical, given the university's own degree-awarding powers, in contrast to the award of a Teaching Certificate by the Board of Education a hundred years ago.

It is interesting to compare the Carnegie Faculty courses with TDA requirements,[23] which provide a good indication of what knowledge the government and bureaucracy deems important for prospective teachers. Here we find evidence of the kinds of knowledge and the hierarchy of knowledge valued by the TDA. Literacy and numeracy remain prominent, and this is matched by the knowledge requirements of the Primary National Strategy.[24] The curricula then and now share the same feature of concurrency of what we might call academic and professional dimensions of study. Now, ITE 'what to teach' knowledge is driven by the National

CITY OF LEEDS
TRAINING COLLEGE

Fig 11
Photo of Library from
CLTC Handbook
(1912). (Source: Leeds
Metropolitan University
Archives)

LIBRARY

22

Curriculum for schools, standards and competencies, so there are compulsory modules in, and increased importance of, school-based experiential learning and support from mentors.[25]

There is also now provision for the study of options, as there was then, even though the options themselves have changed dramatically. For example, students studying primary education can opt to study modules focusing on healthy and active lifestyles, compared to hygiene and physical activity then. Courses also try to reflect a wider curriculum focus through the integration of cross-curricular links, for example, between physical education and science (in respect of pupils' knowledge and understanding of fitness and health) or geography (in regard to students' understanding of basic map work in Outdoor and Adventurous Activities).

Mention also needs to be made about the substantial time devoted to knowledge of 'how to teach', through Professional Studies modules and school placements, which provides a space to engage in professional issues and to reflect upon students' own development as teachers[26] (**Figure 15**).

Fig. 12
Photo of student
common room in a hostel
from CLTC Handbook
(1912). (Source: Leeds
Metropolitan University
Archives)

CITY OF LEEDS
TRAINING COLLEGE

THE GRANGE—STUDENTS' COMMON ROOM

32

An important addition now is the academic study of children, of schooling and of education, including some training in educational research and the conduct of a major independent study by student-teachers (**Figure 16**). The staffing for ITE courses[27] also reflects the changing knowledge emphases.

The undergraduate qualifications from university in turn opens up access to study at Masters and Doctoral levels, options undreamt of by trainee teachers at City of Leeds Training College, although we acknowledge that a number of staff then had gained Masters degree

qualifications. This is matched today by university incentives for staff development, particularly to obtain doctoral qualifications.[28] Depending on the nature of their course work and/or research, this provides another opportunity for academics to get involved in curriculum debates.

So much for a comparison of 'then' and 'now' at this *prima facia* level. At this level, the story would appear to be one of progress for the education and training of teachers, from the Teachers' certificate or sub-degree award to contemporary degree and postgraduate awards, from

Fig. 13
The student
extended
curriculum:
Societies & Sports
from CLTC
Handbook *(1912).*
(Source: Leeds
Metropolitan
University
Archives)

CITY   OF   LEEDS
TRAINING   COLLEGE

SOCIAL LIFE IN THE COLLEGE

WHILE every effort is made to cultivate a home feeling in each Hostel, various Societies have been organised to stimulate a corporate spirit throughout the whole College.

Apart from the Games Clubs, there are the following Clubs of a more social nature—an Art Club, a Photographic Club, a Natural History Club, Literary and Debating Societies, Education Society, Musical and Dramatic Societies and College Orchestra.

A View from Tennis Lawn

33

college to university status, and of a degree of autonomy predicated on the relative loosening of government control.

But again we can ask why is the knowledge offered through the Carnegie Faculty considered appropriate for the 2007 student-teacher? Young[29] made a distinction between mass institutions which are under pressure to develop curricula geared to immediate economic and political demands, and elite institutions which are able to maintain discipline-based curricular.

Behind this analysis one might argue that there has been less progress than might at first appear and indeed that there are discordant undertones that mark the progress that has taken place.[30] ITE in England is now in large part school-based (**Figure 17**) with central control exerted through a combination of an extensive inspection regime conducted by the Office of Standards in Education (Ofsted) and the rigid application of standards to be achieved by all student teachers.[31]

Moreover, the degree of regulation of teachers has more recently

The Leeds Met Experience

Experience Carnegie

Carnegie Faculty starts its work with some of the youngest in our society and continues to do so through to adulthood. Within that we work in partnerships and teams recognising and valuing mass participation as much as world class performance. People within this Faculty help deliver a stimulating and quality learning experience so that all students can use their talents to the full. The Carnegie Experience is delivered across teaching, research, volunteering, sport, all taking place at our prestigious Headingley campus; at the Headingley Carnegie Stadium; in primary and secondary schools; on football pitches; in lecture theatres; the Lake District and beyond.

In Carnegie we take pride in putting our students at the core of everything we do and at the centre of our way of doing things. We look forward to working with all of you to ensure that you experience the full range of opportunities made available by being a member of our vibrant community. From pre application, to joining us at Leeds Met through to life long association with us, in experiencing Carnegie our goal is to ensure that we continually raise our game to influence you for life.

BA (Hons) Education & Professional Development
(Full-time or part-time)

This award provides opportunities for undergraduate study aimed at career development or professional updating. These opportunities will be provided through an appropriately planned individual programme of study to match personal and professional goals.

You will use your own skills and experience to address a wide range of areas related to education. You will develop transferable skills that may be applied to a variety of employment, social and individual contexts. A variety of assessment methods are used including assignments, examinations, case studies, presentations and projects.

KEY FACTS
UCAS code: XX32 BA/EPD
Place of study: Headingley Campus
Start date: September/February
Length of study: Full-time 3 years. Part-time flexible.

ENTRY REQUIREMENTS
UCAS tariff points: 140–220 from 6, 12 or 18 unit awards.
Required GCSEs: English Language (grade C or above) or equivalent.
Other requirements: Students are encouraged to claim for advanced credit. Claims can be made for prior certificated learning or experiential learning. Certificated learning should be current and normally achieved within five years of application for this award.

For an explanation of how your qualifications fit into the **UCAS tariff**, please see the inside back cover. If you have **few or no formal qualifications**, but a wealth of relevant work and life experience, your application will still be considered.

BA (Hons) (leading to QTS) Early Childhood Education (level 2/3 top-up) (Full-time or part-time)

This 2-year route is designed for students who already have 120 level 1 credit points and 120 level 2 credits points. It is particularly relevant as a 'top-up' to students who have successfully completed a Foundation degree in Early Years and transferring from other degree courses (such as Childhood Studies or Primary Education).

It is offered as a full-time route or as a part-time route. Although based on years 3 and 4 (level 3) of the 4-year BA (Hons) in Early Childhood Education,

it has a flexible structure to take account of the different entry profiles that students arrive with.

KEY FACTS
UCAS code: X111 BAQ/nlp2
Place of study: Headingley Campus
Start date: September
Length of study: Full-time 2 years. Part-time 4 years.

ENTRY REQUIREMENTS
Successful completion of two years degree study (240 CATS credit points).
Required GCSEs: English Language, Maths and a science (grade C or above) or equivalent.
Other requirements: Please be aware that you will be required to attend an interview as part of the selection process. Two years' previous successful full-time higher education on a course is required involving a significant amount of study of childhood is required (eg Dip HE Playwork).

For an explanation of how your qualifications fit into the **UCAS tariff**, please see the inside back cover. If you have **few or no formal qualifications**, but a wealth of relevant work and life experience, your application will still be considered.

BA (Hons) (leading to QTS) Early Childhood Education (Full-time)

The Early Childhood Education (QTS) route is specifically designed to train specialist teachers to work with pupils aged 3–7 (Foundation Stage and Key Stage 1). Over the four years of this course, you

will cover both theoretical and practical aspects of early childhood education. The curriculum includes the study of early childhood education and child development, as well as personal and professional development.

In addition, students will undertake placements in schools and a range of other Early Childhood settings and by the end of the course will experience teaching both in foundation stage and in key stage 1.

KEY FACTS
UCAS code: X110 BAQ/nlp
Place of study: Headingley Campus
Start date: September
Length of study: Full-time 4 years.

ENTRY REQUIREMENTS
UCAS tariff points: 240 overall, to include a minimum of 160 from 6, 12 or 18 unit awards.
Required GCSEs: English Language, Maths and a Science (grade C or above) or equivalent.
Other requirements: Please be aware that you will be required to attend an interview as part of the selection process. Checks on applicants' medical fitness and lack of criminal convictions are made after they have been offered a place. Evidence is sought of work experience with children in the Early Years (3–7).

For an explanation of how your qualifications fit into the **UCAS tariff**, please see the inside back cover. If you have **few or no formal qualifications**, but a wealth of relevant work and life experience, your application will still be considered.

Fig. 14 Extract from Leeds Met. handbook on undergraduate courses 2007-8. (Carnegie Faculty office)

still been extended from ITE to include continuing professional development across the teacher's career. Whitty[32] claims that recent government policy decisions, such as the workforce remodelling agenda and the creation of teaching assistant posts, and the instigation of multi-agency work within the *Every Child Matters* legislation, has extended central government control even further into teacher education.[33]

These external influences, as well as changing views about adult learning and appropriate assessment of that learning, are reflected in examples of assignments shown in module handbooks for students (**Figure 18**).

The distribution of physical resources provided for ITE (**Figures 19 & 20**) emphasises the government's current priorities for the curriculum. It also evidences a key shift that Winifred Mercier would have greatly envied in the early 20th century – the burgeoning information revolution.

Example Proforma

Example: Summary of Lesson

Introduction	Development	Plenary

3.3.3. Reflected on activities from previous lesson. Identified general principles through Q&A. Introduced lesson focus. 3.3.3. Could have clearly outlined <u>objectives</u> as set out in the planning and developed Q&A to <u>build on</u> previous knowledge.	3.3.4. Discovery learning: use of a variety of <u>teaching strategies</u>, providing opportunities for creativity and skill development. 3.3.3. Use of reciprocal <u>teaching materials and resources</u> to facilitate learning and peer assessment. 3.3.3. <u>Adapted language</u> for teaching points on task cards.	3.3.7. Teacher led plenary helped <u>manage learning</u> of the group in latter stage of lesson. 3.3.3. <u>Explanations</u> and <u>questions</u> used effectively. 3.3.3. <u>Objectives</u> achieved? Reflect on these 3.3.12. Could provide handouts to summarise key points / set homework task.

Fig. 15
Slide from a mentor training session on improving the quality of feedback in relation to TDA standards. (Source: Chris Bouckley, Partnership Coordinator, secondary Physical Education, Qualified Teacher Status (QTS))

Fig. 16
Module Descriptor from
Level 3 Dissertation
Module Handbook 2007
indicating curriculum
content. (Source:
Carnegie Faculty courses
office)

1 MODULE DESCRIPTOR

Module Title	Dissertation – Individual Study				
	Credits	Hours	Level	Core for:	Optional for:
	30	300	3	All Scheme Undergraduate Awards	
Purpose/Rationale	To engage with the complexities of the research process at first hand and to appreciate the strengths and weaknesses of, and assumptions underpinning, their own and other people's research. Students undertake a small-scale research project of particular interest to them.				
Prerequisites	Successful completion of Level 2 or equivalent.				
Learning Outcomes	On completion of this module students will: • assemble, and analyse critically, key concepts and research findings relevant to their chosen focus; • formulate a research focus/question, and design and conduct a small–scale research project to address that focus/question having due regard to ethical issues; • communicate and appraise their results; and • reflect critically on the process of carrying out their own study.				
Key Skills	Academic and employability. Information literacy. Research.				
Content	The content of the module will cover: • identifying worthwhile and feasible foci for individual projects; • developing, sharing and refining a proposal for investigation; • linking theoretical aspects of research foci: literature reviewing; and research questions; • selecting, designing and implementing research methodology; • ethical issues in conducting research; and • analysing and reporting.				
Assessment Procedures	A dissertation of between 8,000-10,000 words.				
Teaching and Learning Strategy	• Issue-focused lectures at key points during the production of the dissertation. • Small group sessions with supervisor. • Individual support from supervisor.				

H:\CFSR-Archives\EPT-CHC\OFFICE\Module Handbooks 2006-07\Education and Professional Training\Carnegie Education Scheme\FINAL module handbook - Dissertation - Individual Study L3 27.09.06.doc   Page 3 of 19

The Headingley Campus Library with its books, periodicals and access to the world via the internet provides a knowledge resource for both guided and independent learning and for student teachers and their charges unimaginable in 1907. As 2007 BA (Hons) Primary Education student Rachel Settle put it:

ICT comes in to learning so much more now because we have interactive whiteboards in teaching rooms here and we had sessions training how to use them from Year 1 . . . and we have to keep an ICT portfolio.

In closing, it should be said that the trends behind the apparent progress in curriculum provision over the past century are not unique to either Leeds Met or, indeed, to the UK.[34] They appear to be part of a broader process across a range of social institutions towards the regulation of work, education and leisure. When examined in the context of the education and training of teachers, they do appear to suggest a process of 'back-to-the-future'.[35]

The task for Carnegie Faculty ITE staff, as we see it, is to continue to find spaces for curriculum debates about the knowledge question, the new knowledge economy, and global society based on research into policies, programs and practices, and wider disciplinary studies. Sociology, Philosophy, Psychology and History of Education help us make sense of past and present constructions of teacher education, then and now, and the ways our legacy feeds into current work. A key question is how teachers are positioned in relation to knowledge, learners, economic demands, and democratic values.[36] Again, graduate student Rachel Settle speaks volumes:

There is an emphasis on continually looking at what you've done, how you can use it, how you can improve, and it covers everything from teaching a lesson to assessing children, it informs your planning but it teaches you a lot about yourself as well . . . I think you can only really do it that way and if you chose not to look at what you've done and not benefit from reflection then you're not really going to improve and its something that's now spread through to assessment for all children, for pupils, because they now do peer assessment, look at a piece of work and find three good things about this and find one thing that you can find for improvement. That's the sort of thing. It's so beneficial.

Now, as then, staff endeavour to explore ways to develop curricula in line with the principles we hold dear, including the sorts of learning experiences that challenge student teachers to be critically reflective. The final word belongs to our student, Rachel Settle:

It's a great place to come to study and the best thing has been building up a network of friends and future colleagues. In terms of the actual university, it's a world away from a hundred years ago, completely different in every respect. Coming on campus rather than staying in residence, and dealing

with different subjects, more diversity in subjects, more lecturers. It's not just the [National Curriculum] subjects that you're going to need in a primary school but 'Professional Values, Knowledge and Practice', learning about Reflective Practice, and doing research as part of your routine.[37]

The authors wish to give special thanks to Dr Anne Flintoff, Associate Dean Denise Gilchrist, Dr Julia Lawrence, and Dr Sue Warren for thoughtful inputs to this chapter and critical feedback. Also to 2007 Primary Education student Rachel Settle for her valuable contribution.

*Fig. 17
School-based learning by ITE students 2007.
(Source: LeedsMet. Communications: Icon Photography)*

11 ASSIGNMENT DETAILS

A 2000 word report which draws on a specific aspect of SEN, considers the debate on inclusion and the implications for teaching and learning in educational settings. Through their directed activities students will have identified a specific aspect of Special need or disability and focussed on the issues for inclusion, teaching and learning. Through the module the students will have had an opportunity to consider issues raised for and against inclusion and should draw on these ideas to debate the implications for the inclusion of children in general and those children with the learning need identified. It is particularly important that the assignment reflects current policy at school, local and government level and recognises the international perspective, particularly in terms of human and social justice.

11.1 ASSESSMENT STRUCTURE

A report which draws on a specific aspect of SEN, considers the debate on inclusion and the implications for teaching and learning in educational settings. (2,000 words).

11.2 LEARNING OUTCOMES TO BE ASSESSED

On completion of this module students will:

1. identify and describe the key issues in the debates over inclusion in relation to the provision of education in Key Stages 1 to 3, including, for example, the Gifted and Talented;
2. identify and critique governmental policies and practice in relation to educational provision;
3. comment on the relationship between theories on approaches to inclusive education and professional practice (with particular reference to one aspect of SEN); and
4. present the results of an investigation in a form that uses appropriate referencing, grammar, standard English spelling, and punctuation.

11.3 KEY SKILLS TO BE ASSESSED

The following key skills are embedded in Learning Outcomes 1 to 4:

Application and reflection.
Data collection.
Information literacy.
Organisation and planning.
Report writing (including the academic skills of writing and referencing).
Understanding theory and principles.

The key skills will be assessed through the learning outcomes as identified by the assignment.

11.4 GUIDANCE

To prepare effectively for the assignment, students need to complete the Directed Activities which draw together the key aspects of the work.

In identifying a specific area of special need or disability, students should consider an aspect in which they have a particular interest or previous experience. In preparing the presentation, students should research the chosen aspect carefully drawing on both books and other resources. It is important to keep a careful record of these sources and to record carefully the content which either supports or contradicts their personal view.

The debate on inclusion is complex and requires considerable preparation. The earlier directed activities should enable students to identify the specific aspects of the debate and appropriate sources to support the opposing arguments, both from books, journals and web sites. In session 5, students will be asked to present a short statement about the inclusion debate to a small group of peers. Whilst this will not be a formal aspect of the assignment it should enable the key ideas and issues to be clarified.

It is important to plan an outline the assignment, linking together the key issues and avoiding an emphasis either on the specific need or the debate. There will be opportunities for tutorial to support the preparation of the written assignment.

11.5 SUBMISSION DATE AND ARRANGEMENTS

Submission Date/Time: **Thursday 10 May 2007 (Week 41)**

The completed assessment will be submitted via the Assignment Hand-in Box at Course Registry reception in Carnegie Hall. It will be receipted and dispatched to marking tutors by the assessment administrator.

Completed assessments cannot be submitted to any other location or persons.

Return Date: **31 May 2007**
Reassessment Date: **21 June 2007**

Re-assessment will be by re-submission of the above piece of work.

H:\CFSR\Courses\BA BSc (H) Primary Ed (QTS)\Documentation\Module Handbooks\2006-07\FINAL module handbook - PVKP Inclusive Education
Y2 18.12.06.doc
Page 20 of 25

H:\CFSR\Courses\BA BSc (H) Primary Ed (QTS)\Documentation\Module Handbooks\2006-07\FINAL module handbook - PVKP Inclusive Education
Y2 18.12.06.doc
Page 21 of 25

Fig. 18 Example of student assessment schedule for ITE students in 2007 from Module Handbook for Level 2 'Promoting & Supporting Learning and Integration – Inclusive Education'. (Source: Carnegie Faculty courses office)

Fig. 19
Example of resources
available for teachers in
training at Leeds
Metropolitan University
in 2007 – Headingley
Stadium IT facilities.
(Source: LeedsMet
Communications: Icon
Photography)

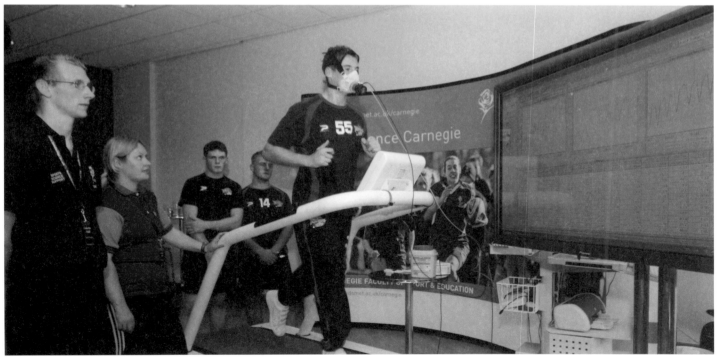

Fig. 20
Example of resources
available for teachers in
training at Leeds
Metropolitan University
in 2007 – Headingley
Stadium PE and Sport
facilities.(Source:
LeedsMet
Communications: Icon
Photography)

ENDNOTES

1 Board of Education (1907) *Regulations and Syllabuses for the Preliminary Examination for the Elementary School Teachers' Certificate* (original copy held by The National Archives ref. ED24/441).

2 See the advice to parents, boys and girls on examinations in Board of Education (1912) *How to Become a Teacher,* London, HMSO and Eyre and Spottiswood, Ltd pamphlet.

3 This concept of curriculum is based on the etymological analyses of D. Hamilton (1990) *Curriculum history* Geelong: Deakin University Press. Hamilton suggested that the word curriculum first appeared in educational texts in the 16th century, at a time when Latin was the universal language of scholarship. In Latin, curriculum referred to chariot racing, and had its root in the verb currere, to run. This 16th-century appropriation of curriculum by educationalists drew on these connotations of running or racing along a course to suggest that in educational institutions such as universities, colleges and schools, students move along or through a course of study. Hamilton argued that by the end of the 18th century the idea was well established in educational circles that the word curriculum was map-related and referred to a map of knowledge, and then later, through the 19th century, to the journey of the learner following particular routes across the landscape of knowledge. By the beginning of the 20th century there was an intermingling of notions associated with a map of knowledge and the journey of the learner. This intermingling of notions around the concept of curriculum is important for our understanding of the curriculum of teacher education at Leeds Met then and now. Hamilton made the interesting observation that some time during the 18th and 19th centuries, the concept of *Bildung* replaced curriculum within German and Scandinavian education. If the curriculum question is 'What should they know?', then *Bildung* responds to a deeper question of 'What should they become?'. The (much later) American appropriation of curriculum, during the first half of the 20th century, led to the further question (influenced by behaviourism) of 'What should they do?'.

4 The second documented the Board of Education's expectations for graduation from training, which would then equip candidates with the necessary qualifications for teaching.

5 Connell, L. (nd) *A Century of Teacher Training in Leeds 1875-1975.* Leeds: Leeds Metropolitan University, p. 95.

6 Samuel Childs' *Demonstration Lessons workbook,* September 1908 (original copy held by Leeds Metropolitian University Archives).

7 Young, M. F. D. (2006) Curriculum Studies and the Problem of Knowledge; Updating the Enlightenment? Chapter 50 in Lauder, H., Brown, P., Dillabough, J., and Halsey, A. H. (eds) *Education, Globalization and Social Change.* Oxford, p. 736/7. See also Higher Education Committee Chairman Fred Kinder's comments about specialists p. 27 in the 1906-1907 Annual Report to the Council of the City of Leeds (original held in Leeds Local and Family History Library. Call no.352.1 L517).

8 Ibid p. 30.

9 City of Leeds Training College (*c.* 1912) Prospectus (original copy held by Lori Beckett). See City of Leeds Training College (n.d) Temporary prospectus (original copy held by WYAS ref. WYL863/7S).

10 Op.cit., p. 87.

11 Simon, B. (1974) *Education and Labour Movements 1870-1920.* London: Lawrence & Wishart.

12 Board of Education Circular 846 *Hygiene and Physical Training. Issue of Statement to Certificated Teachers who included the subject in the Course of Training* (original copy held in West Yorkshire Archive Service [WYAS] ref: LEA file 78).

13 According to Connell op.cit.

14 An image of Conditions of Admission from the CLTC 1912 Prospectus is reproduced in Lori Beckett, with Anne Flintoff and Sue Warren's chapter on the Education and Training of Teachers.

15 Mercier, W. (1909) An experiment in the teaching of history. Paper read to Manchester branch of the Historical Association on 22 January. Printed as Leaflet No.17, June.

16 Mercier, W. (1919) President's Address to the Training College Association. *Journal of Experimental Pedagogy and Training College Record.* Vol.5, No.1. March 5, p. 4.

17 Ibid. p. 5.

18 Ibid p. 5.

19 See Jacqui Dean's chapter on Student Participation, where she uses a 'Remembrance' by Mr E. H. Mitchell, a student resident of St Anne's Hill in 1911, printed p. 12 in Pickering's Part 1 1907-1933 in *A Short History of the City of Leeds Training College 1907-1957.*

20 See TDA at www.tda.gov.uk/Recruit/thetrainingprocess/choosingacourse.aspx

21 As noted in the preceding chapter on The Education and Training of Teachers, the Qualifications and Curriculum Authority (QCA) launched the new secondary curriculum in July, 2007, which has implications for Carnegie Faculty work and academics' debates about the knowledge question.

22 Leeds Metropolitan University *Undergraduate courses 2007-8,* pp. 169-81.

23 See the TDA's new *Professional Standards for Teachers. Why sit still in your career?,* released for implementation in September, 2007, at www.tda.gov.uk/standards

24 See www.standards.dfes.gov.uk/primary/

25 See Jill Adam and Anne Campbell's chapter on Partnerships.

26 In secondary Physical Education, for example, academics work in partnership with teachers engaged as school-based mentors of student teachers. The mentors receive training in a range of locations, including university.

27 An image of the Carnegie Faculty ITE staff, 2007, is reproduced in Lori Beckett's Editor's Introduction.

28 PhD by dissertation or publication; EdD with a strong professional focus, partly taught and with an emphasis on presentation and dissemination of professional knowledge acquired.

29 Op.cit.

30 Ironically, as teacher education became more like university education, by the mid to late 1960s universities 'now began to come under increasing pressure from central government as it sought to remodel the work of these institutions to suit perceived national needs'. Even though the first Bachelor of Education degrees in teacher education had appeared in university Departments of Education in the 1960s, early signs of a shift in momentum back to government control came in the form of the new Council for National Academic Awards (CNAA) B.Ed. degree in the 1970s. While the 1988 Education Reform Act initiated a programme of increased government control over school education and teacher education, 'New Labour's education reforms have built on the "new right settlement" and even gone beyond it'.

31 See the new TDA standards, op.cit. See also Edwards, A., Gilroy, P., and Hartley, D. (2002) *Rethinking Teacher Education. Collaborative responses to uncertainty.* London and New York: RoutledgeFalmer, p. 72ff.

32 Whitty, G. (2006) Teacher Professionalism in a New Era. Text of the first General Teaching Council for Northern Ireland Annual Lecture delivered at Queen's University, Belfast 14 March, p. 4, see www.ioe.ac.uk/directorate/GTC-NIAaddress03-2006.pdf

33 A full discussion of the influences of neo-liberals, neo-conservatives, teacher education professionals and technocrats based on their research into Modes of Teacher Education is to be found in Furlong, J., Barton, L., Miles, S., Whiting, C., and Whitty, G. (2000) *Teacher Education in Transition.* Buckingham: Open University Press, chapter 1.

34 See, for example, J. Furlong et al *op.cit.* Chapter 10, and Young, M. F. D. (1998) *The curriculum of the future,* Chapter 11, 'Towards a New Curriculum for Teacher Education'. London: Falmer.

35 A concept developed by Lori Beckett in her inaugural professorial lecture, The Curriculum Imagination, delivered at Leeds Met on 5 October, 2006.

36 See Edwards et al (2002) op.cit.

37 From transcript of interview with B.A student, Rachel Settle June 2007

CHAPTER 8

Teaching Methods, Pedagogies and Professional Learning

Lori Beckett and Jon Tan

Looking back one hundred years ago, part of the Academic and Professional Training at City of Leeds Training College **(Figure 1)** *was devoted to method instruction in the two-year course and in practising schools, or what we might call professional learning about teaching.[1] Candidates wanting admission to the City of Leeds Training College were required to attend an interview and if they had teaching experience, presumably through their apprenticeship as pupil-teachers or bursars/student teachers, to bring a report as to their aptitude for teaching.[2] This would have included the Headteacher's insights into the candidate's capacity for teaching and becoming a certificated teacher.*

ACADEMIC AND PROFESSIONAL TRAINING

SCHEME OF STUDY THE ordinary course of study is the "Two Years' Course" described in the Regulations of the Board of Education for the Training of Teachers for Elementary Schools.

PRACTISING SCHOOLS THE College is within easy reach of a large number of schools of all types—better class schools, schools in poor districts, special schools, schools for the blind and deaf, and for cripple children, which may be used for observation, demonstration, and practice.

THE COLLEGE YEAR THE College Year begins in September and is divided into three terms, each of about twelve weeks' duration. The year closes at the end of the Final Examination of the Board of Education, which is usually held in the first week in July.

Entrance to Hostel.

11

Fig. 1 Extract from City of Leeds Training College (c. 1911) Handbook. (Source: Lori Beckett)

Fig. 2 (Right top) Front cover of Board of Education's (1912) How to Become a Teacher in a Public Elementary School booklet. (Right bottom) Extract p. 9 from Board of Education's (1912) How to Become a Teacher in a Public Elementary School booklet. (Source: Courtesy of Special Collections, Leeds University, Shelf mark 93/032)

TEACHING METHODS 'THEN'

The Board of Education's regulations[3] specified that during a course in a Training College, students should receive instruction in the Theory and Practice of Teaching and pass a final examination (**Figures 2**), which entitled recognition as a certificated teacher. We learned from the appendices that the Qualifications necessary for Recognition as a Certificated Teacher (**Figure 3**) must include the methods of teaching. It is important to note that the terms 'teaching methods' and 'pedagogy' were used interchangeably then, in official documentation originating from the Board of Education and literature emanating from the academic community.[4] Whatever the preferred term, the focus was on the school classroom, with students learning about teaching, which included the subject matter and the practices employed, of which drilling and rote learning are the most famous.

BOARD OF EDUCATION.

HOW TO BECOME A TEACHER

IN A

PUBLIC ELEMENTARY SCHOOL.

LONDON:
PUBLISHED BY HIS MAJESTY'S STATIONERY OFFICE.
To be purchased, either directly or through any Bookseller, from
WYMAN AND SONS, LTD., FETTER LANE, E.C.; or
H.M. STATIONERY OFFICE (SCOTTISH BRANCH), 23, FORTH STREET, EDINBURGH or
E. PONSONBY, LTD., 116, GRAFTON STREET, DUBLIN;
or from the Agencies in the British Colonies and Dependencies,
the United States of America, the Continent of Europe and Abroad of
T. FISHER UNWIN, LONDON, W.C.

PRINTED BY
EYRE AND SPOTTISWOODE, LTD., EAST HARDING STREET, E.C.,
PRINTERS TO THE KING'S MOST EXCELLENT MAJESTY.
1912.
Price Fourpence.

6. Students in Training Colleges.

(5) During their course in a Training College, students receive instruction in the Theory and Practice of Teaching, and also instruction of a general character in preparation for their Final Examination at the end of their course. Success in this Final Examination entitles the students to recognition as Certificated Teachers, subject to their satisfying the requirements of the Elementary School Teachers Superannuation Rules, 1899 (*see* Section (8) 3). Under certain conditions, students may follow special courses of training with a view to obtaining recognition as Certificated Teachers in schools for blind, deaf, or mentally defective children.

E.

QUALIFICATIONS NECESSARY FOR RECOGNITION AS A CERTIFICATED
TEACHER.

1. In order to be recognised as a Certificated Teacher, the candidate
must satisfy the Board of Education, in the manner prescribed by the
Elementary School Teachers Superannuation Rules, 1899, of his or her age
and physical capacity, and must possess one of the following qualifications :—

He or she must either—

    (i) have been trained in a Training College recognised under the
Regulations for the Training of Teachers for Elementary
Schools and have passed the Board's Final Examination of
Students in Training Colleges or an Alternative Final Exami-
nation sanctioned under those Regulations ;

or (ii) have passed the Certificate Examination of the Board for Teachers
in Elementary Schools ;

or (iii) have been recognised as a Certificated Teacher by the Scotch
Education Department after passing the Certificate Examination or satisfactorily completing the period of training
prescribed by the Regulations of that Department ;

or (iv) be certificated in the First Class by the Irish Commissioners of
National Education ; or be reported by them to have passed
the revised examination and to have received a Diploma from
them ; provided in either case that he or she has been trained
in a Training College, and that no adverse report is received
from the Commissioners ;

or (v) have passed a final examination for a degree, held by a University
in the British Empire and recognised by the Board for this
purpose, or be an Associate of the Royal College of Science ;
provided in each case that he or she holds one of the following
certificates of proficiency* in the Theory and Practice of
Teaching :—

    (1) The Diploma of the University of Oxford in the
Theory, History, and Practice of Education.

    (2) The Certificate of the University of Cambridge in
the Theory, History, and Practice of Teaching, if accompanied
by the Certificate of Practical Efficiency in Teaching.

    (3) The Teacher's Diploma of the University of London.

    (4) The Durham University Certificate of the Theory
and Practice of Teaching.

    (5) The Teacher's Diploma of the Victoria University of
Manchester.

    (6) The Diploma of Associate, Licentiate, or Fellow of
the College of Preceptors, if accompanied by the Special
Certificate of ability to teach.

    (7) The Schoolmaster's Diploma granted to Graduates
by the University of Edinburgh.

* The continued recognition of these certificates of proficiency is under consideration. Candidates desiring recognition in virtue of certificates of proficiency
granted on courses of study and training begun on or after August 1st, 1908, may
be required to show that their courses have included the methods of teaching all the
subjects ordinarily taught in Public Elementary Schools, and a definite period of
practice in teaching in Public or other Elementary Schools.

The prominence of teaching methods, inextricably linked to
curriculum and questions of knowledge, is further reflected in a number
of documentary sources. In a list of early salaries (**Figure 4**), we see that
Master of Method, Mr T. P. Holgate received £225 in 1907 and was
second only to Principal Mr Walter Parsons, who received £500. The list
of Methods staff show they were the most numerous and most qualified
at the City of Leeds Training College, as recorded in the prospectuses
and handbooks.[5] The various qualifications, Masters and Bachelors of
Arts and Science and a Higher Froebel Certificate, suggest that such
expertise was highly valued and the achievement of such status required
significant commitment.

5.

4. Early Salaries

The earlier records seem to have been very carefully maintained with
the possible exception of changes in the College appointment, which
sometimes look incomplete. Section 12, total annual emoluments, must
have kept the recorder busy. It showed initial salaries and all
subsequent changes, including annual increments. Here are the first
ten

1. W. Parsons.   Principal. 7 October 1907. £500, altered later to
£750 with house, presumably when the new
College was built.

2. T.P. Holgate.   Master of Method. 7 October 1907. £225. This
to £240 from April 1914.

3. H.T. Todd.   Science Tutor. 7 October 1907. £200.

4. R.H. Parker.   Art Tutor. 26 September 1910. £200.

5. W. Taylor.   Tutor for Mathematics and Geography. 7 October 1907. £200.

6. G.C. Dent.   Tutor for English and History. 7 October 1907. £200.

7. G.E. Wilkinson.   English Tutor. 7 October 1907. £185.

8. J.E. Parkinson.   Lecturer in Mathematics. 7 October 1907. £185.

9. C.H. Jarvis.   Lecturer in History. 26 September 1910. £150.

10. P.J. Cooper.   Assistant Master of Method. 26 September 1910. £140.

*Fig. 4 Loose page found
in Carnegie archives*

This is substantiated by biographical details of City of Leeds
Training College Vice Principal (1913-16), Winifred Mercier,[6] a pupil
teacher before doing a two-year course at Maria Grey Training College
and the exam for the Cambridge Teachers' Syndicate, where she was
placed in the first class of both the theoretical and practical parts of the
examination. She had been working towards an external London degree,
abandoned when she went to Somerville in 1904. The following year she
won the Margaret Evans Historical Prize given by the Association for the
Education of Women at Oxford, and went on to matriculate and complete
her degree when Oxford made degrees available to women.

Grier[7] noted she had an intense respect for and appreciation of
scholarly work, but did not welcome University Honours Graduates into
the elementary schools because of their subject specialisms. Indeed she
is credited with saying 'they think they will have to teach subjects and
forget they have to teach children'. One can only speculate that Miss
Mercier would have had something in common with Miss Eggar, a
member of the Methods staff at City of Leeds Training College, given her
qualifications. Putting children at the centre, closely configuring the

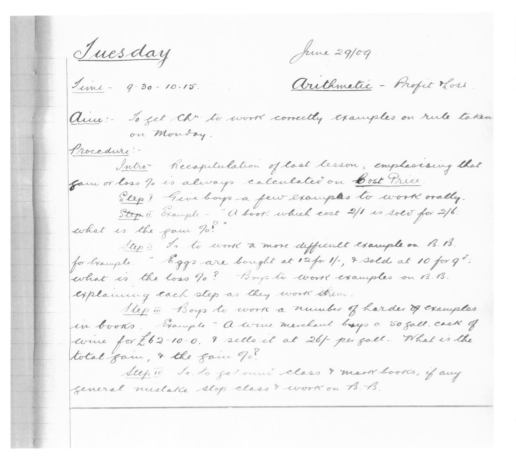

progression of teaching with their development, and giving ownership to the learner in self-discovery is at the core of these ideas, echoing the seminal work of Friedrich Froebel in the field of elementary education.[8]

Such approaches are clearly evident in Mercier's work prior to her appointment at Leeds. Writing as a teacher at the Manchester Girls High School, Mercier drew attention to the expectations of teachers to 'know how to do it' and to make sense of the advice and example that surrounds their day-to-day practice. In a classroom-based pedagogical experiment,[9] she addressed the challenges associated with what we might now term motivation and engagement in the teaching of history. Concerned with 'set lessons' and the anxiety generated by an obligation to 'produce a certain result in knowledge', she explored an alternative way of promoting pupil's learning through the stimulation of debate, through deeper engagement with material and texts, and through clear messages about progress and achievement. Her account of the 'experiment' provides us with a rich descriptive analysis of different approaches to teaching and learning, marked by pupil centred debate and group work, and significantly the idea of the teacher as a facilitator of learning, rather than an instructor.

This approach to teaching and learning was professionally popular at the time, though not without its contrasts. According to Dr C. Spearman,[10] a Reader in experimental psychology at the University College, London, in 1912 there were contrasting ideas as to the balance of theory and practice of pedagogy: one seeing that it *should follow, not idle theory, but real experience; it should make tests not phantastically artificial, but thoroughly practical*. Spearman's discussion makes for interesting reading, providing a valuable commentary on the relationship between learning about teaching and teaching practices. While he confined his analysis to the teaching of arithmetic, seemingly a common practice at the time, his comments are noteworthy: . . . *a method of instruction is a very complex thing (because) success depends not only on the method being mental or not, but also on many other important factors, such as the relative predominance of concrete, schematic or symbolic material, the interplay of induction and deduction, the degree of monographical treatment, and so on.*[11] The fact that Spearman used a very specific example prompts us to think further about the application of method to different subjects, different schools, and different learners' needs.

Then, as now, it was normal for elementary teachers to be asked to teach across a broad range of subjects, but learning about the subject matter being taught and learning about teaching was far from easy. We can see this challenge in the work book on demonstration lessons[12] of City of Leeds Training College student, Samuel Childs, who demonstrated the links between professional knowledge of arithmetic, teaching methods, and the importance of experiential learning (**Figure 5**). His 1907 school practice book[13] provides insights into his professional learning, but also insights into the Supervisor's ideas in regard to teaching about teaching (**Figure 6**).

The Board of Education final examination[14] on Principles of Teaching (**Figure 7**) provided the best indication of the distinction between learning what was being taught and the ways it was being taught. In Section III, candidates were asked to describe the main principles for a scheme of arithmetic they constructed, based on the *Suggestions to Teachers,* and illustrate each point noting its superiority to other schemes. We presume from this question there was advice on teaching provided from bodies like the Board of Education, that it was mandatory knowledge for Training College students, and they were expected to not only demonstrate this knowledge but also argue the merits of the scheme.

Other elements of the 'learning about teaching' agenda at the time are also evident in the same examination, because if we study the questions we see reference to the school and classroom environment; expertise and age-specific teaching approaches, which recognise a

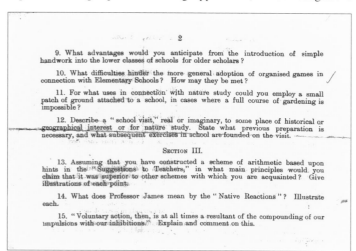

Fig. 7
Final Examination, 1909. Principles of Teaching Syllabus No. 1. (Source: West Yorkshire Archive Service ref. WYL863/40)

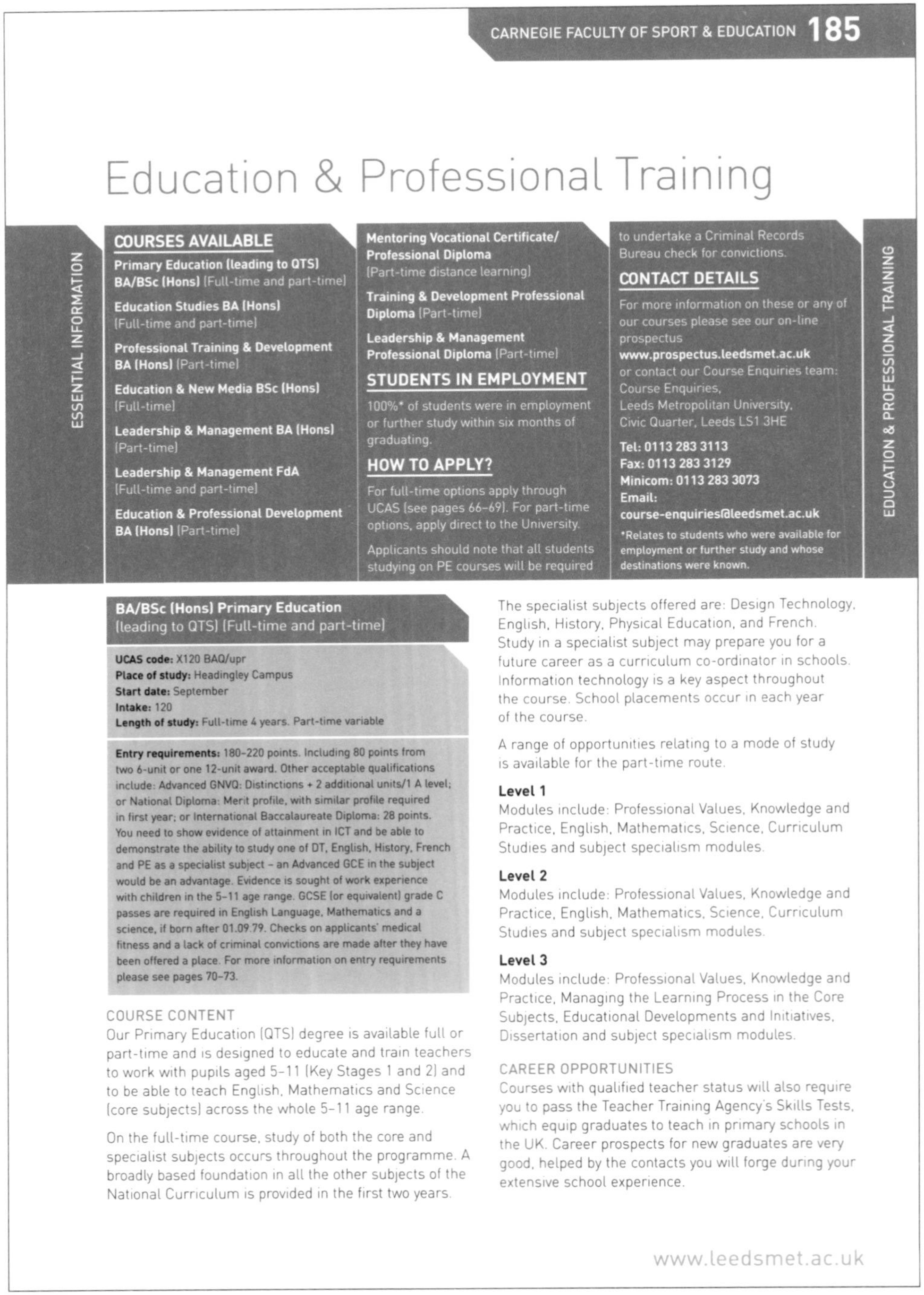

Education & Professional Training

COURSES AVAILABLE

Primary Education (leading to QTS)
BA/BSc (Hons) (Full-time and part-time)

Education Studies BA (Hons)
(Full-time and part-time)

Professional Training & Development
BA (Hons) (Part-time)

Education & New Media BSc (Hons)
(Full-time)

Leadership & Management BA (Hons)
(Part-time)

Leadership & Management FdA
(Full-time and part-time)

Education & Professional Development
BA (Hons) (Part-time)

Mentoring Vocational Certificate/
Professional Diploma
(Part-time distance learning)

Training & Development Professional
Diploma (Part-time)

Leadership & Management
Professional Diploma (Part-time)

STUDENTS IN EMPLOYMENT

100%* of students were in employment
or further study within six months of
graduating.

HOW TO APPLY?

For full-time options apply through
UCAS (see pages 66–69). For part-time
options, apply direct to the University.

Applicants should note that all students
studying on PE courses will be required

to undertake a Criminal Records
Bureau check for convictions.

CONTACT DETAILS

For more information on these or any of
our courses please see our on-line
prospectus
www.prospectus.leedsmet.ac.uk
or contact our Course Enquiries team:
Course Enquiries,
Leeds Metropolitan University,
Civic Quarter, Leeds LS1 3HE

Tel: 0113 283 3113
Fax: 0113 283 3129
Minicom: 0113 283 3073
Email:
course-enquiries@leedsmet.ac.uk

*Relates to students who were available for
employment or further study and whose
destinations were known.

ESSENTIAL INFORMATION

EDUCATION & PROFESSIONAL TRAINING

BA/BSc (Hons) Primary Education
(leading to QTS) (Full-time and part-time)

UCAS code: X120 BAQ/upr
Place of study: Headingley Campus
Start date: September
Intake: 120
Length of study: Full-time 4 years. Part-time variable

Entry requirements: 180–220 points. Including 80 points from
two 6-unit or one 12-unit award. Other acceptable qualifications
include: Advanced GNVQ: Distinctions + 2 additional units/1 A level;
or National Diploma: Merit profile, with similar profile required
in first year; or International Baccalaureate Diploma: 28 points.
You need to show evidence of attainment in ICT and be able to
demonstrate the ability to study one of DT, English, History, French
and PE as a specialist subject – an Advanced GCE in the subject
would be an advantage. Evidence is sought of work experience
with children in the 5–11 age range. GCSE (or equivalent) grade C
passes are required in English Language, Mathematics and a
science, if born after 01.09.79. Checks on applicants' medical
fitness and a lack of criminal convictions are made after they have
been offered a place. For more information on entry requirements
please see pages 70–73.

COURSE CONTENT
Our Primary Education (QTS) degree is available full or
part-time and is designed to educate and train teachers
to work with pupils aged 5–11 (Key Stages 1 and 2) and
to be able to teach English, Mathematics and Science
(core subjects) across the whole 5–11 age range.

On the full-time course, study of both the core and
specialist subjects occurs throughout the programme. A
broadly based foundation in all the other subjects of the
National Curriculum is provided in the first two years.

The specialist subjects offered are: Design Technology,
English, History, Physical Education, and French.
Study in a specialist subject may prepare you for a
future career as a curriculum co-ordinator in schools.
Information technology is a key aspect throughout
the course. School placements occur in each year
of the course.

A range of opportunities relating to a mode of study
is available for the part-time route.

Level 1
Modules include: Professional Values, Knowledge and
Practice, English, Mathematics, Science, Curriculum
Studies and subject specialism modules.

Level 2
Modules include: Professional Values, Knowledge and
Practice, English, Mathematics, Science, Curriculum
Studies and subject specialism modules.

Level 3
Modules include: Professional Values, Knowledge and
Practice, Managing the Learning Process in the Core
Subjects, Educational Developments and Initiatives,
Dissertation and subject specialism modules.

CAREER OPPORTUNITIES
Courses with qualified teacher status will also require
you to pass the Teacher Training Agency's Skills Tests,
which equip graduates to teach in primary schools in
the UK. Career prospects for new graduates are very
good, helped by the contacts you will forge during your
extensive school experience.

www.leedsmet.ac.uk

Fig. 8 Extract Leeds Met handbook on undergraduate courses 2006-7. (Source: Carnegie Faculty office)

chronology of child development in learning; pastoral responsibilities that identify and attend to children's welfare, moral and physical; an understanding of the different needs of individual pupils, coupled with the ability to implement appropriate teaching strategies; teaching pupils and planning for their educational progress with reference to external standards and measures of quality; strategies for classroom behaviour management; and knowledge of approaches to assessment. We see, then, that professional decisions about appropriate teaching methods and pedagogical approaches were significantly complex and required a broad consideration of social, environmental and school factors impacting on learning.

Writing years after she left City of Leeds Training College, Winifred Mercier[15] was critical of some teaching methods. *'Chalk and talk' was stigmatised long ago as an educational failure, and we need not discuss its evils'*. Mercier's concern was for the system of training, a vocational course primarily directed towards fostering creative power. *'The imitative, the repetitive, the mechanical processes must be limited; the reflective, the inventive, the creative encouraged'*. She called this the development of a central intellectual interest, evidence of her concern for developing a pedagogy of teacher education.[16] *'In the courses in geography or history, etc, the development of the student's own knowledge of the subject should proceed together with her study of its possibilities as a teaching subject'*.

There are many messages about approaches to teaching methods that we can glean from the archival materials. Mercier, working all those years ago, not only provided us with invaluable insights into classroom practices and experiment, a nascent form of teacher research, but she provoked us to think deeply about teaching and learning about teaching. She is saying to us that students of teaching (student teachers) and teachers of teaching (academics) need to be consciously working at two levels, on the nature of the content to be examined in the teaching and learning environment; and on the nature of teaching being employed.[17]

PEDAGOGY OF TEACHER EDUCATION 'NOW'

A substantial part of the Carnegie Faculty Initial Teacher Education (ITE) programmes are devoted to Professional Studies, which are intended to facilitate student teachers' critical learning about teaching and teaching styles, alongside curriculum and knowledge questions. They provide the

Left form:

	Leeds Metropolitan University			MODULE APPROVAL/DESCRIPTOR FORM FOR USE FROM November 2006	
1	Module Title	Pedagogical Perspectives for Learning, Teaching and Assessment			
2	Short Module Title (30 characters or less)	Ped Persp for LTA	3	Date of Approval	02/05/07
4	Version Number	1	5	Date of Version	02/05/07
6	Level	2	7	Credits	15
8	Status		9	Notional Hours	150
10	Course code (Banner)		11	CRN	

28	Module aims	The aims of this module are to enable students to develop their learning in Introduction to Teaching. Students will review and extend their knowledge of teaching styles; forms and methods for assessment for learning will be investigated with consideration of the theoretical and practical implications of inclusive education
29	Learning outcomes	By the end of this module, students should be able to: • Analyse the relationship between theory and practice in the roles and responsibilities of teachers with respect to planning and assessing learning in the medium-term in ways which respond to different learning needs • Select and critique a wide range of current and appropriate literature related to assessment for learning • Select and evaluate relationships between theory and practice related to a range of teaching and learning styles, including strategies for understanding and managing troublesome behaviour, bullying and harassment in educational contexts • evaluate and reflect upon their individual learning and development through this module and practical experiences of planning for learning, teaching and assessment in a form which correctly uses the Harvard referencing system, Standard English grammar, punctuation and spelling
30	Key Skills developed and/or assessed in the module (Please specify which are developed and which are assessed)	Application and reflection assessed Communication assessed Group/interpersonal assessed Organising and planning assessed Technical skills developed Data collection and interpretation assessed Theory and Principles assessed
31	Indicative content	• pedagogical approaches to teaching, learning and assessment, matching learning and teaching styles effectively, responding to a range of individual learning needs • Planning, teaching, assessing, reporting in the medium term; target setting for individualised learning and development • Forms of assessment for learning: formative, diagnostic, summative, ipsative; choosing appropriate strategies • Strategies for reflecting on individual learning and progress in theory and practice • Classroom organisation and management, including managing behaviour
32	Teaching and Learning Strategies	A variety of teaching and learning strategies will be employed: lectures, workshops, practical experience in school, on-line and directed activities
33	Assessment	Formative: directed activities to support and develop learning, peer, self and

H:\CFSR\Course Registry Education\Validation documentation\Modules\L2 Pedagogical Perspectives for LTA.doc
2

Right form:

	Leeds Metropolitan University			MODULE APPROVAL/DESCRIPTOR FORM FOR USE FROM November 2006	
1	Module Title	Pedagogical Perspectives for Learning, Teaching and Assessment			
2	Short Module Title (30 characters or less)	Ped Persp for LTA	3	Date of Approval	02/05/07
4	Version Number	1	5	Date of Version	02/05/07
6	Level	2	7	Credits	15
8	Status		9	Notional Hours	150
10	Course code (Banner)		11	CRN	

	(Please detail all components)	tutor assessed Summative: Portfolio containing a reflective statement of learning and development with completed supporting directed activities, plans and evaluations of tasks in school. 2000 words equivalent, 100% *(including % of final mark)*
34	Rationale for assessment and relationship of assessment methods to learning outcomes	The rationale for a spread of formative and synoptic summative assessment in this module is to allow for smarter assessment processes and engage the students in the process of formative assessment through the use of self-, peer- and tutor assessed activities. The formative and summative processes will assist in reflection on and the completion of the PDP section together with the review of the TDA Standards in the School Experience 2 module.
35	Indicative sources (texts / web based)	Black, P, Harrison, C, Lee, C Marshall, B & Wiliam, D (2003) *Assessment for Learning: Putting it into practice* Maidenhead: Open University Press Clarke, S (2001) *Unlocking Formative Assessment* London: Hodder and Stoughton Clarke, S (2003) *Enriching Feedback in the Primary Classroom* London: Hodder and Stoughton DfES (2001) *Learning and Teaching – A Strategy for Professional Development* DfEE 0071/2002 London: DfES Gipps, C and Stobart, G (1997) *Assessment: a teachers guide to the issues* London: Hodder and Stoughton Hayes, D. (1999) *Planning, Teaching and Classroom Management in Primary Schools.* London: David Fulton Hoodless, P. Bermingham, S., McCreery, E. & Bowen, P. (2003) *Meeting the professional Standards for QTS: Teaching Humanities in Primary Schools.* Exeter: Learning Matters. Hall, K & Burke, W M (2003) *Making Formative Assessment work: Effective Practice in the primary classroom* Maidenhead: Open University Press Mitchell, G (2001) *Practical Strategies for Individual Behaviour Difficulties* London: David Fulton Overall, L & Sangster, M (2006) *Assessment: a practical guide for primary teachers* London: Continuum Roffey, S (ed) (2002) *School Behaviour and Families: frameworks for working together* London: David Fulton Suschitzky, W & Chapman, J C (1998) *Valued Children, Informed Teaching* Buckingham: Open University Press

H:\CFSR\Course Registry Education\Validation documentation\Modules\L2 Pedagogical Perspectives for LTA.doc
3

spine of the BA (Hons) and Postgraduate Certificate of Education (PGCE) programmes for Early Childhood Education and Primary Education, leading to Qualified Teacher Status (QTS). This work is developed and contextualised in core subject modules (English, Mathematics and Science) as well as in modules on subject pedagogies (that is, how to teach the subjects) (**Figure 8**). In the newly approved courses,[18] one Level 2 module is entitled Pedagogical Perspectives for Learning, Teaching and Assessment (**Figure 9**). Professional Studies is similarly apparent in the BA (Hons) and PGCE programmes for Physical Education (**Figure 10**).

Candidates wanting admission into ITE are required to attend an interview and report on their experiences of working with children in educational settings. It is essential they have some experience, given they

Fig. 9
Extract from Leeds Met Carnegie Faculty Module Descriptor. (Source: Carnegie Faculty Archives)

Physical Education

ESSENTIAL INFORMATION

PHYSICAL EDUCATION

COURSES AVAILABLE

Physical Education BA (Hons)
(Full-time)

Secondary Physical Education BA (Hons) (leading to QTS)
(Full-time)

Physical Education with Outdoor Education BA (Hons)
(Full-time)

RELATED COURSES

Sports Development & PE
(see page 203)

PE & Sport & Exercise Science
(see page 198)

STUDENTS IN EMPLOYMENT

100%* of students were in employment or further study within six months of graduating.

HOW TO APPLY?

For full-time options apply through UCAS (see pages 66–69). For part-time options, apply direct to the University.

Applicants should note that all students studying on PE courses will be required to undertake a Criminal Records Bureau check for convictions. Certain convictions would result in students not being eligible to work with children and therefore any such students would be unable to complete the requirements of the course.

CONTACT DETAILS

For more information on these or any of our courses please see our on-line prospectus
www.prospectus.leedsmet.ac.uk
or contact our Course Enquiries team:
Course Enquiries,
Leeds Metropolitan University,
Civic Quarter, Leeds LS1 3HE

Tel: 0113 283 3113
Fax: 0113 283 3129
Minicom: 0113 283 3073
Email:
course-enquiries@leedsmet.ac.uk

*Relates to students who were available for employment or further study and whose destinations were known.

BA (Hons) Physical Education
(Full-time)

UCAS code: X390 BA/PE
Place of study: Headingley Campus
Start date: September
Intake: 120
Length of study: 3 years

Entry requirements: 260 UCAS tariff points. Including 220 points from two 6-unit or one 12-unit award. Other acceptable qualifications include: International Baccalaureate: 28 pts; or Advanced GNVQ distinction + 2 additional units or an A level. Mature applicants with suitable profiles will be assessed on ability to benefit from the course. GCSE passes (grade C or above) in Mathematics and English Language are required. All applicants for this course must attend an interview, these will be held in the spring term and decisions on places will only be made once all interviews have been completed. For more information on entry requirements please see pages 70–73.

COURSE CONTENT
This degree focuses on lifelong physical education. Central to the course are the strong links between theory and practice, with practical work and student interaction at the heart of the student experience.

The course will develop your ability to analyse human movement and physical activity through a variety of disciplinary perspectives, in a range of different contexts. These contexts include physical education, and sport and physical activity with options to select practical electives to meet your individual interests and needs.

You will consider the holistic multi-disciplinary study of the physical education through theory and theoretical applications, in a variety of themes and issues. In years 2 and 3 of the course, you can select theoretical and practical modules to develop your personal interests and career profile. Although the course does not lead to qualified teacher status, it does provide an excellent first degree for entry onto postgraduate courses for secondary physical education leading to QTS.

The nature of the course will require you to take part in all forms of physical activity, including swimming. You are expected to contribute to the cost of the first year residential induction. All students will be engaged in a structured tutorial programme over 3 years, leading to the production of a personal development file. The tutorial programme is designed to help you develop key skills and enhance your employability. The expectation is that you maintain a physically active lifestyle at Leeds Met and contribute to sport at the University and our extensive programme of volunteer work.

BA (Hons) Secondary Physical Education
(leading to QTS) (Full-time)

UCAS code: XC16 BAQ/sec4PE
Place of study: Headingley Campus
Start date: September
Intake: 48
Length of study: 4 years

Entry requirements: 260 UCAS tariff points. Including 220 points from two 6-unit or one 12-unit award. Other acceptable qualification include Advanced GNVQ: Distinction + 2 additional units/1 A level; or National Diploma: 4 Distinctions & 3 Merits from final year units, with a similar profile required in the first year; or International Baccalaureate Diploma: 28 points. Applicants should have a relevant GCE A level. Alternative qualifications or experience will be considered where applicants have not taken a GCE A level in PE or Sports Studies. GCSEs (or equivalent) passes are required in English language & maths. Applicants must have the ability to take part in all forms of physical activity. Checks on applicants' medical fitness and lack of criminal convictions are made after they have been offered a place. For more information on entry requirements please see pages 70–73.

COURSE CONTENT
This 4 year course is specifically designed for those wishing to teach Physical Education in secondary schools. The course will equip individuals to meet the demands of Key Stages 3 & 4 and Post 16 teaching of the subject.

The subject integrates theory and practice in teaching the National Curriculum in PE. Teacher trainees are encouraged to become competent in the performance and teaching of the full range of activities up to and including A level and to appreciate the importance of

PE to all children's fitness, health, and moral personal, social and cultural development.

You will cover such areas as how pupils learn, adolescent development, language in the classroom, behaviour and discipline, effective teaching and the National Curriculum. Other topics covered include the assessment of pupils and the wider responsibilities of schools and teachers. Issues surrounding teachers legal liabilities and responsibilities are addressed throughout the course. On this course there is a requirement to apply subject and professional knowledge in teaching contexts in order to develop practical teaching skills.

FACILITIES
Facilities available include the Carnegie Regional Gymnastics and Tennis Centre, extensive playing fields, two sports halls, two squash courts, fitness areas, two gymnasia, two synthetic turf pitches, a swimming pool and sports science laboratories. Trainees also have access to the University's learning centres, which integrate facilities such as library provision, Internet labs and PC suites. There is also a dedicated IT suite within the School of Education and Professional Development.

ASSESSMENT
You will be assessed against the standards for Qualified Teacher Status (DfEE Circular 02/02), which are phased across each of the teaching placements, in years 1 to 4. There is a strong emphasis on integrating theoretical studies with practical teaching skills. You will spend time in school every year. In the initial phase of the

www.leedsmet.ac.uk

www.leedsmet.ac.uk

Fig. 10 Extract Leeds Met handbook on undergraduate courses 2006-7. (Source: Carnegie Faculty office)

are required to demonstrate their critical thinking about their understanding of teaching.

In September 2007, a new suite of Professional Standards for Teaching was implemented.[19] Designed to be applied to all stages of a teaching career, these Standards map the characteristics of teachers at each career stage from the award of QTS; through to teachers on the main scale (Core); teachers on the upper pay scale (Post Threshold); Excellent teachers; and finally Advanced Skills Teachers.

At the level of award of QTS, the framework of professional standards is organised into three key, interrelated sections: firstly, professional attributes essential for QTS to be granted include an awareness of the statutory framework, policies and practices, effective communication

to undertake a review of the literature that informed the development of these standards. We take caution with prescriptive standards and testing in schools, only because they need to be scrutinised by teachers working with the school-community, students of teaching (student teachers) and teachers of teaching (academics) in the process of professional learning.[23] At the same time we celebrate the new emphasis on pedagogies in schools as long as it is linked to rigorous dialogue about pupil performances, classroom practices, and their alignment.[24]

Carnegie Faculty Associate Dean (Initial Teacher Education) Denise Gilchrist (**Figure 11**), like most staff, insists on teacher education, not teacher training, as a key to our approach. *In Carnegie we are about teacher education and teacher training is part of what we do.*[25] Such a distinction

Left, Fig.11 Photo Carnegie Faculty Associate Dean (Teaching and Learning) Denise Gilchrist. (Source: Ian Kaplan)

with children, young people, parents and carers and colleagues, and having a commitment to reflecting upon and improving their practice. Secondly, under *'Professional Knowledge and Understanding'* there is reference to knowledge of assessment, understanding social and human development factors that mediate learners' progress, and awareness of policies and guidelines concerning learners' welfare. Finally, the framework describes specific *'professional skills'* such as planning for *'progression across the age and ability range for which they are trained'*, the use of *'a range of teaching strategies and resources, including e-learning, taking practical account of diversity and promoting equality and inclusion'.*[20]

Significantly, while *'teaching strategies'* is mentioned, section Q14 specifically names pedagogy, stating that *'those recommended for the award of QTS (Q) should: Q14 Have a secure knowledge and understanding of their subjects/curriculum areas and related pedagogy to enable them to teach effectively across the age and ability range for which they are trained'.*[21]

It is interesting to note the terminology. The emphasis on trainee teachers and initial teacher training (ITT), evident in the earlier regulations,[22] is absent in the new version of standards, and while it has not been replaced with student teachers and/or teacher education, a shift in emphasis from 'teaching methods' to 'pedagogy' is noticeable. This reflects the theoretical framework of the new standards, which in many respects is a more coherent approach to professional learning. It would be interesting

Fig. 12 Mini-poster for pan-university invitational seminar. (Source: Carnegie Faculty Marketing Manager Michael Ainsworth)

www.leedsmet.ac.uk

leeds metropolitan university

Pan-university invitational seminar

Teacher Education Pedagogies
Supported by TQEF-RIT grant

Distinguished visiting professors and researchers share their expertise in academic pedagogy/scholarship of teaching

Professor Bob Lingard (University of Edinburgh)
Associate Professor Martin Mills (University of Queensland)

This invitational seminar supports the development of the research culture at Leeds Met and efforts to promote research-informed teaching. Funded by TQEF, it is focussed on teaching and learning in the school and teacher education settings.

Lingard & Mills are world-class scholars and well known co-researchers, heavily cited in national and international research literatures, and well placed to provide generic research training and in-depth engagement with research ideas. They will help facilitate building the pan-university research culture, including the areas identified for the 2008 RAE

In association with
Headteacher Jill Wood (Little London Community Primary School)
Principal Fran Dawning (Lyneham Primary School, Canberra)
Dr Lesley Saunders (General Teaching Council)
Chris Edwards (Chief Executive, Education Leeds)
Dorothy Smith (Strategic Manager, School Improvement, Education Leeds)

From: 3 to 5 July 2007
Venue: Headingley Campus

CARNEGIE RESEARCH INSTITUTE

For further information contact:
Samantha Armitage
Tel: 0113 812 6293
Email: s.armitage@leedsmet.ac.uk

35843_

Fig. 13
Photos students working
in maths lesson.
(Source: Jane Barber)

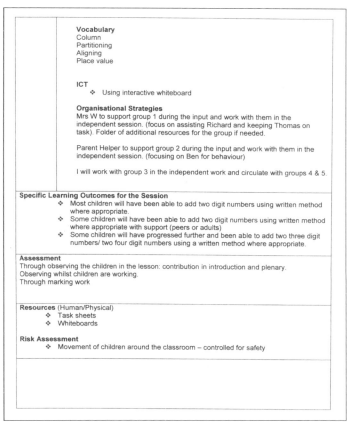

Fig. 14
Short-term lesson plans.
(Source: Jane Barber)

is more in keeping with Hoban's[26] argument that in emphasising professional learning, one has to move from a view of teaching as simply the development of expertise to one that considers it as being the development of scholarship. Similar conceptualisations of scholarship and its application to the teaching profession can be found in contemporary theorist Lee Shulman's[27] work and this too has struck a chord with Carnegie Faculty Senior Lecturer Andy Bowles' efforts to develop the idea of signature pedagogies across Initial Teacher Education. This is part of the Carnegie Faculty project to develop research into pedagogies, in the university and school settings (**Figure 12**).

Contemporary theorist of teacher education pedagogies John Loughran[28] argued the development of critical conversations and the nurturing of mentorship should be a concern for teacher educators and students of teaching alike. He pointed out that critical conversations and mentoring need to be infused in teacher education practices so that an expectation to further both is inherent in teaching as a profession.

We find evidence of these two components in the Carnegie Faculty, where there is a longstanding commitment to the development of critical reflective practitioners. There is significant emphasis in ITE on support for students engaging in research into their own school practice on *'critical reflection on learning about the process of research and the contribution to further and extended study'*.[29] Such efforts are shared as part of professional dialogue, for example, *'formative reflective practice in initial teacher training might be supported by the development of a reflective analysis framework'* and that *'making these connections*

Fig. 15
Examples of different
pedagogies for maths
lesson. (Source: Jane
Barber)

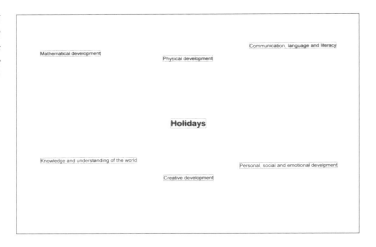

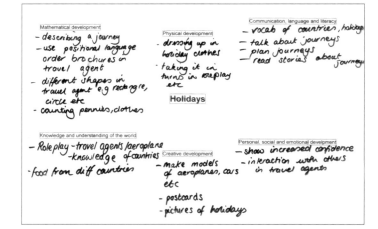

Far right, Fig. 16
Extract from Carnegie
Faculty School
Experience Handbook,
p. 9. (Source: Carnegie
Faculty partnership
office)

between research and practice within Education is essential if we are to better inform the development of strategies that support, not only teacher training, but also the refreshing of professional expertise'.[30]

A further example of critical conversations is found in ITE primary education work on mathematics[31] (**Figure 13**). Student teachers are encouraged to critically engage with the nationally-configured curriculum and associated guidelines to consider more deeply such things as the importance of developing mental strategies, knowledge of manipulating number, how number systems operate, and pedagogies geared to how children best learn (**Figure 14**). This is distinct from following procedures learned by rote. Starting with an audit of student teachers' prior knowledge, drawing up a programme of learning tailored to

Roles and Responsibilities

SCHOOL BASED TUTOR

This is the member of staff who has responsibility for the trainees in school. They will make the necessary arrangements for the trainees' placement and will liaise with the University's Link Tutor and Carnegie Placement and Liaison Office in matters concerning the trainees. The School Based Tutor has an important role in structuring the trainee's school based learning. They will act as a critical friend to enhance the trainee's teaching skills as well as personal reflection and evaluation.

Before the Block Experience

- Attend School Based Tutor training
- Make arrangements for trainee to be placed in a class
- Ensure class teachers are aware of the implications of having a trainee in their class
- Check documentation in place.

Trainee's Preliminary Visits

- Welcome trainee to school and induct them into the life of the school
- Provide relevant policies
- Set out school specific expectations
- Discuss targets for School Experience and strategies for meeting them
- Check and approve file. Where planning is unacceptable, liaise with the Link Tutor at Leeds Metropolitan University, to provide tutorial support and ensure arrangements are made for starting the School Experience at a later date if necessary.

During the Block Experience

- Inform and liaise with class teachers to support planning and teaching, utilising this School Experience handbook
- Check School Experience file to approve planning and evaluation each week
- Arrange a specific weekly allocated time for formative verbal and written feedback to trainees indicating strengths and targets for development
- Write the Summative School Experience Report in relation to module objectives and standards in 'Qualifying to Teach' (02/02) on the forms provided
- Return to Leeds Metropolitan University copies of summative School Experience reports as indicated

BA (Hons) Primary Education

Theme	Professional strand		Age phase strand			Core subject strand	ubject strand
Year 4 Looking forward to employment and CPD	Leading learning in Educational Settings(15)	School Experience, Standards and Professional Development Portfolio 4 (30)	Alternative educational placement (15)	Major Independent Study (30)		Option (15)	Option (15)
Year 3 Teachers in the wider world; working with other professionals; globalisation	Wider Perspectives for Teaching and Learning (15)	School Experience, Standards and Professional Development Portfolio 3 (15)	Research Methods and Ethics (15)	Multi Agency Practice for Children (15)	Creativity in the Core Subjects (30)	Option (15)	Option (15)
Pedagogical approaches; assessment and inclusive education	Pedagogical Perspectives for Teaching, Learning and Assessment (15)	School Experience, Standards and Professional Development Portfolio 2 (15)	Concepts and Strategies for Inclusive Education (15)	Social Perspectives in Education (15)	Core Subjects in Key Stage 2 (30)	Foundation Subjects 2 (30)	
The school as a community; roles and responsibilities	Introduction to Teaching (15)	School Experience, Standards and Professional Development Portfolio 1 (15)	Introduction to Learning and Development	Education Policy and Practice (15)	Core Subjects in Key Stage 1 (30)	Foundation subjects 1 (30)	

Modules shared with BA (Hons) Early Childhood Studies (4 year route)   Modules shared with BA (Hons) Education Studies

Module shared with BA (Hons) Education Studies, BA (Hons) Early Childhood Education (4 year route)

Fig. 17 Extract from Carnegie Faculty Programme Specification for BA (Hons) Primary Education (Leading to QTS) p. 6 of 17. (Source: Carnegie Faculty office)

individual progression, and finishing with a reflection on the learning process makes explicit the learning journey. Critical discussion reveals an empathy with the challenges children encounter, and produces strategies to support learning mathematics (**Figure 15**).

Loughran[32] considers that *'mentoring is important in demonstrating community appreciation of the fact that studying practice requires a personal commitment to public sharing so that professional critique might lead to enhanced knowledge building for all involved'*. So too the School Experience Handbook for BA/BSc (Hons) Primary Education[33] draws particular attention to the importance of school-based mentors, having *'an important role in structuring the trainee's school based learning'* and acting *'as a critical friend to enhance the trainee's teaching skills as well as personal reflection and evaluation'* (**Figure 16**).

FIRST YEAR ASSESSMENT TASK
UNDERSTANDING PHYSICAL EDUCATION MODULE

WORKING IN GROUPS OF THREE, SELECT ONE OF THE FOLLOWING AND PRODUCE A POSTER TO ILLUSTRATE ITS IMPACT ON YOUNG PEOPLE'S EXPERIENCES OF PE OR SPORT:

• GENDER • 'RACE' • SOCIAL CLASS •

YOU SHOULD BE PREPARED TO ANSWER QUESTIONS RELATING TO YOUR POSTER TO OTHER STUDENTS AND TO YOUR TUTOR IN THE POSTER PRESENTATION SESSION.

Fig. 18 Example of Assessment task from module handbook for first-year student teachers in secondary BA (Hons) Physical Education leading to QTS. (Source: Carnegie Faculty office)

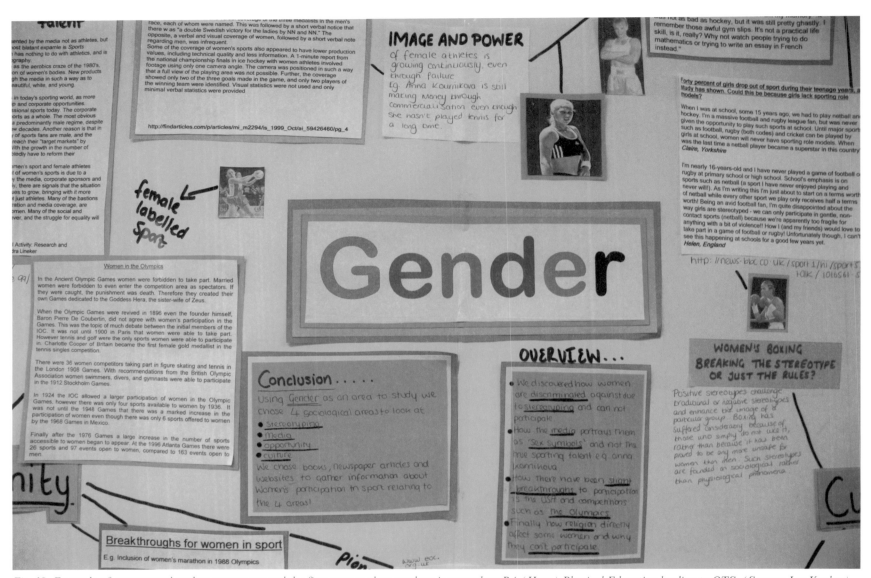

Fig. 19 Example of poster produced as assessment task by first-year student teachers in secondary BA (Hons) Physical Education leading to QTS. (Source: Ian Kaplan)

Other documentary sources reflect a Carnegie Faculty version of pedagogy of teacher education. For example, the Course Structure Description in the Course Handbook for BA (Hons) Primary Education (Leading to QTS) (**Figure 17**) shows a progression in professional learning with a year one focus on the school as a community, and pedagogies for teaching and learning; year two developing wider perspectives on teaching and learning, incorporating such things as global perspectives on education; and in year three, focusing on leading learning in professional settings. This speaks to the pedagogic imperatives described by LaBoskey:[34]

'Educators need to be thoughtful about their work, which means that they must question assumptions, consider multiple perspectives, avoid judgements, recognize complexity, and be primarily concerned with the needs of their students'.

The needs of teacher education students are carried into a wide variety of assessment tasks in ITE provision, moving beyond the simple staging of examinations to the use of such means as assessed presentations, formative directed activities and major independent studies that rely on critical and reflective engagement in small-scale research that centres on practice.[35] For example, first year student teachers in secondary BA (Hons) Physical Education are expected to engage a socio-cultural analysis of young people's experiences of physical education and sport through research (**Figure 18**), and produce their findings in the form of a poster[36] (**Figure 19**).

CONCLUSION

Loughran's idea of critical conversations helps us make sense of plotting the storyline of teaching methods at City of Leeds Training College and Carnegie Faculty pedagogy of teacher education. Engaging teacher educators and theorists past and present in critical conversations about teaching methods and pedagogy contributes to our professional learning. There is significant complexity to grapple with in teaching and learning about teaching. As both Mercier and Loughran, among others, pointed out, we need to illuminate the detail of teaching practices in schools and teacher education, especially the relationships and exchanges between teacher and learner. The challenge for teacher education is to '*make clear all of that which has hitherto been unseen and unappreciated*'.[37]

Thanks to Dr Anne Flintoff, Dr Sue Warren, Jane Barber, Andy Bowles and Sarah Squires for thoughtful inputs and critical feedback on this chapter.

ENDNOTES

1 For extended discussion see Loughran, J. (2006) *Developing a Pedagogy of Teacher Education. Understanding teaching & learning about teaching*. London: Routledge.

2 See p. 19 Key to Diagram (on following page) and p. 20 Diagram (pathways to) Certificated Teacher, Board of Education (1912), reproduced in Lori Beckett, David Kirk, and Iain Poole's chapter 7 on Curriculum for Teacher Education and Training.

3 Board of Education (1912) *How to Become a Teacher in an Elementary School*. London: His Majesty's Stationery Office.

4 See, for example, Sonnenschein's *Cyclopaedia of Education* (1889), in the entry on 'Pedagogy', a debate about considerations of pedagogy seemingly out of favour in England. Perhaps its use suggested an over-theoretically based approach to the business of teaching, and that methods sat more easily with the sense of teaching being practical and experientially grounded. Yet such material makes claim that it is pedagogy that provides the status of the educators 'profession', affording it the proper label and associated knowledge that makes it distinctive from it just being an occupation into which people drifted. These concerns are reflected in the seminal essay, Why no pedagogy in England?, Chapter 4 in Simon, B. (1985) *Does Education Matter?* London: Lawrence and Wishart.

5 See references in Beckett et al's chapter on Curriculum, ibid.

6 See Grier, L. (1937) *The Life of Winifred Mercier*. Oxford; also Lori Beckett's presentation, Winifred Mercier at CLTC, delivered at the centenary event *Winifred Mercier and first-wave feminist contributions to teacher education – their legacy*, International Women's Day, 8 March 2007.

7 Grier (1937), ibid.

8 See entry on Froebel (1782-1852) in Palmer, J. A. (ed) (2001) *Fifty Major Thinkers on Education. From Confucius to Dewey*. London and New York: Routledge.

9 Mercier, W. (1909) An Experiment in the Teaching of History. The Historical Association. June Leaflet number 17, p. 1; also reported in Beckett et al's chapter on Curriculum, op.cit.

10 Spearman, C. (1912) The Way to Develop Experimental Pedagogy. *The Journal of Experimental Pedagogy & Training College Record*, Vol 1, p. 1.

11 See Spearman (1912) ibid p. 2.

12 Copy of Childs' workbook on Demonstration lessons held by Leeds Metropolitan University Archives. As Jill Adam and Anne Campbell noted in their chapter on Partnerships, student teachers were supplied with two stout exercise books. One was for brief notes of the lessons given, together with Supervisor's criticisms; the other was for a record of the work other than actual teaching done, according to a circular from City of Bradford Education Committee (1915) *Scheme for the Training and Supervision of Student Teachers*. Original copy held in the Brotherton library, Leeds University (ref. 93/032).

13 Original copy of Childs' School Practice book held by Leeds Metropolitan University Archives.

14 Final Examination, 1909. Principles of Teaching, Syllabus No. 1 original copy held by WYAS (ref. WYL 863/40).

15 Mercier, W. (1928) The Training College Curriculum. Reprinted from *The Forum of Education*, vol VI, no.1. Original copy held in archives at Whitelands College, Roehampton University.

16 See Loughran's (2006) discussion of a pedagogy of teacher education where teachers and students of teaching pay careful attention to the subject matter being taught, simultaneous to the manner in which they knowledge is being taught, op.cit. pp. 3-4.

17 See Loughran, op.cit. pp. 6-7.

18 The university-based approval process, normally undertaken every five years, involves reviewing the curriculum of current courses, updating them in the light of recent research and policy initiatives, according to academic regulations regarding degree-level quality assurance.

19 See www.tda.gov.uk/standards; also Beckett et al's chapter on the Education and Training of Teachers.

20 See Training and Development Agency (2007) *Professional Standards for Teachers. Why sit still in your career?*, ibid, esp. Q1-Q33.

21 Ibid. Q14.

22 Previous TDA regulations specified Standards for the Award of QTS. Following the requirements under the headings 'Professional Values and Practice', and 'Knowledge and Understanding', comes 'Teaching' with a note that those awarded QTS must be able to demonstrate planning, expectations and targets; monitoring and assessment; and teaching and class management. It is in this latter requirement that we find a mention of methods, first described in relation to a capacity to teach the National Curriculum and the National Literacy and National Numeracy Strategies competently and independently. As the focus shifts to later Stages, 'relevant frameworks, methods and expectations' are named, but in relation to specific strategies and national programmes of study. Finally, there is a more conscious emphasis on methods. In the section 'Requirements for Initial teacher Training', there is no specific mention of methods and/or pedagogies under 'Training and Assessment', but an implicit recognition that this is part of trainee teachers' training, because providers such as Carnegie Faculty must meet the requirements.

23 We agree with concerns expressed about 'naming and shaming', 'standards', 'effectiveness', etc, especially where they preclude positive developments and insightful understandings about teaching and learning. See Mahony, P. and Hextall, I. (2000) *Reconstructing Teaching. Standards, performance and accountability*. London and New York: RoutledgeFalmer.

24 See Michael Apple's Introduction to Hayes, D., Mills, M., Christie, P., and Lingard, B. (2006) *Teachers and Schooling Making a Difference*. Sydney: Allen and Unwin.

25 From transcript of interview with Denise Gilchrist (Associate Dean, Carnegie Faculty), February, 2007.

26 See Hoban (2002) cited in Loughran (2006) op.cit.

27 See Shulman (1999) cited in Loughran (2006) op.cit.

28 Loughran (2006) op.cit.

29 Example provided by Principal lecturer Dr Sue Warren and Senior lecturer Dr Jon Tan from the Module Handbook for Dissertation – Individual Study (2006/7) Section 10.4 Assessment Criteria.

30 Example provided by Dr Jon Tan and former Carnegie Faculty PhD student (now Dr) Pam Jarvis (2005) Constructing a Reflective Analysis Framework within Teacher Training. Leeds Met Research Reflection, 11 March 2005 at www.leedsmet.ac.uk

31 Examples provided by Senior lecturer Jane Barber, briefing on pedagogies, June 2007.

32 Loughran (2006) op.cit. p. 170.

33 School Experience Handbook, Year One. BA/BSc (Hons) Primary Education, p. 9.

34 See LaBoskey, V. (1997) Teaching to teach with purpose and passion: Pedagogy for reflective practice, chapter in Loughran, J. and Russell, T. (eds) teaching About teaching: Purpose, Passion and Pedagogy in teacher Education (pp. 150-163). London: Falmer Press, cited by Loughran op.cit. p. 172.

35 Carnegie Faculty hosted the first regional conference of the National Teacher Research Panel (NTRP) conference in September 2006, and invited Professors Bob Lingard (Edinburgh University) and Susan Groundwater-Smith (Sydney) to do keynote addresses. See http://www.standards.dfes.gov.uk/ntrp/

36 For example, Fig. 18 shows an example of a first year assessment task in secondary Physical Education (leading to QTS), prepared for the module *Understanding Physical Education* by Sarah Squires. Students are asked to engage with the social and cultural issues that influence young people's responses and experiences of PE and sport. This assessment task helps students address one of the Professional Standards for Teachers, #Q18: *Understand how children and young people develop and that the progress and well-being of learners are affected by a range of developmental, social, religious, ethnic, cultural and linguistic influences*. Figure 19 shows an example of a student's response to the task.

37 Loughran (2006) op.cit. p. 173.

CHAPTER 9

Student participation

Jacqui Dean

When the co-educational City of Leeds Training College was opened in 1907 it fulfilled a real need – in its first year there were 1,100 applicants for 137 student places. The college expanded rapidly: by 1913 there were 480 students on the new Beckett Park campus, at a ratio of women to men of 5:3. The residential students lived in eight hostels, with 60 students per hostel. There was also 'a large number' of day students who lived in the West Riding. The residential students came from all over England, though predominantly from Yorkshire, Lancashire and Tyneside.[1] For women, training as teachers represented one of few paths into reasonably paid professional employment (professions such as law, accountancy, surveying, were closed to them until after World War I). It has been argued[2] that at this time the very act of becoming a teacher was a feminist act, part of the struggle for equal citizenship. For both men and women teacher training also offered a route out of traditional working class occupations, a socially respectable career and a step up the class ladder.

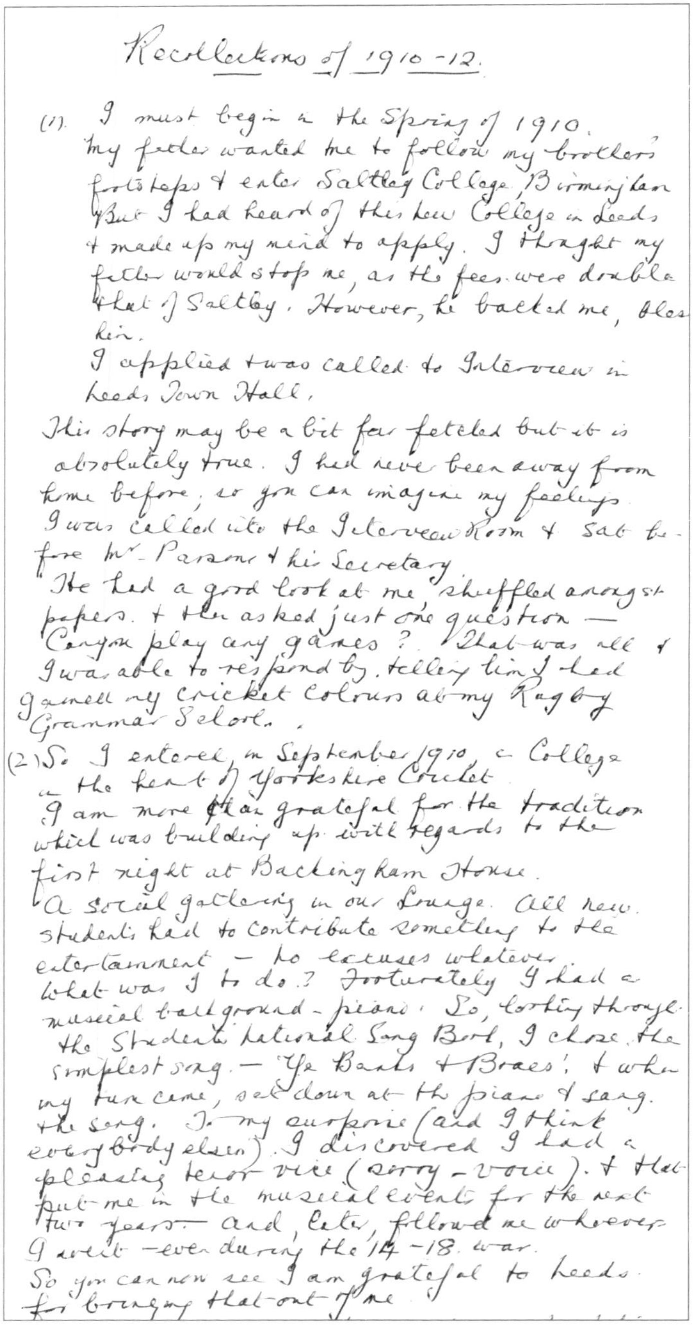
Recollections of 1910-12.

(1). I must begin in the Spring of 1910. My father wanted me to follow my brother's footsteps & enter Saltley College, Birmingham But I had heard of this new College in Leeds & made up my mind to apply. I thought my father would stop me, as the fees were double that of Saltley. However, he backed me, bless him.

I applied & was called to Interview in Leeds Town Hall.

This story may be a bit far fetched but it is absolutely true. I had never been away from home before, so you can imagine my feelings. I was called into the Interview Room & sat before Mr Parsons & his Secretary. He had a good look at me, shuffled amongst papers. & then asked just one question — Can you play any games? That was all & I was able to respond by telling him I had gained my cricket Colours at my Rugby Grammar School.

(2) So I entered, in September 1910, a College in the heart of Yorkshire Cricket. I am more than grateful for the tradition which was building up with regards to the first night at Buckingham House. A social gathering in our Lounge. All new students had to contribute something to the entertainment — no excuses whatever. What was I to do? Fortunately I had a musical background — piano. So, looking through the Students National Song Book, I chose the simplest song — 'Ye Banks & Braes', & when my turn came, sat down at the piano & sang the song. To my surprise (and I think everybody else's) I discovered I had a pleasing tenor vice (sorry — voice). & that put me in the musical events for the next two years — and, later, followed me wherever I went — even during the 14-18 war. So you can now see I am grateful to Leeds for bringing that out of me.

Fig. 1 An extract from Thomas Halliwell's handwritten recollections. (Source: Leeds Metropolitan University Archives)

THEN: 1906-1915

INTRODUCTION

A picture of the nature of student participation in the first years of the City of Leeds Training College can be formed from college documents, student publications and the reminiscences of two of its students: Thomas Halliwell[3] (**Figure 1**) and E. H. Mitchell.[4] These two first-hand accounts of student life are from a male student's perspective; we can only infer what participation in college life was like for women from surviving official documents about a female student, Rachel Ross, from the writings of Winifred Mercier, and from the student magazine *The Owl* (**Figure 2**).

BECOMING A STUDENT

The college was for young men and women destined to become teachers in public elementary schools. There were two routes to qualification as a teacher: a one-year and a two-year course. (For details of elegibility for admission see chapter on The Education and Training of Teachers above.)

The surviving documents tell us that in July 1914 Rachel Ross passed the University Matriculation examination in six subjects, thus qualifying for a training college place. However, she did not begin training at college until two years later – we have no surviving clues to the reason why. At her matriculation in July 1914 the City of Leeds Education Department awarded her a bursary to attend Thoresby High School for a year (**Figure 3**), and for the subsequent year, 1915-16, she was appointed as a student teacher at Meanwood Road County Girls Elementary School, at a salary of £20 per annum. While there, she continued to have her studies 'directed' at Thoresby High School every Tuesday and Friday morning. Rachel finally began her two-year teacher training course at the City of Leeds Training College in the autumn of 1916, graduating in 1918 (**Figure 4**).

Thomas Halliwell also took the two-year course. His father wanted him to attend Saltley College in Birmingham, where his brother had studied. However, young Thomas clearly had a mind of his own: *'I had heard of this new College in Leeds and made up my mind to apply.'* His father backed his choice, despite the fact that the Leeds fees at £15 per annum were double those of Saltley. In his college interview, Thomas found that the sporting interests of the Principal, Mr Parsons, were the deciding factors in his acceptance:

'I was called into the Interview Room and sat before Mr Parsons and his Secretary. He had a good look at me, shuffled amongst papers and then asked just one question – Can you play any games? That was all and I was able to respond by telling him I had gained my Cricket Colours at my Rugby Grammar School'.[5]

Lists of student names printed in *The Owl* suggest that students were overwhelmingly of white Anglo-Saxon or Celtic stock, though the names alone could be deceptive. For example, we have a tantalising hint of a non-British background in Rachel Ross's documents (**Figure 5**). Her father, an egg merchant in North Street, Leeds, was an immigrant, a naturalized citizen. In the late 19th century Jewish immigrants fleeing persecution in Eastern Europe were settling in England, many in Leeds. Given Rachel's first name, she may well have been Jewish. Many immigrants anglicised their surnames, and Rachel's father could have done this.

EXPECTATIONS OF THE STUDENTS

In general, training college students were treated more like school pupils than like university students.[6] Vice-Principal Winifred Mercier called the students 'pupils', and prefects were appointed (one of E. H. Mitchell's duties as a junior prefect was to wind the hostel's grandfather clock). The tone of the college handbook is both authoritarian and paternalistic to 21st-century eyes. The students had supervised study sessions in Hall every weekday evening from 6 to 9 pm. Lecturers supervised the hostels, and were definitely *in loco parentis*. Thomas Halliwell remembers being allowed out until 9.30 pm at weekends. If students wished to attend a concert or theatre in Leeds, they had to obtain special permission.[7] There was no student representation in the governance of the college. In 1913 *The Owl* printed a proposal to form a Students' Representative Council, but one was not formed until 1922.

Leeds was a non-denominational college, but attendance at church or chapel and twice-daily prayers, bible readings and hymns in Hall was expected. The college handbook is clear: *'Students are required to state to the Resident Tutor on Sunday evenings the Place of Worship at which they have attended.'*[8] Thomas Halliwell remembers a less authoritarian approach: in the Principal's talk to new students:

Fig. 2 Cover of THE OWL, *1911. (Source: Leeds Metropolitan University Archives)*

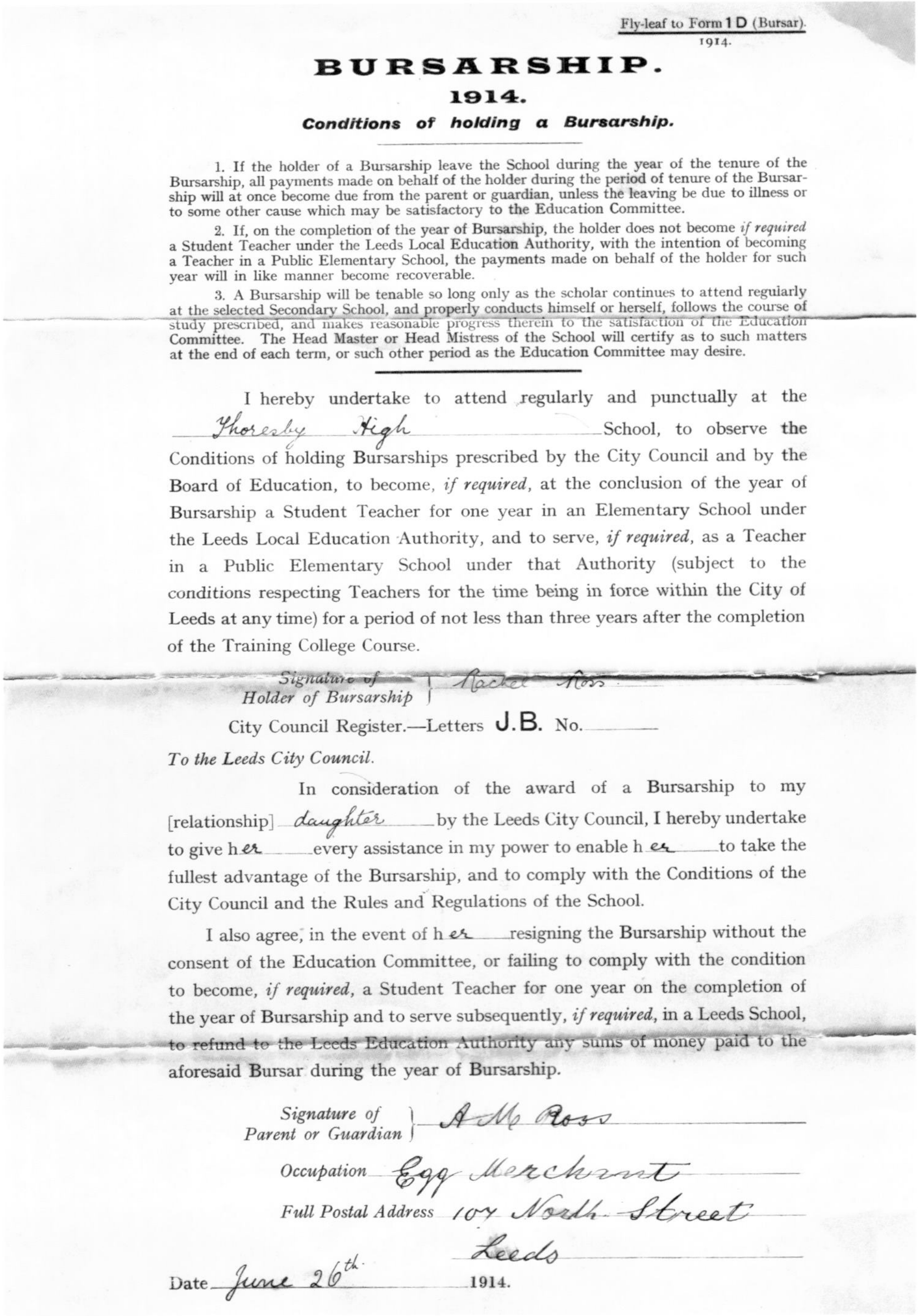

BURSARSHIP.
1914.
Conditions of holding a Bursarship.

1. If the holder of a Bursarship leave the School during the year of the tenure of the Bursarship, all payments made on behalf of the holder during the period of tenure of the Bursarship will at once become due from the parent or guardian, unless the leaving be due to illness or to some other cause which may be satisfactory to the Education Committee.

2. If, on the completion of the year of Bursarship, the holder does not become *if required* a Student Teacher under the Leeds Local Education Authority, with the intention of becoming a Teacher in a Public Elementary School, the payments made on behalf of the holder for such year will in like manner become recoverable.

3. A Bursarship will be tenable so long only as the scholar continues to attend regularly at the selected Secondary School, and properly conducts himself or herself, follows the course of study prescribed, and makes reasonable progress therein to the satisfaction of the Education Committee. The Head Master or Head Mistress of the School will certify as to such matters at the end of each term, or such other period as the Education Committee may desire.

I hereby undertake to attend regularly and punctually at the *Thoresby High* School, to observe the Conditions of holding Bursarships prescribed by the City Council and by the Board of Education, to become, *if required*, at the conclusion of the year of Bursarship a Student Teacher for one year in an Elementary School under the Leeds Local Education Authority, and to serve, *if required*, as a Teacher in a Public Elementary School under that Authority (subject to the conditions respecting Teachers for the time being in force within the City of Leeds at any time) for a period of not less than three years after the completion of the Training College Course.

Signature of Holder of Bursarship | *Rachel Ross*

City Council Register.—Letters **J.B.** No._____

To the Leeds City Council.

In consideration of the award of a Bursarship to my [relationship] *daughter* by the Leeds City Council, I hereby undertake to give h *er* every assistance in my power to enable h *er* to take the fullest advantage of the Bursarship, and to comply with the Conditions of the City Council and the Rules and Regulations of the School.

I also agree, in the event of h *er* resigning the Bursarship without the consent of the Education Committee, or failing to comply with the condition to become, *if required*, a Student Teacher for one year on the completion of the year of Bursarship and to serve subsequently, *if required*, in a Leeds School, to refund to the Leeds Education Authority any sums of money paid to the aforesaid Bursar during the year of Bursarship.

Signature of Parent or Guardian | *A M Ross*

Occupation *Egg Merchant*

Full Postal Address *107 North Street Leeds*

Date *June 26th* 1914.

Fig. 3 Rachel Ross's bursary letter. (Source: Leeds Metropolitan University Archives)

'He put us on our honour to attend at least once on a Sunday. To my knowledge this honour was generally accepted.' There were exceptions to the general rule: conscientious objectors were granted exemption from attending religious services.

DIFFERENCES BETWEEN THE SEXES

A 'dual' system prevailed at City of Leeds Training College. The treatment of men and women differed in terms of both rules and activities. Two examples illustrate this. Women students' church attendance was recorded, unlike men's, and women were only allowed into Leeds centre on Wednesday and Saturday half holidays. They were clearly perceived as needing more control than men. Here we see the historical system of differential positioning of men and women in operation, illustrated by a bitter little question in *The Owl*: *'Wanted to Know . . . Why sympathy is extended to men and sarcasm to women for the same offence – making a mess of a crit. lesson?'* [9]

Separation was the norm in the academic sphere, too. In most subjects, men and women were taught separately. Even the library and gymnasia were planned *'so that they may be used by men and women at separate times'.* [10] Winifred Mercier believed that the men and women distracted each other from their studies. However, *'There were joint classes in some special subjects . . . and for my first two years there was a mixed class.'* [11]

Respectability was paramount. The authorities could not risk liaisons forming between male and female students. Surprisingly, before the outbreak of war in 1914 there were fairly frequent mixed socials on a Saturday evening. Male and female hostels were located in close proximity to one another, so separation of the sexes was not effective in terms of daily intercourse.

In the eyes of the public, 'proper' behaviour had to be seen to be in place. This was achieved through unwritten conventions. Winifred Mercier again:

'We had to have a great many understandings, we had to see that the men and women did not arrange to spend half-holidays in expeditions together; did not go out for walks together in public; did not invite comment by being seen too much together in public. This practically amounted to no association outside the grounds'. [12]

There were punitive consequences for those who broke these 'understandings', as Thomas Halliwell remembers:

'Although a mixed College, on no account were we to associate either with a College girl – or one outside. The penalty for this would be severe. One of my year did get caught and was sent down for a week – if caught again expulsion'.[13]

And Mitchell, too comments vividly:

'But what of the monastic rule which, in a mixed College, forbade us to mix or to make private assignments with 'women students'? . . . their persons, except for an annual dance, mysterious and unknown'.[14]

When the Great War broke out in September 1914 the male students enlisted *en masse,* only 42 remaining on campus. Thus, during the war Leeds City Training College students were almost entirely women.

EXTRA-CURRICULAR ACTIVITIES

Sport and fitness played a large role. The men's sports were: rugby, soccer, hockey, swimming, running, tennis, cricket, water polo, cycling. According to Thomas Halliwell, lectures only took up the mornings, with the afternoons *'mostly free, and most of us took to games; football, hockey or Harriers'* (**Figure 6**). His account of college cricket reveals how long-standing is the Yorkshire tradition of choosing only Yorkshiremen to play: *'Most of the 1st XI were Yorkshire lads and how a Warwickshire man got into the XI I do not know.'* The college XI played their home games on *'the Sacred Headingley Cricket Ground'*. Thomas also spent time walking on the moors.[15] According to Mitchell, the Principal took the men climbing, with intimate teas *'at the Inn after an Ingleborough climb and a dizzy rope-held peer into Gaping Ghyll'*. He also remembers a strict swimming regime, with the *'compulsive instructive figure on the side of the swimming bath sending us into cold water at seven a.m. all the year round.'*[16]

The women did hockey, badminton, basketball, tennis and swimming. Men's sports dominated, however, and this was resented by at least some of the women, who wanted to know: *'Why the minority should have a monopoly of "The Sports"'*[17] (**Figure 7**).

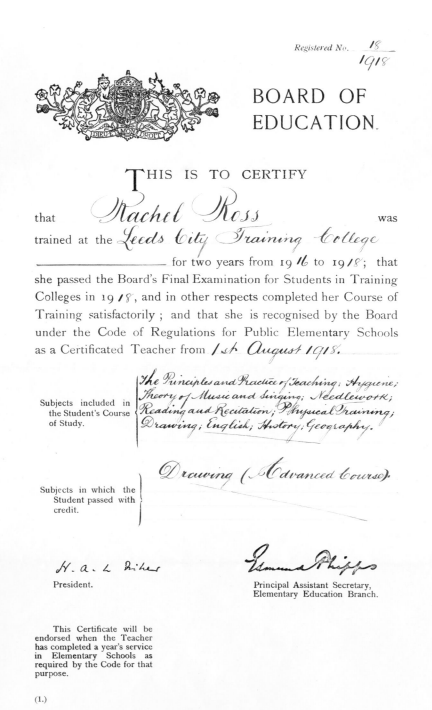

Fig. 4 Rachel Ross's graduation certificate. (Source: Leeds Metropolitan University Archives)

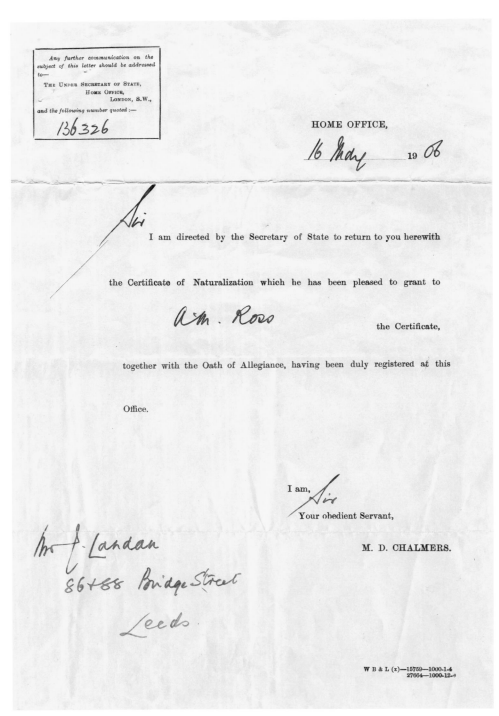

Students enjoyed a range of social events and customs. Music was an important part of the student community: Thomas Halliwell and fellow students attended concerts, joined music clubs and sang the college song, *Yip-i-du-da*. E. H. Mitchell remembers *'delicious evenings'* of Chopin in his hostel common room. Chess was another hostel pursuit. Many tutors lived on site, and played a prominent part in student life. Every society had one or more members of staff in key roles, and there was a wide range of such clubs and societies. They were separate for men and women, with a few mixed exceptions: eg the Art Club, the Browning Society. The societies held serious social and political debates, eg about equal pay; women's suffrage; the relative happiness of women and men; whether England would become a republic.

A real controversial debate entered student life in 1916. In the wake of James Graham's assertion that the students had been subject to propaganda, and the resignations of Winifred Mercier and eight women tutors:

The women prefects of the Training College wrote an indignant letter about Mr. Graham's comments on conduct. Some junior students wrote protesting against any suggestion that propaganda had been introduced into their tuition. They said: 'Individual political opinions have never been impressed on our minds. We think it quite necessary that political and social questions should be dealt with in connexion with certain subjects.'[18]

Overall, students identified strongly with their individual hostels and with the college, referring to themselves as 'Owls'. College alumni clearly felt a continuing sense of identity with their *alma mater:* there were frequent reunions, sports matches against current students, involvement in student societies such as the Arts society. Alumni also had their own societies (eg the Old Students' Dramatic Society); and they both subscribed and contributed to *The Owl.* Halliwell closes his reminiscences with the words: *'To me Leeds T. C. was a very happy place and I am proud that I am still a Wise Old Owl.'*[19]

Fig. 5 Naturalisation letter. (Source: Leeds Metropolitan University Archives)

NOW: 2000-2007

INTRODUCTION

Significant movements in the 20th century have led to changes in student participation and have stimulated a continuing debate about it. Currently fair access and widening participation in HE are key policy drivers in the UK,[20] with a current government target of 50 per cent participation in HE by 18-30-year-olds by 2010. In response, universities have developed a range of initiatives to increase diversity and widen participation.

Leeds Metropolitan University's efforts to remove barriers to HE and to widen participation by under-represented groups since 2001 have had significant success. Notable WP projects are kids@uni; Widening the Horizon; the increasingly successful Progression Module; and two projects aimed respectively at recruiting Asian girls and Afro-Caribbean boys into HE.[21]

With the introduction of tuition fees in 2006, nationally student applications to HE dropped by 3 per cent. In contrast, that year LeedsMet saw a record increase of 8.3 per cent, followed by a 12.3 per cent rise for 2007, compared to the national average of 6.4 per cent. This can be largely attributed to its decision to charge tuition fees of £2,000, instead of the majority charge of £3,000 per annum.

We are fortunate to have the views and stories of two students in this section. The first is Jodie Tumelty (**Figure 8**), who in 2006 graduated as a primary school teacher, specialising in history. In March 2007 she was elected for the second year running as LeedsMet's Student Union president.

The second is Phillip Garnett, now in his third year of training as a primary teacher, specialising in Physical Education[22] (**Figure 9**).

STUDENTS IN INITIAL TEACHER EDUCATION (ITE)

Originally training teachers specifically for elementary school teaching a century ago, Leeds Metropolitan University now trains secondary PE, early years and primary teachers, on one-year postgraduate and four-year undergraduate courses. Applications for ITE places are buoyant. (See Admissions Data 2007 figures quoted in the chapter 'The Education and Training of Teachers'.)

Teaching is now a wholly graduate profession in the UK. It is also a feminized profession, particularly in primary schools and early childhood

Fig. 6 Photograph of the CLTC Harriers team, with Thomas Halliwell seated second from the right. (Source: Leeds Metropolitan University Archives)

Fig. 7 Playing fields for women students in CLTC Handbook *(1912). (Source: Leeds Metropolitan University Archives)*

settings. This feminization has existed for over a century and is both sustained and international.[23] In the Carnegie Faculty, women make up over 85 per cent of ITE students, with the highest proportion in ECE and the lowest in secondary PE. The preponderance of women in primary schools concerns both Jodie and Phil, and both think it important to attract more men to primary teaching *'especially if young children haven't got fathers at home …they need to have a respectable male'* as a role model. For Jodie the major widening participation need in ITE is to address the gender imbalance.[24]

In 2003/04 11.7 per cent of ITE students came from the most disadvantaged group in society, ie those who are most under-represented in higher education.[25] According to Jodie, this disadvantaged group comprise mainly 'second chance' learners. Teacher training courses do indeed attract many mature students; Carnegie ITE currently has 125 students over 21, with 54 of those over 25. Phil at 25 is a second chance learner. Having left school without A-levels, he went travelling. He decided to become a teacher after working in summer camps in America – it *'changed my life basically'*. He took an access course at HCAT, managing to pass the two-year course in one year.[26]

In 2006/07, 42 (4.5 per cent) full-time ITE students were from ethnic minorities: Asian, Black, Chinese and Mixed. This proportion is lower than the university average. Despite the New Labour government's high profile campaign to make the profession attractive to a wider range of people, it seems that ethnic minorities do not regard teaching as being as desirable as law, medicine, business or accounting. This said, the Faculty's flexible education routes to Qualified Teacher Status, which provide a range of opportunities for non-standard students, have been successful in recruiting diverse mature learners. For example, 15 Jamaican teachers are currently working towards English Qualified Teacher Status through their enrolment on a modular Independent Programme of Study – one of Carnegie's many flexible awards (**Figure 10**).

NATURE OF PARTICIPATION WHILE A STUDENT, AND INFLUENCES ON THIS

Finance is an issue in deciding to enter higher education, and it remains a significant factor for many ITE students throughout their time at university. We have no accurate figures about how many students have to work to make ends meet, though *'the figures are high – a lot of students actually have full-time jobs as well as studying, and especially mature students with dependants;*

they tend to be balancing a lot more than the traditional student'.[27] Phil shares this perception: *'A lot of students do have to work part-time, and that's a struggle for them, to balance that, especially if they're working in bars or clubs, so it's late nights and early morning lectures'.* He says that the vast majority of people on his PE specialist course work part-time in the evenings, as he does.[28] This work is driven partly by fees and debt, but also serves *'to maintain a lifestyle'.* Watson supports this claim by pointing out that almost half of UK students drive cars.[29]

Phil's parents help him by paying his tuition fees, so LeedsMet's lower fees were an incentive to come here. He finds his student loan doesn't go far, so part-time work is essential to pay the rent. He argues strongly that it is unfair that ITE students taking the four-year route have to pay four years of tuition fees, while PGCE students are given a 'golden handshake' by the government for their one year of training.[30]

Jodie also highlights the difficulties experienced by distance learners on her primary course, some living in Sheffield or Newcastle. One mature student *'had to take two trains and cycle to college every day – really dedicated student'* but she found it very difficult to participate fully. *'I find that generally students are strategic in missing lectures, if they're distance learners and they're coming in for one two-hour session, they won't come in for that one,'* though they will if a fuller day is timetabled.[31] One hundred years ago there was no provision for participation by students with disabilities, in terms of either access or support. Today, the situation is transformed, with support available for both physical and mental disabilities. Among current ITE students, dyslexia is almost the only recorded disability, with 30 students so registered.

As a student representative, Jodie has regular discussions with the governors of the university about a technology-infused future, with students interacting with lecturers through personal laptops and other devices. But she emphasises that face-to-face learning is *'vital – one thing we have stressed whenever we have these discussions is that you can't lose the contact,'* stressing the power of face-to-face discussion. She says that students have concerns about contact hours and thinks it imperative that these are maintained, otherwise there is no reason for students to come into university. Jodie emphasises the importance of the personal touch, brought home to her in her first year, when she was walking along a corridor in Carnegie with a friend from another faculty. Three or four members of staff passed them, and all said: *'Hi Jodie'.* Her friend was astonished. In her faculty *'I don't think*

anybody knows my name'. This was because her course was impersonal, delivered via big lectures. The personal was lost. For Jodie, the key strength of her course was that *'people get to know you . . . That's really important in teaching, knowing every student. And because our lecturers all knew us, we learnt it was important and carried it over into schools'.* The message to those promoting wide use of technology for delivering learning is that it can be a great learning tool, but it is no substitute for personal relationships, support and face-to-face debate. For Phil, too, it is the relationships that matter: the most important thing for him is the friends he's made as a student, friends he will keep for life.[32]

Both Jodie and Phil enthuse about their school experience. This is in marked contrast to the students of 100 years ago, who, if articles in *The Owl* are any guide, experienced school practice as a special form of torture.[33]

Fig. 10
Photograph of three of the Jamaican teachers, Camille Banks, Thayapary Thissaverasingan, and Denise Coke at Leeds Metropolitan University, 2007 – with Val Tarbitt and Sue Warren (standing) and Emma Nettleship. (Source: LeedsMet. Communications: Icon Photography)

EXTRA-CURRICULAR ACTIVITIES

As we have seen, for many students today, part-time work tends to take up time that might otherwise be spent in extra-curricular activities. Despite this, there is a plethora of student clubs and other activities and campaigns across the University (**Figures 11, 12 & 13**). For teacher trainees the main issue with joining is time. Phil and Jodie are both more actively engaged in extra-curricular activities than the average student, Phil in sport, Jodie in student

Fig. 11 Enjoying the Kaiser Chiefs' concert at LeedsMet. (Source: LeedsMet. Communications: Icon Photography)

Fig. 12 The Language and Culture Fiesta, April 2007. (Source: LeedsMet. Communications: Icon Photography)

politics. Phil is captain of the University badminton team. Sport is *'always on my mind'*. He plays tennis too, and with his part-time job has no time for much else, apart from *'a few drinks after work'*. His food tends to be *'Super noodles for tea, super noodles for breakfast . . .'*

Jodie *'was a quite abnormal student, I was a different student in terms of the average student who didn't get involved . . . I suppose I'm a lot more political than most other students.'* She participated right from the start: she was her course representative for four years and was on the Student Union (SU) council, becoming involved in their campaigns and debates and going to general meetings. She deplores the fact that so many students don't even know what the SU is, *'a bugbear of mine, because we do so much for students and nobody knows about it'*. Students don't come to the general meetings, so miss their chance to influence developments. She concludes

that all the SU can do now is concentrate on student welfare, as that's what is relevant to students today. The culture over the years has changed. Drinking is part of the socialising aspect of university life (exceptions tend to be religious, distance and mature students).

Both Jodie and Phil identify strongly with LeedsMet and feel a sense of loyalty to the University. Phil, discussing the rivalry with other universities in sport; said: *'You wear your badge with pride.'* Significantly, these were both engaged students, playing active roles in student life.

What is important to today's teacher training students as they go through their training? With a plethora of assignments to write, tests to pass and standards to meet, ITE students are under relentless pressure. Back to that personal touch: Jodie has a treasured memory about her personal tutor when she was overwrought and had three assignments to finish.

Fig. 13 Students at the Great Student Run in fancy dress. (Source: LeedsMet. Communications: Icon Photography)

I knocked on his door and he said: 'Jodie, you look awful, what's wrong?' I was hysterical; I started crying and I said, 'I can't do it I've given up, I can't do it, just fail me now.' He said, 'No, don't be so stupid.' He took my assignment off me, opened the door; all my friends were outside. He gave the assignment to them and he shut the door and he said, 'Look, you're not to do any work for the next three hours. You're to go home, you're to go to sleep, you're going to eat some food, you're going to watch the TV – whatever you want, to completely clear your mind. Once you've done that phone me, and we'll talk about it. We'll go through it bit by bit. You're to go to bed early and tomorrow we'll have all day and it'll be done. And I just think that for support, that sums up the support that I got[34] **(Figure 14)**.

JODIE ALEXANDRA TUMELTY

has been awarded the Degree of

BACHELOR OF ARTS

with Second Class Honours (1st Division)

having followed an approved programme in

PRIMARY EDUCATION LEADING TO THE AWARD OF QUALIFIED TEACHER STATUS

14 June 2006

VICE-CHANCELLOR   CHANCELLOR

LEEDS METROPOLITAN UNIVERSITY

748538

Fig. 14 Jodie Tumelty's graduation certificate from Leeds Metropolitan University. (Source: Jodie Tumelty)

ENDNOTES

[1] City of Leeds Training College, *Coming of age celebrations souvenir handbook, 1907-1928.*

[2] Delamont, S. and Coffey, A. (1997) Feminism and the Teacher's Work, in B. J. Biddle et al. (eds) *International Handbook of Teachers and Teaching,* Kluwer Academic Publishers, pp. 199-236.

[3] Thomas Halliwell, at the age of 96, wrote nine pages of recollections of college life and the student experience between 1910 and 1912 for the History Department at City of Leeds and Carnegie College in February 1986. He donated this, with several photographs, to the college (mss. in Leeds Metropolitan University Archives).

[4] E. H. Mitchell's recollections are recorded in City of Leeds College of Education, *A short history of the City of Leeds Training College, 1907-1957* (p. 12).

[5] Halliwell, op.cit., p. 1.

[6] Grier, L. (1937) *The life of Winifred Mercier*, London, Oxford University Press, p. 135.

[7] Halliwell, Ibid, p. 5.

[8] City of Leeds Training College, *Handbook* (1913).

[9] *"The Owl"*, Summer 1914, p. 10.

[10] *A short history of the City of Leeds Training College 1907-1957* (1957).

[11] Grier, op.cit., p. 137).

[12] Grier, Ibid., p. 138).

[13] Halliwell op.cit., p. 3.

[14] Mitchell op.cit.

[15] Halliwell op.cit., p. 6.

[16] Mitchell, op.cit.

[17] *"The Owl"*, Summer 1914, p. 23.

[18] Grier, op.cit., p. 127.

[19] Halliwell, op.cit., p. 9.

[20] HEA website at http://www.heacademy.ac.uk accessed 11/01/2007.

[21] Leeds Metropolitan University (2005), *Monitoring 'Widening Participation': Applications and Student Statistics for Academic Years: 2001/02; 2002/03; 2003/04.*

[22] The author would like to thank the following students and staff for their help and contributions to the 'now' part of this chapter: Michael Ainsworth, Phillip Garnett, Paul Hurst, Andy Knaggs, Rachel Sykes and Jodie Tumelty.

[23] Delamont and Coffey, op.cit., p. 210.

[24] Jodie Tumelty, interviewed by the author in 2007.

[25] Leeds Metropolitan University, 2005.

[26] Phillip Garnett, interviewed by the author in 2007.

[27] Jodie Tumelty, op.cit.

[28] Phillip Garnett, op.cit.

[29] Watson, D. (2005) *A new university world?: the landscape of higher education in the twenty-first century,* open lecture for University Centre Hastings, 17 January 2005, Brighton: Education Research Centre, University of Brighton.

[30] Phillip Garnett, op.cit.

[31] Jodie Tumelty, op.cit.

[32] Jodie Tumelty, op.cit. and Phillip Garnett, op.cit.

[33] *"The Owl"*, Winter 1911, p. 15; Winter 1913, p. 26; Summer 1914, p. 26.

[34] Jodie Tumelty, op.cit.

CHAPTER 10

'Play Up Coll!': Rugby and Football at the College

Ian Richards, Karl Spracklen and Tony Collins

Anyone walking around the brand new Beckett's Park campus in the years before World War One would have regularly heard the shout of 'Play Up Coll!' coming from spectators assembled around its many sports pitches. 'Coll' was the abbreviation for the college that was used by staff and students alike to voice their support for its wide variety of sports teams.[1]

G. H. Callard

B. H. Lewis   P. S. Campkin   J. H. Collins   D. Roe   H. Winspear (*Linesman*)
H. S. Warrington   J. Walker   A. Poppleton   W. Stancliffe   S. J. Morgan

G. H. Gibson (*Secretary*)   A. Booth (*Capt.*)   Mr. Parsons (*President*)   R. Wake (*Vice-Capt.*)   Mr. Harrison (*Hon. Treasurer*)

G. E. Tindall   R. A. Jones   E. Thomas-Griffiths

Fig. 1 The College's rugby football team of 1914-1915. (Source: Leeds Metropolitan University Archives)

'Play Up Coll' was heard often because sport played a vitally important role in the daily life of Beckett's Park. Although there were a wide variety of artistic and literary activities available to students, it was games that occupied a special place in the ethos of the young training college. In *The Owl*, the college's student magazine of the time, reports of sporting events feature prominently. The photograph of the college's Rugby football team of 1914-1915 (**Figure 1**), taken just before the outbreak of the First World War, is typical of the period: its survival demonstrates the importance of sport at the college, but the photograph also hints at the way in which sport played a key role in preserving maleness and Englishness.[2]

This was an era in which discussions about the value and purpose of sport dominated discussions of pedagogy and educational philosophy. Dating back to mid-Victorian books such as *Tom Brown's Schooldays*, some commentators believed that games were vital to develop the moral character of young men – and later, in a slightly different way, young women (**Figure 2**) – through the promotion of 'Mens sana in corpore sano': a healthy mind in a healthy body.[3]

Team sports in particular were seen as valuable in making men fit – physically and morally – to serve the needs of the British Empire. By the time the college opened Association football, or soccer (nowadays popularly known as football), had spread from the upper classes of England to the industrialised working class. It is no surprise to see soccer being played at Beckett's Park in the early years, as the game had an almost universal appeal.[4] But Rugby football, or at least the version of rugby played under the rules of the Rugby Football Union, was still viewed in England as a game for middle-class men.

The importance of games and physical recreation was spelt out in the college's first handbook for prospective students. A whole section was devoted to describing how the college looked after the physical welfare of the student, including the taking of regular physical measurements and stimulating 'the cultivation of hygienic habits'. But it would have been when the new students arrived at Beckett's Park that they would have seen how extensive the sports facilities were.

For soccer, there were two pitches and three training grounds (**Figure 3**). Rugby had one pitch and a training ground. There were two women's hockey pitches, one more than for the men, and twenty-six tennis courts. Cricket had two pitches, one for men and one for women, plus a practice ground. There was also a croquet lawn, swimming baths, two gymnasia and a general 'field for games'.

Reflecting the bias in favour of men's sports, use of the facilities cost male students one pound and five shillings, but was fifteen shillings and sixpence for women. On top of the annual tuition and board fee of twenty pounds, this was a considerable sum for the time, roughly the equivalent of one week's wages for an unskilled manual worker.

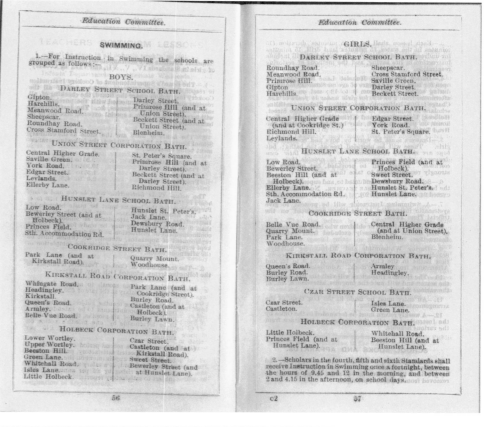

Above, Fig. 2 From the 1899 Official Yearbook of Leeds School Board. (Source: Leeds Metropolitan University Archives)

Fig. 3 A page from the College's 1912 Handbook. (Source: Leeds Metropolitan University Archives)

The most important sport for the college at this time was soccer. In these early years it could sometimes turn out four teams during a season, all of them very successful. In 1911 the student magazine *The Owl* reported that the first team (**Figure 4**) was unbeaten, scoring forty-four goals to twelve. In the 1913-14 season the side was even more successful, losing just two matches out of twenty-six and scoring 108 goals to twenty-two.[5]

The popularity of soccer was also helped by two other reasons. Many students who came to Leeds were from areas where soccer was strong – for example in 1914, the team captain and vice-captain came from Sheffield and Essex respectively – and were not interested in rugby.[6] Moreover, the college's mission was to train students 'who intend to become teachers in public elementary (ie state) schools' (**Figure 5**) in which soccer was overwhelmingly the most popular game and where it would be advantageous for a teacher to be able to play and coach the game.[7]

Before the First World War, rugby union was less popular than soccer among the students. The first serious match that the college played was against the Yorkshire Wanderers in November 1911, which was lost 16-11. The college club was only founded in 1911 and it tended to have somewhat erratic fixture list.[8] In 1913 it joined the Yorkshire Rugby Union, bringing to six the number of clubs in Leeds in membership, and had the honour of one of its players, R. Bland, being selected to play for his home county of Cumberland (**Figure 6**).[9]

*Right, Fig. 5
The college magazine,*
The Owl, 1911, *lists the
schools where students
are now teaching.
(Source: Leeds
Metropolitan University
Archives)*

THE OWL. 37

"THE OWL," welcomes Mr. Jackson as a permanent member of the College Staff, and wishes Miss Martin and Messrs. Firth, Lacey, and Relton to accept its hearty "Welcome to C.L.T.C."

Please note the following change of address : Mr. J. E. PARKINSON, Simonstone, Padiham.

The following "List of Appointments" is, unfortunately, not complete. We hope to publish a supplementary and final list in our next issue. Will those whose names are not included kindly notify the Principal, and enclose "the appointment" ?

LIST OF APPOINTMENTS.

MEN.

Mr. S. Barraclough, Parish Church School, Leeds.
Mr. J. W. Bateman, Ardsley (Barnsley) Council School.
Mr. A. M. Black, Collierley Council School, Dipton.
Mr. H. W. Carter, St. Augustine's Church of England School, Bradford.
Mr. J. Child, Leeds Hunslet Carr Council School.
Mr. B. Cohen, Darley Street Mixed Council School, Leeds.
Mr. A. Coulter, Ingram Road Council School, Leeds.
Mr. R. Dickinson, West Herrington Council School, County Durham.
Mr. H. E. Gibson, Brudenell Council School (Handicraft), Leeds.
Mr. E. Heley, New Shildon Church of England School, County Durham.
Mr. J. K. Heywood, Swalwell Council School, County Durham.
Mr. T. Hillcoat, Belle Vue Road Council School, Leeds.
Mr. F. Hobson, Belle Vue Road Council School, Leeds.
Mr. W. L. Jones, South Elmsall Council School.
Mr. H. B. Kitchen, Southdale Council School, Ossett.
Mr. G. W. Mann, Brudenell Council School, Leeds.
Mr. A. Nettleton, Woodlesford.
Mr. E. R. Nuttall, Leeds, Hunslet National School.
Mr. F. H. Pearson, Greenside Council School, Pudsey.
Mr. W. Postlethwaite, Ordsall Council School, Salford.
Mr. A. Smith, Central Council School, Hebden Bridge, Yorks.
Mr. C. G. Smith, Stamford Road Council School, Kettering.
Mr. P. R. Smith, North Helton Council School.
Mr. H. Tunnicliffe, High and Low Bishopside Council School, Pateley Bridge.
Mr. W. Wilkinson, Whitehall Road Council School, Leeds.
Mr. J. E. Wilson, Cudworth.
Mr. H. Wofflindin, Rothwell Stourton Council School, West Riding.
Mr. E. W. Woodhead, Lye Valley Road Council School, Stourbridge, Worcester.

WOMEN.

Miss G. Abbey, Slaithwaite National School.
Miss F. Adair, Quarry Mount Council Girls' School.
Miss L. Aines, Hunslet Moor Council School, Leeds.
Miss E. Almond, Gower Street Council School, Leeds.
Miss M. Atkinson, Lofthouse National School, Rothwell.
Miss M. A. Baker, Brownhill Council School, Leeds.
Miss C. Birdsall, Jack Lane Council Girls' School, Leeds.
Miss A. Birkby, Farnley Council School, Leeds.
Miss H. Buckle, Castleton Council School, Leeds.
Miss A. Burke, Ellerby Lane Council School, Leeds.
Miss D. Casson, Stanningley National School, Leeds.
Miss S. I. Clegg, Queen's Road Council School, Leeds.
Miss M. F. Cook, Richardson Dees Council School, Wallsend-on-Tyne.
Miss M. L. Dearlove, Great Houghton Council School, near Barnsley.
Miss A. Denison, Quarry Mount Council School, Leeds.
Miss M. Dockray, Bridge Street Council School, Morley.
Miss M. W. Dykes, Bowling Back Lane Council School, Bradford.
Miss E. Fawcett, South Hetton Council School.
Miss N. Firth, Darfield Council School, Leeds.
Miss J. Fletcher, Kerber Council School, Leeds.
Miss E. M. Fox, Penkhull Council School, Stoke-on-Trent.
Miss M. Green, Gipton Council School, Leeds.
Miss L. A. Hardcastle, Prince's Field Council School, Leeds.
Miss B. Hardy, Lovell Road Council Mixed School.
Miss B. Hayhurst, Dewsbury Road Council School, Leeds.
Miss M. Holt, Warley Town Council School.
Miss G. E. Hope, Armley Council School, Mixed.
Miss C. L. Hopkin, Park Lane Council School, Leeds.
Miss E. Hopkinson, Bradford.

Rugby union, of course, was not and is not the only version of rugby. Rugby league, or Northern Union as it was called before 1922, was not played at the college. At that time, and until 1995, anyone playing rugby league was banned by the Rugby Football Union from playing rugby union. This could have been a serious social and career handicap for a young man entering the teaching profession, and this

A. B. Ross
H. S. Dougherty, *Linesman*
R. Wake   S. Shaw   T. G. Wood   J. Wilson   W. Best
H. L. Holliday   T. J. Watkins   H. Smith   G. H. Gibson   W. Stancliffe
M. H. Mossop, *Secretary*   J. Y. Williamson, *Captain*   Mr. Parsons, *The Principal*   T. Masters, *Vice-Captain*   Mr. H. Harrison, *Treasurer*
A. H. Bretton   A. Toon   R. Bland   A. Booth

Fig. 6 The college men's rugby union team in 1913. With county player R. Bland seated to the right of the ball. (Source: Leeds Metropolitan University Archives)

Fig. 8
The women's gym in CLTC, pictured just after the first world war in CLTC Handbook, 1912. (Source: Leeds Metropolitan University Archives)

Fig. 7
The Owl, 1911, *reports on the activities of women's sporting clubs. (Source: Leeds Metropolitan University Archives)*

42

Changes always accompany the end of a College year, and we have already elected our new secretary and treasurer, Misses M. Hughes and S. Cartner, to whom we offer our hearty congratulations, and wish them every success in their work.

We are extremely sorry that we must bid " farewell " to the Naturalists' Society; we hope that during the next year, so many pleasant evenings will be spent there, that our Juniors will be quite as sorry to leave as we are now.

D. M. BATESON.

WOMEN'S TENNIS CLUB.

Captain—A. MERIGOLD.　　Hon. Sec.—E. G. THOMPSON.

Senior Committee :—A. BLACKBURN, N. DAVIS, C. GALLEWAY, R. KIRTLEY, A. MERIGOLD.

Junior Committee :—M. BEEVERS, M. DOCHERTY, R. HOPE, D. HANCOCK, F. NASH.

Miss Crawshaw has been appointed President of the Tennis Club, and our thanks are due to her for the interest she has taken in our Club.

Tennis this year is most popular, the courts being in great demand.

Inter-Hostel matches have been arranged, most of which have already been played.

RESULTS OF INTER-HOSTEL TENNIS MATCHES.

May 6th—Leighton won (88 games) against Priestley (72 games). Macaulay won (102 games) against Caedmon (53 games).

13th—Leighton won (79 games) against Bronte (73 games). Priestley won (91 games) against Caedmon (63 games).

20th—Leighton won (101 games) against Caedmon (47 games). Macaulay won (93 games) against Bronte (63 games).

27—COLLEGE v. UNIVERSITY.

The match was played on the College courts, and after a keen game the University won by 5 rubbers to 4 rubbers. We hope to be more successful in the remaining matches.

" Everything comes to him who waits " was the motto of the Senior tennis players when they beheld the attractive looking new courts—but they have at length realised that they must adopt the new motto, " Take care of the old courts and the future generations will take care of the new." Good luck to next year's players.

E.G.T.

48

WOMEN'S SWIMMING CLUB.

Captain—Miss DOROTHY DAVIES.

Vice-Captain—Miss DOROTHY CAKEBREAD.

Secretary—Miss BEATRICE DEWHIRST.

Committee—Miss G. DOBSON, Miss G. SHEPHERD, Miss N. WINTER, Miss E. WHITTEY, Miss E. JORDAN, Miss N. GEBHARD, Miss D. KIRKLAND.

The Swimming Club has been very popular throughout the year. There are a great many members, and under the excellent tuition of Professor Boyd and Mrs Wilson, the number of experts increases month by month, as the Medallion Classes become more popular. The enthusiasm displayed by the majority promises well for the continued success of the Club.

During this year we have gained 6 silver and 11 bronze medallions, a decided advance upon last year, which was the first in which we entered any of our members for any of the examinations of the Royal Life-Saving Society.

The present Bronze Medallion Class numbers 35 members, several of whom we hope will gain their Medallion before the close of the season.

The opportunity which has been ours this year, of using the Swimming Bath throughout the winter terms, has proved a decided advantage. It is one which will add much to the success of the club if continued in future.

Several displays have been given before distinguished visitors to the College, and each one seemed to give as much satisfaction to the audience as to the performers.

ATHLETIC SPORTS.

These were held on May 23rd. The ground had been hard for a full fortnight before the day, but during the morning of the 23rd, a heavy downpour of rain continued from 9 o'clock until noon. Fortunately the weather became more conducive to running, although the ground was now in anything but a good condition.

The points gained by the respective hostels in the winter games were :—

Fairfax　...　...　30
Cavendish　...　25
Grange　...　...　35

Together with these numbers, Fairfax had obtained 19 points for medallions, Cavendish 11, and Grange 11.

Thus, the competitors began the events with the points standing :—

meant that rugby league was not widely played in further or higher education until the 1970s.

In 1907 the biggest, most popular version of football in Leeds was the version of rugby played by the Northern Union. Association football (soccer) had yet to take a firm hold in Leeds – no sports journalist of the time could ever have predicted the dominance of Leeds United in later years. Just across Beckett's Park and down Headingley Mount were the Loiners, the Leeds club that then, as now, flaunted its wealth and attracted crowds from across the north of the city. South of the river, two more professional Northern Union clubs ensured the local press was always full of reports about the rugby played by the Northern Union. Opposite Headingley, and visible from Beckett's Park, the suburb of Bramley proudly reminded everyone of its independent past with its club the Villagers. A few miles to the east, the working-class industrial district of Hunslet, then and now a heartland of rugby, had its own club. In the year of Leeds Teacher Training College's birth, Hunslet Northern Union Football Club started an all-conquering season that would see them become the first professional rugby club to win all the trophies on offer.[10]

The rugby played by the Northern Union, what became the game now known as rugby league, permeated the lives of the working-class families of Headingley, Kirkstall, Burley, Bramley, Armley, Wortley, Holbeck, Beeston and Hunslet. The other version of rugby, played by the amateur gentlemen of the Rugby Football Union, survived in Yorkshire in pockets of middle-class suburbia, but the formation of the Northern Union in 1895 had left rugby union weak where the northern

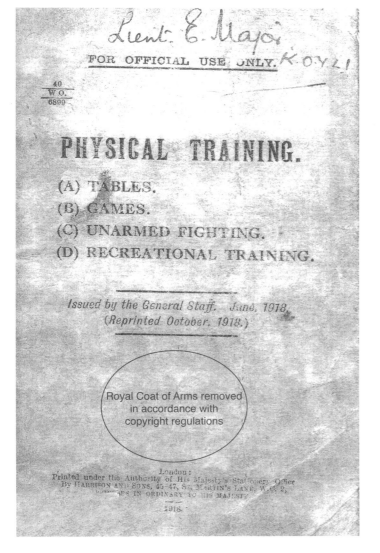

game was strong. This was especially true of the industrial parts of the West Riding.[11]

And yet the rugby played by the students at Leeds Teacher Training College was not the version that their future pupils would talk about. The professional code of the Northern Union, and its working-class roots and culture, barred this version of rugby from being played at the new college. Instead, the students of the college played to the rules and the values of the Rugby Football Union. And those values, as well as the rules, clearly defined and delineated the working-class rugby from the middle-class game nurtured and played by the students of the college. In the slow build-up to the First World War, patriotic and masculine values became more and more prominent in British society, and it is no surprise that rugby union, the football of the middle-classes, reflected this.[12]

Although there was strict segregation between the sexes for physical training and games, women were encouraged to participate in sport. Women had their own gymnasium too, as can be seen in

Fig. 9
The all-conquering women's hockey team in action in 1911. (Source: Leeds Metropolitan University Archives)

Left, Fig. 10
An army physical training manual from 1918 that belonged to Lieutenant E. Major who became the first Principal of Carnegie College. (Source: Leeds Metropolitan University Archives)

Fig. 11
Representative Jersey and
photo of Henry Sharp,
one of the pioneers of
Carnegie Rugby League
Club, from the reception
area of the Carnegie
Sports Centre. (Source:
Keith Rowntree)

Fig. 12
Leeds Met win the BUSA
Men's Rugby League
Final at Headingley
Carnegie 28/03/2007.
(Source: LeedsMet.
Communications: Icon
Photography)

(**Figure 8**). In the first years of the college, clubs were established for swimming, hockey, tennis and badminton, as can be seen in (**Figure 7**). Most of these were played between 'hostels', as the halls of residence were then known. As an indication of the status of sport at the college, and its perceived superiority over other cultural forms, it is interesting to note that for a time badminton was played in the art gallery in the Main Education Building.[13]

Hockey was the most prominent sport for women. By 1911, can the college could field two sides against local opposition (**Figure 9**).

Fig. 13 The Carnegie Challenge Cup. CEO Rugby Football League,
Richard Lewis and Vice-Chancellor Professor Simon Lee. (Source:
LeedsMet. Communications: Icon Photography)

Led by Miss F. Smith, the first team went through autumn and winter unbeaten, scoring twenty-five goals to two. They played matches against teams from across West Yorkshire and regularly defeated the Leeds University side.[14]

Despite the success and obvious skill of the players, the team had a male coach, a Mr Mansfield. As with many women's sports at this time, there was also some disquiet at women playing a game that could be seen as violent and masculine. A minor scandal ensued in 1913 during the Staff versus First Team match when someone in the crowd shouted 'Rough it, Chaps!', implying that the players were somehow less than feminine.[15]

Nor were women's sports free of the growing tensions as the First World War approached. Reports of the women's hockey club in 1914 were headlined 'play up, play up and play the game,' after the famous lines in Sir Henry Newbolt's jingoistic poem 'Vitai Lampada'.

When war was declared on 4 August 1914, many of the young men who had hurled themselves around the college's rugby and soccer pitches rushed to the nearest recruitment office to enlist. Sport eventually became part of military life (**Figure 10**), but despite what the enthusiastic recruits may have imagined, war was not a 'greater game' and many of them tragically did not return to take up their teaching careers after the war.

Now, of course, rugby league is played at Beckett's Park alongside rugby union and the version of football that became so popular it took the name 'football' for itself. Students from one rugby background often opt to explore the other version, and of course these days rugby is played by women students as well as men. In 2007 all three codes of football are flourishing at the University. Student teams currently compete with distinction and success at regional and national level. Sport is still an integral part of the student experience. The most significant changes since the early 20th century have been the introduction of Rugby League in the 1980s and the advent of women's football and rugby teams in the 1990s. The football codes at Leeds Met have also reflected the wider changes in the structure of sport in Britain

Left, Fig. 14
First Round of the 2007
Carnegie Challenge Cup
Wigan St Patrick's v
Leeds Met 05/02/2007.
(Source: LeedsMet.
Communications: Icon
Photography)

Left, Fig 15
Leeds Met Carnegie FC.
(Source: LeedsMet.
Communications: Icon
Photography)

Fig. 16
Colin Stephens,
Carnegie Director of
Rugby Union.
(Source: LeedsMet.
Communications: Icon
Photography)

Fig. 17
The launch of Leeds
Carnegie 14/05/07.
Chairman Leeds Rhinos,
Paul Caddick, CEO
Leeds Rugby, Gary
Hetherington, Director
of Rugby, Leeds
Carnegie, Stuart
Lancaster, Vice-
Chancellor Professor
Simon Lee. (Source:
LeedsMet.
Communications: Icon
Photography)

and in particular the relationship between the two codes of rugby. The establishment of high profile ground breaking partnerships across all three codes has also benefited the sports significantly.

The relationship between the two codes of rugby continued to be acrimonious until the end of the 20th century. The Rugby League Club was only formed as late as 1981.[17] The recollections of Henry Sharp (**Figure 11**) illustrate that the formation itself of the rugby club is indicative of the relationship between the codes and of the internal Student Union politics of Carnegie College and Leeds Polytechnic. In the late 1970s students at Carnegie College were not able to play for the Leeds Polytechnic Rugby Union team. This resulted in county standard rugby union players being unable to play whilst at university. As a protest against their exclusion from the Polytechnic's teams, a group of players got together to form a Rugby League team in 1981. Since its inception the Rugby League team has been one of the most successful student teams in the country, with numerous players moving on to play professionally and picking up international honours.

Recently Leeds Met Rugby League teams have established themselves at the top of the student game winning the BUSA title several times[18] (**Figure 12**). This position has been cemented by the appointment of the first full time Director of Rugby League at a British university, in 2005[19] and the partnership developed between Leeds Met

Fig. 18
Leeds Met Women's
football team in action.
(Source: LeedsMet.
Communications: Icon
Photography)

Fig 19
Carla Cantrell, winner
of the Fresher of the
Year award at the
inaugural Athletic Sports
Awards, May 2007,
receives her award from
Vice-Chancellor
Professor Simon Lee.
(Source: LeedsMet.
Communications: Icon
Photography)

and the Leeds Rhinos Academy. The club has made an impact beyond the student game by qualifying for the Rugby League Challenge Cup for the first time in 2005/06. In 2007 the Leeds Met team made sporting history as part of Leeds Met's partnership with the Rugby Football League. This has seen the university becoming the first Higher Educational establishment to enter into a partnership with a National Governing Body and to sponsor a major knock out competition. Leeds Met's rugby league were victorious over one of the most famous amateur clubs in the game Wigan St Patrick's (38 to 24) in the First Round of the 2007 Carnegie Challenge Cup[20] (**Figures 13 & 14**).

The men's football team mirrored its position with regard to other sports prior to the First World War by remaining one of the most prominent sports teams within the institution during the latter half of the 20th century. The 1970s was one of the high points of the club's history

with several appearances in the FA Trophy.[21] The club currently has four men's teams and plays in the British Universities Sports Association (BUSA) Premier League. From the 2007/08 season the club will play in the Northern Counties East League First Division. Matches in this division are staged at Farsley Celtic's ground (**Figure 15**). The facilities and capacity of the ground will enable the club to move up the football pyramid.[22] The profile of football at the University has also been raised through the partnership with the Irish Football Association and the sponsorship of the Carnegie Premier League in Northern Ireland.[23]

The men's Rugby Union club currently has three teams with the first team playing in the BUSA Premier League. The club also won the Yorkshire Cup in the 2005/06 season. The club has benefited in recent years from the partnership with Leeds Tykes and the Academy. Many students currently play for the Leeds Carnegie Academy A Team and 1st Team. Like their league counterparts they have also benefited from a full time Director of Rugby[24] (**Figure 16**). The University's acquisition of Leeds Rugby's Union Team in May 2007 and the renaming of this team as Leeds Carnegie will see the club playing as Leeds Carnegie in the Guinness Premiership and European Competitions (**Figure 17**).

The men's football, rugby union and rugby league teams have also undergone a process of professionalisation, as the institution has begun to mirror some of the developments and features of the American Collegiate sports system. One of the most obvious manifestations of this process has been the appointment of full time performance directors and coaches.[26] The teams have also begun to adopt more professional methods of training and preparation by utilising the expertise of the University's staff in areas such as sports science, strength and conditioning, physiotherapy and sports medicine. Alongside catering for the elite student footballers and rugby players, University Sport also provides opportunities for students to participate in rugby and football at a recreational level through the intramural programme and for students to take coaching qualifications.[27]

One of the most significant developments has been the growth in women's sports at the University. This has included a growing range of sports being offered to female students and in particular the advent of women's teams and clubs in football and rugby union, in what were previously considered the embodiment of masculinity and an important part of 'making men'.[28] The growth of football and rugby union within the University has reflected the growth of these sports nationally and internationally and the advent of World Cups. The British Universities Sports Association (BUSA) and its various forerunners, such as, the Universities Athletic Union (UAU) and British Polytechnics Sports Federation, have played a major role in promoting these sports to women who may not have had the opportunity to play them prior to coming to university.

Women's football emerged in Britain at a similar time to the establishment of the City of Leeds Teacher Training College mainly taking place in the public schools. Following the First World War women's football led by teams such as Dick Kerr Ladies in Preston, attracted crowds in excess of 50,000. In response to this perceived threat to the men's game, in December 1921 the FA banned women's teams from using the grounds of affiliated clubs.[29] The FA Council deemed the game to be unsuitable for women. The Women's FA was founded in 1969, but it was not until the late 1980s that the women's game began to experience a significant level of growth and recognition from the men's game. The growing popularity of the women's games is illustrated by the fact that at Leeds Met the women's football club was able to raise a 2nd team in the 2005/06 season (**Figure 18**). The club plays in the BUSA Premier League and the Yorkshire County Cup and has strong links with Leeds United Ladies.[30] Several of the students, such as Carla Cantrell also play for Doncaster Belles, one of the top teams in the country and in March 2007 was selected for the senior England Squad[31] (**Figure 19**).

Women's Rugby was first played seriously in Britain in the late 1970s, with the majority of early teams established through the student network. The Women's Rugby Football Union (WRFU) was formed in 1983.[32] The women's rugby team at Leeds Met was formed soon afterwards. The Women's 1st XV is one of 80 student sides across the country and they currently play in the BUSA Premier League (**Figure 20**). The club has also produced a number of international players. Compared to rugby union, women's rugby league is relatively underdeveloped, with a small number of clubs mainly being

concentrated in the game's traditional heartlands of Yorkshire and Lancashire.[33] Unlike rugby union there is no BUSA competition. Despite having a number of international women's rugby league players, Leeds Met does not yet have a women's rugby league team.

Fig. 20 Leeds Met Women's Rugby Union 1st XV, 2006-07 Season. (Source: LeedsMet. Communications: Icon Photography)

CONCLUSION

The changing face of football and rugby at Leeds Met reflects changes in wider society: the growth of football on campus reflects the widening of higher education to all social classes and the emphasis on sport for all. The growth of rugby league demonstrates the close links the University has with the surrounding region, exemplified by the partnership announced with the Rugby Football League in 2007. The growth of women's football and rugby is a recognition of the excitement of sport, and a shift of attitudes away from the imperialist, masculine ideals of gentlemanly amateurs trained to be junior officers. Despite the significant growth and development of women's football and rugby, there are however, several things that have not changed since the early years of the City of Leeds Teacher Training College. Like the women's hockey team of 1911 the women's football and rugby teams are still coached by men. Like their counterparts of 1913, female students playing football and rugby are still subject to stereotypes that question their femininity and sexuality.[34]

ENDNOTES

[1] 'Play Up Coll' is noted in *The Owl*, Winter 1911, p. 23.

[2] For the importance of sport to Victorian and Edwardian education see J. A. Mangan *Athleticism in the Victorian and Edwardian Public School*, Cambridge, 1981, Bruce Haley, *The Healthy Body and Victorian Culture*, Harvard, 1979, D. E. Hall and G. Beer (eds), *Muscular Christianity: Embodying the Victorian Age*, Oxford, 2006, Philip Mason, *The English Gentleman: the Rise and Fall of an Ideal*, London, 1993 and Tony Collins, 'English Rugby Union and the First World War' *The Historical Journal*, vol. 45, no. 4, December 2002.

[3] On the importance of *Tom Brown's Schooldays* to education, see E. C. Mack and W. H. G. Armytage *Thomas Hughes*, London, 1952, W. E. Winn, 'Tom Brown's Schooldays and the Development of Muscular Christianity' *Church History*, vol. 29, no. 1 (March 1960), pp. 64-73, Isabel Quigley, *The Heirs of Tom Brown: The English Public School Story* London, 1982 and Richard Holt, *Sport and the British*, Oxford, 1989, pp. 86-97.

[4] On the appeal of soccer in the north of England, see Dave Russell, *Football and the English*, Preston, 1998, Tony Mason, *Association Football and English Society 1863-1915*, Brighton, 1981, and Tony Collins, *Rugby's Great Split*, London, 1998, ch. 5.

[5] *The Owl*, Winter 1911, p. 34 and Summer 1914, p. 42.

[6] For details of the home addresses of students, see *The Owl*, Summer 1914, pp. 34-39.

[7] City of Leeds Training College, *Handbook*, 1912, p. 2.

[8] *Leeds Mercury*, 24 November, 1911, p. 16.

[9] *The Owl*, Winter 1913, p. 44.

[10] For a detailed exploration of rugby league in this period, see Collins, *Rugby's Great Split*, ch. 6.

[11] Collins, *Rugby's Great Split*, ch. 5 and Tony Collins, 'The Ambiguities of Amateurism: English Rugby Union in the Edwardian Period', *Sport in History*, vol. 26, no. 3 (Dec 2006).

[12] See Collins, 'English Rugby Union and the First World War' plus Derek Birley, 'Sportsmen and the Deadly Game', *International Journal of the History of Sport*, vol. 3, no. 3 (Dec 1986) and his *Playing the Game: Sport and British Society 1910-45*, Manchester, 1995.

[13] *The Owl*, Winter 1913, p. 42.

[14] For reports on the many successes of the hockey team see *The Owl, passim*. Miss Smith's captaincy of the side is discussed in the October-November 1911 of *The Owl*.

[15] The name of the male coach is revealed in *The Owl*, Summer 1914, p. 26. *The Owl*, Winter 1913, p. 18.

[16] *A grand finale for BUSA rugby league champions* (30/03/06), published online at http://www.lmu.ac.uk:81/the_news/mar06/busa_grand_final.htm (accessed 25/06/07); *Leeds Met win the BUSA Men's Rugby League Final at Headingley Carnegie* (28/03/2007) published online at http://www.leedsmet.ac.uk/the_news/mar07/busa grand final.htm (accessed 25/06/07); *BUSA 2006/2007 Season* (28/03/07) published online at http://www.leedsmet.ac.uk/the_news/busa/index.htm (accessed 25/06/07).

[17] Interview with Henry Sharp, 30 January 2007.

[18] *A grand finale for BUSA rugby league champions* (30/03/06), published online at http://www.lmu.ac.uk:81/the_news/mar06/busa_grand_final.htm (accessed 25/06/07); *Leeds Met win the BUSA Men's Rugby League Final at Headingley Carnegie* (28/03/2007) published online at http://www.leedsmet.ac.uk/the_news/mar07/busa grand final.htm (accessed 25/06/07).

[19] *Paul Fletcher*, published online at http://www.leedsmet.ac.uk/carnegie/sport/pfletcher.htm (accessed 25/06/07).

[20] *Students pass Wigan exam* (05/02/07), published online at http://www.leedsmet.ac.uk/the_news/feb07/challenge_cup_firstround_postevent.htm (accessed 25/06/07).

[21] *Leeds Met Carnegie FC – History*, published online at http://www.leedsmet.ac.uk/carnegie/sport/11110.htm (accessed 25/06/07).

[22] *Football*, published online at http://www.leedsmet.ac.uk/carnegie/sport/10399.htm

[23] Irish Football Association in partnership with Leeds Metropolitan University, (25/10/05), published online at http://www.leedsmet.ac.uk/the_news/oct05/irish_football_league.htm (accessed 25/06/07).

[24] *Men's Rugby Union*, published online at http://www.leedsmet.ac.uk/carnegie/sport/10396.htm (accessed 25/06/07).

[25] *Deepening partnership between Leeds Rugby and Leeds Met Carnegie*, published online at http://www.leedsmet.ac.uk/the_news/may07/tykesannouncement.htm (accessed 25/06/07).

[26] *Paul Fletcher*, published online at http://www.leedsmet.ac.uk/carnegie/sport/pfletcher.htm (accessed 25/06/07); *John Hall*, published online at http://www.leedsmet.ac.uk/carnegie/sport/10355.htm (accessed 25/06/07).

[27] *Intra Mural* published online at http://www.leedsmet.ac.uk/carnegie/sport/9926.htm (accessed 25/06/07); *Health & Fitness Classes* published online at http://www.leedsmet.ac.uk/carnegie/default/Health%20&%20Fitness%20Classes.htm *Carnegie Sports Awards* published online at http://www.leedsmet.ac.uk/carnegie/default/9758.htm (accessed 25/06/07).

[28] John Nauright, 'Sustaining Masculine Hegemony: Rugby and the nostalgia of Masculinity', in, John Nauright and Timothy Chandler, *Making Men. Rugby and Masculine Identity*, London, 1996, pp. 227-244.

[29] Dave Russell, *Football and the English*, Preston, 1998.

[30] *Football*, published online at http://www.leedsmet.ac.uk/carnegie/sport/10399.htm

[31] *England call up for Carla*, (25/03/07) published online at http://www.leedsmet.ac.uk/the_news/mar07/carla.htm (accessed 25/06/07).

[32] *RFUW: A Brief History*, published online at http://www.rfu.com/index.cfm/fuseaction/RFUHome.Community_Detail/StoryID/7125 (accessed 25/06/07).

[33] *Women & Girls*, published online at http://www.therfl.co.uk/community/page.php?id=128&areaid=40 (accessed 25/06/07).

[34] Pat Griffin, 'Changing the game: Homophobia, sexism and lesbians in sport*', in, Sheila Scraton and Anne Flintoff (eds.) *Gender And Sport: A Reader*, London, 2002, p. 199.

CHAPTER 11

Footsteps That Pass:
The Military at Beckett Park from 1914 to 1945

Keith Rowntree with Frank Atkins

Prior to the beginning of the First World War arrangements were made to establish a network of military hospitals throughout the country consisting of six General sectors; Eastern, London, Northern, Scottish, Southern and Western with five Northern General Hospitals; Newcastle, Leeds, Sheffield, Lincoln and Leicester.[1] The Territorial and Reserve Forces Act of 1907 aimed to provide a medical service for the Territorial Forces formed in 1908.[2] The Royal Army Medical Corps met the medical needs of the Regular Army.

Fig. 1
T. J. Neilson. 1916.
(Source: George
Sprittles' Scrapbook,
Leeds Metropolitan
University Archives)

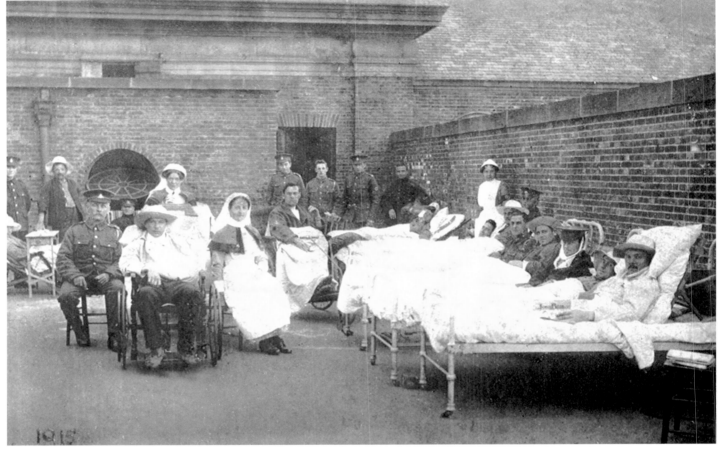

Fig. 2
Flat-roof Ward. c. 1917.
(Source: George
Sprittles' Scrapbook,
Leeds Metropolitan
University Archives)

A world-recognised reputation in medical and surgical sciences existed in Leeds. For this reason the 2nd Northern General Hospital was based in the city. The original plan would house the hospital within the Leeds Institute on Cookridge Street and other selected Leeds schools, but in 1912 when Major J. F. Dobson took command he realised that this plan was inadequate.[3] Meanwhile the Leeds Education Committee was in the process of building modern teacher training facilities at Beckett Park, which eventually saw a number of boys and young men enrol for war service (**Figure 1**). Dobson saw potential in housing the hospital on one large site. On 4 August 1914 the authorities approved his scheme and the City of Leeds Training College was established as the 2nd Northern General Hospital. The site quickly became a military establishment with barbed wire on the Acre and the Red Cross hoisted above the Education Building

(James Graham Building).[4] The opening week of the war saw beds provided in the Great Hall, the Library and other suitable rooms, while the flat roofs and quadrangles (now in-filled with Lecture Theatres and Library) became open-air wards[5 6] (**Figure 2**).

The plan to staff the hospital with a matron, twenty-two sisters and sixty-eight nurses changed as the number of casualties increased, more use being made of Voluntary Aid Detachment staff[7 8] (**Figure 3**). In time senior nursing staff, nurses, doctors and surgeons, after gaining valuable experience, were being posted to front line positions (**Figure 4**). Often elderly and retired doctors volunteered to fill gaps in hospital personnel. In 1915 Lieutenant-Colonel Dobson was replaced, due to illness, by Lieutenant-Colonel Harold Littlewood who remained as Administrator until 1919[9 10] (**Figures 5 & 6**).

1914 presented the College with the problem of providing teaching and living space for students. The only answer was to rent other buildings and implement a system of half-time working in schools where the training college shared facilities.[11] Thoresby High School (**Figure 7**) functioned as the Education Building during the afternoons while the school operated in the mornings.[12] Caedmon moved to Torridon (**Figure 8**), a house on Headingley Lane, now demolished. Priestley moved to Whinfield, while Fairfax was split between Spring Bank and The Elms (**Figure 9**). College accommodation was ever changing, The Grange later became the Administration and Educational Centre. Lectures were held in Cavendish Library and the Sports Pavilion.[13][14] The editor of the college magazine *The Owl*, in the summer of 1915, lamented changes forced on the college: 'The military occupation of the Education Building has dealt such a blow that compared to last year we are practically non existent.'[15] Meanwhile at Beckett's Park the remaining students were almost all women, the majority of male students now in the Army. This juxtaposition between women students and convalescing soldiers did not pass without controversy. James Graham, Director of Education at Leeds, held strong opinions about what he perceived as terrible behaviour by women students 'disporting themselves in unseemly ways'. Frequently soldiers were found gathered around tennis courts watching the women play. Graham thought the students were not behaving appropriately, but he appears to have laid no blame on the soldiers.[16][17] 1917 saw further College moves throughout Leeds including to Brudenell School, Leeds Clergy School and The Wesleyan College.[18]

The first convoy of wounded, most had been caught up in fighting at Mons, arrived at Leeds Midland Station on 17 September 1914 to a Civic Welcome by the Lord Mayor, Sir Edward Brotherton. Well-wishers, lining City Square and the streets of Leeds, threw tobacco and cigarettes to the wounded men. In time a fleet of 25 ambulances, established by public contributions, were assigned to ferry the wounded between Leeds centre, Beckett's Park and the other hospitals around the

Left, Fig. 3
Sister Pratt and VAD
Hodgson, 1917.
(Source: George
Sprittles' Scrapbook,
Leeds Metropolitan
University Archives.)
Voluntary Aid
Detachments were
formed in 1909 to
support trained nurses.

Right, Fig. 4
Nurses on Steps, c. 1916.
(Source: George
Sprittles' Scrapbook,
Leeds Metropolitan
University Archives)

Fig. 5
*Lt-Col Littlewood, 1919.
(Source: George
Sprittles' Scrapbook,
Leeds Metropolitan
University Archives)*

Fig. 6
*Lt-Col Littlewood's
farewell. (Source:
George Sprittles'
Scrapbook, Leeds
Metropolitan University
Archives)*

LT.COL. H.LITTLEWOOD'S FAREWELL.

Fig. 7
*Thoresby High School.
(Source: Keith
Rowntree, 2007)*

district[19] (**Figure 10**). Initially the West Riding hospitals of the 2nd Northern General in Leeds and 3rd Northern General in Sheffield absorbed war casualties, but gradually auxiliary or extension hospitals were set up.[20] This included the East Leeds War Hospital, formerly Leeds Union Workhouse on Beckett Street (renamed St James's Hospital in 1925).[21] Other auxiliaries were established in Bradford, Dewsbury, Halifax, Huddersfield and Keighley. Ultimately the total number of beds administered from Leeds numbered 6,500.[22]

In 1915 it became clear that Beckett Park required hospital extensions and recreation facilities. A committee including the Hospital Administrator Lieutenant-Colonel Littlewood, Rupert Beckett, Joseph Watson, F. J. Kitson and F. Kinder, eminent men with Leeds interests (some of whom had played a part in the forming of the City of Leeds Training College) raised £26,000. As a result of the fund raising, The Grand Duchess George of Russia opened the large YMCA recreation hall,

Left, Fig. 8
Remaining gate post of
Torridon. (Source:
Lou Charnley, 2007)

Fig. 9
Spring Bank, one of the
houses used to
accommodate the
College. (Source:
Lou Charnley, 2007)

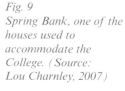

Fig. 10
Ambulances ready to
ferry patients in Leeds,
c. 1917. (Source: George
Sprittles' Scrapbook,
Leeds Metropolitan
University Archives)

known to patients and staff as the 'YM', in 1915 equipped with cinema apparatus; concerts, lectures, plays and billiard tournaments took place there[23][24] (**Figure 11**). The hall and chapel (**Figure 12**) stood on the site of the Design and Technology Centre to the south of Carnegie Hall. On 30 March 1916 a 700-bed annexe to the hospital was opened in temporary huts on the college playing fields.

The Royal family visited the hospital at various times, the most notable being those of King George V.[25] He arrived on 27 September 1915 accompanied by HRH Princess Victoria and the Grand Duchess George of Russia, when they met with patients and staff.[26] Later the King visited the hospital accompanied by Queen Mary on 31 May 1918 presenting several officers and men with medals (**Figure 13**).

Sergeant George Sprittles (**Figures 14 & 15**) a medical orderly based at Beckett's Park during the First World War left a unique pictorial record of the Hospital in the form of a scrapbook.[27] George was born in 1894 at Wakefield where his father, Charles, originally from Northampton, was a Coach Smith.[28] George's elder brother Joseph Sprittles was to become a prominent local historian and was president of

Above left, Fig. 11
The Cheerio Boys, one
of the entertainment
groups at the hospital,
1918. (Source: George
Sprittles' Scrapbook,
Leeds Metropolitan
University Archives)

Above right, Fig. 12
Postcard showing view of
the Chapel interior, c.
1917. (Source: George
Sprittles' Scrapbook,
Leeds Metropolitan
University Archives)

Fig. 13
Medal ceremony with
King George V and
Queen Mary, 1918.
(Source: George
Sprittles' Scrapbook,
Leeds Metropolitan
University Archives)

Left, Fig. 14
George Sprittles on the
right, c. 1917. (Source:
George Sprittles'
Scrapbook, Leeds
Metropolitan University
Archives)

the Thoresby Society for many years, writing a history of the New Grange Estate, where the Training College would be built. The Sprittle family connection with Beckett's Park continued with George's niece Joyce Pogson who was Principal Lecturer in History at The City of Leeds and Carnegie College until her retirement in 1975.

In September 1919 Capt. H. S. Carter noted in his first editorial of *The Blue Band, Magazine of the 2nd Northern General Hospital* that, 'Beckett's Park are a small township of something like 2500 souls . . . it is incredible that we should live from month to month with no organ to chronicle our doings, the humour, pathos and endless variety that constitute the life of a great hospital'. These sentiments reflect staff and patients' perception that they formed a distinct community. The magazine described itself on the front cover as 'A compendium of wit and wisdom of humour and pathos with some pithy comments on the sayings, doings and beings of today'.

The first issue cost 3d or 2d for patients, the Christmas double issue of 1919 cost 4d. There were regular contributions about pensions for veterans, entertainment and cinema notes, boasting that films shown in the YMCA hall had not previously been seen in Leeds. Gallows humour was in evidence with stories such as; Private X who '. . . was so full of bullets that they took him back to base in an ammunition wagon instead of an ambulance . . .' The Christmas Double issue paid special notice to a consignment of bananas gifted to the hospital by J. B. Allsop, Esq with the message 'Good Luck'.[29]

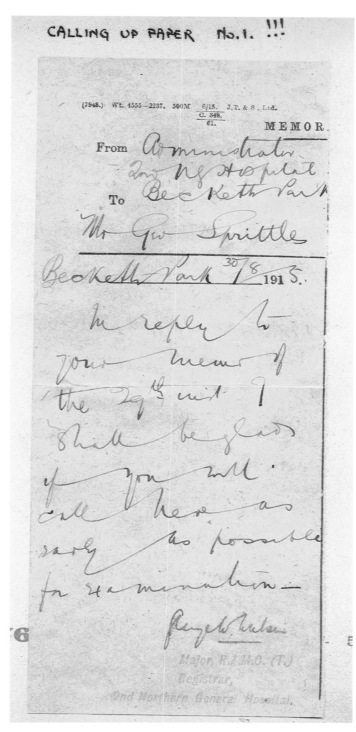

Fig. 15
Call up papers of George
Sprittles, 1916.
(Source: George
Sprittles' Scrapbook,
Leeds Metropolitan
University Archives)

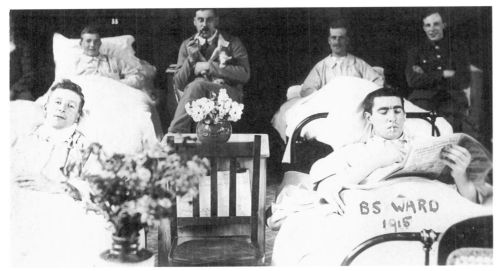

As the number of invalided soldiers grew Beckett's Park was converted into a specialist surgical hospital, requiring more extensions and specialist equipment. Pioneering orthopaedic, jaw and face injuries departments (**Figures 16 & 17**) were established in May 1916.[30][31] In 1917 the Extension Committee reformed to raise £16,000 towards operating theatres and X-ray rooms. An increasingly important hospital function was rehabilitation of injured men. Workshops (**Figure 18**) were equipped to train patients in a diverse number of new skills including: basket making; blacksmithing; tailoring; shoemaking; shorthand; and typing skills. With this new emphasis at Beckett's Park, East Leeds hospital took over the responsibilities of receiving wounded soldiers to Leeds.[32] Beckett's Park provided a stream of qualified and experienced personnel with skills much needed at the Front. This exodus required staff to replace them, many were American medics brought in as their English counterparts were reassigned. On 11 October 1917 Walter Hines Page (**Figure 19**), United States

Fig. 16 BS Ward 1915. (Source: George Sprittles' Scrapbook, Leeds Metropolitan University Archives)

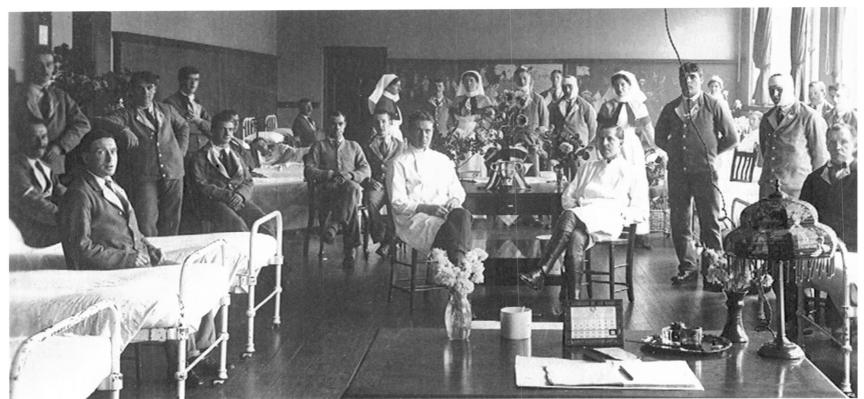

Fig. 17 Jaw Ward, 1916. (Source: George Sprittles' Scrapbook, Leeds Metropolitan University Archives)

Ambassador to Great Britain, visited the Military Hospital to formally open the new facilities.[33][34][35]

After November 1918, Leeds Education Authority was keen to return Beckett's Park to its original purpose as a Training College.[36] Factors concerning them were: schools forced to work half-time wished to return to normal working; the Authority was uncomfortable having a men's hospital co-located with women students; owners of properties rented to the College wanted their properties back.

By September 1919 the Education Authority had secured assurances from the War Office that Beckett's Park would be handed back to them by December 1921. Throughout 1919 and 1920 meetings were held with the Authority and the Ministry of Pensions (who had taken over the hospital from the War Office) and some compromise was reached. Two hostels would be released; one immediately and parts of the Education Building would be vacated gradually.[37][38] By the end of 1921 there was no sign of the hospital moving and another compromise was reached. The hospital would retreat to the temporary wooden huts and doctors and nurses would be accommodated in Caedmon and Priestley.[39]

The Ministry of Pensions in late 1923 asked for a further extension. By March 1924 the Leeds Education Authority, frustrated by what was perceived in-action by the Ministry to seek alternative accommodation, sent a deputation to London to meet the Minister of Pensions in person. At this meeting the Minister outlined the difficulties of finding alternative accommodation and requested that the Education Authority be prepared to have the hospital on site for a further five years. The Leeds delegation pointed out the suitability of a hospital site at Ripon. This site was investigated but appears to have been demolished regardless of reports suggesting its suitability. Despite these problems all students were back in residence at Beckett's Park by 1924 although the hospital continued in accommodation on the playing fields until 1927[40] (**Figure 20**).

It was estimated that 97 per cent of male former students were in the Forces at some point, and seventy-seven had been killed in combat.[41] Matthew Hudson Mossop was one of those who died, now remembered on the City of Leeds Training College War Memorial.[42] Mossop was born in 1890 at Seascale in Cumberland, the son of Isaac Mossop and Ann Hudson, Ann died shortly after he was born.[43] An active sportsman during his time at the City of Leeds Training College he appears in a photograph of the CLTC Rugby team of 1913-14 (**Figure 21**). He joined the 15th Battalion West Yorkshire Regiment (Prince of Wales Own), the Leeds Pals.[44] His regiment was part of the Somme offensive when the Leeds and Bradford

Left, Fig. 18
Workshop at the
hospital, c. 1916.
(Source: George
Sprittles' Scrapbook,
Leeds Metropolitan
University Archives)

Right, Fig. 19
Visit of American
Ambassador, Dr Page,
1917. (Source: George
Sprittles' Scrapbook,
Leeds Metropolitan
University Archives)

Fig. 20
Hospital Extension Huts
with Fairfax on the left.
(Source: George
Sprittles' Scrapbook,
(Leeds Metropolitan
University Archives)

Fig. 21
Close up of Matthew
Mossop, 1913-14.
(Source: Leeds
Metropolitan University
Archive)

Pals formed part of the attack on the village of Serre, a German stronghold, the 15th were the lead battalion and were decimated by machine gun fire before they had advanced very far towards the German lines.[45][46] At the time of his death on 1 July 1916 Mossop had been made Acting Sergeant and was posthumously awarded the Military Medal for bravery in the field. He is buried at Serre Road Cemetery No1, Beaumont-Hamel.[47][48][49]

HRH Princess Mary opened the 200-bed Chapel Allerton Hospital in May 1927, built in the grounds of Gledhow Grove, to accommodate patients from Beckett's Park, and the military finally vacated the college site.[50] Only twelve years later the whole drama seemed about to repeat itself.

In the years leading up to the Second World War, especially after the Munich Agreement in 1938, plans were drawn up to convert the City of Leeds Training College site back into a hospital.[51] On 3 September 1939 a requisition order was pushed through and according to R. W. Rich, the Principal, the college was in military hands before lunchtime that day.[52]

Beckett's Park became the 1/4th General Hospital later renamed the 18th General Hospital, and was partially equipped for this purpose, involving structural changes to many College buildings. Sluices were positioned in wards, walls knocked down, new doorways opened and a lift built in the northeast corner of the Education Block.[53] By 1 November 1939 the military sought to double capacity in the hospital to 1,200 beds.

But abruptly work was ordered to stop. New priorities meant that a major hospital along the lines of WW1 was redundant. On 1 December 1939 Beckett's Park was transformed into the No.11 Depot for the RAMC.[54] Personnel from the 18th General Hospital were split, the more experienced sent off to form the 28th General Hospital, the remainder posted to France in February 1940.[55] In June 1942 the 21st Primary Training Centre was opened providing training for officers and other ranks. The Training Centre shared the site with No.11 RAMC Depot. Lieutenant-Colonel Watt remarked that the two units cooperated to the benefit of both. He also noted that the PTC endorsed this teamwork by presenting the RAMC with two side drums for the Pipe Band.[56]

The College buildings were utilised by the Military for varying purposes. The swimming pool was converted into a training area where recruits were taught how to carry casualties over water. The Grange was used as an Officers' Mess and Fairfax as an NCO training facility.[57] At some point Carnegie Hall was used for the instruction and accommodation of the Auxiliary Territorial Service, referred to as the Women's Army, later the ATS were housed in the Grange.[58] Caedmon and Carnegie acted as Officers' Messes with Brontë becoming the Sergeants' Mess.[59] The Education Block was the hub and named the Training Establishment. It housed Barracks, the Chief Instructor's Office, Quartermaster, Isolation Ward, Psychiatrist's Office, Engineer's Office, Stores and Butchery Department. It also boasted a fully equipped Operating Theatre, Resuscitation Unit and Dispensary, a legacy from the earlier hospital refit, retained in case enemy action disabled local hospitals.[60]

Training at the Depot included a three-week Officers' Course and a four-week NCO/Cadre course. There was an intake of recruits at two-week intervals, who endured physical training, field exercises, drill and lectures. The depot also handled, drafting, a process of training men and women for foreign service where they would be documented, re-clothed and inoculated.[61] Evidence of part of this training was discovered in the roof space of Carnegie Hall, a set of wooden guns including a replica mortar weighted by a metal plate simulating the actual feel of the equipment.[62]

Plans were discussed, in 1939, to disperse the College to Loughborough in the event of war; this was not realised as many students were exempted from military service thereby creating an accommodation problem. The Training College made its own plans and gained approval to move to Scarborough.[63][64] Carnegie had been closed at the start of the war and would not reopen until 1946.[65][66] Malcolm Rowntree, a local councillor, negotiated with the North Riding County Council and five hotels were approached to provide accommodation. The college tried to maintain the integrity of its hostels by moving them as units to the participating hotels. The Grange moved to the Villa Esplanade, Fairfax to Brooklands, with Cavendish being split between the two. Macaulay moved to Red Lea, Brontë to Southlands and Leighton making use of both these hotels.[67]

By 1 November 1939 the college had implemented a full timetable and sported the new address of: The City of Leeds Training College, High Cliffe, Filey Road, Scarborough. High Cliffe became the new Education Block for teaching and administration and Victoria Hall, part of the Holy Trinity Church, was used for Physical Training. Negotiations with Scarborough College allowed the Leeds college access to various playing fields.[68] When the war ended the Scarborough hoteliers commissioned

Scarborough born artist Kenneth Rowntree to paint a scene of the South Bay, Scarborough to be presented to the College when it left in December 1945.[69]

Towards the end of the war the Beckett's Park site had many functions including a remedial unit for the rehabilitation and retraining of misfit soldiers, while part of the playing fields were populated with tents to house repatriated POWs. These fields had to be carefully picked clean of razor blades and fragments before any college games could be played.[70] Rich wrote on his return to Beckett's Park that the recently vacated buildings were in need of attention, structural changes made by the military were much in evidence, doors had been removed, and little maintenance work had been undertaken. Despondently he also noted that fifty-five students had been killed.[71]

The fifty-five lives lost were added to the seventy-seven, claimed by the First World War, commemorated on the City of Leeds Training College War Memorial[72] (**Figure 22**).

Fig. 22
City of Leeds Training College War Memorial. (Source: Keith Rowntree, 2006)

ENDNOTES

[1] Light, S. (2006) The territorial force nursing service 1908-21. *Stand To! The Journal of the Western Front Association*. 75. January, pp. 11-13.

[2] Ibid. pp. 11-12.

[3] Scott, W. (1922) Leeds in the Great War 1914-1918: a book of remembrance. Leeds. p. 204.

[4] Rich, R. and Pickering, H. (1958) A short history of the City of Leeds Training College 1907-1957. Leeds. p. 16.

[5] Scott, W. op.cit., p. 205.

[6] Sprittles, G. (no date) *Scrapbook*. Unpublished scrapbook. (Leeds Metropolitan University Archives, BPL/SP.

[7] Storey, N. (2007) The auxiliary war hospital nurse. *Family Tree Magazine*. April, pp. 6-9.

[8] Territorial army nursing service. *The British Journal of Nursing*. September 1931, p. 252.

[9] Scott, W. op.cit., p. 205.

[10] Sprittles, G. op.cit.

[11] Rich, R. and Pickering, H. op.cit. p. 17.

[12] *Proceedings*, 1914-15. Leeds. Leeds Education Committee.

[13] City of Leeds Training College (1916) City of Leeds Training College temporary prospectus. Leeds.

[14] City of Leeds Training College (1928) *City of Leeds Training College coming of age celebrations souvenir handbook 1907-1928*. Leeds. Held at Leeds Metropolitan University Archives, BPL/3.

[15] Rich, R. and Pickering, H. op.cit. p. 16.

[16] Meyer, W. (1985) *Introduction to the papers of Leeds Education Authority 1903-60*.

Leeds, School of Education, Leeds University. p. 15.

[17] *Mercier papers*. Held at Leeds Metropolitan University Archives, BPL/A.

[18] Rich, R. and Pickering, H. op.cit. p. 17.

[19] Scott, W. op.cit., p. 208.

[20] Light, S. op.cit.

[21] Bedford, P. and Howard, D. (1985) St James's University Hospital: a pictorial history. Leeds.

[22] Scott, W. op.cit., p. 207.

[23] *The Blue Band Magazine of the 2nd Northern General Hospital*. 1 (1-5) September 1919-January 1920.

[24] Sprittles, G. op.cit.

[25] King cheers up wounded. *The British Journal of Nursing*. 2 October 1915. p. 278.

[26] Sprittles, G. op.cit.

[27] Ibid.

[28] Census (1901) *All Souls, Leeds, West Riding*. RG12/4231 75.

[29] *The Blue Band Magazine of the 2nd Northern General Hospital*. op.cit.

[30] Scott, W. op.cit., pp. 212-213.

[31] Sprittles, G. op.cit.

[32] Scott, W. op.cit., p. 215.

[33] Ibid. p. 214.

[34] Sprittles, G. op.cit.

[35] Care of the wounded. *The British Journal of Nursing*, 8 September 1917. p. 148.

[36] *Proceedings*, 1918-19. Leeds. Leeds Education Committee.

[37] Leeds Education Authority (1924) *Beckett's Park hospital. statement of the Leeds Education Authority*. Held at Leeds Metropolitan University Archives. BPL/62/1.

[38] Memorandum relating to the present position of the City of Leeds Training College. (1921) Held at Leeds Metropolitan University Archives, BPL/62/2.

[39] Ibid.

[40] Leeds Education Authority (1924) op.cit.

[41] Rich, R. and Pickering, H. op.cit., pp. 17-18.

[42] *City of Leeds Training College war memorial*. James Graham Building. Headingley Campus. Leeds Metropolitan University.

[43] Census (1891) *Seascale, Cumberland*. RG13/4897/72.

[44] Milner, L. (1991) Leeds pals: history of the 15th (Service) battalion (1st Leeds) the Prince of Wales' Own (West Yorkshire Regiment), 1914-18. Barnsley, Wharncliffe.

[45] World War One Battlefields. *The Somme: Serre*. [Internet] Available from: <http://www.ww1battlefields.co.uk/somme/serre.html> [Accessed 12 January 2007].

[46] Wood, S. and Price, A. *The Leeds pals*. [Internet] Available from: <http://www.leedspals.co.uk/> [Accessed 10 January 2007].

[47] *Commonwealth War Graves Commission*. [Internet] Available from: http://www.cwgc.org/ [Accessed 31 March 2006].

[48] Military medal awards. *Supplement to the London Gazette*. 28 July 1917. p. 7772.

[49] *Silent cities: a guide to the cemeteries and memorials of the first world war in France. Serre Road Cemetery No. 1*. [Internet] No longer available. <www.silentcities.co.uk> [Accessed 31 March 2006].

[50] Connell, L. (1994) *A century of teacher training in Leeds 1875-1975*. Leeds, Leeds Metropolitan University, p. 153.

[51] Platt, T. and Bramley, G. (1952) *The story of the 18th General Hospital 1939-45*. Leeds, Privately Published.

[52] Rich, R. and Pickering, H. op.cit., p. 27.

[53] Platt, T. and Bramley, G. op.cit.

[54] National Archives (1942) *No XI depot and training establishment RAMC, notes by Lieut-Colonel R N E Watt – Commandant*. WO 222/258.

[55] Platt, T. and Bramley, G. op.cit.

[56] National Archives (1942) op.cit.

[57] Platt, T. and Bramley, G. op.cit.

[58] Morell, P. (2003) *Alberts war: at war with the Royal Army Medical Corps 1941-44*. [Internet] Available from: http://www.far-eastern-heroes.org.uk/alberts_war/index.htm [Accessed 30 March 2006].

[59] National Archives (1942) op.cit.

[60] National Archives (1942) op.cit.

[61] National Archives (1942) op.cit.

[62] *Wooden training guns* (c. 1945) Found in roof space of Carnegie Hall. Held at Leeds Metropolitan University Archives, BPL/ML/2-5.

[63] *Proceedings, 1939-40*. 12 October 1939, Leeds, Leeds Education Committee.

[64] Letters/memos from R. W. Rich and two letters from George Guest regarding the evacuation of the College. Summer/Autumn 1939. Leeds Metropolitan University Archives, BPL/40.

[65] Connell, L. (1983) *A history of Carnegie College and School of Physical Education 1933-76*, Leeds, Carnegie School of Physical Education and Human Movement Studies.

[66] Furlong, B. (1983) *Carnegie 1933-1983, college and school*. Liverpool, Liverpool University.

[67] Rich, R. and Pickering, H. op.cit., pp. 29-30.

[68] *Proceedings, 1939-40*, 16 December 1939. op.cit.

[69] Rich, R. and Pickering, H. op.cit., p. 40.

[70] Ibid. p. 39.

[71] Ibid.

[72] *City of Leeds Training College war memorial*. op.cit.

CHAPTER 12

Character Forming

Simon Lee

Character is the running stream that flows through this history of one hundred years of education. It would be a false dichotomy to apportion responsibility for the character of the institution, or the influence of this character on students, staff and the wider community, to either the pioneering vision of the college's founders or the beautiful setting of the City of Leeds Training College. For the former led to the latter. One way or another, however, the atmosphere enduring over one hundred years in first this college and now this campus of a wider university is worth exploring.

Fig. 1 Graduation day on the Acre, Headingley Campus, July 2006. (Source: Leeds Met. Communications: Icon Photography)

To the extent that environment makes a difference to our learning, our characters, our lives and our society, it is not only the aesthetic appeal of the campus that gives it such a distinctive character but also the combination of being a hidden treasure yet being only yards away from major roads and from one of the most frequently used and famous sporting stadiums in the world. The history of an institution set in rural isolation would be very different, as would the fate of a college that dominates the centre of its city. In contrast, being part of Leeds brings a certain worldliness through constant interaction with the vibrancy and diversity of urban life while being hidden in Headingley brings a certain humility, or at least weariness, at not being seen and, by virtue of the combined cricket and rugby grounds, not even being the most prominent element in a tiny village or suburb within the city.

Even more disconcertingly, the City of Leeds Training College has, for most of the one hundred years we are celebrating, not even been the most well known occupant of the campus it created. It gave way to other uses in times of war, gave space in the 1930s to Carnegie College which rapidly became identified with sporting excellence and most recently gave in to a merger in the 1960s and 1970s with first Carnegie and then the polytechnic, which became in the 1990s Leeds Metropolitan University. So, whether the campus is known as Headingley or Beckett's Park or Leeds Met or Carnegie, it is unlikely to be identified nowadays as the home of its founding college. More fundamentally, in any of these manifestations, people who have over decades used the Otley Road or ring road daily or attended the stadium weekly might never have strayed from their regular paths to see it for themselves.

In this, there is a lesson for life which, if discerned or even subliminally absorbed, will have stood generations of alumni in good stead as they taught, often without external acclaim, in schools in less glamorous settings. In each student, each pupil, each person, each community, each society, there are hidden talents that can be missed by those too busy, too blinkered or too haughty to see for themselves. Alumni will have known that they had enjoyed a good education in a glorious environment, just as the first vice-principal, Winifred Mercier, knew she was right not to settle for second best and was ultimately vindicated. As was intended by the founders, this splendid setting for education has been character-forming. The lasting impression arises, however, partly from the unintended surprise in first beholding the hidden campus and later contrasting the quality of its education with the challenge of its invisibility.

The focus of the merged institution in the last decades of the twentieth century was in the centre of Leeds, where four formerly independent colleges had been brought together right next to the local authority that initially controlled the polytechnic. On either side of the turn of the century, the original City of Leeds Training College halls of residence around the Acre were, one by one, year by year, being turned into offices and teaching space, with student accommodation provided elsewhere, principally the wonderfully restored and converted Kirkstall Brewery. The liveliness of the campus in Headingley suffered, however, and it seemed peripheral to the university in the city centre. On the other hand, at the end of the twentieth century, the university rescued and merged with Harrogate College. This created some challenges but had the side-benefit of putting Headingley in between the two other campuses in the centre of Leeds and in Harrogate.

Three changes seemed necessary to me. First, the university itself needed to take this campus more seriously, drawing people to it. Second, the campus had to be connected to the most famous part of the surrounding neighbourhood of Headingley, namely the stadium. Third, extending the hint of an idea from the Harrogate merger, the combination of the stadium and the campus needed to be seen not as on the fringes of the city of Leeds but as the epicentre of the wider North and capable of attracting people from around the world. Steadily, we are working towards each of these, in the spirit of the original college, which was established to make a difference not just in the locality but far further afield. Thus, the college was not only character forming when it was an independent institution, shaping students who became teachers and thus influencing also pupils and their world, but even now, its distinctive characteristics and high ambitions are shaping the vision and character of a much wider-ranging university.

HEADINGLEY CAMPUS

The first step was to ask, before taking up my post in September 2003, that my office should not be in the city centre, as had become

*Fig. 2
Geoffrey Boycott, Stewart Regan, Mike Gray and visiting Professor Doune MacDonald (University of Queensland) at a reception at Queenswood. (Source: Leeds Met. Communications: Icon Photography)*

customary, but should be on this campus. This was achieved in the first few weeks of the 2003/2004 academic year in the temporary location of North Lodge. In July 2004, we held graduations on the campus, renaming it Headingley and creating a temporary village on The Acre, in the style of golf's open championships. Although previously the practice was to hold graduations in winter in the Town Hall, graduations have been held here ever since, bringing graduands and their families to the site of the college, even if they have studied in town, for one of the most important days of their lives (**Figure 1**). The re-naming of the campus was a declaration of intent, linked to the other two changes. The campus could be unlocked by connecting it to the stadium known around the world and together they could be the hub or focal point of a regional university network. In the autumn of 2004, the original building, the Grange, became home to my office, with reception and meeting rooms drawing people into the oldest building on the campus. My wife, Patricia, and I moved from a flat in Kirkstall Brewery into a flat within the original principal's residence, Queenswood, on the campus and began inviting students, staff and guests into its reception rooms and glorious gardens (**Figure 2**). By

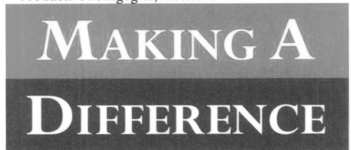

*Fig. 3
Book cover: Debra
Hayes, Martin Mills,
Pam Christie and Bob
Lingard,* Teachers and
Schooling Making a
Difference: Productive
pedagogies, assessment
and performance,
*published by Allen &
Unwin, 2005.*

2007, the main building at the head of The Acre, has not only had its exterior cleaned but has been transformed internally. It now includes state-of-the-art creative music technology studios, a reordered library and a restored hall. We have plans to bring back students to live on campus in the numbers first envisaged one hundred years ago and to create a Carnegie Clubhouse as the pivot between the original campus and the developments of the 1930s.

It is not only what is added but what is subtracted which makes a difference. Blots on the landscape strangely known by two inappropriate terms, either as 'mobile' or as 'temporary' classrooms, have been removed after a decade of obscuring the view. Cars have also been removed from surrounding The Acre and the long road in to the campus from South Lodge. What matters most is who comes on to the campus and how they raise awareness of its surprising inspiration. Estelle Morris, for example, made such a difference to schools at the turn of the century as Minister and then Secretary of State for Education that it was important for her to see our setting when she received an honorary doctorate to great acclaim in 2004. It matters that a leading educationalist such as Professor Bob Lingard, the Andrew Bell Professor of Education at the University of Edinburgh, has been a regular visitor in recent years (**Figure 3**). It is significant that Dame Kelly Holmes (**Figure 4**) was often on campus even before she won her gold medals at the 2004 Olympics in Athens. Indeed, she came to receive treatment and support from Alison Rose, the leading physiotherapist in the world of athletics, in the run-up to her double gold medals in Athens and has returned to receive an honorary doctorate (**Figure 5**) and to inspire others to become champions. Amitabh Bachchan, the doyen of Indian cinema (**Figure 6**), was among many leading figures in that creative industry who saw the campus at its very best in the summer of 2007, receiving an honorary doctorate and re-naming our restored Great Hall as the Gandhi Hall, in honour of the International Indian Film Academy (IIFA) bringing its annual awards to Yorkshire, with our university as their official education partner (**Figure 7**). Open days, Freshers' Festival and our Staff Development Festival have all brought thousands to the campus.

It was, however, national policy and our reaction to it which drew most attention to the campus. In 2003/2004, the government reneged on its manifesto promise not to introduce top-up fees, then we had to set our fees in the next academic year, following which the media have taken great interest in student applications for succeeding years. We stood out against the government and then became the only university in the country to adopt a fee of £2000 with our governors' 'low-charging, high impact' policy which has led to dramatically increasing applications and great public interest. Every time the media wanted to represent this, they have been showing images of our Headingley Campus, especially The Acre and James Graham facade, instead of the tower blocks in town, which are now being demolished. This led to an era of award-winning recognition where the same images were used repeatedly. Unlocking the first class setting of the City of Leeds Training College in Beckett Park, now our Headingley Campus, came just in time to capture media interest in the seeming paradox that the lowest-charging university in the country had the high impact of a beautiful environment, much to the surprise of those who expected newer universities to be wallowing in abject surroundings. This echoed and took to a far wider audience the surprise experienced in person on beholding the original campus for the first time, with which this chapter and this college began.

HEADINGLEY CARNEGIE STADIUM: 'MAKING A STAND FOR EDUCATION'

The story of sporting partnerships has been told in part in a previous chapter. For these purposes, what is significant is that the campus is opened up by closer and closer association with the neighbouring stadium which pre-dates the City of Leeds Training College. The

Fig. 4
Dame Kelly Holmes with Malcolm Brown and Alison Rose outside The Grange. (Source: Leeds Met. Communications: Icon Photography)

Fig. 5
Dame Kelly Holmes having received her honorary doctorate with Chancellor, Brendan Foster MBE. (Source: Leeds Met. Communications: Icon Photography)

Fig. 6
Amitabh Bachchan
receiving an honorary
doctorate, summer 2007.
(Source: Leeds Met.
Communications: Icon
Photography)

space surrounding the campus became crucial after the First World War as the country needed a physical education teacher training college. In the centre of the United Kingdom, Leeds was chosen to receive funding from the Carnegie Trust and the campus was expanded in the 1930s accordingly. This enabled even closer relationships with the famous cricket and rugby grounds in Headingley, although sport was already central to the life of the original college.

Taking this part of our heritage into the 21st century, my inaugural lecture about partnerships, entitled 'Beyond Boundaries',

was given at the cricket ground in 2003[1]. A partnership with the three professional sporting teams at the stadium followed at the start of 2004. On my first day, I had signalled the intention to recover the best of the university's heritage and we duly brought back the name 'Carnegie', now as the prefix to the Faculty of Sport and Education, when faculties were adjusted during the year. By the start of 2006, the cricket and rugby grounds had become Headingley Carnegie. By the end, they featured the first significant building works in 75 years at the rugby ground, with the Carnegie Stand incorporating teaching and meeting space for the university (**Figure 8**). In 2007, the university

acquired a controlling interest in the professional rugby union team on its return to the premiership and its name changed from Leeds Tykes to Leeds Carnegie. The association between the twin pillars of an emerging Headingley Quarter, the campus and the stadium, was best illustrated in both 2006 (**Figure 9**) and 2007 (**Figure 10**) by the Carnegie Great Student Run bringing so many people from the stadium to and around the campus, savouring its atmosphere. The next challenge is, by the turn of the decade, to build a Carnegie Pavilion as the entrance to the cricket ground, at the closest point to the campus.

WORLD-CLASS REGIONAL UNIVERSITY

In Australia, India, New Zealand, Pakistan, South Africa, Sri Lanka, the West Indies and throughout the cricketing world, the cricket ground at Headingley, now Headingley Carnegie, is more famous than our host city of Leeds. Closer to home, in what can be a fiercely competitive environment of city rivalries, such a Test venue is seen as more of neutral capital of the north than as a partisan competitor in the regional economy. So it is natural that our Headingley axis of campus and stadium should attract all-comers, such as our regional

Fig. 7
The Great Hall restored in 2007 is re-named the Gandhi Hall in honour of the International Indian Film Academy. (Source: Leeds Met. Communications: Icon Photography)

*Fig. 8
Launch of the Carnegie
Stand, Headingley
Carnegie Stadium, 2007
professional rugby union
team Leeds Carnegie
2007. (Source: Leeds
Met. Communications:
Icon Photography)*

university network and other partnerships. An example would be that so many head-teachers and aspiring head-teachers are now engaged in continuing professional development through The Northern Partnership. This brings the successors to the original students of the City of Leeds Training College on to our Headingley Campus and to Headingley Carnegie. International students (**Figure 11**) are the university's guests at every Test match and one day international game, as well as at special events such as IIFA's celebrity cricket match. Likewise, regional university network partners are invited when their local teams are playing rugby at the stadium. Other major events held by our Great North Uni at the stadium include the Northern Design awards, won this year by a student from Hull College, which is set to take over responsibility for Harrogate College in the coming year.

CHARACTER

The university's vision was set by governors in the 2003/2004 academic year as striving to become a 'world-class regional university, with world-wide horizons, using all our talents to the full' (**Figure 12**). The Governors' succinct account of the character of the university followed in 2006/2007. The front cover of our 'Vision & Character' shows Dee Caffari, an alumna, becoming the first woman in history to sail solo, non-stop, round the world the so-called 'wrong way', against the prevailing winds and currents (**Figure 13**). It begins by drawing an analogy between the Great North Run, created by our Chancellor and alumnus, Brendan Foster, and our notion of a Great North Uni, that in long distance running or lifelong learning, it is possible to combine mass participation and high performance (**printed inside back cover**).

We are developing a 'Headingley Carnegie Scorecard' to record outstanding achievements in the spirit of that vision and character. The front cover shows our women's cricket team during their victory over Cambridge in 2007 (**Figures 14**). An example of national honours for student group work is the achievement of landscape architecture students winning gold at the Royal Horticultural Society's Chelsea Flower Show in 2006 with the best courtyard garden. Truly exceptional work by students this century includes Charlotte Harris winning the National Portrait Gallery Prize in 2003 with a painting of her grandmother that was part of her final degree show. For an

Fig. 9
On the Acre after the Great Student Run 2006. (Source: Leeds Met. Communications: Icon Photography)

Fig. 10
The Carnegie Great Student Run, Fun Run 2007. (Source: Leeds Met. Communications: Icon Photography)

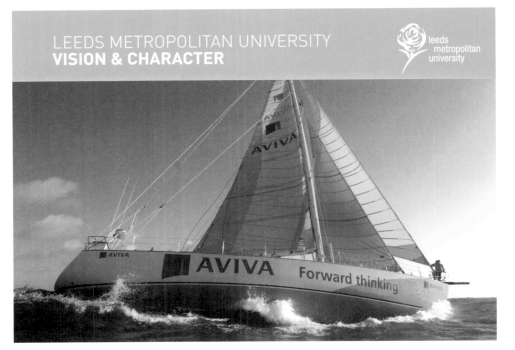

undergraduate to win this most prestigious of national competitions against all-comers gives some indication of the extraordinary talents of our students. The painting, together with one of Charlotte's sister and one of her self-portraits, was acquired by the university and is on permanent exhibition.

I commissioned Charlotte to paint portraits of Students' Union and Athletic Union sabbatical officers who have served the maximum term of office of two years. These portraits, of Anne-Marie Watkinson, Louise Sweeney and Leanne Creighton (**Figure 15**), on the one hand, and Emma Beith (**Figure 16**), on the other, are on the walls of my office in The Grange, alongside an image of Winifred Mercier. They start to balance The Grange's collection in the neighbouring Parlour and Panel Room of portraits of my predecessors as heads of this institution and of its forerunner, the City of Leeds Training College. The portraits that look over my shoulder seem to depict a determination to make a difference that is emblematic of the character of both the women concerned and of the original college's vision.

The university continues and broadens the tradition of

*Fig. 13
Solo sailor and Leeds
Met alumna Dee Caffari
with her family prior to
receiving an honorary
doctorate photographed
in the Parlour, the
Grange, July 2006.
(Source: Leeds Met.
Communications: Icon
Photography)*

*Fig. 14
Leeds Metropolitan
University, Headingley
Carnegie Scorecard.
(Source: Leeds Met.
Communications: Icon
Photography)*

educational institutions as patrons of the arts also in other ways. The success of our cultural partnerships was illustrated by becoming the only university in the country to win a national Arts & Business award with Northern Ballet Theatre Company in 2007. In 2006, the university also won gold in the Times Higher Education Supplement's award for 'the outstanding contribution to the local community' by a UK university, for our work connecting Bradford City Football Club to its local Muslim community (**Figure 17**), and silver in the overall 'university of the year' category (**Figure 18**). In 2007, the same paper had a front page headline declaring that, 'Leeds Met tops first UK green rankings' and another one reporting that, 'Leeds Met enters a league of its own', while the BBC News website also had a front page headline referring to the university, 'The UK has gone Carnegie crazy'.

Our statement of vision and character concludes by calling for us to attract more and more students and staff with the attitude to make a difference. Another publication, 'Leeds Met Acts', shows the attitude, character and talents that we seek. The front cover shows one of our students making a difference in the summer of 2007 in Indonesia

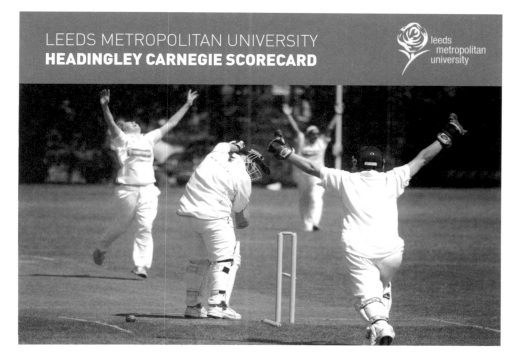

Fig. 15 Commissioned portrait of Student Union Sabbatical Officers, Anne-Marie Watkinson, Louise Sweeney and Leanne Creighton by Charlotte Harris. (Source: Leeds Met. Communications: Icon Photography)

(**Figure 19**). In marking this centenary, the university has created opportunities for a hundred students to volunteer for diverse projects in different continents and we have funded one hundred new doctoral students, strengthening the commitment to research for generations to come.

At our best, then, we are growing into the style established by our founders, not only in the sense that our campus is worthy of being the headquarters of the equivalent on this side of the Atlantic of a

Fig. 17 Baroness Warwick of Universities UK presenting the Times Higher awards for the 'outstanding contribution to the local community' to Jim Brown of Bradford City Football Club and to Inder Hunjan and David Ward of Leeds Met. (Source: Leeds Met. Communications: Icon Photography)

Fig. 16 Emma Beith, AU president presented with her commissioned portrait by Charlotte Harris. (Source: Leeds Met. Communications: Icon Photography)

Fig. 18 Jo Piddington, Jodie Tumelty, Leanne Creight, Emma Beith, Anne-Marie Watkinson and Louise Sweeney, at the Times Higher awards. (Source: Leeds Met. Communications: Icon Photography)

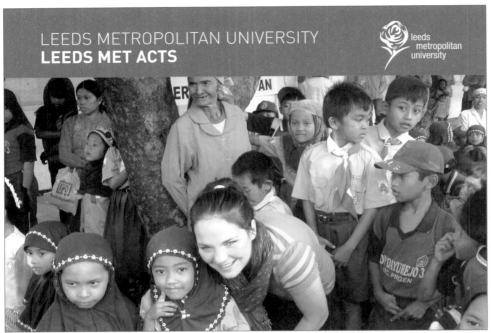

Fig. 19 Front cover of Leeds Metropolitan University Leeds Met Acts. (Source: Leeds Met.
Communications: Icon Photography)

major American state university system. Our approach to partnerships (**Figure 20**) is also radical in the true sense of fidelity to our original roots, extending the founders' commitment to educational partnerships to the broader reach of the university's activities, especially in creating cultural, sporting and business partnerships (**Figure 21**). It is not the beauty of the campus or the boldness of the original vision that forms character alone but the long walk, the long run, the hundred years of history, the context, the capacity to surprise and the stimulus to reflection that is so refreshing and character-forming.

The author wishes to acknowledge and thank Sarah Hicks for her assistance.

ENDNOTE

[1] See the transcript at http://www.leedsmet.ac.uk/the_news/docs/proflee_inaugural.pdf

Record Partnerships

September 2006
Carnegie Stand opened by Sports Minister who paid tribute to the pioneering partnership between the university, Leeds Rugby and Yorkshire County Cricket Club.

October 2006
The Northern Partnership with the universities of Manchester and Teesside began continuing professional development of existing and aspiring head-teachers   Won Varsity Games v University of Leeds by 15 sports to 5

November 2006
Won gold in the 'outstanding contribution to the local community award' for community engagement with Bradford City Football Club and silver in the 'university of the year' overall category at the Times Higher awards

December 2006
Hull College joined regional university network   Prime Minister met Chancellor & Vice-Chancellor in recognition of successes

January 2007
Governors agreed distinctive statement of the university's vision and character Rugby Football League announced partnership including the Carnegie Challenge Cup, with its return to Wembley finals, our campus base for full-time referees and Great Britain's coaching team, the Carnegie World Club Challenge and the Carnegie Champion Schools' Cup, engaging 25,000 school-girls and school-boys in the world's biggest rugby league tournament

February 2007
Sustained our record increase in undergraduate applications As the reigning university champions, our own students qualified for the Carnegie Challenge Cup, defeating one of the strongest teams, Wigan St Pat's, in the first round.

March 2007
Only university to win a national Arts & Business award, for our partnership with Northern Ballet Theatre Company

April 2007
Senator George Mitchell was the first public speaker in our transformed Old Broadcasting House, celebrated the start of work on the £50M Rose Bowl development for our Leeds Business School with SU Associate President and students, began with SU President and post-graduate students the demolition of the tower blocks inherited from Leeds Polytechnic, which are giving way to a new complex including the Senator George Mitchell Centre for Peace & Conflict Resolution, in partnership with Peace Museum.

May 2007
'Leeds Met enters a league of its own', front page headline, Times Higher and 'The UK has gone Carnegie crazy', front page BBC News website, as the university took a controlling interest in the premiership professional rugby union club, now Leeds Carnegie.

June 2007
'Leeds Met tops first UK green rankings', front page headline, Times Higher Official education partner, International Indian Film Academy, Amitabh Bachchan re-named Gandhi Hall, a restoration flanked by new industry-acclaimed music studios and a radical re-ordering of our library, responding to student feedback   Northern Design awards supported widely, from Sotheby's to the Chair of Yorkshire Forward, with students from across the North.

July 2007
Recruited one hundredth funded doctoral student to mark our Headingley centenary, appointed more professors in the year than there were in the whole university in 2003.

A balanced scorecard goes beyond financial indicators which can be seen on the university's website and in a dedicated publication   In summary, the accounts for 2005/6 showed an historic cost surplus of £2M on a turnover of £142M, with a net cash inflow of £8M A £44M exceptional receipt secured on leasing student residences was the biggest contribution towards funding the transformation of the estate In 2007, the revaluation of the estate showed an improvement from £250M to over £300M.

As well as positive external recognition of, and praise for, our pioneering partnerships, we also know that we are setting the pace and making a difference when there is a certain kind of criticism or copying Examples during the year included attacks on the scale and pace of our change and on our insistence that attitude is vital, together with attempts by several universities to copy aspects of our sporting and cultural partnerships Somewhere between criticism and praise there is also some bemusement at our pioneering developments in pursuit of our Vision & Character as a Great North Uni, as shown, for instance, by the current media interest in our Masters of Northern Studies Our scorecard does not suggest other universities as benchmarks or competitors Rather, our distinctive Vision & Character is to be the front-runner, establishing pioneering partnerships which others might follow, in striving to be a world-class regional university, with world-wide horizons, using all our talents to the full

Fig. 20 Statement from Leeds Metropolitan University Headingley Carnegie
Scorecard. (Source: Leeds Met. Communications: Icon Photography)

www.leedsmet.ac.uk

Fig. 21 Jo Piddington (SU Associate President & Governor),
Senator George Mitchell (Visiting Professor, Peace Studies), and
Jodie Tumelty (SU President and Governor). (Source: Leeds Met.
Communications: Icon Photography)

As human beings, our greatness lies not so much in being able to remake the world ... as in being able to remake ourselves

Mahatma Gandhi

Acknowledgements & copyright

The editor and contributing authors would like to give their thanks and acknowledgements to the following people and organisations for their help with this book, including permission to reproduce images.

Every attempt has been made to acknowledge copyright and obtain consent where required. Where this has not been possible we apologise for any infringement and ask the persons concerned to contact the publishers to make arrangements.

Allen & Unwin

Jane Barber

Chris Bouckley

British Library Catalogue of Illuminated Manuscripts

Ian Crossland

Education Leeds and Leeds City Council

Jim Farmery

Girton College, Cambridge, Mistress and Fellows

Phillip Garnett

Lord Grimthorpe

David Hall

Deakin University

Hotel Villa Cimbone (www.villacimbrone.it)

Hulton Archive/Getty Images

Robert Ingpen

Jarrold Publishing

Ian Kaplan

Leeds Library and Information Services

Leeds Metropolitan University Archives

Lou Charnley

Leeds Met. Communications: Icon Photography

Leeds Museums and Galleries (Temple Newsome House).

Leeds University Library, Special Collections Department

Michele LeFevre, the Local Studies Manager at Leeds Library and
    Information Services

Mr Bill Bennett and Julie's Antique Prints

Susannah Marshall

National Archives

National Portrait Gallery, London

Nevil Shute Norway Foundation

Oxford University Press

Iain Poole

Roehampton University and especially Gilly King, Whitelands
    College archivist

Keith Rowntree

Rachel Settle

Chris Sheppard and Hilary Diaper for help obtaining the portraits of
    John and Jane Marshall from the University of Leeds Art Collection

Richard Thomson and the license for reuse under this Creative
    Commons Licence: http://creativecommons.org/licenses/by-sa/2.0/

Thoresby Society and especially Peter Meredith and Eve Bradford
    for their help

Training and Development Agency for Schools 2007

Jodie Tumelty

West Yorkshire Archive Service, Leeds and Leeds City Council and
    especially Alexandra Eversleigh and Daniel Sudron who helped
    obtain the 1829 plan from West Yorkshire Archives Service

W.T. Pike and Co., 19, Grand Parade, Brighton, 1902 [Pike's New
Century Series, no.6]

Yorkshire Post Newspapers Ltd.

Leeds Metropolitan University Board of Governors, 2007